EMOTIONAL INTELLIGENCE 2.0

THIS BOOK INCLUDES:

DARK PSYCHOLOGY - MENTAL MANIPULATION – NLP -

HOW TO ANALYZE PEOPLE – EMPATH - REWIRE YOUR BRAIN.

THE INDISPENSABLE GUIDE TO IMPROVING YOUR SOCIAL SKILLS

MARK SMITH and **JACK GOLDMAN**

TABLE OF CONTENTS

PART ONE

Introduction

When you learn about psychology in school, you are introduced to a whole new world. You learn all about how the brain, perhaps the most complicated organ within the human body, functions, and ultimately, everything that everyone does is eventually broken down into nothing but electrical impulses created by neurons that are passed on to other neurons, and the entire impulse eventually spreads enough to create the action, feeling, thought, or sensation that you become aware of. Every complicated bit of yourself, your decisions on what to do or say, or how you feel when you see a certain person, can be explained by those same neurological impulses, no matter what the sensation. It is, at its simplest, the way that the body passes information from place to place. Despite how daunting and complicated humans may seem, we are actually surprisingly simple.

Humans follow a surprisingly simple sequence of thoughts, feelings, and behaviors, which feed into each other in a constant loop, with thought influencing how one feels, which influences one's actions, which in turn again influence their thoughts. When you understand that constant cycle, you will begin to recognize that it is surprisingly simple to hijack a person's mind. That is where dark psychology comes into play.

What is Dark Psychology?

Dark psychology takes an understanding of how people's minds work, understanding their most intrinsic, unconscious motivations, and using them. By understanding what motivates a person to behave in certain ways, regardless of whether it is in a positive or negative manner, you can take control of the person, preying on those motivations and turning them into something that can be influenced.

Those with the darkest personalities seem to understand this process innately, recognizing exactly how to identify a target, read a target, and ultimately, snare a target without needing a guide. Their own predatory instincts are honed naturally, making them incredibly effective at what they do. Dark psychology recognizes that those with dark personalities, narcissists, sadists, or psychopaths, seem to be inherent masters at manipulating others, usually managing to stay behind the scenes as they do so. These masters of manipulation are so skillful that no one ever suspects that they are doing what they are doing until it is too late, and the damage is done. They utilize their inherent understanding of psychology and how it works in order to manipulate others, getting the results they need and making it seem effortless in the process.

Psychologists recognize these skills, seeking to further understand the process of manipulating other people, in breaking someone down so thoroughly that they are no longer someone they recognize in the mirror, and how they do so in ways that are so sneaky that they are frequently entirely overlooked. Psychologists recognize that this potential, this propensity to behave in ways that harm or control others, resides within each and every person in the world, though the vast majority of us keep it under lock and key. Every person around you has the potential to be a monster, behaving in ways that are harmful simply for the sake of predatory behavior.

However, psychologists have also come to recognize that, with the right motivations behind your actions, these dark psychology skills can be used for a myriad of good reasons. It can offer a defense—when you understand it, you are less susceptible to the tactics utilized. It can offer the skills that lead you to success when persuading people to give you better jobs or to take a chance with you. It can provide you the skills necessary to ensure that you are a better friend and family member. Psychologists have come to understand that just because you are using the same skills as those within the dark triad or with other dark personality types does not mean that you, yourself, must also give in to the darkness. You can take a look into the darkness without succumbing to it, allowing you to gain valuable skills that can be utilized to your benefit without becoming a predatory monster.

Principles of Dark Psychology

Those who utilize dark psychology frequently persuade, manipulate, deceive, coerce, seduce, and control the people around them. They want what they want and do not care about the cost. To them, the ends justify the means, even if the means they are using to reach that end are the wellbeing and happiness of those around them. To many of those within the dark triad, the only person whose happiness matters is their own. They may even be thrilled by hurting other people, gaining pleasure out of the suffering of those around them.

Oftentimes, those who are acting out in ways that utilize dark psychology techniques do so out of impulse—something in their unconscious encourages them to do so, so they do it with no regard to the consequences. They may see the other person as innately weaker than them, choosing to target them much like how a wolf would target weaker deer. They seek to make those that are weaker than them their prey. This is likely due to evolutionary instinct. Humans have three driving instincts that are massive motivators to their behaviors, culminating into what is referred to as the biological imperative, or the purpose of life in general: Sex, aggression, and self-preservation. These are quite self-explanatory: Sex is for procreation, allowing for genetics to pass through the generation. Aggression allows for the protection of territory, the self, and mates, and self-preservation is the instinct to ensure survival at all costs.

Those who give in to dark psychology are typically acting upon one of these, either wanting to preserve the falsified images of themselves that they have been wearing like a mask, alleviate the aggressive drives they feel, or coerce someone into fulfilling sexual desires. However, the vast majority of people recognize that such devious, harmful methods have to be used in order to ensure survival.

Most people recognize the constraints of society and live within them, knowing that their biological imperatives can still be achieved and fulfilled.

Though the dark psychology wielder is likely to be aggressive, he will still be tactful in his targets, seeking out the weakest targets that are the least likely to hurt them back in return. The same biological imperatives that encouraged them to lash out in the first place also restrain them to an extent, causing them to want to remain hidden and the only way they can remain hidden is if they remain unchallenged. For that reason, they seek out those who are the least likely to attempt to challenge them.

Ultimately, dark psychology can be identified by the following five traits:

It is universal: Every human being has the potential for dark psychology manipulation within them, and every human being shares the potential to behave in violent and predatory manners

It studies the way people think and feel, as well as how willing they are to utilize their understandings of the world to target other human beings

It recognizes a spectrum of behaviors, with some behaviors being deemed as worse or more dark or evil than others

That same spectrum is dependent upon how evil or inhumane the intentions behind the action were

Understanding dark psychology allows for it to be controlled or restrained, while also recognizing just how useful dark psychology principles can be.

Examples of Dark Psychology

Imagine that you have just landed a job selling houses. You want to be successful at it, but recognize that it is a huge purchase for the vast majority of people, taking up a massive amount of money and requiring a long-term commitment. You also know that the more expensive the house you sell is, the more money you get, and the happier you are with your larger commission check. You then decide to learn how to persuade people and influence them with your body

11

language to convince your clients to buy houses that are always just slightly outside of their original suggested max price they were willing to pay. This is dark psychology, appealing to dark persuasion techniques as well as using body language to influence.

Perhaps you are in an interview and you are asked a question that you cannot answer honestly without tanking your chances at getting the job. You instead utilize the art of deception, subtly sidestepping the issue altogether while also utilizing some of the techniques you learned about how to use mind games to completely distract the interviewer. You then skip over the question altogether, saving yourself the hassle of answering.

Maybe you are interested in getting someone to love you, but they will not give you the time of day. Through understanding persuasion tactics as well as how to seduce people, you can essentially hijack the other person's mind, making the other person interested enough to give you the chance to earn their love. Through skills such as knowing how to make yourself seem more interesting than most would give you credit for, to understanding just how to utilize eye contact to force an intimate connection, you will find your luck with those who interest you skyrocketing as you learn how to portray yourself and how to seduce successfully.

All of these are ways that dark psychology could be used to get the results you want with relatively little effort. Understanding the art of dark psychology can make walking through life a breeze, allowing you to shortcut your way to success, love, power, and anything else you wanted out of life. From here, you will begin to look at the wide array of ways that dark psychology can be utilized in order to lead the life you want to live.

Dark psychology is the art of using manipulation and mind control over others. It is the study of human conditions about how people prey on others. We all have the potential to oppress other human beings and creatures. Most of us restrain this feeling, but some utilize it. Dark psychology tries to find out the perceptions, behaviors, and thoughts that lead to this preying behavior. In most cases, dark psychology has found that 99.99% is goal-oriented, and the remaining 0.01% manipulate others with no purpose and with no influence from religious dogma and science. Therefore, dark psychology is the trend in which people use techniques like persuasion, manipulation, and motivation to get their way. What is a dark psychology triad?

Dark psychology triad is the seeking to foretell the criminal behavior and manipulation in relationships. These triads are narcissism, which is the grandiosity, egotism, and lacking empathy, psychopathy, which is using charm and friendliness, but lacking empathy, selfishness, and remorsefulness to get what you want and Machiavellianism, which is manipulating others with deception and lacking morality in your manipulation. Nobody wants to be manipulated, but in today's world, we are prone to be manipulated. It does not have to be in extreme cases like the dark triad above, but we are manipulated in simple actions that may seem harmless and normal. You will find this manipulation in sales techniques, in the internet ads, and our children when they seek to get what they want. People we love and trust a lot apply dark psychology to us.

Dark psychology involves everything that human beings are in their dark part. We all have a masked side within us from birth that is evil. Dark psychology has found out that these people who do these acts never do it for sex, power, retribution, or any other purpose. They commit these heinous acts with no goal in mind. They violate and harm others just for the thrill of it. Like I mentioned, we all have that potential in us. The potential to harm others without explanation or reason. Dark psychology takes this potential to be difficult and complex to explain. Let us look at the 0.01% manipulators in dark psychology.

Basics. Of Dark Psychology

The mind is one of human nature's most complicated elements. The functioning of the brain is something that, as soon as we know, has both perplexed and fascinated humanity. The mysteries of the mind have been unraveled by philosophers, psychologists, and researchers. It is usually believed that our conduct and deeds are influenced by natural perceptions. A bunch of studies has, therefore, been carried out to understand the cognitive cycle of individual experiences, whether subtle or evil, before adopting the intervention.

Some efforts to study the human mind have focused on the brain. These trials examine the physical elements of the body with an emphasis on the collection, processing, interpretation, and storage of data. In essence, they aim to understand more in-depth of how the body can influence the thinking of a person. These surveys have led to advances in the management of weakening circumstances such as Alzheimer's, perception problems, and even memory loss.

Psychology is the best-known element of research into the human mind.

We have interviewed a psychiatrist at some stage in our life, or we have met someone who had to ask him to conduct our harder mental fights. Life encounters many occasions that break us down in respects that we are unable to repair ourselves. Sometimes the disintegration comes as a consequence of some of our relatives ' biological indicators. Emotions such as depression, anger, and dread are rendering it hard for our everyday lives to flourish. We can defend ourselves from the shadows in a mixture of medicines and treatment.

But in others, what about the obscurity?

All can do excellent work. We are capable of doing a single wrong, as well. Underlying feelings like sorrow, anxiety, joy, and happiness is a deep-seated urge that can intentionally damage others when those desires are not controlled. The lighter wishes stem from more basic calls such as our plane or fighting reaction, which fosters our existence. There is sometimes only one term that qualifies the response of the natural being to these hostile emotions.

Dark sociology is a research of the natural situation concerning animal psychology. Dark psychology investigates in a lay sense this part of the human nature that enables us to act intentionally and willingly to damage our peers. Bearing this in mind, the use of prey does not merely result in a person's physical harm, although there is a wholly devoted part of dark Psychology.

We will comment shortly on these fields in the following segments to understand the subject faster.

You may have found words or sentences in films or novels that refer to "blackness inside." This was also pointed out by some of the most famous philosophers. The holy book of Christians speaks of the "urgently evil core of god." We have all found that a person we have defined as extremely calm or socially restricted only to perpetrate such a devious deed by that same person that it is hard to relate this behavior with that specific person. We're that person sometimes. It's not entirely shocking, however surprising it may seem.

These instances are only reactions to internal circumstances. The cup was so stirred, and the sad feelings under it cooled to the ground. Usually, when the command is exercised, they get back. If the correct switches are pressed, everyone has the latent inclination to be a little unwelcome or just an utter bad. On the other side, some other people regulate black feelings thoroughly. They eat, nurture, and unleash them voluntarily at the cost of someone who provides their ends.

These feelings are sometimes groomed from a young era. The kid knows that the parents hurry to make an offer if it shouts in a particular manner. When parents don't feel the wrong way about the kid at an early stage, the kid brings up believing that individuals can be handled in their life to do their job. The weeping would stop being a gun but proceed in manipulative forms. They use emotions to chastise their victims if they don't use cries. Therefore, it becomes an obscure need to regulate what began with harmless juvenile conduct.

The length of time this person controls would identify the strength of his behavior. Dark psychology is all about learning a person's way of thinking. It aims to know why these activities are based on the models shown before the deeds

The Framework of Dark Psychology

Both in the past and our daily life, we have cruel, evil, and selfish people. Psychologically and in the language which we use regularly, we have multiple designations for various Dark Behaviors, especially for psychopathy (absence of compassion), narcissism (excessive absorption of ourselves), Machiavellianism, so-called' dark triads,' and so on. It implies that most dark characteristics are aromatic representations of one essential trait: the dark portion of the personality. It means that you are more likely to show one or more of those dark personality traits, as well. The latest research demonstrates that the common denominator of all dark features, the D-factor, can be defined as the general patterns of maximizing one's utility — ignoring or recognizing others or leading to a wicked disutility

In other words, the general trend of people's own goals, concerns about others and the delight of injuring one another can be attributed to all the darkness together with a variety of viewpoints that act as justifications and thus discourage emotions of guilt, disgrace or the like. Research shows that in particular, dark characteristics are seen as cases of this prevalent heart even if they may differ in the common elements (for example, the narcissistic justification element is compelling, whereas a malignant disutility is mainly characterized by sadism).

Compared with the evidence that Charles Spearman has approximately 100 years previously that people who hold high places on certain kinds of intelligence exams typically also execute exceptionally on a different type of intelligence tests, researchers are following the common criterion D. "Intellectual" or "device-oriented trends are frequently called the Dark components of personal personality. But you can identify that the person has an elevated D coefficient by defining the popular title for the distinct dark features. It is because the D-factor indicates that a person who has one or more of the dark characteristics is more inclined to take part in other unlawful activities as well (like cheating, lying or robbing); in fact that this means that someone who has some evil behavior (likes beating others) is more inclined to be part of another heinous procedure (such as cheating, lying or robbery).

Dark Persuasion Methods

Trigger methods are often used by other names and are called forced strategies and stimulating tactics. There is only one way to convince someone to think or act in a particular way, which by persuasion. Persuasion can talk to the subject while providing evidence. To change the mind of the object, they can use some kind of force or pull on the object. And they can do some service for this problem or use different tactics. This segment details the different stimulation modes available for each method and their effectiveness.

Use of violence

In some situations, persuaders may decide that it is better to use some form of violence to reflect on the problem. This can happen if the ideas don't fit properly, if regular conversations don't work, or if the agency is fit. Dissatisfaction or regret about the mode of conversation. Violence is often used as a kind of horror tactic because the topic has less time to think logically than during normal conversation. Coercion is often used when persuader has little success with other coercions. However, violence may be available. Otherwise, you can use violence when the agent feels out of control or when the agent provides contradictory evidence, and the agent is angry.

Using violence with respect to violence is often not the best idea

For the stimulation process. This is because many subjects view the use of violence as a threat because they have no choice but to require the use of violence. The attraction you want is to choose a path to the lesson, but as power is added to the mix, you lose the freedom to choose. Instead of feeling threatened. If the material is perceived as intimidating, the agent is less likely to hear or think about the agent. For these reasons, the use of violence in the area of coercion is generally not recommended and not avoided. Different from other mental controls.

Influence weapon

Another method that can be used to convince a subject to lean in a particular way is to use available impact weapons. Robert Chardini created these six influences in his influential book. Techniques of persuasion have six goals. Persuaders can accomplish these. The six weapons of influence are reciprocity, commitment and persistence, social evidence, empathy, empowerment, and lack. It is very important that the agent is part of these six influential weapons

mutually

The first weapon of influence is mutual politics. The principle is that when a persuader offers something to another person. If there is a value, the object tries to return the agent. This means that a persuader occasionally feels obliged to perform a similar service for the agent when a persuader provides a service in a matter. Although the two services are not the same, they are the same.

Everybody is equal.

The tour ultimately creates a sense of duty for the subject and can be a powerful tool if persuader wants to use the trigger. Interactive rules are very useful as they help the agent get the subject in the right mood for coercion. Inject the sense of duty into this thing and drown it. In this case, a feeling of duty tends to make persuader believe that they will act or behave in a certain way.

Another advantage of persuader is the use of interactions

A moral position to impose obligations on objects; This is a position supported by social norms. Persuader does not have to worry about whether there is an appropriate code of ethics to return the favor. If the subject does not consider this necessary, persuader has various tools at its disposal to implement them. As a community, people hate people who don't pay back or pay for free gifts and services. If persuader doesn't feel that classes are going to and from them, they can involve them in their social group. You can do this by telling other friends and colleagues how you like the topic. However, the material will not be returned if necessary. Persuader is now promoting socialization classes by turning to helpers, further increasing their chances of persuading them to do something.

In most cases, the lessons are readily returned to the agent

Without the need for external strength. If it is found, the agent looks for ways to repay the agent. The score becomes uniform and does not appear greedy or selfish. Persuaders can provide an easy solution to repay these debts. The lessons appreciate this simple solution, and persuader is more likely to do what they want.

Commitment and sustainability

Persuader must use both if they want to persuade someone to change. From their point of view. When things are smooth, they are easy to understand, and the lessons help them improve their results. It does not change the fact that persuaders always use it or change other information that requires material to process. Instead of helping. The process of persuasion, which maintains consistency, makes the agent look like a liar or an untrustworthy person, which leads to the failure of the induction process.

One of the most important aspects of the stimulus process is persistence.

Reason:

Hard work is invaluable in society: in most cases, people want things to be a certain way.

There are many types of everyday life, but people believe that the whole thing is more consistent.

They can remember what happened, know what to expect, and be prepared for change. If there is no consistency available, it is very difficult to plan things,

It is always a confusing problem. If you want to believe in a topic, you need to make sure your facts are consistent and meaningful.

Stable

It benefits the everyday attitude of most people. Have you ever tried to plan a day when something unexpected happens? It makes things almost impossible and ends. Feel like a disaster. People love patience because they know what to expect and what to do.

They know when to eat when to work and when to do other things.

Stability provides an invaluable summary of the issues of modern existence. Life is enough without it

Then add those that aren't. If people can live a sustainable life, things will be much easier.

Sustainability is a great tool because it can make the right decisions and process information. If so, the agent wants to successfully persuade the topic. He needs to make sure the message is consistent. There is no room for false evidence to appear later and destroy the entire process. Keep the facts true and accurate and believe that the topic is very good.

Related to permanence is engagement. It takes some commitment to know that the title is really concrete and worth the effort. Advertising means buying a product, and politics means voting for product-specific candidates. Commitment depends on the type of trust. Under the concept of sustainability, a person may value a commitment if involved in writing or verbally turned out to be more true written duties, titles can be very psychologically specific, and there is solid evidence that they have agreed to the promise. It makes every sense.

Many people verbally promise, fix, or do something, but they don't. Of course, some people will do what they said.

You are more likely to make verbal promises than if you do not, but often it is difficult to achieve the desired result. Furthermore, there is no way to confirm this because there is only one verbal agreement, there is disagreement, and no one can win. On the other hand, if the agent can confirm in writing, they have enough evidence that the thing is over.

It is very important that persuader agrees to the obligation, as subjects are more likely to act in a manner that meets this obligation when a new approach is committed. Afterward, the important thing is that the topic continues, and you can convince yourself of this. You and others will provide a variety of reasons and reasons to support your involvement to avoid agent problems. If the agent can solve the problem in that location, there is little that the agent has to do.

Social evidence

Stimulation is a form of social interaction, so it must follow the social rules that occur. This thing is influenced by those around you. What they want others to do instead of doing it themselves. In classes are based on their beliefs and actions, what others around them do, how the same people behave, and how they feel. For example, if your subject grew up in a city, you behave more like the rest of the neighborhood. On the other hand, those who grew up in a very religious community

Time to pray, learn, and help others.

With this belief, the term "power of the crowd" is very useful. Classes always want to know what others are doing around them. It is almost hysterical to do what others do in this country. How people differ and what they want to be as individuals must agree.

Examples of what people do are heard on the phone because other people are doing something. Host "Waiting for the operator; please call now." You can feel like an operator is sitting there doing nothing because nobody is calling. This makes it more difficult for them to make a call because they should not make a call when there is no one on the phone. The host changes only a few words, and instead: "If the operator is busy, call again." Very different results. Here the Chancellor assumes that the operator calls several clients. The system must, therefore, be appropriate and systematic. Subjects are more likely to make calls regardless of whether they pass or need to be suspended immediately.

Induction technology

The effects of social evidence can be very useful in situations where the object is uncertain, or there are many similarities to the situation. In ambiguous or uncertain situations with many choices or possibilities, the subjects often choose what others are doing. The decisions are very similar, so they all work, but assume that the decisions made by others are correct. Another way to use social evidence is with some similarities. For example, classes are about some people, and they are more likely to change. If someone resembles a responsible person, the person is more likely to listen to and follow them than the responsible person is very different. Persuaders can use social resource ideas to support the process of coercion. You are the first way to do this

Look at the words they say. In the Game Show example, the two quotes were the same, but changing the words had two different meanings. Both are wrong. You have triggered a variety of reactions. When persuader can see their words from things, they can get the right answer from the subject and force the subject to adopt the same ideas and beliefs.

In addition, persuaders will be more successful if they are able to share ideas with people like themselves. That is why politicians want to fight in groups for similar ideas. If you want to reach larger groups, change your ideas to address these new groups. Cause or that; if the subject wants a persuader, they are more likely to say yes. There are two main factors that influence a material agent's preference. The first is physical attraction, and the second is unity first if the agent is physically very attractive in this regard.

Changing the attitude of others makes it easier for you to get what you want, so you will feel confident. This fascinating factor has been shown to be effective in transmitting cheap messages and other attributes of the agent, such as intelligence, kindness, and ability.

Narcissism, Sadism, Machiavellianism, Psychopaty

Machiavellianism

This is a technique that traces its origins from the famous political philosopher known as Machiavelli. His established works on influence and political power, "the prince", Machiavelli shares with the rest of the world his version of ideas, principles, and tactics that have saved the purpose of a sort of blueprint for those individuals who might be looking for influence throughout the course of history. Based on this, we then ask ourselves what this Machiavellian person actually is and how he comes about. What puts this particular tactic on the map is basically the manipulator's affinity to only focus on one's self-interest at all times, the exercise of ruthless power and cruelty, one's understanding of the importance of image and the perception and superficial appearance.in a nutshell, Machiavellian individuals are people whose approach to life is widely strategic. Meaning that, the ramifications and consequences that they take are usually well thought out and assessed in terms of how they might end up impacting their lives if they do it in a particular way .you may simply identify a Machiavellian individual since their speech often revolves around something like, "how will this benefit me, and how will my public reputation be impacted by this result?"

Machiavellian individuals are pros at doing that which personally serves their interests while at the same time skillfully managing to maintain the best public image without anyone being the wiser. Perhaps one of the biggest examples of one such individual is that of the former president of the United States, bill Clinton. He succumbed to his sexual desires while in office time and time again, while at the same time managed to keep the people's admiration for him stronger than ever. This is really an advantage he had over the majority of politicians with the same lifestyle but is frowned upon by the public. Another example in the political arena is also that of President Barrack Obama, and George W Bush. Barrack Obama while in office cultivated and capitalized on his love for peace while Bush solidified his image as that of a guy who always had war on his mind. Obama was able to manipulate the masses building a public perception that served his one interest evil bush did to even try.

Psychopathy

To be able to tell you in black and white what psychopathy really is would be difficult but the vary basic definition of what psychopathy really is ,or rather who a psychopath really is, is that particular individual who seems to be suffering from a type of psychological disorder which heavily involve a superficial charm, impulsivity and a lack of commonly held "human" emotions such as empathy and remorse .these psychopaths can be regarded as the most dangerous people on the face of the earth as they are the best examples of two faced sons of bitches. Pardon my language. When the majority of people hear the mention of these individuals, the first image that usually comes to mind is of a haggard looking individual wielding a machete and wearing a mask like John Wayne Agency. But the reality of their identity is far from this. They are most likely to be very handsome strangers who win over their victims by being just the right amount of charming, before eventually ruining or even ending their victims' lives. Surprisingly, based on a series of tests, experiments, and observations, it has been discovered that there exists a high number of these individuals at the very helm of the business world. A majority of people are just now beginning to view psychopathy as more of a problem to the whole society that for the very psychopaths owns selves. They are usually programmed in such a way that they can survive in any field they chose to go into. This is mainly attributed to their indifferent views they have regarding normal human feelings of love, compassion and so forth.

Narcissism?

If you ask anyone who they think a narcissus is, I can bet on it that the most likely answer you are likely to receive is that of an individual who simply loves themselves. This is along the correct lines but not accurate enough, particularly when narcissism is understood through the dark triad lens. Without being a narcissist, you can have self-love. So, what are some of the differences between a highly self-esteemed individual and someone who is narcissistic to the extent that they are regarded in the Dark Triad range? Someone who meets narcissism's medical diagnostic requirements, to the point that they are deemed to have a psychological disorder, is likely to continuously display a variety of the following characteristics. They are usually captives of the inflated sense of self-worth which manifests itself f in a number of ways .these include seeing their lives as the most special and important to have ever existed., seeing that they're of a biter spaces hire in status than that of "normal people". This behavior often reflects their sense of self-worth.

Narcissists are likely to have an excessively inflated self-worth, such as seeing their life as special and one of the most important in history, often the most important. Narcissists are not, in their own minds, only special—they are superior. They are a better species of person, higher in status than "normal" people. Their behavior reflects their sense of self-worth. Some of narcissism's prevalent outward manifestations are an inability in any manner to tolerate criticism or dissent. The need to be flattered is similar to this need to be agreed. Narcissists need continuous praise, endorsement, and appreciation and tend to organize their life in a manner that provides them continuous access to others who meet this need.

Having looked at the base of this particular behemoth theme of dark psychology, let us now dive in headfirst into how the dark triad manifests itself into the behaviors of these indifferent human beings.

Machiavellian characteristics

We know that a Machiavellian person is a political schemer who is mainly concerned border lining obsessed with his public image. These particular groups of individuals are considered to be the most cold-hearted in their pursuit of self-interest above all else. What then could be said about the behavior of these types of individuals? Due to their master level skill of masking their true intentions from the public eye, their behaviors might be abetted hard to decipher.

For most individuals who do not fulfill Machiavellianism's clinical definition, their public persona is generally a reflection of their true personal self. Everyone polishes their picture and conduct in public a little, but in general, the outward picture of most people is nothing more than a polished portrait of who they really are. They often have a fine line as to what they truly are and the person who they often pottery themselves to be in the public eye. Perhaps the best example to be given here is that of serial killers. The best has often been able to escape the grip of the law because of their outward image being the furthest thing from their morbid fascinations. The most famous example that can be given on this is that of a renowned serial killer, Ted Bundy. He was a very handsome man according to those who knew him. He was also very eloquent and just wall presented that no one imagines him to have a single bad bone in his body. This is what enabled him to murder an upwards of 30 women before he was eventually caught.

Examples of such a distinction between intent and appearance can be found in areas less extreme than serial murder. There are countless tales of leaders in the world of business who manage to ruthlessly cut jobs and pursue profit over people whenever possible. In terms of Machiavellianism, the very best of these bosses can actually get individuals to purchase into the idea that they behave by necessity or even compassion! Such rulers are almost role models for those who only want to serve their own wishes while simultaneously appearing to be a "person of the individuals."

A willingness to exploit people is another hallmark of Machiavellian individuals. Let us look at an example to have a better understanding of this. A newcomer in a particular office who possesses these Machiavellian traits would see each individual colleague, boss or team member as a resource or piece of a puzzle to use and utilize. The Machiavellian person would see a sequence of strategic threats and weaknesses to handle, exploit, or neutralize instead of seeing others as fellow human beings. This is a big component of the reason why Machiavellians are so conscious of how they find themselves. They understand that this outward depiction is the key to exercising impact and exploiting everybody they come across effectively.

Psychopathic characteristics

It is in all aspects to know how this group of individuals manifest themselves so as to detect them early and putting up the necessary defenses against them. Charm is one of a psychopathic person's most prevalent behaviors. It must be understood that this charm is superficial rather than profound, real charm. If you think of a truly charming individual from your lifetime, you will probably acknowledge that they have favorable characteristics that underpin outward behavioral displays. However, if an n individual genuinely displays a charming persona as an expression of kindness, they should not be labeled as psychopaths. Psychopaths can show all the outward indications of charm such as physical appeal, obvious warmth, and interest in others. The inward motive behind these outward displays is why it's such a red flag. Psychopaths see charm as part of an equation. The manipulator usually asks himself as to whether if displaying a particular emotion towards the victim makes them feel in a particular euphoric way and also if the result will prove to be advantageous or themselves. They are very calculative people who are numb to normal human feelings. Lying is another trait that really makes psychopaths really stands out. We all lie in our day to day lives. This doesn't necessarily mean that we are all psychopaths. However, it can show a psychopathic personality when coupled with other characteristics.

Lying comes for a psychopath as naturally as breathing for most individuals who are psychologically healthy. A psychopath can convincingly present the reality in a specific time as anything they need it to be. Also, psychopaths do not demonstrate outward indications of lying because they do not have any emotional attachment or emotions of shame, guilt or excitement about their lies. Lying is just "doing what's required at the moment" for psychopaths.

Narcissistic characteristics

One of the most prevalent characteristics in almost all narcissists is the fantasies of their absolute power and an elevated sense of importance. Most of these individuals lay blame on the constant praise they got as children while talking about these fantasies.as adults these individuals will still demand praise from all around hem since they have nurtured the feeling of being most important of their peers to the maximum.

The inflated sense of self-worth experienced internally by narcissists also has consequences for their external reality. This typically manifests in two ways— the need for consent and praise, and criticism or rejection hate. For the narcissistic ego, praise and consensus are like oxygen, while criticism and dissent are like poison. Picture a dictator in a hermit state in order to comprehend what narcissism looks like when taken to its logical conclusion. Such individuals request worship from those over whom they have authority, statue building in their likeness, and full obedience and recognition. Any act of dissent or disagreement shall be punished quickly and brutally. North Korea would be an ideal contemporary illustration of narcissism's extreme manifestation. That nation's rulers request reverence like gods and execute and torture anyone who even dares to convey a thought or concept that is not entirely consistent with the formal doctrine of the state.

Common Techniques & Tricks Used In Dark Psychology

Thus far, we have talked about techniques that are used in dark psychology. Indeed, we have only skimmed the surface as there is quite a bit to discuss when it comes to manipulation tactics. You will find that some of the techniques we will get into a very common and rather overt while others are rather subtle and go unnoticed. In fact, some of these tactics are so subtle that you don't even know they are there; but they are. They will find a way to make it into your mind.

Now, the reason why dark psychology techniques are effective lies in the way they interact with your psyche. The human psyche is structured in such a way that it is capable of filtering out stimuli that somehow don't conform to the patterns, beliefs and values that permeate the psyche. For instance, if you believe in peace, your mind will reject any notion of violence. By the same token, if your mind is centered on greed and avarice, you may place very little restrictions on schemes aimed at getting money.

However, the subconscious mind, the layer that exists beneath the conscious mind, is unfiltered but equally able to process the stimuli that enter it. This is why the manipulator's true goal is to access your subconscious and implant ideas at that level. When that happens, the chances of ideas and beliefs sticking are very high.

This is why advertising is so repetitive. Think about it. If you only head an advert once, the chance of you recalling it would be very slim. However, if you hear adverts over and over, there will come the point where your conscious mind will stop putting up a fight. When that occurs, the message can seep through into your subconscious. This is the secret of brand positioning. So, if you think advertising, at least good advertising anyway, is about selling stuff, guess again. Good advertising is all about getting you to constantly think about a brand or a product.

Persuasion

Earlier, we talked about how persuasion is the act of convincing someone to do something. In order for persuasion to work, your tactics need to somehow resonate with your target audience. In order for that to work, your message needs to reflect the values and beliefs of these folks.

So, your argument and reasoning could be so compelling that your logic would be undeniable. But would that still be enough to get people to do what you want? What if you are the best candidate for a job but the company decides to hire someone else anyway?

These are the considerations that persuasion looks to deal with. Persuasion works when you are able to resonate with the target audience in such a way that you evoke feelings in them. A simple example may be a political candidate going into a town that's desperate for jobs to unveil a plan to create more jobs. This would be a rather overt attempt at getting folks to vote for them. And while folks may be skeptical about the candidate's ability to actually create jobs, they may feel compelled to vote for them out of desperation and hope.

Another powerful emotion that you can trigger is fear. Any time fear is evoked in people, their primal survival instincts kick in. This might compel people to go along with you simply because they fear the outcome if they don't. While this may also be associated with coercion, the fact of the matter is that your ability to trigger these feelings will allow you to get ahead.

Manipulation

However, persuasion doesn't always work even when you are able to trigger emotions. In such cases, you may have to take things up a notch. In this case, manipulation becomes the most immediate means at your disposal.

Manipulation can be as blatant as you would like it to be. You can be quite overt, that is, do very little to conceal your true intentions, or you can be much more subtle. The fact is that it depends on the situation you are in. There are times when you can be overt while at other times you can be very subtle.

Consider this situation.

A supervisor knows that many of the workers in their department are desperate for jobs. They really need their income and will do just about anything to keep their current job. Knowing this, the supervisor will coax them into working overtime on a regular basis. Sure, they are paid for their overtime, but the truth is that they are being exploited. However, the workers will say very little because they need the job. And even when they know they are being exploited; they have little choice but to go along until they can find another job.

Another good example of manipulation can be seen in relationships. One partner can manipulate the other by using statements such as, "no one else can love you as I do." This is rather overt manipulation. As such, the victim, over time, will internalize the fact that there is no one else that will love them in the same way. This can lead to creating a type of dependency among partners, thereby limiting the will of the victim.

Emotional Manipulation Techniques

Emotional manipulation can happen at various levels. We already know that fear is a very powerful emotion. But that's not the only one. How about greed? That works just a good as fear. People who are driven by ambition can be easily had with statements such as "think of all the money you could make." Such a statement would drive a greedy person over the edge.

By the same token, if you're dealing with someone who is overly frugal, a statement such as "think of all the money you could save" would hit their sweet spot. The point here is that you need to know the person you're dealing with in order to make your manipulation attempts ring true.

So, let's take a look at some emotional manipulation tactics which you can use in a given situation.

The Bait and Switch

This technique is predicated on a person pretending to be someone they are not until they get what they want. For example, a person who is interested in gaining something from another may pretend to be romantically interested in this person. The victim, who is desperate for love and affection, will go along with the hopes of entering a meaningful relationship. The manipulator then gets close enough to their target until they extract the benefit they seek. Once the manipulator gets what they want, they pull the bait and switch; that is, they revert to their true self.

This type of technique is used to prey on the emotional needs of a person and is not limited to romantic relationships. This can also occur when a manipulator senses that someone is desperate to make money. The manipulator then uses this need to manipulate the victim with the promise of easy money or a steady income. The victim goes along only to be defrauded at some point.

In a manner of speaking, the manipulation takes place every time the manipulator is able to strike a chord with the victim. The victim falls prey for the empty promises of the manipulator until either the manipulator reveals their true self, or just moves on.

The Blame Game

This is very common in the workplace. There are folks who are experts at pinning everything on someone else. For instance, when something goes wrong, the manipulator will find a way to shift the blame to someone else. The ablest manipulators are able to produce compelling evidence against others thereby clearing their name of any responsibility. Then, there are folks who are just full of excuses for the shortcomings. These folks tend to wear out their welcome quickly and need to move on sooner rather than later.

The blame game can happen in relationships, business dealings, and politics. Politicians who find someone else to blame for the problems happening in their country often present themselves as saviors and heroes for their people. They are the ones who have a solution for everything, yet when you drill down on their track record, they really don't achieve much of anything.

Guilt

Guilt is one of the most powerful manipulation techniques known to humankind. Guilt can be used to manipulate people by making them feel inferior for the help and support they have received at some point. Guilt can also be used to get others to feel inadequate for a condition they possess. Think of all those times you hear people say, "things would be different if you weren't sick." That is one of the most rudimentary means of making someone feel guilty, yet it is highly powerful. Also, you may hear others say things like, "remember when you needed my help? Now, I need your help." This is a clear attempt at coaxing someone to go along with the manipulator's intentions.

The White Knight

This game is used by skilled manipulators. In this game, the manipulator purposely creates a problem and then rushes to the rescue. The intention is to create dependency among those around them as the manipulator is the only one who can solve the problems they encounter. However, the victims may not be aware that the problems are artificially fabricated by the "white knight" to make themselves look good.

This is an expression of the problem-reaction-solution technique. In this technique, manipulators create a problem or exacerbate an existing one, then get people to react in a certain manner so that they can come to the rescue with the miracle solution.

How To Use Manipulation Techniques

1. Establish Similarity

Establishing similarity is one of the most effective ways to get someone to do something you want them to. Whether you're trying to impress a man or woman you've just met a party or your boss into giving you a raise, go all out to establish a strong sense of familiarity. People quickly take to others who are much like them. They subconsciously develop a strong sense of affiliation for the other person and are more likely to do what he or she wants them to.

Observe the way they talk and try using similar words and phrases. Similarly, notice the way they hold their drink or lean against the wall, and follow suit. Sip your drink immediately after them or shift your weight from one leg to another just like they do.

However, when you are mirroring people's words and actions to reinforce that you are just one among them, do it in a more subtle and nonobvious manner. If the act of mirroring is too obvious (or in your face), people will be offended by the notion of you imitating them, which can backfire hugely.

When you want to influence or manipulate people into thinking and doing things in a certain way subtly mirror everything from their body language to intonation to words and expressions. This method works wonderfully well when you are trying to manipulate someone in a professional or official situation since emotions seldom work in such settings.

2. Sign up for a Drama or Theatre Workshop

One of the biggest hurdles when it comes to manipulating people is to master not just your emotions but also expressions, voice, and body language to convince people of your contrived or created feelings.

Have you tried practicing appearing distressed or disillusioned when you want to have your way? What about faking various emotions and expressions? Taking a theatre, drama or acting class is a great way to hone your manipulation powers.

Ensure that you do not let people know you've signed up for a theatre class lest they stop believing in the genuinely of your rather practiced emotions and expressions.

To be a master manipulator, you've got to know and master your emotions. Practice being in control of your emotions, otherwise, you will end up manipulated instead of being the manipulator. You will have to cry when required, laugh at the drop of a hit and basically learn to put on a variety of acts according to the demands of the situation. Recognizing and using your emotions/expressions at will is an important skill for any manipulator to pick.

3. Develop Charisma

The concept of charisma is hard to explain yet it can be quickly recognized or identified when you see it. Charismatic folks have an effortless and inherently smooth tendency to get people to do exactly what they want. They often seamless work their charm to hypnotize people into their way of thinking and behaving. Do you radiate a warm and friendly vibe? Do you have a more approachable, affable and open body language? Can you hold people into a compelling and arresting conversation even if you've only just met them?

People well-versed in the art of manipulation practice their conversation skills. They complement others generously and make them feel exclusive and special. Make eye contact with people you desire to influence. Give them the feeling that you are truly interested in getting to know about their feelings, emotions, and interests. Demonstrate that you care to take the trouble to know them better (even when you clearly do not).

Confidence is a huge charisma booster. Charismatic folks and people who wield magnetic personalities are aware of their effect on people during interactions, which makes them even more confident. This confidence, in turn, makes them appear even more charismatic. Thus, it is a circle of each positive leading up to the other. If you have explicit faith in yourself or your abilities, you are likelier to be successful in influencing or manipulating people into thinking or behaving like you.

If you are confident of yourself, you inspire the faith and trust of other people too. People tend to take your words and actions more seriously if they are convinced that you know exactly what you are doing, and that comes only with practiced confidence. Be glib when you are talking to people you want to manipulate, whether you are speaking the truth or fabricating something to accomplish an objective.

4. Practice Reading People

Each individual has a distinct personality, and a unique spiritual, psychological and mental make-up. Everyone is not likely to respond to your manipulation techniques in a similar way. Every person has a different trigger point that drives them into thinking, feeling or behaving in a certain way. Before you begin putting together an elaborate plot for manipulating someone, take some time to thoroughly study their personality. What makes him or her tick? What is the most suitable and effective approach to get them to do what you want them to? What are the person's most compelling fears, motives, and needs?

Here are a few tips for reading people accurately.

Identify if people are more prone to emotional responses. These folks may turn out to be easier to manipulate emotionally or psychologically. They are typically people who sob while watching movies, feel an instant connection with animals, display strong sympathy for people and a high sense of empathy for other's problems. To get them to do something specific, you have to tap into their emotions until they feel a sense of pity for you and give in to your wishes.

Some people are more open to a logical or rational approach. They need facts, figures, statistics, and evidence if they have to buy into what you say. If for instance, you realize that someone keeps themselves updated with news reports frequently or requires hard facts and figures before making important choices or decisions, you'll have to be more calm, persuasive and fact-oriented while trying to influence them. There will be a greater need to speak in a more composed, balanced and rational manner without resorting to an overt display of emotions. You'll at best have to use subtle, calm and gentle persuasive powers to manipulate them into the way you want them to think and behave.

5. Follow an Unrealistic Request with a Reasonable One

This is a classic and proven manipulation technique that we've all used at some point or the other. It is super simple yet works like a charm! It begins with the manipulator making a highly unreasonable request, quickly followed by a more reasonable and realistic request. In doing so, what you actually end up doing is give the other person an opportunity to compare one request against the other and be far more psychologically relieved with the second request after being shaken or disturbed by the first.

There is a huge surge of tension caused by the first request, followed by instant relief following the second request. This make makes it easier for the person to give in to a reasonable request.

6. Induce Fear then Relief

Plenty of marketers, brand managers, advertisers and business owners' prey on the fears of consumers to manipulate them into buying from them. Make the person imagine the worst situation, followed by helping them feel relieved. This sneaky little trick will help you to get them to do precisely what you want them to.

For instance, you could say something like, "When I wore your dress for the prom night, I thought I heard a horrible sound of the dress tearing. I was sure I had torn your beautiful dress. However, I realized that it was just a video one of the girls was watching on her phone. Isn't that truly funny?" Oh, and this reminds me, can I borrow the dress again for an upcoming weekend bash if you do not mind?

See what we did there? We simply took the person on a whirlwind of emotions from fear to immediate relief that the dress is still in good condition after all. They will be in a more positive and receptive frame of mind, which will increase your chances of having your way with them.

7. Induce a Feeling of Overpowering Guilt

Guilt is another excellent tool for manipulating someone into your way of thinking, feeling and doing. This works even more effectively on people who aren't sure of themselves, do not possess a very high self-confidence (or sense of self-worth) level or are generally indecisive by nature.

People also feel an overpowering guilt in their partners by saying something like, "It is all right, I didn't expect anything else from you." This implies that he or she is always letting you down, and you do not really expect anything better than that from them.

Notice how some senior people induce guilt among their children and manipulating them into doing what they want them to by stating that the children do not spend enough time with them or do not do much for them or that they aren't going to live for too long now even though the grown-up children go out of their way to spend time with them in the midst of their busy schedules and domestic duties.

8. Play Victim

Playing the victim card is another time-tested manipulation strategy. Often a group of people to gain political or social or some other benefit will portray themselves as a disadvantaged group to attract the support of masses. They will manipulate popular opinion in their favor by demonstrating the unfairness they've been subjected to or the disadvantages they faced on account of belonging to a particular group, class, community, tribe, race or religion.

Use this technique carefully and cleverly to get it right, without overdoing it. Basically, you are telling others that you're a wonderful and giving person or group or community and that the entire universe is against you.

Rather than arguing, fighting or squabbling with people to have your way, simply act calm and like you've accepted the situation. For example, if a co-worker refuses to give you a ride back home from the office, tell them it is all right. "I could do with the exercise since no one is willing to help. It is absolutely fine."

9. Do Not Admit to Using Manipulation Tactics

Some people are really smart and experienced cookies. They sniff manipulation from miles and more so if you've been using the same techniques on the same set of people over and over again. If a friend, manager or spouse calls you out for using sneaky, manipulative strategies for having your way, never ever admit to it. Just open your mouth wide open, gape and say, "I do not believe you actually said that." Act horrified (now you know the importance of signing up for that acting class) and hurt.

Saying something like, "I do not believe you think like this about me" will make the person feel really bad about accusing you of resorting to manipulative techniques. Under no circumstances should you ever admit to using manipulation because it will be extremely hard to manipulate the individual into doing what you want again.

10. Flirt

We all have done this more than once. Flirted our way into people's hearts and minds to get them to do what we want. You can't simply issue orders and tell them to do what you want them to. People can't really be forced to do what they want. They have to like you or even better adore you if you want to cast a spell on them and drive them into thinking or behaving in a particular manner. You invoke positive emotions and give yourself the power to make a more favorable impact on the other person.

Characteristic Of Manipulators

Who has never come across people who take on the most different psychological traits? People who at every hour act in a way, adjusting the situations and the moments, all to quickly achieve their goals? We call this psychological manipulation behavior. It is the influence exerted through mental distortion and emotional exploitation. The manipulator uses these tricks to steal the balance of a person or group of people, inducing, shaping and conducting behaviors, all to gain their own benefits.

Manipulators use the power of oration. They are good at using clever tactics to convince their victims that their lives have changed for the better after meeting them. They are masters at selling their "qualities" and convincing everyone that they are the best people in the world, the most honest, the coolest, and the sweetest.

A manipulator is the famous "wolf in sheepskin". They seem like a nice person, the kind we always want to have around. A born manipulator sees no one as a friend. For him, people are mere "bridges" that will lead them toward their goals. Manipulators enter the intimacy of their victims.

Types of Manipulation

People dissatisfied with their social, loving, professional and family lives are real oceans of possibility for manipulators to exercise their "talents". There are different forms of manipulation, one for each situation:

The Idiot: This word is not very well known. Deceiver, liar, and crook are the meanings. The talkative manipulator has political, financial, and even sentimental goals;

The Brute: The rough manipulator has psychological problems. Owners of narcissistic and perverse personalities. It makes their victims feel emotionally dependent;

The Good: Unlike the other modalities, the good manipulator believes that he has noble feelings and that he can change the world according to his rectitude of character.

Abilities of a Manipulator

Lying: Manipulators have, in "lying", their main weapon. They invent truths convenient to the moment and the people they encounter. If you suspect something is not true, they feel offended;

Put You Down: They discover what you love, what you hate, everything to gain your trust. They ardently celebrate their achievements and get very upset when things go wrong. They convince you that you are worthy of the best and that the moments of "lean cows" are enormous injustices committed by cruel people. Manipulators use their findings against you;

Favors: Prepare to rely on a willing person to help. The manipulator may perform repairs or arrange for someone to do this. They may follow you in the doctor's office. Manipulators help compulsively. But they will know when and how to charge for these favors.

Promise: Manipulators promise heaven and earth. They swear eternal friendship and love.

Hide things: A manipulator knows everything about you. Without realizing the victim reveals the address, landline and cell phone, e-mail, where he studied, shoe size, measurements, weight. However, when they feel that the information is not coming at the desired speed, they use family and friends of the victim to speed up the process, bringing one more person to his or her web. The manipulator knows strictly about you, however, there is no reciprocity.

Manipulation vs. Spirituality

Manipulation is against love. Manipulators are people who consciously choose their victims, using them without even showing a minimum of remorse, with great pleasure in seeing their prey increasingly surrounded by the web of seduction. We can say that manipulators are incapable of loving.

Spirituality has its explanations for manipulative attitudes. They are still in the early stages of spiritual learning. They still do not realize that the evils we provoke will one day be turned against us. Manipulators are the fruits of a society that every day departs more from what really matters, that immensely values material goods and elects as winners those that can accumulate a financial fortune.

In this context, manipulative people are considered "toxic people". Toxic because they hypnotize us in such a way that we need them, and we come to wonder how we can live without them. The "toxic people" steal personal information and intimate details, our identity. Additionally, since we become dependent on the company and the "friendship", we lose our autonomy, therefore, we cannot take a step without consulting their opinion. Manipulators steal our energy.

Manipulators Are Everywhere

It is worth noting that manipulative people don't always come out of nowhere. Often, we find individuals with this behavior in the workplace, at school, and in the family. The characteristics presented above are shaped according to the mode of conviviality. Here's how to deal with manipulative people in these environments:

At Work

In a professional environment, the manipulator is the employee always ready to help. But remember, it's a compulsive help. He stays at the heels of colleagues, reinforcing at all times how much he loves helping colleagues who have difficulties in their tasks. The manipulator on the desktop is able to stay up later, and even take a break in the office, all for the "pleasure of helping others". The targets of "goodwill" are charmed with such dedication.

The manipulator is seen as the legal person of the company, employee and fellow stick to, for all work. However, this establishes a relationship of dependence. Whoever is the target of "goodwill" is being placed in a web. The one who receives the "help" loses his autonomy since he cannot act without asking for the manipulator's opinion, and consequently loses confidence and does everything to not lose this "friendship". When the victim begins to perceive himself as such and tries to escape, the manipulator reverses the roles and convinces his prey that he is bad. The prey, in turn, accepts such a condition and follows the will of his tormentor.

- How to get rid of the manipulator at work?

Be firm and kindly dispense unsolicited favors. When the manipulator takes the day off to flatter you, return the compliments, but make it clear that you are just doing your duty, and anyone else would do the same. The manipulator will be amazed at your steadiness.

In School

At school, the manipulator is the perfect colleague. The manipulator targets unpopular students who are constantly ridiculed.

The manipulator praises the high notes, you are sure that the "new friend" is the best student. When his grades are low, he places the blame on the teacher, because the teacher certainly did it in order to harm him. He does not hesitate to defend injustice. There is no bad time that prevents you from helping with the activities and the manipulator makes a point of doing the work with you. The target of such unknowing friendship reveals what time he leaves home, what time it takes to drive there, reveals possible enmities with other students, tells of his fears and anguish. The manipulator reveals nothing about his life.

When the victim begins to realize that something is strange and tries to disengage, the manipulator feels extremely offended. He places the "friend" as an unjust person, unable to recognize true friendship. The manipulator depreciates the "friend", listing his defects, and claims that he will return to be a solitary person and will be ridiculed if the friendship ends. The prey, who already had low self-esteem, is even more vulnerable. Thus, the victim believes the manipulator, apologizes and no longer measures their efforts to do all the will of the manipulator, so afraid of losing the "friendship".

- How to get rid of the manipulator in school?

If you feel that you are being cheated again, move away slowly. Speak only as necessary and ask other people's opinions on how to deal with the situation.

In the Family

In the family, the manipulator sticks close to that shy relative and is considered good by everyone. It may be that cousin who always gives compliments, even when the victim has done something that isn't so great. The manipulator justifies the blockades of his "object of affection", believes that his target is wronged. He insists on telling us how much he loves us and is happy to be with such special people.

The manipulator is always ready to go to the mall, help with school activities, go to the doctor's office and do some repairs. However, when the target begins to be bothered by the excessive clinginess and flattery, the manipulator turns the tables and lowers his victim. The manipulator underscores his lack of social skills and how he is seen as lonely, poor, and a failure unable to have friends. The sentences that the victim says will continue to be seen as unimportant. The already emotionally unstable target agrees with everything, apologizes and resumes "friendship", doing everything according to the will of his tormentor, afraid of not being able to count on such a valuable person.

Weapons Of Persuasion

What are you trying to do when you try to persuade someone? In its very nature, persuasion is the ability that allows you to influence your goal in allowing a new belief in your system. You do this by making sure the belief you instill in your target fits the way he thinks. You also do this by challenging the authorities he listens to and assuming that you are the authority of the new belief that you want him to acquire.

At this point, you will begin to realize that persuasion is a very powerful tool. Persuasion allows you to move in and drop your target's defenses by placing them in a situation where their beliefs would be changed.

Beliefs are very powerful in creating what is comfortable for people, which in turn dictates what they had done over and over again. They are not 100% correct, and according to experience, they are malleable. Because they can change depending on one's world experience, you, the controller, will be able to challenge them and make your expectations view their environment as something else. It sounds easy, but it is not, of course.

The obstacle you face as you step into persuasion is your goal's definition of comfort. People would always want to believe what makes sense to them, such as their religion, their choice of products, and their entire lifestyle. We do not care about anything else. Now, you should dispute the notion and offer damning evidence that some (or all) of your convictions may be incorrect. How are you doing this? You need to find a way to get them to listen and make sure you are on the same page and get them to accept that you make sense. You should step in for the kill when that happens.

One of the most effective ways to convince the target is by admitting a weakness, downside, detriment, or disadvantage before the other person does. For hundreds of years, this principle has been known, understood, and applied. The reason you admit a flaw in your case, or you state that you seem to be more truthful to the other party and your target by doing so.

For today's society, where everyone is cynical, this will be useful. By being skeptical, it is meant that people in today's society will usually not believe a case or claim if the only advantages, benefits, and other arguments are admitted in their favor. As such, they usually expect people to be on the lookout for a capture. In other words, you will be automatically regarded as an honest and trustworthy person by accepting a negative, fault, or drawback of your argument, idea, or case at the outset.

This strategy is one of most people who sell their proposals or services using the best tactics; this works well because the dealer would always give a personal brand testimony by making his current experience so much better than his previous life. The comparison makes the objective more conscious of what he wants–he never wants to experience the trouble you have been through, and anything you have tried and used personally will save him the trouble.

Why is this tactic going to work? Because this makes them know that you can make mistakes that make them feel you do not have your defenses all the time, and you can relax in front of them. Moreover, your target will feel more comfortable with your presence because you do not seem too enthusiastic about persuading him or her to buy your claim, proposal, or case. Instead, you are providing them with an opening they can test. So, which makes the entire statement a very exciting proposition–it becomes something very fascinating about which they would like to find out more. As such, the moment you are trustworthy in the eyes of your target is the moment to strike perfectly!

You can better convince your target if you have done something that is going to be in his or her favor.

Offer your assistance. Any form of help is appreciated. The target will be more comfortable with you in this way. The target will also have a certain relation to you–implying that he sees you just like him or her. Once your goal becomes comfortable with you, your mental defenses will be lowered; this is the perfect time to convince him or her in your plan, statement, or case at the end of the day when he or she lowers his or her mental defenses.

Here's what a lot of self-help gurus would do–they are giving themselves a little background, and that'd always be about the time they weren't successful. Once they find an easy way to change their lives, they turn up and tell you. They had told you their methods worked because they were trying the hard way to do things. They are willing, however, to show you how to do things that would make your life tremendously better just the way you want it –the easy way. The technique appeals to many people because these accomplished people are willing to share what they have been through and are willing to share the secret without the recipient having to go through the bad experiences to gain the information.

It would also be advisable to point out that you are like your target as well and offer your claim because you think you are very similar. By making people think that people with the same rank can easily exchange experiences, you can always persuade people. Now, they had found they could relate to an expert like you!

Knocking off the socks of your target means you are giving it a pleasant surprise. How are you going to do this? Blow off your goal with an amazing fact, an amazing statement, or just something that only a few people would learn. Make a claim, case, or suggestion that you can make. Or, there is something you can teach them that has never been done before; this can also be something that can change the way the idea or statement is perceived; this will open their minds in such a way that they will accept new ideas and thoughts. It positions them in a state of relaxation and acceptance, in other words.

The psychology behind this is that people enjoy being pleasantly surprised in general. If your target has been pleasantly surprised, making him or she say yes to your proposal, claim or case will be relatively easy. Why do you know? Because if you help such a person discover some amazing new reality, deciding to pursue another person (you) will always be relatively easier. It will be relatively easy to decide to give in to your statement or suggestion because you intend to feel more comfortable and receptive.

There is a reason why people believe in success stories. In essence, everybody wants always to find the easiest way to do things, and they are willing to buy anything that a person used to get out of a terrible situation that is also likely to happen to them. When you sell a parachute, the belt that people usually use is made of strings used to hold a parachute together, keep in mind that they likely wouldn't find themselves falling out of a plane and using a parachute to save their lives. However, if you tell people that a parachute can hold more than 500 kilos of weight so that they can use it tow their cars, and that it is the favorite bracelet for hunters and adventurers because it can serve as a tourniquet, a fishing line, or something to tie up their tents, they had to buy one from you for three times the price. That is because these are the information that would make you think the service is much more important than it appears.

Another useful tip linked to this technique of persuasion is the last introduction of the plan you want to be accepted or the item you want to purchase; this indicates that you have spent a considerable amount of time asking for approval of a plan or buying an item from your target. Because of your actions, the target would usually have to accept a single item or service after you have been removed from the start of the discussion. As such, placing your most important proposal or product at the end of the presentation or conversation would be strategically advantageous.

Be precise. You should be precise and specific in specifying details to your target audience if you want to add an element of credibility and credibility to your statements. The explanation for this is that if your words contain clear and detailed information, it means you know how they affect other things. When you understand how certain issues can be influenced by your plan, argument, or event, your claims are more difficult to attack. Moreover, most people unconsciously feel better when very specific and accurate information is given to them.

Why are figures and percentages of all sorts of convincing people? It is because they get a sense of security from specific numbers. Of course, people do not think that 100 percent of the time, something would work. They had wanted something that is almost foolproof because the "almost perfect" object they might get is even better than all the other products they've tried.

That is why consumers often prefer to buy items use numerical adjectives like most, almost all, and 9 out of 10. But if you insist that your product is perfect, notice the number of questions you get. That is because people do not think about perfection. They would rather get something that can be flawed, but if they fulfill the conditions, they are still guaranteed to work. That makes the brand more interesting and trustworthy for people.

Suppose you are a consultant for operations management, for example. How can you apply the principle to your target dealings? Okay, you can say your target that his or her revenue will increase by 46 percent in 6 months through the use of your consultancy services. That is unique now! But if you tell someone you can promise a hundred percent increase in his revenue, then your goal will be more likely to go away. That is because you do not get your target as a buyer unless you can show him some big-time customer who can back up your story.

Benefits Offer: What is a good offer? An offer should look like it is, not just for your benefit, for the benefit of your target. You need to make an offer that would build the same appeal for that reason.

Bear in mind that most people are more self-interested, not you. They are more likely to be aware of themselves, and they definitely wouldn't be following your interests. If you are going to make them act on what you are thinking of, make sure you make it look like they are getting more benefits than you would.

Emotional Influence

Understanding the basic dynamics of manipulative and abusive relationships is important for everyone. Any type of relationships can be characterized by specific types of behavior. Psychologists have identified many specific techniques of behavior modification commonly employed by emotional manipulators. Some of these techniques include:

- Positive reinforcement: This technique was identified by the behavioral psychologist B.F. Skinner, whose theory of operant conditioning resulted from his experiments with small animals placed in cages. In his experiment to prove the theory of positive reinforcement, he used cages equipped with two levers—one lever did nothing, while the other produced a food pellet whenever the small animal pushed it. Soon, the animals learned - through positive reinforcement - which lever to push to get the reward.

Emotional manipulators employ positive reinforcement in their strategies by using techniques such as praise, false and superficial demonstrations of emotions such as charm and sympathy, excessive rewards including gifts, money, approval, and attention, and other outward demonstrations of emotion meant to make the victim feel good.

- Negative reinforcement: The other part of Skinner's experiment proved the effectiveness of negative reinforcement. For this part of his experiment, small animals were again placed in cages, which were again equipped with two levers. This time, the cages were charged with a mild voltage of electricity that caused slight discomfort to the animals that were placed in them. Once inside the cages, the animals would press one of the two levers. One of the levers did not produce any results, while the other stopped the electrical current, relieving the discomfort. Soon, the animals learned to press the lever that lessened their pain.

Emotional manipulators employ negative reinforcement in their strategies by using techniques such as removing someone from a difficult situation or relieving them of the responsibility to complete an agreed job or task in exchange for some type of favor.

- Intermittent reinforcement: Intermittent reinforcement can be either positive or negative and is used to create doubt, fear, or uncertainty. An emotional manipulator may "train" his or her victim by imposing inconsistent reward and punishment mechanisms to lessen the victim's sense of confidence, control, and autonomy. For example, in a romantic relationship, the predator may condition the victim to wear certain clothing, listen to certain music, eat certain types of food, and work at a certain type of job. As the victim in this relationship gains confidence, the predator may begin to discourage their victim, who will be caught off guard. As the victim scrambles to respond, the manipulator may again change tactics.

- Punishment: Punishment is a very basic form of emotional manipulation that may involve an entire range of psychologically and emotionally negative and damaging behavior, such as threats, yelling, nagging, complaining, intimidation, insults, guilt, and other forms of emotional blackmail. Skilled predators may find a way to incorporate this abusive and controlling behavior into the relationship over time, so that the victim will develop a tolerance for abuse.

- Traumatic one-trial learning: This technique is related to the use of punishments, but rather than a feature of a long-term relationship, these techniques involve discrete episodes in which the manipulator uses verbal abuse, demonstrations of anger, and other forms of dominance and intimidation to discourage the victim from certain types of behavior.

Specific Types of Emotional Manipulation

Within these major categories of emotional manipulation techniques, psychologists have also identified a wide range of more subtle variations that we all likely encounter on a daily basis.

These techniques include:

- Lying: Dark Triad personalities, particularly psychopaths, are highly skilled at lying and cheating, so often we may not detect their intent until it is too late. Beware of those who have demonstrated a pattern of dishonesty.
- Lying by omission: Lying by omission is a little more subtle. The predator may not say anything that is untrue but may withhold information that is necessary in an effort to cause you to fail.
- Denial: Often the damage from emotional manipulation is inflicted after the fact. When you confront someone with evidence of their dishonesty and abuse, their refusal to admit wrongdoing can cause even greater psychological harm.
- Rationalization: The increase in popular news media has led to the growth of public relations and marketing firms who produce "spin" to deflect criticism in both political and corporate environments. Rationalization is a form of spin, in which a manipulator explains away his or her abuse.
- Minimization: Like rationalization, minimization is a form of denial in which the predator understates the seriousness of his or her offense.
- Selective attention and/or inattention: Manipulators will pick and choose which parts of an argument or debate should be considered so that only their views are represented.
- Diversion: Manipulators often resist giving straight answers to questions, particularly when they are confronted by their victims. Instead, they will divert the conversation to some other topic or change the subject altogether.
- Evasion: More serious than diversion, a manipulative person confronted with his or her own guilt will often completely evade responsibility by using long rambling responses filled with so-called "weasel words," like "most people would say," "according to my sources," or other phrases that falsely legitimize their excuses.
- Covert intimidation: Many manipulative people will make implied threats to discourage further inquiries or resolution.

- Guilt tripping: A true form of emotional manipulation, a manipulator will exploit the integrity and conscientiousness of the victim by accusing them of being too selfish, too irresponsible, or not caring enough.
- Shaming: Although shaming can be used to bring about social change when large corporations or governments advance abusive or discriminatory policies, manipulators may attempt to intimidate their victims by using sharp criticism, sarcastic comments, or insults to make them feel bad.
- Blaming the victim: This tactic has become increasingly common. When a victim accuses a predator of abuse, the predator will attempt to turn it around by creating a scenario in which the victim alone is responsible for the harm that came to him. The predator may also try to accuse the victim of being the aggressor by complaining about the violation.
- Playing the victim: Using the opposite tactic of blaming the victim, the predator will lure a conscientious person into a trap by pretending to have been grievously wounded and cultivating feelings of sympathy. The real plan, however, is to take advantage of the caring nature of the conscientious person by toying with their emotions.
- Playing the servant: This tactic is common in environments marked by a strict, well-established chain of command, like the military. Predators become skilled at manipulating this system by creating a persona of suffering and nobility, in which their bad actions are justified as duty, obedience, and honor.
- Seduction: This technique does not always have to involve sexual conquest or intimacy. Emotional predators may use flattery and charm to convince people to do their bidding, and they often look for people with low self-esteem.
- Projection: This term is used in psychotherapy. Predators who use this technique will look for victims to use as scapegoats. When the manipulator does something wrong and is confronted, he or she will "project" his or her guilt onto the victim in an effort to make the victim look like the responsible party.

- Feigning innocence: This technique can be used as part of a strategy of denial. Under questioning, the manipulator will "play innocent" by pretending that any violation was unintentional or that they were not the party who committed the violation. A skilled manipulator who lacks morality and empathy can be very successful at planting the seed of doubt.

- Feigning confusion: This technique can also be used as part of a strategy of denial. Under questioning, the manipulator will "play dumb" or pretend to be confused about the central point of the conflict or dispute. By creating confusion, the manipulator hopes to damage the confidence of his or victim.

- Peer pressure: By using claims, whether true or not, that the victim's friends, associates, or "everyone else" is doing something, the manipulator will put pressure on his victim to change his or her behavior or attitude.

Specific Examples of Emotional Manipulation

- Insisting on meeting at certain locations: Manipulators may try to get the upper hand by insisting on a so-called "home court advantage," thereby forcing you to function in a less familiar and less comfortable environment that diminishes your personal negotiating power.

Examples:

- Premature intimacy or closeness: The manipulator will immediately shower you with affection and reveal all sorts of intimate secrets.

Examples:

- Managing conversations by always requiring you to speak first: In professional relationships, this is commonly used as a sales and negotiation technique to mine you for your information to make a more lucrative sale.

- Distorting or twisting facts: Whether in personal or professional relationships, manipulators will use conversational techniques to distort facts in an effort to make you doubt yourself and back down.

- Intellectual bullying: An emotional manipulator may use an unnecessarily large volume of statistics, jargon, or other types of factual evidence to impose a sense of expertise.

Example:

- Bureaucratic bullying: This technique is similar to intellectual bullying. Unfortunately, this technique may indicate that someone is abusing their position of authority by insisting on placing as many obstacles, red tape, or other impediments in the way of what should be a straightforward resolution.

Example:

- Passive aggression

There are many examples of passive aggressive behavior in conversation in both personal and professional relationships to force you to back down to the predatory efforts of a manipulator.

- Insults and put-downs: Manipulators are good at following up rude or mean-spirited comments with sarcasm or some other attempt at humor to make it seem like they were joking.

Mind Control And Techniques

Our mind is very powerful, it is possible to put a thought in the mind, feel the emotions related to, train your mind and it would respond accordingly. Every individual has different aims in their life and even the concept of happiness as well differs from each other. Our subconscious mind knows our sources of happiness but at times our conscious mind is not able to comprehend it. To equip our complete potential, it is important for both conscious and subconscious mind works together. By doing this it becomes easier for us to control our mind and our will too.

Have you ever thought that how many thoughts do we have in one day? It is around 50,000 on an average and 75,000 for people who think too much. The worst part about it is that most of them are negative, repeated or have no purpose at all. But the fact is that your thoughts affect the feeling for others and if we say as a whole, it affects your life. For a few people learning mental techniques and skills are a luxury, instead, they are a necessity, and everyone should be aware of them.

It is your turn now to know and learn about the mind control techniques so that you free yourself from negative thoughts and do not stay distracted because of any argument. Here are the best techniques for you which were written after a great study-

1) Meditation- It is said to be one of the oldest techniques which are used for controlling the mind. This method has been used by our ancestors and their ancestors too. This method undoubtedly has positive results and brings peace to your mind. In meditation, we calm our mind and empty all the thoughts, so that we can focus on positivity and light. The best part about meditation is that it awakens

our subconscious mind and makes it easy for us to listen to its voice. Not only this, it was scientifically proved that the alpha rays which are produced by our mind, they are at its peak after meditation. These rays bring creativity and positivity to our minds. By doing meditation you would be able to control your mind by just thinking of the present and core things. It eliminates negative and baseless thoughts fro out mind.

2) Think of the opposite- This is another way of attracting positive thoughts and disposing of negative thoughts of your mind. This method is very simple, as you know that usually, the distracting thoughts are negative, so you just need to think it's the opposite. For example, if you had a fight with your friend in the morning and you are getting distracted at your work thinking about it. In this case, think of the good time spent with your friend or things they have done for you. So, this means that if you are feeling angry think of things which make you happy, such as your favorite place, food, etc. Just make a note that whenever negative thoughts surround you, do not let it control and think of good things.

3) Visualize- Always visualize yourself about doing good things or achieving success. We should always prepare our mind to think of victory and work towards it. It is very true that positive energy can be attracted, no matter how difficult our goal is but making our visualization positive we attract good luck. This technique is used everywhere be it sports, education and even in offices to get the work done. There are many books on it as well which state that whatever you ask the universe it gives to you if you are positive about it. So, if you think of the good it would come to you and if you think it cannot be done. Then it would not be done, so urge for positive results and work towards it by thinking right.

4) Physical Movement- Try to do physical work as much as possible, this keeps you busy and lets the unnecessary thoughts out of your mind. Try and go out for a coffee break, take a deep breath, do exercise (if possible) or take a deep breath. You can also listen to some

music that you like. Doing these things keep you busy and would help you attract positivity which may flush the bad thoughts.

5) Talk to yourself- You can be your best friend and enemy both. Talk to yourself in the mirror, ask questions to yourself as you yourself have a solution to all the problems. If we give ourselves positive answers and encourage ourselves, then our minds would work towards the goals. On the other hand, if you feed bad thoughts in your mind it will lead you to a wrong path. So, if you want to make yourself a better person, talk to yourself and strive towards achieving success in your life.

6) Distancing- This technique is imperative for each one of us. It is not easy to maintain distance from repeated, useless and negative thoughts but once you learn how to do that it would make your life trouble-free and full of happiness. Here you need to slide thoughts from your mind by not attaching to them. You just need to think that thoughts are just thoughts, they cannot control your mind until you let them. Just think that you do not have to act according to them and just let go of them. So, this would empty your mind and make a place for other good things. I can assure you learning this trick would make you and others around you lively.

7) Stop over-generalizing- This means that thinking of one negative experience again and again and connecting it to future experiences and then thinking that how would be your future. Stop thinking of the same thing again and again and relating it to the future. It not only hampers your future but your present too. For example, few people think that my parents divorced because they did not have a great understanding and start thinking that relationships are of no use and do no good. In fact, you should become positive and think of changing this perspective, you should give your best in your relationship, love them, care for them and understand them. Always give yourself a chance by thinking in a positive manner. So stop over-generalizing as it will make you a negative person. Just go with the flow and give your 100%.

8) Personalization- We should always avoid taking everything personally. We start taking the blame for things which we have not done or felt the insults that no one sees. For example- if a person is not in a mood to talk and avoids you. You would start thinking that he does not like you or is not talking to you because you must have done something wrong. You should always be positive and think maybe he was busy or not in a good mood. Stop taking responsibility for things that are not in your control. Always try to think in a logical and positive manner to see if it was actually your fault, this would help you in being fair to yourself and avoiding the unnecessary blame that you wanted to take on you.

9) Reward yourself- whenever you are successful in controlling your mind reward yourself. The reason behind it is that it would keep you motivated to do this in the future as well. For example, you do not feel like going to work, but go to work and reward yourself by having good lunch or order something you like and make yourself happy. Do not even do it excessively but initially to motivate yourself this is a good technique.

10) Punish yourself- This is the opposite of the above-mentioned point. If you are not able to control your mind then punish yourself for the failure, so that it would remind you in future if you are unable to control. Also, studies tell that punishments can lead to more self-control in people. For example, you can ask any of your family members to punish you if you are unable to control your mind. These things are important to keep you moving and motivated.

All these above-mentioned techniques can be learned by practicing. Every time you come across a situation which makes you anxious or angry, try to control your mind by any of the technique. Try to be calm and patient, all this can be achieved by eradicating negativity from your mind which would, in turn, bring peace. You are the only one who can decide if you want to keep negative thoughts in your mind or let it out.

Hypnosis

B rains aren't designed to get results; they go in directions. If you know how the brain works, you can set your directions. If you don't, then someone else will."

-Richard Bandler

Hypnosis is pretty easy to understand if you know how it works. Of course, it takes practice to master hypnotizing others; however, simply understanding how it works is very useful in being able to observe dark psychology and manipulation in practice.

Hypnosis tends to be misunderstood as a parlor trick that requires someone to be asleep or in a nearly asleep state to become hypnotized. Then, when they are under the spell of hypnosis, they can be made to cluck like a chicken or bark like a dog or repeat any number of embarrassing phrases for a cheap laugh. Hypnosis happens every day because all hypnosis means is that someone has entered into an altered state or a trance state.

We enter trance states every day. All it takes to enter a trance state is to affix your attention on one thing so intently that some or all of your peripheral awareness can be shut out. Most people, for instance, enter a hypnotic state every day at work or zoning out while on the subway.

Hypnosis can be a potent tool for getting people to compromise their critical faculties, and it ties into what we have been talking about so far in terms of polarization and eliciting the desired response from someone.

Stages of Hypnosis

Stage 1: Absorb Attention

The first step into altering someone's conscious state (hypnosis) is grabbing hold of their full attention. Believe it or not, there are verbal and non-verbal forms of this first stage of hypnosis. Take, for example, the situation mentioned above in which a person can be so zoned in at work that everything around them sort of just fades away.

This is a prime example of the way that our psychological states are changed when we are intently focused on something and of non-verbal hypnosis.

Of course, gaining someone's complete attention can be a bit easier if you are using words. People tend to cling more completely to someone's words when they are describing images or telling a story. It is a lot like how some people prefer visual learning over textual learning. The human mind can follow along better when pictures and mental images are involved because their visual sense is engaged.

You can practice this first stage of attention absorption in everyday speech. Go out with a friend or coworker and see how much more they pay attention to you when you say you have a story for them. Tell them a story, either true or made up, and be sure to include a lot of details. Paint the picture with your words, use a lot of adjectives to describe the scene. The more senses you can engage, the better. Give their mind and imagination something to engage with.

When you have them wrapped up in your story, you have successfully absorbed their attention which will lead you into the 2nd stage of hypnosis:

Stage 2: Bypass the Critical Faculty

The conscious mind is a rather limited entity. It takes in the data that is thrown at you every day, and it processes it rationally. The unconscious mind, on the other hand, is a lot more whimsical. It does not get bogged down with matters of reality. Consider, for example, that your unconscious mind is active when you dream. You may have never seen a purple, flying turtle in real life, but your unconscious mind is free to consider such things as completely real and viable.

The conscious mind deals with what is feasible. In hypnosis, this is what is known as the critical faculty. Think of the critical faculty as a guardian at the gate to the subconscious mind. The critical faculty is what alerts your mind to things that are impossible, unreasonable, and unlikely. If you are attempting to hypnotize someone, the critical faculty is the enemy of hypnosis. The point of hypnosis is transferring a person's mind from a fully conscious state to an unconscious or at least an altered state, and the critical faculties make it impossible for this switch to occur, so it must be bypassed.

Bypassing the critical faculties can be achieved by first absorbing the full attention of a person using simple techniques such as maintaining intent eye-contact with the subject and speaking a little slower and in a low tone than you normal.

Speaking in a hypnotic tone can go a long way in inciting a trance state and bypassing the critical faculty. If you are hypnotizing someone, you want to watch out for signs that your subject is in a trance state. Most importantly, do not give any hypnotic suggestions until you are certain you are past the critical faculty, and your subject is in a trance state. Otherwise, your suggestion will be rejected by the critical faculty.

Step 3: Activate an Unconscious Response

Activating an unconscious response does not have to be as extreme as getting a person to cluck like a chicken. It can be as subtle as evoking a laugh or making someone clap their hands to their mouth in shock. An unconscious response is an action carried out that a person is not aware of or is only aware of after the action has been made. In other words, it is a response that has not been regulated by the conscious mind.

Eliciting an unconscious response is very easy when a person has entered a hypnotic state. Look for dilation of the pupils, a change in breathing rate, or flushing of the skin. These are all signs that your subject has let their critical faculty guard down and have been ushered into a hypnotic state.

Once you observe this, try eliciting an unconscious response; maybe describe in vivid detail a delectable steak dinner so that their stomachs growl in hunger or a swarm of bugs overtaking someone's body so that their skin crawls with goosebumps.

Stage 4: Lead to Your Desired Outcome

This is the point where you, the hypnotist, can lead the subject towards the desired outcome through hypnotic suggestion or associated metaphors. This stage of hypnotism is all about speaking directly to the unconscious mind and taking advantage of the altered state to either help the person or to lead them to a conclusion, outcome, or decision that is favorable for you.

One example of this stage is called priming. Say, for example, that you want to go swimming and you want the subject to go swimming with you. Try telling them a story involving cool, cascading, and refreshing water overcoming oppressive heat. This could lead to a post-hypnotic reaction that has been geared towards your desired outcome.

Pattern Interrupts & Rapid Induction Techniques

The concept of pattern interrupts very simply. Consider each word individually: the first word in the phrase being "pattern." A pattern can be anything you do mindlessly or habitually. Getting up in the morning, brushing your teeth and taking a shower is likely something you do every day that you don't even really think about. This is an example of a pattern. A pattern can also be called a routine. Getting in your car and driving to work can be considered a routine.

Now consider the second word in the phrase: "interrupt." An interrupt in this context is anything that breaks your normal routines or patterns. Interrupts are conscious efforts to change the way you do things, the way you think or the way you act.

The major difference between the two words – the two concepts of "pattern" and "interrupt" – is that one involves an unconscious or passive state of mind, and the other involves a very conscious and active state of mind.

Pattern interrupts are often used in behavioral psychology and NLP to help people break harmful habits and routines in their lives. Routines often give us a sense of drive and purpose. Still, they can be detrimental when we get so used to them that we switch off our brains while doing them, thereby becoming vulnerable to hypnotic suggestion and manipulation.

The average human has about 50,000 thoughts per day, but the majority of these are repeat thoughts. Pattern interrupts are very effective ways to induce new thoughts, which helps the brain develop their ability to think critically. It is the difference between letting your brain atrophy and exercising it.

To get back to basics, consider pattern interrupts a way to alter yours or someone else's mental state from a conscious to an unconscious mode. This is precisely why patterns can be used for hypnosis and NLP.

In particular, the pattern can be very useful for rapid hypnotic induction or getting someone into a hypnotic state very quickly. This may be because of a slight disconnect in a person's mind when a pattern interrupt is used on them. The switch from passive to active brain function isn't seamless. There is a lapse in which the unconscious and conscious mind meld for a brief time, and it is in this time that a person enters a hypnotic state and is susceptible to suggestion.

Consider it a state of confusion that a person enters for a brief time when one of their patterns or thought processes is abruptly interrupted. Confusion tactics are very common and potent methods of rapid hypnotic induction.

Getting someone riled up about a certain subject is similar to putting someone into a confused state where their routine has been suddenly broken. It is in this state that a skilled hypnotist can implant unconscious suggestions and therefore predict a certain outcome.

Pattern interrupt techniques have become very popular in hypnosis and manipulation because they are fairly simple to carry out, and they can be done in virtually any setting and sometimes without the person even realizing it. It happens in an instant and garners the desired results in an instant, which is why it has become such an oft used tool to hypnotize and manipulate people.

The most popular method of pattern interrupts hypnotic induction is the handshake technique. In this technique, the hypnotist will go in for the very mundane act of shaking someone's hand. At the last second, before the hand's touch, one person abruptly disengages from the handshake and grabs the other person by the wrist.

Getting up and getting ready for work is a routine that could take hours, and shaking someone's hand only takes a few seconds, but they are both patterns and they can both be broken, and when they are, the mind enters an altered state.

This altered state is the goal of pattern interrupts and why they are such a powerful tool for inducing hypnotic trances.

Other Benefits Of Hypnosis

Boosting Performance

I n our day-to-day life, we are always looking for ways to improve our performance. Many things could hold us back from living our best life and achieving our greatest potential. If we are not careful, we can be held back by the many distractions in our life. One of the ways to increase performance is by indulging in hypnosis. It helps improve our focus and attention and prepares us for success. People who practice hypnosis have reported improved concentration and capacity to utilize their full potential. If one is struggling in any area of your life, be it academics or professional, hypnosis can be helpful.

Healing Anxiety

Let us face it; we live in a world that is full of stimulations everywhere you turn. These stimulations can have a negative impact on the emotional health of an individual. More precisely, they can cause an individual to feel anxious. When you are anxious, most of the time, you are going to be less productive, and have a hard time interacting with other people. However, we are social animals and we need to stay in contact with other people in order to fulfill our important emotional and physical needs. One of the ways to get rid of anxiety is through indulging in hypnosis. This exercise prepares one mentally to overcome the negative emotions and ascend from the bondage of anxiety. It also helps the individual acquire a high level of self-awareness, so that they are aware of who they truly are.

Boosting Self-Confidence

One of the major problems that most people face in the world is a lack of self-confidence. In addition, when one is lacking in self-confidence, it does not matter what their potential might be, but they are not in a position to accomplish their life goals. Before you can succeed, you need the input of other human beings. Then you have to be confident in your capabilities so that other people may come in. So many people end up wasting their potential because of their low self-confidence. One of the best ways to turn around this condition is through practicing hypnosis. In this way, the individual gets a boost in their self-confidence, and finally, they have the power to become who they want to be.

Eradicating Negative Habits

One of the things that stop us from becoming the best version of ourselves is our negative habits. We acquire these negative habits from either spending time with the wrong crowd or consuming negative material. Either way, negative habits affect our productivity and discourage us from being the best we can be. But then overcoming these negative habits is not something you can do at the snap of a finger. One of the exercises you can take to overcome these negative habits is hypnosis. Hypnosis helps kill the urge to revert into your old negative habits.

Helping Stop Addictions

It's one thing to have a negative habit, but it's another thing to have an addiction. When you are addicted to something, it means that you cannot function in a normal way unless you get your fix. Addictions not only kill any potential we might have but they also drive people into early graves. It is very crucial that someone overcomes their addiction because if left untreated soon they are reduced to nothing. Overcoming an addiction through willpower is a tall order. Hypnosis is one exercise that can help you fight away addictions so that you have a new chance to pursue your dreams and be the best you can be. Some terrible addictions that entrap most people include sex, alcohol, gambling, and video games.

Fighting Away Phobias

If you have a phobia about something, there's a reason behind it. But then phobias stop you from experiencing what life has to offer. Phobias cause you to be affected by things that do not affect normal people. Struggling with phobias means that there are many potential situations you are not comfortable with. In addition, this can complicate your life in far many ways. One of the best ways to fight away your phobias is through hypnosis. This exercise helps you overcome your fears and start living in a healthy fashion.

Eliminating PTSD

People go through a lot of emotional pain on a daily basis. You only need to turn the news in order to see how people are suffering around the world. It does not matter how lofty one might be in society, but they have been traumatized in one way or another. These tough experiences that we go through leave us emotionally broken. They leave us traumatized. In addition, this usually predisposes us to post-traumatic stress disorder. One of the ways to get rid of PTSD is through hypnosis. Performing this exercise on the regular helps, us gain understanding as to what we really are, the root cause of our emotional disturbance, and helps us gain awareness of how to put our emotional vulnerabilities in check.

Fighting Off Dysfunctions

One of the worst conditions that could plague a human being is a dysfunction. It simply means that one cannot perform as they are expected to. Having dysfunctions of any kind can take away the pleasures of life. In addition, this causes the person in question to become dissatisfied with the quality of their life. Overcoming a dysfunction is not something you would achieve in a snap of a finger. However, performing hypnosis on the regular has been proven to help people overcome their dysfunctions and start leading their best possible lives.

Eliminating Relationships Issues

A famous man once said that in order to be happy, one needs work to do, and someone to love. As human beings, we cannot get away from love, because it is the main point of living. However, far often, we find ourselves with the wrong person. We get into abusive relationships and hey ruin our self-esteem. Then sometimes we get into relationships that are perfect in the beginning only to grow worse at a later time. If we are paired with the right person, but due to our negative habits or mindset we start ruining the relationship. It makes sense to salvage the relationship instead of throwing it away. Hypnosis can help people come back into being the best partner and this allows them to have a powerful relationship going.

Settling Family Issues

Most people will tell you that their family comes first. However, if you would take a close look at most families, you would notice patterns that give rise to conflict. As human beings, conflict is just one decision away. Just because a family is, having problems does not mean that the whole family is helpless. It is rather an opportunity for the family members to work out their differences and start leading their best lives. Hypnosis is one of the exercises that helps fight away their family issues.

How to Find People Who Are Easy to Hypnotize?

Hypnosis is guarded by a number of principles. Once you observe these principles, your target should fall under your power, so that you can plant suggestions into their mind. Then the capacity for people to be hypnotized differs. Some people are easy to hypnotize, and others are not so easy. In order to be successful in your efforts, you have to first profile your target, so that you are sure they are easy to hypnotize, for this makes your work a lot easier. The following are some of the factors that point to people who are easy to hypnotize.

They like Fantasy

If someone is captivated by the world of fantasy, they are a good candidate for hypnotism. One needs to have an active imagination for the best chances. In addition, someone who is into having fantasies or enjoys fantasy-related things is likely to have a high imaginative drive. It is important to have a conversation with this person as you try to find out who they really are as it gives you a glimpse into whether or not they are inclined to fantasy-ridden ideals. The more a person is into fantasy, the better candidate they are for hypnosis.

Having Strict Parents

In your interactions with your target, you might want to find out what their parents were like. Generally, someone who had strict parents has grown into someone who follows instruction pretty easily, and that makes them a better candidate for hypnosis, as opposed to someone whose parents were never there for them. When you really think about it, hypnosis is about issuing instructions, making the person assimilate your ideas, and if they had strict parents, it means they are not new to receiving instructions.

Age

Technically, hypnosis flies better with extremes in terms of age i.e. People who are either on the young side or the elderly side. This is not to mean that any other person cannot fall into the power of hypnosis; but rather, it works better with people who are either young or elderly.

However, the greatest determinant of success in hypnosis is the observance of the principles. Ensure that you are following the rules and it doesn't matter who your target might be, but they will fall into your power.

Brain Washing

Much has been said about brainwashing in the past, both through its portrayal in popular media and as a focus in conspiracy theories. What's more, there is a reason to believe that government and military programs during the cold war era experimented with brainwashing. The now infamous MK ULTRA experiments sought out to find if mind control on human subjects was possible. But today, most notions of brainwash have been exaggerated by fiction.

Brainwashing devices do not exist as they are portrayed in cartoons and movies. But brainwash to an extent is possible. The issue boils down to definitions of it. What is a meaningful way to describe brainwash as a mode of being? Does a brainwashed subject have any conception of free will at all, or are they under the total and complete control of someone else?

Most likely, this form of brainwash does not exist in real life. For a human to give up all agency doesn't make sense given that we all have our unique set of needs and desires. Giving up some human agency, however, is more feasible. It is believable to say that a person's mind can be interfered with, molded with propaganda, or shaped through torture.

Military applications of brainwash are evident from the recruitment process to the captivity of prisoners of war. Soldiers must learn how to develop an obedient mindset, take copious amounts of mental and verbal abuse, and forget about their status as civilians.

Almost every major intelligence agency on earth is in some way or another thought to be involved in brainwashing techniques. The CIA, MI6, the KGB and so on are rumored to dabble in it. Under these contexts, both intelligence agencies and militaries of the world have direct access to coercive force, namely through firearms.

Force plays an important and often overlooked role in brainwashing techniques. What kind of behavioral change could an organized group induce if they had the freedom to do anything to their subjects? What would the psychological effects be if prolonged starvation, sleep deprivation, torture, and constantly repeating propaganda? Doubtless, some form of brainwash would be possible under these contexts.

Torture itself may create trauma-based personality changes. These changes can then be directed in whatever way the torturers want in order to influence behavior. Just like a child will learn not to touch a hot pan after being burned, a subject may respond in a certain way to stimuli if they are reminded of the torture they had to endure.

But trauma-based brainwashing and conditioning go beyond the scope of dark psychology, at least as presented in this book. From the perspective of a dark manipulator who prefers to operate in the shadows, using force or the threat of force may not work as intended. What trauma-based brainwashing tells us, though, is that behavioral change is definitely possible.

Non-Trauma Induced Brainwash

A subject who is conditioned through experimentation and the fear of punishment will act in a certain way. They will want to avoid the stimuli at all costs because their body reflexively knows what is coming. With non-trauma induced brainwash, you may get results where an individual acts out of personal belief rather than fear. The ultimate end of any type of brainwash is belief change, whether that is created by love or fear is irrelevant.

A non-trauma-based model of brainwash is similar to the kind using force but isn't so imposing on the target. The first step is to strip this person of their identity. Normally, it takes years for somebody to form a good idea of who they are. Somewhere around the mid-twenties, a person knows more or less who they are. To get rid of that identity can take a much shorter amount of time.

When the sense of identity is stripped, the subject is less in control of the ideas that enter their heads. They are no longer guarded and experience a sort of open-mindedness that they didn't have before.

The malleable state makes them susceptible to suggestions from their attacker or in many cases, their captor. Now, all that the attacker has to do is replace that identity with a new one. Anything from political goals, religious radicalization and conspiracy-based narratives can be conveyed to the subject, for the purpose of subversive control.

Attacking the Self

A human mind can be broken down so that all notions of truth are questioned. The popular adage to "question everything" can be turned on its head to become "question yourself." That will be the basic angle an attacker will take to start the processes of softening the target. Target selection is important because these techniques will not work on everyone.

When coupled with emotional and physical trauma, standard gaslighting works well. Fear-based attacks are more effective. They don't necessarily have to be a threat-based either. Convincing someone that a group of people is out to kill them and their families, for example, doesn't involve a direct threat. Such techniques have been used in the past by kidnappers to demoralize their victims. Somewhere between their traumatized mind and the sudden friendliness of their captors disorients their mind and they are more likely to believe what is being said.

Isolating the Self

Second to the breakdown of the notions of self-identity is the concept of isolation. Any brainwashing attempt must involve an element of isolation, both from friends and family and the rest of society as a whole. Friends and family are often the first to go, through a series of gaslighting attempts and deception campaigns.

Disinformation, spreading lies and rumors about the target's closest relationships instills a sense of doubt. they must be physically isolated from them, if possible. For the kidnapper this much is obvious. The non-violent manipulator must think about ways to create this distance without raising alarms. It could be finding a "third place" away from the home that they associate with their message.

Religious radicalization can take place in mosques, and other religious gathering places, for example. Physical isolation can also be convincing someone to move far from the place where most of their close relationships reside.

If physical isolation proves too difficult, another avenue to take is emotional isolation. This involves turning the target against their family and vice versa. A deep understanding of the familiar structure, as well as a mapping of local support systems, will be necessary to disrupt this balance. An attacker who has knowledge of these things picks up a massive number of secondary targets to manipulate or turn against the target. Disinformation and rumor spreading are the ways to go.

A broken support system means that there is nobody left to get in between you and the target. You can unload whatever mixture of manipulation techniques you deem fit, and there will be minimal interference. Getting to this stage is already winning half the battle. Just as much energy should be put into isolating the individual as put into the brainwashing part.

Conditioning the Mind

It is only after the self has been adequately broken down and possible support systems destroyed that an attacker should begin to target conditioning. This is the part where the target is introduced to new beliefs, new realities, and a world that is of your making.

The standard techniques of dark persuasion are useful in this regard. Another possibility is to use the carrot and the stick method. Reward the target when they say or do something that reflects your agenda and punish them when the contrary happens.

An Arab man might be convinced that they are at war with the western world and must commit atrocities in the name of their religion. An abused spouse may be made to believe that her relationship with her husband is not abusive at all. It really depends on what the objectives of the manipulator are.

Classical conditioning follows the reward and punishment scheme that is common in behavioral therapy. The target is somehow rewarded for admitting whatever the manipulator wants them to admit. There is some gray area whether coercive persuasion is a type of punishment. It certainly doesn't seem like a reward when the target must admit to something, so they don't want to. But because the manipulator has them cornered; they have no choice.

After a prolonged period of conditioning, the target may start experiencing complete changes in their belief system. They may start taking actions on their own behalf, without the manipulator having to instruct them. But if they do not, it is possible to give out commands to motivate them. These commands, if resisted after the conditioning phase, can be complemented by additional gas lighting.

Toxic People

The ideal goal of someone who is a manipulator is to get into a relationship with their target, one they can maintain for a long term, and that they can have full control over the other person. This is a very unhealthy relationship to deal with because it is just going to benefit the manipulator and not the target in any manner.

A healthy relationship is going to involve an equal amount of giving and take between the people who are in it. But if you are in a relationship where it feels like you are always the one giving, and never actually receiving something, you may be in a relationship that has someone who is manipulative in it. A manipulative relationship is going to be really tough to identify because the manipulation is going to be more subtle compared to some of the other relationship types that are toxic.

Psychological manipulation can happen when one person tries to create a power imbalance in the hopes of exploiting another person. Manipulation is going to have several methods that it can manifest, but the one theme that is going to keep on showing up between them all is that one person, the manipulator, is going to be the one who benefits, and the other person, the victim, is not and may even get harmed.

There are a lot of times when someone is going to end up in a toxic relationship, and not even realize it. The relationship may have started out perfectly normal, without any of the drama or the issues that you will later have to face when dealing with the manipulator. This is going to be part of the process that comes with the manipulator because it allows them to get in with target, and take control, without the other person realizing.

Of course, the relationship is not going to start out with the drama or the drain on self-confidence or any of the other tactics that the manipulator is going to use later on. If they started out with this, then the target would see right through them in the beginning and would run the other way. the manipulator is going to take a different approach. One that is slower and more thought out.

In the beginning, they will have no problem with love bombing and showing lots of affection. When the target is invested in the relationship, and often in love, then the manipulator will start to switch tactics. This will not be overnight and can take place over many weeks so that the target doesn't really notice the changes until it is too late. By this point, the target is so invested in what is happening in the relationship and around them that they will tolerate more of the manipulation and the problems than they would in the past.

There are actually a few different signs that can come up that show a manipulator may be at work in your own relationship. If you are uncertain about whether someone in your relationship is toxic and causing problems for you, or if they are a manipulator, it is important to take a look for these signs:

They push you to go out of your comfort zone in many different manners. The manipulator is going to do this financially, physically, and emotionally in order to make sure their target is off balance. This allows the manipulator to be the one with the upper hand, and then they can be the one in control along the way.

They will try to get rid of your confidence. When we start to have low self-confidence, we are going to be more easily manipulated because we are looking for ways to make ourselves feel better. This is why a manipulator is so interested in chipping away at our confidence levels to make us feel smaller and like we are never good enough. The manipulator can take our vulnerability and use it to their advantage.

The silent treatment. This is where the manipulator is going to take any small slight that you do and turn it into a big deal. And to punish the target, they are going to use the silent treatment and ignore them. This includes all emails, chances of talking, phone calls, messages, and more. The manipulator gets to maintain all of the control with this, and they will decide when the silent treatment is done.

The guilt trips. None of us want to feel guilty about something, and if we are feeling this guilt, then we are going to do every action we can think about in order to make that guilt go away. The manipulator is counting on this and will throw as much blame and guilt on the target as they can, even blaming the target for things that they had nothing to do with.

They will ignore or gloss over problems that are unresolved. Unhealthy relationships are going to thrive with lots of unresolved conflicts because there is no communication, or because the manipulator will deliberately not want to solve these conflicts. This is because manipulating you into thinking that the discussion was over and done with is going to be easier and more convenient for them than working to resolve that problem with you in the first place.

Now, we can imagine that this is not that healthy of a relationship type to be dealing with. None of us want to get caught up in this kind of relationship where we feel trapped and like the other person is always in control, taking advantage of us and doing what they want in the process. We want to be able to have control over our own lives. And we want to find a partner who is willing to let this happen, without taking full advantage of us in the process.

Before we go too far into all of this though, there are a few questions that we need to ask ourselves in order to help establish were we stand in a relationship if we think our partner is a manipulator.

The questions that you should ask yourself here include:

Am I being respected?

Are the expectations and the requests set upon me by my partner reasonable? Would I let someone else give me these same requests and be fine with it?

Is the giving and the receiving equal in the relationship? You don't have to go out and do a tally sheet, but there shouldn't be an obvious disparity here.

Do you feel good about yourself when you are around this person?

By the time we have gone through this guidebook, you should already be pretty sure about whether your relationship is a manipulative one or not. If you are in one of these types of relationships, some of the things that you can do to protect yourself include:

Know your rights. If you have been in this kind of relationship for a long period of time, it is sometimes hard to remember how to stand up for yourself. Remember that, no matter what the manipulator has said to you, you do have some fundamental rights that need to be respected. These rights include the right to have others treat you with respect, the right to express some of your own feelings, needs, and opinions, the right to set your own priorities without someone else controlling you, and the right to tell another person no. It is also your right to have an opinion that is different than another person, to help make sure you are protected physically, mentally, and emotionally, and that you are able to have your own life apart from someone else if you choose.

These are rights that the manipulator is going to try and take away from you in the long term. This allows them to maintain the control that they want and will ensure that you are able to do what they say. But the time that you are around your partner who is a manipulator, remember your own rights, take in a deep breath, and then try to execute them. You are the only one who gets to be in control of your life.

Stay away. The thing that you need to focus on doing here is to stay away from the other person. It is always best if you can keep your distance from someone who is manipulative. If it is too late for this one, see if you can at least get a bit of distance between the two of you. Every time that you do need to have some engagement with someone who is manipulative, you are simply giving them another chance to learn about you, figure out your weaknesses, and find a way to get into your life.

Staying away from this person is the first and the best way to protect yourself from someone who is manipulative. If you start to feel some kind of impulse to try and help them, run the other way. Remember that the manipulator wants you to fall for this, and they want you to feel bad for them so that they can get you back into the relationship and can take advantage of you again. Remember your own worth and stay away from the manipulator, and don't fall for the trap of wanting to feel bad for them or wanting to help them.

Remember that it is not your fault. One thing that a manipulator is going to work with is trying to look for the best ways to exploit the weaknesses that you have. When the manipulator finds what these weaknesses are, they are going to be able to take full advantage of these and will use it against you. This makes it easier to feel inadequate and the target will often end up blaming themselves on a regular basis for how much you end up disappointing the manipulator.

The manipulator does this on purpose. They know that you are going to be looking for ways to avoid guilt. And they know that they can always move the goalposts so that no matter how hard you work, and how long you work for it, you will never meet the standards that are set. This allows them to keep control the whole time, and to take advantage of their target for as long as possible.

Preventing Manipulation

1 Ground rules.

What you have read so far will help you to identify the difference between persuasion and manipulation. Persuasion may be for yours or the team's own benefit, manipulation is always for the controller's benefit. Examples could be: is what you are being asked to do within your normal remit? Are they asking you to rush something through for the team, or for their own personal remit? Will this benefit you, or make you look bad? Do you like and trust this person?

Manipulative people can seem to be everywhere. Most manipulation is not necessarily oppressive. Not every stranger asking you to do something is a controlling manipulative person.

Everyone can be a little manipulative when they need to be, so not every manipulative person is bad.

Take your time to identify a person whom you suspect to be a control freak. Do they come across as selfish? Are they approachable? Do they seem excessively bossy?

There are ways you can deal with a manipulator, should you have the misfortune to meet one.

2 Observe a manipulator before you label them.

It is not unusual in the workplace to have people telling you what to do. So long as they ask in the correct manner and they have the authority. Authority comes in many guises. It could be because they are your managers, or they are close work colleagues. If the request is genuine, then it should not be a problem. If someone is constantly demanding you to do things with aggressive coercion, then you are right to be suspicious. Don't jump the gun though, take your time. You don't want to overreact and ruin a workplace relationship unnecessarily.

Observe their behavior whenever you can, without them realizing what you are doing. Keep your distance because you don't want to attract this character's attention. It is important to identify this person for what they are, so you to keep them at a distance in the future.

3 Never let them see your own weaknesses.

If you recognize someone to be a controlling manipulative person, it might be best that you have as little contact with them as possible. This can be difficult in a working environment but try to restrict personal contact with them. That way, you are not likely to ever divulge your personal life or any problems you may be having. The last thing you want is for them to recognize any of your own weaknesses. They may use that information to gain a hold over you.

4 Never allow them to put you down, especially in front of others.

A common psychological phenomenon often exploited by manipulator's is Imposter syndrome. This is a phenomenon that has been well studied. At least 70% of people will suffer from Imposter syndrome at some time in their life (6a). It includes that dreaded feeling of inadequacy at whatever you attempt to do. Even if there is evidence that shows you otherwise, such as your own success at your work. You feel a fraud and you are simply waiting for someone to announce it. That someone may very well be the office manipulator. Except, of course, they are not uncovering you because you are perfectly proficient at your job. What they are actually doing is working on your own feelings of inadequacy. It's how manipulators work, especially the more invasive ones.

When you stand up to a manipulator, they can become abusive. A forceful manipulator will not let people stand in the way of their primary objective. Everyone is fair game in their attempts at power-play. If there is one in your work environment, it will only be a matter of time before they turn their attention to you.

What can you do?

Show them your confident side, especially if this person is constantly putting people down. You know them for what they are.

Convince yourself that anything they say is untrue.

Do not allow them to break you, and do not bend to their will. Try not to be confrontational with them, that could make matters worse, but stand up for yourself.

Sometimes, the best strategy is to take it on the chin and walk away. If their schemes and plans do not affect you, they will soon lose interest.

Don't bluster in front of them, that is a sign of weakness.

Show your strengths and the attitude that you have no care about what they think or say.

Then pat yourself on the back and walk away.

It is important that any conversation you have with them is never on a personal level. They may try to make it personal, but you must steer them away.

If someone does not treat you with respect, then show your contempt in a respectful way. Then, turn your back on them.

If someone is making unreasonable demands of you, stay clear of them whenever you can. If you can't meet their needs and they complain, be brave. Explain the truth of the situation but not in a defensive manner. Try not to be hostile or confrontational in any way, but don't allow them to walk all over you.

If you are successful at rebutting their attempts to manipulate you, they may become aggressive and personal. Now they may attempt the Imposter syndrome. This is where the insults of incompetent, inadequate and useless may come at you. Keep your calm and keep a distance of space between you. Don't apologize, that's what they want you to do. Trust in your own instincts and advise them to go to your supervisor with their complaints. If they are your supervisor, then let them know that you may need to take this further up the ladder of management. If you say this with commitment, they may falter. If you say it with fear, it may be time to walk away and indicate that you will speak with them once they calm down.

If the situation gets to this point, you may want to find someone you can trust to help you calm down. Tell them what happened so you can get it off your own chest. It was a disturbing situation, but you must be able to move on from it. Don't brood and don't be fearful of them.

They may not calm down and start making you a target of their abuse. Now is the time to be looking at making that complaint to those in a higher authority. Before you do that, begin to document your evidence of any future events involving you both. This will provide you with evidence for the day you decide to go ahead and report them. Whether your boss will accept your complaint is irrelevant. You have evidence to back up your argument and it could be enough for the manipulator to back off. Sadly, they will only find someone else to pick on unless the senior management accepts that there is a problem.

If you are regularly under the spell of a narcissistic manipulator, then will have low self-esteem. You MUST build up your self-confidence and become more powerful within yourself. Only then will you be able to break the chains they have wrapped around you.

5 How to leave a control freak

For many people, especially women, this can happen in the family home. For such victims, trying to break free is the most difficult. Not the least because the victim may, in fact, love their toxic partner or parent. If you are in such an unhappy situation then you must consider your own wellbeing and safety. Only if the perpetrator can admit that they have a problem and seek help, can they begin to mend. If they learn to compromise and accept your input, then it will be a great step forward. Such openness may save a two-way partnership. The problem is though, such a manipulator cannot see that they are making your life a misery. If they are so blind, how can they ever accept that something is wrong? Indeed, if you approach them, they may become defensive and aggressive. This is because they perceive you as having insulted their integrity and pride. How dare you accuse them of anything!

Unfortunately, if you are in such a relationship then the only way you will be free is to make the break yourself. The adage, "You only have this one life, live it to the fullest," is never after than in this situation.

How though, do you find the courage to leave? That is exactly what it will take to be rid of such an overpowering partner. They may even continue to threaten you after you have dared to leave. That is one of the reasons why you dare not make that move.

How then do you build up your confidence to finally leave the relationship?

6 Begin with building up a support network.

It is vital that you have support from friends and family. This can be a difficult one though. It could be that the very partner you have just left, browbeat you to severing all personal ties. If this is your situation and you are unable to pick up those ties, then there are organizations that you can turn to. These agencies can guide you in dealing with your situation.

It is going to be a rough ride and you may even need a safe house where your partner does not know where to find you. Don't feel ashamed. If you have children it will be even harder, but for their sakes, get them away. They can make contact again in later years if they so wish. Then they may better understand what happened. Bear this in mind that if you feel stifled, then almost certainly they do too.

That is, of course, the worst scenario. No matter how hard it is for you to leave, you must take the time for yourself, and recoup.

7 Don't forget your own health needs.

Do things that help you relax, if possible. Get outside and take short walks. You need personal space so you can consider your situation. Listening to music you like or immersing yourself in a book or a TV program, is good if it helps you to switch off. Avoid overeating or drinking too much alcohol. Your problem will become tenfold if you take that route. All these points are double stressed if you have children. You need to stay strong for them, and for yourself.

8 Accept that you will feel scared.

If your partner has sensed anything, they could revert to being overly nice to you. Don't be fooled, you know without anyone having to tell you that it will not last. It will only be natural to hesitate in your actions, whether it is out of fondness, pity, or fear. Fear of being on your own is natural. Fear of your partner's violence is not. If that's something you feel, then you are most certainly making the right choice. If you do leave, then you must make it quick and clean, leaving no trace of where you are going. Manipulative, obsessive partners will attempt to track down fleeing partners, even if only to punish them. You have broken their self-ego and now they have no one left to control. If they do find you, they may try the extra-nice approach and beg you to return, or they may be violent and angry. You don't want to be there for any confrontations whatsoever.

Understanding Deceptions

What is Deception?

How can deception be defined? Deception, alongside subterfuge, mystification, feign, deceit and beguilement, is an art employed by an agent to spread beliefs in the subject which are untrue, or truths coated with lies. Deception involves numerous things, example dissimulation, sleight of mind, suppression, cover-up, propaganda etc. The agents win the favor of the subjects, they trust him and are unsuspecting of his propensity to be dubious. He is able to control the subject's mind having won their confidence and trust. The subjects have no doubts about the agent's words, in fact the subjects trust the agent completely and possibly plan their affairs based on the agent's statements.

The deception practiced by the agent can have grave consequential effects if discovered by the subjects. How? The subjects will not be disposed to hearing his words, neither will they accept them anymore, no wonder the agent must be skilled at the deception technique. He must create an escape route to cover up if things boomerang and still retain the trust his subjects have in him.

Types of Deception

1. Lies: This occurs when the agent manufactures information or provides information that is not similar to the truth. They will give this information to the unsuspecting individual as the truth and the individual will then see this lie to be fact indeed. However, this can be unsafe as the person being given this false information would have no idea about the falsehood; most likely, if the subject understood that they were being given information that was not true, they would not be on talking terms with the agent and no deception would have occurred;

2. Equivocations: This is the point at which the agent will make statements that are differing, unclear, or not direct, such that the

subject becomes confused and does not understand what is going on. Also, it can help the agent to preserve their reputation, saving face if the subject later returns to blame them for the falsehood;

3. Concealments: It is the most frequently used form of deception. It refers to when the agent leaves out information that is related or critical to the situation on purpose, or they display any such behavior that would cover up information that is of importance to the subject for that exact situation. The agent won't have lied straightforwardly to the subject, they will, however, have ensured that the vital information required never gets to the subject;

4. Exaggeration: Exaggeration occurs when the agent emphasizes too much on a fact or stretch the truth just a little so as to twist the story to suit them. Although the agent may not directly be lying to the subject, they will manipulate the situation such that it appears as though it is a bigger deal than it actually is, or they may twist the truth to make the subject do whatever they need them to do;

5. Understatements: This is the inverse of the exaggeration tool in the sense that the agent will present part of the fact as less important, telling the subject that an event is less of a deal than it actually is when in it really could be what decides whether the subject gets the opportunity to graduate or gets a huge promotion. As such, the agent will be able to return to the subject saying they had no idea how huge a deal their omission was, they get to keep their reputation leaving the subject to look petty if they protest.

The above are only some of the forms of deception that there are. To reach their final goal, the agent of deception will make use of any means that are available to them, same as what happens in other types of mind control. These methods mentioned are however not limiting, as the agent would use any means to get to their goal.

The agent of deception (who is going to be good at what he does) can be dangerous since the subject will be unable to know what the truth is or lie.

Reasons for Deception

It has been confirmed by researchers that there are 3 major reasons for deceptions found in intimate relationships. These consist of motives focused on partner, motives focused on self-focused, and motives focused on a relationship.

In the case of the partner focused motives, the agent will use deception to keep their partner from harm. Also, they could make use of falsehood to save their partner's relationship with an outsider, thereby protecting the subject from worry, or keep the subject's confidence intact. This reason for deception is often seen to be of benefit to the relationship and socially respectful.

In comparison with some of the other reasons for deception, this one is not as bad. If the agent finds out about something terrible that the subject's closest friend said about them, the agent may remain quiet about it. Although this is a type of deception, it not only saves the subject's friendship but also keeps the subject from feeling terrible for themselves. This is the type of deception that is often found in most relationships and also if found out, might not cause a lot of damage. To protect their partner, a larger percentage of couples would use this form of deception to protect their partner.

The self-focused motive for deception is not thought to be as noble as the partner focused motive for deception, and as such, is not as acceptable as the other methods. Rather than stressing over the subject and how they are doing, the agent is going to simply consider how they are doing, and about their very own self-image. Here, the agent makes use of deception so as to protect the agent from criticism, shame or anger. Using this form of deception in a relationship is typically seen to be a very serious issue and offense than in the case of partner-focused deception. This is because the agent chooses to act in a manner that is self-centered instead of working to protect their relationship or their partner.

Lastly, the relationship focused motive of deception. The agent makes use of this form of deception to prevent any harm coming to the relationship basically by staying away from deception relational disturbance and quarrel. This type of deception will either help or harm the relationship depending on the circumstances. This form of deception could be harmful because it makes things rather complex. For instance, if you do not reveal just how you feel about dinner to prevent a quarrel, this might just help the relationship. Then again, if you keep to yourself the fact that you took part in an extra-marital relationship the situation is only going to become more complex.

No matter the motive of deception in the relationship, deception is not advised. The agent is holding back details that may be vital to the subject; when the subject discovers it, distrust in the agent will set in and they are left to ponder what other details the agent is keeping from them. The subject would, however, not be too worried for the reason behind the deception, they will simply be vexed that they have not been told some things, causing a split in the relationship. Usually, it is best to stick with truthfulness in the relationship and not encircle yourself with individuals who don't put deception into practice in your social circle.

Primary Components of Deception
Camouflage
The major component of deception is camouflage. It is the point at which the agent is attempting to hide the truth in such a way that the subject is unaware of the fact they are missing. Usually, this method is used when the agent gives information that is only partly true. Until these facts are uncovered one way or the other, the subject will not know that camouflaging has taken place. The agent will be so talented in hiding facts, with the goal that it is not easy for the subject to realize the deception has taken place by chance.
Disguise
This is yet is another component that can be found in the process of deception. In this case, the agent tries to pass across the idea that they are something or another person. This occurs in such instances when the agent holds back details about themselves, for example, their genuine name, what they do for a living, the people they have been

with, and what they do when they go out. This is more than simply changing the clothing that a person wears in a play or film; when the disguise is employed in the process of deception, the agent is attempting to deceive the agent by changing their entire personality and appearing as somebody else.

There are quite a few models that can show the use of disguise in the deception process. The first is in relation to the agent masking themselves, often as someone else, with the goal that they are not recognized. The agent may do this so as to be accepted into a group of individuals that do not like him, change their persona to make somebody like them, or for the purpose of achieving their selfish interests. Now and again, the word disguise can simply be referring to the agent masking the real nature of a proposal with expectations of hiding an impact that is not agreeable with that proposal. Most times this type of disguise is found in propaganda or political spin.

Disguise can be harmful for the reason that it is concealing the genuine nature of what is happening. When important details are held back from the subject, it clouds their thinking since they don't have the correct information to settle on logical decisions. While the subject may imagine that they are settling on logical decisions all on their own, the agent has, however, removed important information that may change the subject's decision.

Simulation

This is the third component of deception. Simulation involves presenting false information to the subject. Three methods that can be used in simulation include; mimicry, fabrication, and distraction.

In mimicry, otherwise defined as the copying of another model, the agent will without thinking be giving a picture of something that is like themselves. They may have a plan that is like another person's and rather than giving credit to the other person, they will say that the plan is all their doing. This type of simulation can happen regularly through sound-related, visual, and other methods.

Fabrication is yet another means of deception. Here, the agent takes something found in reality and changes it until it becomes different.

They may tell a tale that did not take place or add to a true story to make it better or worse. While the heart of the story might be true, agreed they got a poor score on a test, it will have some additional things put in, for example the teacher gave them a poor score intentionally. While in reality, the agent got a poor score because they failed to read.

Lastly, distraction is another type of simulation in deception. In this case, the agent makes an effort to get the subject to concentrate on other things, but not the truth; usually done by offering the subject with something that may be more tempting than the truth that has been hidden from them.

For instance, if a cheating spouse thinks the wife is beginning to suspect, he may bring home a precious stone ring to distract her from the matter even for a short while. The problem with this method is that it is not usually long-lasting and as such, the agent has to look for a new way to trick the subject if they are to keep the process going.

How To Use Dark Psychology In Your Daily Life

People use psychology within their daily lives, so why not use Dark Psychology and the tactics to protect yourself in everyday life. There are quite a few personality traits that can be very harmful if you get caught up in them. Sadists fall under this category. For instance, this personality type enjoys inflicting suffering on others, especially those who are innocent. They will even do this at the risk of costing them something. Those who are diagnosed as sadists feel that cruelty is a type of pleasure, is exciting, and can even be sexually stimulating.

We do have to face the fact that we manipulate people and deceive people all the time . When it comes to deception, people are deceiving not only others on a daily basis, but they are also deceiving themselves. People often lie to gain something or to avoid something. They might not want to be punished for an action, or they might want to reach a goal, and they self-deceive to get there.

Here are some examples of how people can deceive themselves:

Having a hard time studying - this is a common occurrence. When people are trying to study, they find a lot of things that can distract them, especially cell phones and social media apps. They will find just about anything to distract them from the task at hand. These types of people seem to have a phobia of not studying long or well enough and they are afraid that they will come home with a bad grade and it will show how unintelligent they are. So, they take the art of self-deception and come up with the idea that will help prevent them from studying. This excuse will weigh better in their mind if they do end up getting a bad grade on their test. The person's subconscious is telling them that it is better for them to get bad grades for lack of studying than to study and failing and therefore having to blame their intelligence. They couldn't live with that.

Here are other ways that we regularly deceive ourselves:

Procrastinating – People often waste time when they do not want to study or do something important. However, the main reason for procreating could be the phobia against failing and procrastinating was just an excuse. Self-confidence can be an issue as well.

Drinking, doing drugs and carrying out bad habits -People often fall into bad habits, drink, or do drugs just to have something to blame if they fall again. This type of person will try to convince themselves that if they could stop doing drugs, they could be very successful. When they are the ones deceiving themselves and standing in their own way.

People often hold back because life is unfair. They tell themselves that we all live in a big lie that most people believe in, but not them. It is easier to blame it on life being unfair, then hold ourselves accountable for not reaching our goals.

If you realize that you have been deceiving yourself, here is a couple of things that you can do to change that.

Remember that you are smart and the fact that you have been able to deceive yourself reaffirms it. If you were not smart, there would have been no way that you would have been able to come up with some of those ideas.

It is important to learn how to face your fears. If you are running from a certain trauma, or not wanting to take a test, you have to remind yourself that you are stronger than this and that you can beat it.

Lastly, once you face your fears, your self-confidence and courage will grow.

Manipulation in our daily lives

Manipulation is an underhanded tactic that we are exposed to on a daily basis. Manipulators are people who want nothing more than to get their needs met, but they will use shady methods to do so.

Those who grew up being manipulated, or being around manipulation, find it hard to determine what is really going on because if you are experiencing it again, it might feel familiar. Maybe you were manipulated in a previous relationship, or the current relationship that you are in reminds you of your childhood.

This is important because manipulation tactics break apart communication and break a person's trust. People will often find ways to manipulate the situation and play games rather than speaking honestly about what is going on. However, others value communication only to manipulate the situation to reveal the weaknesses of the other person, so that they can be in control. These types of people do this often in conversation. They have no concern with listening to others talk about anything about themselves. And they are not there to help those people get through whatever it is that they are going through. It is all about dominance in this case and that's it.

Here are some of the tactics that can be used on an everyday basis:

Some of the common techniques that we can experience are:

Lying – White lies, untruths, partial or half-truths, exaggerations, and stretching the truth.

Love Flooding – Through endless compliments, affection or through what is known as buttering someone up.

Love Denial – telling someone that they do not love you and withhold your love or affection from them until you get what you want.

Withdrawal – through avoiding the person altogether or giving them the silent treatment.

Choice Restriction – Giving people options that distract them from the one decision that you don't want them to make.

Reverse Psychology – Trying to get a person to do the exact opposite of what you want them to do in the attempt to motivate them to do the direct opposite, which is what you really wanted them to do in the first place.

Semantic Manipulation – Using common words with a person and later telling them that you have a different view of the conversation that you just had.

Being Condescendingly Sarcastic or Having a Patronizing Tone – To be fair, we are all guilty of doing this once in a while. But those who are manipulating us in conversation are doing this consistently. They are mocking you; their tone indicates that you are a child, and they belittle you with their words.

Speaking in Universal Statement or Generalizations – The manipulator will take the statement and make it untrue by grossly making it bigger. Generalizations are afforded to those who a part of a group of things. A universal statement is more personal.

Luring and Then Playing Innocent – We, or someone we know, is good at pushing the buttons of our loved ones. However, when a manipulator tries to push the buttons of their spouse and then act like they have no idea what happened. They automatically get the reaction that they were after and this is when their partner needs to pay close attention to what they are doing. Those who are abusive will keep doing this again and again until their spouse will start wondering if they are crazy.

Bullying - This is one of the easiest forms of manipulation to recognize. For example, your spouse asks you to clean the kitchen. You don't want to, but the look they are giving you indicates that you better clean it or else. You tell them sure, but they just used a form of violence to get you to do what they wanted. Later they could have told you that you could have said no, but you knew you couldn't. It is important to note that if you fear that you cannot say no if your relationship without fearing for your safety, then you need to leave the relationship.

Using Your Heart Against You – Your spouse finds a stray kitten and wants to bring it home. The logical thing to do would be to discuss being able to house and afford the cat. But instead, they take the manipulative approach. Their ultimate goal is to make you feel bad about not being able to take care of the animal. Don't let anyone, even your spouse, make you feel that you cannot make the best choice for you. You do not have to take care of the kitten if you don't want to. Bottom line. Meet their manipulations with reasonable alternatives.

"If you love me, you would do this" – this one is so hard because it challenges how you feel about your spouse. They are asking you to prove your love for them by giving them what they want from you, making you feel guilt and shame. The thing you can do in this instance is to stop it altogether. You can tell your spouse that you love them without having to go to the store. If they wanted, you to go they could just ask.

Emotional Blackmail – this is ugly and dangerous. The idea that someone will harm themselves if you leave them is harmful at the core. They are using guilt, fear, and shame to keep having power over you. Remember that no one's total well-being is your responsibility alone. You have to tell yourself not to fall for it. This will always be a manipulation tactic. However, you can tell them that if they are feeling like they are going to harm themselves that you will call an ambulance to help them.

Neediness When it's Convenient – Has your spouse started to feel sick or upset when they didn't get what they wanted? This is a direct form of manipulation. For instance, they don't want to go somewhere with you and have a panic attack, that you have to help them through, so that they don't have to go at all. This is not healthy at all, and if this persists you should think about ending the relationship.

They Are Calm in Bad Situations – When someone gets hurt, or their conflict, somebody dies, your spouse always seems to not react with any feeling. They are always calm. This type of manipulation makes you think that perhaps how you are reacting is a bit much. Maybe your emotions are a little bit out of control. This is a controlling mechanism because no one should be able to tell you how to feel. This might seem like they are questioning your mental health and maturity level, and you find yourself looking to them and how to respond in certain situations. If this something that happens often and you see that you keep falling for it, you might need to go and see a therapist. This way, they can help you work on your emotional responses and find your true feelings again. This manipulation method can be very damaging to your psyche. At the moment, learn to trust your gut. It will not steer you wrong.

Forcing Their Insecurities on To You – Your spouse will manipulate you into thinking that their insecurities are now your problem and will use them in a way to control you. They will tell you that they have been cheated on before, and that's why they don't like that you have male friends and that you should stop. Or they use them when they act a certain way, controlling your behavior because they don't want to lose you. When it comes to this situation, you have to find a balance. You can care for someone and make sure that you are considerate of their feelings, but you should not be manipulated into feeling what your spouse wants you to feel. Their manipulation is ruled by guilt.

Start Hacking The Mind, Persuasion Techniques And Manipulation Techniques

The Basics Of Mind Reading

A high number of people aren't aware of mind reading, thought transference and how best to analyze people. Lately, scientists have been running studies and further hypothesis about the truth. Ignorance still shielded people into not believing such things as mind-reading ever existed. These beliefs made people so skeptical about any thinker that wants to employ these tools of reading people's minds.

The world keeps revolving and today we have a different application and thoughts towards the subject. This new science has come to stay with us as the world now revolves around several relationships and the art of reading intentions.

To read someone's mind, there are two possible facts to uphold - the instant change in the brain of the party suggesting and the respective change in the brain of the other party B who is the recipient of the proposed opinion. Between these two occurrences, there is supposed to be a pause to question whether to consider the suggestion of the mind. This has a lot to do with the sequence of thoughts and how they unfold.

The structure of the brain is so connected to conceive impulses as fast as it receives it which brings a connecting channel to what one believes and what it is. As brain nerves keep expanding as it sees any iota of reasoning, it is never right to say the brain reaches a limit for thinking. However, as the action of thought gets more tedious in deciding the way to follow, there are physical vibrations that show the extreme capabilities of reasoning.

With the strange outlook of assumptions and the bewildering stances of getting what the brain is interpreting, mind-reading occurs subconsciously. This belief brings the human closer to all tools of observation, hypothetical nuances and the feeble analysis that comes with reasoning.

As this takes a different shape in thinking, it is safe to say that the universe is about embracing the fashioned way of analyzing the mind, human behaviors and what is left behind as options. Doing this fortifies the mind into higher tasks of deciding the possibilities to rely on thereby justifying the judgment of the heart.

Non-verbal communication conveys in a split second and easily an individual's solace or distress in a given circumstance. An individual's outward appearance or position can alarm others to peril. For example, let's say someone opens the fridge and grabs a liter of soured milk. A bent articulation and eyes full of caution immediately send the message, "Don't drink that!" saving the first person from the disgusting experience of drinking soured milk.

An old piece of the mind called the limbic cerebrum is for the most part in charge of communicating implicit assumptions utilizing motion, facial changes, and wild eye-widening. Miniaturized scale articulations are momentary and pass on distinct emotions even in grown-ups who can buy and considerable control their outward appearances somewhat

Techniques Used in Mental Manipulation

Persuasion Technique

Persuasion is controlling the human mind without the knowledge of the manipulated party. This technique accesses your right mind, which is imaginative and creative, while the left side is rational and analytical. In persuasion, the perpetrator distracts your left brain and occupy it. It leaves you in an eyes-open altered state but still conscious, making you move from Beta awareness to Alpha. This technique is famous for politicians and lawyers.

Subliminal Programming

These are masked suggestions that can only be understood by your subconscious mind. They can be suggestions in audios, airbrushed visual suggestions, and flash images on your television quickly so that you do not consciously notice them. Some subliminal programming on audio makes suggestions on low volume. Your subconscious mind will notice these suggestions, but no one can monitor them even with equipment. The music we listen to can have a second voice behind it to program your mind. In 1984, a newsletter called Brain-Mind Bulletin that 99% of our activities are non-conscious.

Mass misuse - During mass meetings, the attendees go in and out of consciousness. If you have no idea, you cannot notice what is happening to you. It is a mental manipulation of the mass through vibrations. These vibrations produce Alpha, which makes the mass vulnerable. These make them accept any suggestion of the speaker as a command.

Vibrato - Vibrato is some effect installed on instrumental music or vocal, which makes people go in a distorted state of mind. In English history, some singers who had vibrato in their voices were not given chances to perform because of the effect they had on the public. Some listeners would have fantasies, mostly sexual fantasies.

Neurophone - Dr. Patrick Flanagan invented Neurophone. It is a device that can program your mind when it gets in contact with your skin. When this device gets in contact with your skin, you lose your sense and sight for a moment. It is because the skin has sensors for pain, touch, vibration, and heat. The message to manipulate your mind is played through Neurophone, which is connected and placed in the ceiling and no speakers. This message goes directly to the brain of the audience, and the manipulator can easily manipulate their mental state.

Medium for take-over - When you know how humans function, you get the ability to control them. Medium take-over is happening in the televisions we watch. When people are put in a distorted state of mind, they function on the right brain, which releases brain opiates and makes you feel good, and you want it more. The broadcasts in our televisions induce the Alpha making us accept the broadcast easily. It makes viewers translate suggestions as commands. Every minute spent on watching television conditions us.

The Best Techniques of Persuasion

Before we dive deeper into the major facets of persuasion, we have to comprehend the meaning of persuasion. Persuasion refers to the psychological influence which affects the choice that an individual ought to make. With persuasion, an individual is often inclined to make you buy his or her school of thought in a bid to change your thought process. To effectively achieve persuasion, there are a number of things that need to be kept in mind. When we go beyond the natural human framework and get a grasp of what moves others, then we are positioned to achieve effective persuasion. This is because you are aware of the pressure points and how best to manipulate them.

When exploiting the art of persuasion, there are various pointers that can come in handy:

Mimicking

As human beings of reason, we tend to vary from one individual to another. The diversity of this is what makes us appear in the discrepancy of others. You will find that as individuals, we are more drawn to be warm and welcoming to those people who exhibit the same characteristics as us. It could be a physical trait or just the way an individual carry themselves. When an individual has the feelings of liking towards someone, he or she is in a position to be swayed by your influence.

In a bid to elaborate on this technique, we are going to employ the use of this scenario. In the hotel industry, especially in the most advanced and high-end ones, you will find that the allocation of a waiter is dependent on the customer. High-end hotels in the industry have high customer feedback and thus they tend to treat their clients in a manner that suggests so. A client, for instance, would be allocated a particular type of waiter who matches their description. For instance, French waiters are renowned for their exquisite service. Putting the client first is at the top of the list when it comes to this particular field. Many professionals have succeeded in this area owing to the manner in which they treated clients. This is because the clients are the main source of business. Putting the client into consideration goes a notch higher to even saying the exact words that the client has said. With this, they are able to gather that you have aptly decoded what they meant.

In order to achieve this particular technique, an individual ought to do a number of things. First, he or she may consider doing in-depth research into the particular field of the question in order to see to it that what is required of them. Before you can achieve persuasion by the use of this technique, one ought to be well versed with the individual that he or she ought to persuade. This type of expertise should be keen enough to make sure that it elicits major points that may come in handy during the process of persuasion.

Social Proof

When it comes to persuasion, social proof has repeatedly proven its dominance. Social proof refers to the process by which an individual's feelings and thought process are affected by the way other people have reacted to the same issue. An individual who is the persuader, draw his or her basis from the acts that others have engaged in time and again. It could be the norm. With human beings, the danger that occurs is the feeling of wanting to be associated with a group of people. Humans crave a sense of belonging to a group and this is what puts them at risk of being influenced easily.

Employing social proof when persuading an individual will mean that you have a basis of a norm that has been used repeatedly by the people whom we consider to be in the same class. This basis must be something that most people engage in. Take, for instance, there are newbies in the estate who are looking for service providers. This newbie would first be inclined to know what other people in the estate are using. Although they might not settle on the same option as the rest of the estate, this will be somewhat a buildup on to what choice they may choose to settle upon. Rather they may end up embracing what others have used. The trick lies whereby you ought to create a distinction in the manner in which an individual sees himself or herself as per against others. You will only achieve persuasion by convincing this individual that the desired option is one that has been embraced by a large group of individuals.

Reciprocity

When it comes to this technique, one needs to understand that a good deed was done to another individual no matter how remote, tends to go a long way. "Reciprocity" refers to the process by which an individual is able to respond to a good deed by performing a good deed in return. With this type of technique, we will find that most people fail to notice at its onset not until you are obligated to return the favor. In the world today, it is almost as rare as the sun rising from the west as it is to find someone who will extend warmness and care towards you. Except for the people to whom we are closely related, we tend to feel differently when an individual who is not even in our circle of friendship extends warm-hearted feelings.

Dark Persuasion

Persuasion is an interesting topic. There are lots of persuasions that are considered just fine in society. They are acceptable, and even some people hold jobs where they will spend a lot of time trying to persuade others. Any attempt by one person to influence someone else to do some action can be persuasion. A salesperson at a car dealership is using persuasion because they try to persuade someone to purchase a new vehicle. This isn't seen as something sinister or bad. The difference here is that this persuasion and other similar examples of persuasion benefit both parties. The car dealer makes a sale and some money, and the "victim" is going to get a new vehicle.

There are a lot of legitimate types of persuasion that aren't considered part of dark psychology. The car dealer above is an example. If a negotiator uses their skills to persuade a terrorist to let their hostage go, this is a good form of persuasion. If you convince someone to come along to an event that they will enjoy, then this is a good form of persuasion. This type of persuasion is seen as positive persuasion. But then, what would count as dark persuasion?

Understanding Dark Persuasion

The first difference you will notice between positive and dark persuasion is the motive behind it. Positive persuasion is used in order to encourage someone to complete an action that isn't going to cause them any harm. In some cases, such as with the negotiator saving a hostage, this persuasion can be used to help save lives.

But with dark persuasion, there isn't really any form of moral motive. The motive is usually amoral, and often immoral. If positive persuasion is understood as a way to help people help themselves, then dark persuasion is more of the process of making people act against their own self-interest. Sometimes, people are going to do these actions begrudgingly, knowing that they are probably not making the right choice, but they do it because they are eager to stop the incessant persuasion efforts. In other cases, the best dark persuader is going to make their victim think that they acted wisely, but the victim is actually doing the opposite in that case.

So, what are the motivations for someone who is a dark persuader? This is going to depend on the situation and the individual who is doing the persuading. Some people like to persuade their victims in order to serve their own self-interests. Others are going to act through with the intention just to cause some harm to the other person. In some cases, the persuader is not going to really benefit from darkly persuading their victim, but they do so because they want to inflict pain on the other person. And still, others enjoy the control that this kind of persuasion gives to them.

You will also find that the outcome you get from dark persuasion is going to differ from what happens with positive persuasion.

The benefit goes to the person who is being persuaded.

There is a win/win benefit for the persuaded and the persuader.

There is a mutual benefit for the person who is persuaded and a third party.

All of these outcomes are good because they will involve a positive result for the person who is being persuaded. Sometimes, there will be others who benefit from these actions. But out of all three situations, the persuaded party is always going to benefit.

With dark persuasion, the outcome is going to be very different. The persuader is the one who will always benefit when they exercise their need for influence or control. The one who is being persuaded often goes against what is in their self-interest when they listen, and they are not going to benefit from all this dark persuasion.

In addition, the most skilled dark persuaders are not only able to cause some harm to their victims while also benefiting themselves, but they could also end up harming others in the process.

Unmasking the Dark Persuader

At this point, you may be curious about who is using these dark methods of persuasion. Are there actually people out there who are interested in using this kind of persuasion and using it against others to cause harm?

The main characteristics of a dark persuader are either an indifference toward or an inability to care about how persuasion is going to impact others. Such people who use this kind of persuasion are going to be often narcissistic and will see their own needs as more important than the needs of others. They may even be sociopathic and unable to grasp the idea of someone else's emotions.

Many times, this kind of dark persuasion is going to show up in a relationship. Often one but sometimes both partners are going to be inclined towards trying to use dark persuasion on each other. If these attempts are persistent and endure, then this type of relationship is going to be classified as psychologically abusive, and that is not healthy for the victim in that relationship. Often, they will not realize that there is something going on or that they are darkly persuaded until it is too late, and they are stuck there.

There are many examples of using this kind of dark persuasion in a relationship. If one partner stops the other partner from taking a new job opportunity or doesn't allow them to go out with friends, then this could be an example of dark persuasion. The dark persuader will work to convince the victim that they are acting in a way that is best for the relationship. In reality, the victim is going through a process that harms them and the relationship.

The Power Of Persuasion

There are many times when the human mind is pretty easy to influence, but it does take a certain set of skills to get people to stop and listen to you. Not everyone is good with influence and persuasion, though. They can talk all day and would not be able to convince others to do what they want. On the other hand, there are those who could persuade anyone to do what they want, even if they had just met this person for the first time. Knowing how to work with these skills will make it easier for you to recognize a manipulator and be better prepared to avoid them if needed.

The first thing that we need to look at is what persuasion is. Persuasion is simply the process or action taken by a person or a group of people when they want to cause something to change. This could be in relation to another human being and something that changes in their inner mental systems or their external behavior patterns.

The act of persuasion, when it is done in the proper way, can sometimes create something new within the person, or it can just modify something that is already present in their minds. There are actually three different parts that come with the process of persuasion including:

- The communicator or other source of the persuasion
- The persuasive nature of the appeal
- The audience or the target person of the appeal

It is important that all three elements are taken into consideration before you try to do any form of persuasion on your own. You can just look around at the people who are in your life, and you will probably be able to see some types of persuasion happening all over the place.

Experts say that people who are good leaders and who have good persuasion powers will utilize the following techniques to help them be successful:

- Exchanging
- Stating
- Legitimizing
- Logical persuasion
- Appealing to value
- Modeling
- Alliance building
- Consulting
- Socializing
- Appealing to a relationship

The above options are all positive ways that you can use persuasion to your advantage. Most people will be amenable to these happening. But on the other side, there are four negative tactics of persuasion that you can do as well. These would include options like manipulating, avoiding, intimidating, and threatening. These negative tactics will be easier for the target to recognize, which is why most manipulators will avoid using them if possible.

Now, you can use some of the tactics above, but according to psychologist Robert Cialdini, there are six major principles of persuasion that can help you to get the results that you want without the target being able to notice what is going on. Let us take a look at these six weapons and how they can be effective.

The six weapons of influence

Reciprocity

The first principle of persuasion that you can use is known as reciprocity. This is based on the idea that when you offer something to someone, they will feel a bit indebted to you and will want to reciprocate it back. Humans are wired to be this way to survive. For the manipulator to use this option, they will make sure that they are doing some kind of favor for their target. Whether that is paying them some compliments, giving them a ride to work, helping out with a big project or getting them out of trouble. Once the favor is done, the target will feel like they owe a debt to the manipulator. The manipulator will then be able to ask for something, and it will be really hard for the target to say no.

Commitment and consistency

It is in the nature of humans to settle for what is already tried and tested in the mind. Most of us have a mental image of who we are and how things should be. And most people are not going to be willing to experiment, so they will keep on acting the way that they did in the past. So, to get them to work with this principle and do what you want, you first need to get them to commit to something. The steps that you would need to follow to get your target to do what you want through commitment and consistency include:

● Start out with something small. You can ask the target to do something small, something that is easier to manage the change, before they start to integrate it more into their personality and get hooked on the habit.

● You can get the target to accept something publicly so that they will feel more obligated to see it through.

● Reward the target when they can stick to the course. Rewards will be able to help strengthen the interest of the target in the course of action that you want them to do.

Social proof

This is another one that will rely on the human tendency, and it relies on the fact that people place a lot of value and trust in other people and in their opinions on things that we have not tried yet. This can be truer if the information comes from a close friend or a person who is perceived as the expert. It is impossible to try out everything in life and having to rely on others can put us at a disadvantage. This means that we need to find a reliable source to help us get started. A manipulator may be able to get someone to do something by acting as a close friend or an expert. They are able to get the target to try out a course of action because they have positioned themselves as the one who knows the most about the situation or the action.

Likeability

We all know that it is easy to feel attracted to a certain set of people. This can extend to friends and family members as well. So, if you would like to get others to like you and be open to persuasion from you, you first need to figure out how to go from an acquaintance to a friend. This will work similarly to the reciprocity that we talked about earlier, but some of the basic steps that you will need to follow to make this work include:

• The attraction phase: You need to make sure that there is something about you that instantly draws the other person to you.

• Make yourself relatable: People are more likely to be drawn to you if you are relatable to them in some way. It is also easier to influence another person if they consider you their friend.

• Communicate like a friend: Even if the two of you are not quite friends yet, you will be able to make use of the right communication skills so that the target will associate you as a friend.

• Make it look like you are both in the same groups and that you are fighting for the same causes: This can make it easier to establish a rapport with them.

Authority

If you want to make sure that you can influence another person, then you need to dress and act the part. This means that you should wear clothes, as well as accessories, that will help you look like you are the one in command. Some of the ways that you can do this include:

• Wear clothes that are befitting to what people will perceive an authoritative figure would wear.

• When you communicate with the target, you need to do so in a commanding fashion.

• Make sure that you can use the lexicon and the language of experts in that field.

When you can position yourself as the authority figure, people will look to you for the answers that they need. It does not matter how well they know you or not. You will have a great opportunity to influence them the way that you want them to behave.

Scarcity

The last weapon that you can use for persuasion is known as scarcity. Humans like the idea of being exclusive and are drawn to anything that they are not necessarily able to find anywhere else. When you make something exclusive, you have a chance of making it appear more valuable. People are also going to become fearful when something they desire starts to disappear. This whole idea is part of the supply and demand principle. If you have something that is abundant, then it will be perceived as having a lower value and cheap. But if it is rare, then it must have a higher value and be more expensive.

This can work for human beings and for products in the same way. Some things that you should keep in mind when you want to use the scarcity principle with persuasion include:

● Always imply that the thing you are offering is not going to be available to the target anywhere else.

● If you can, it is a good idea to implement a countdown timer on what you are offering. This gives a physical indicator to the target that what you are offering is truly going to disappear.

● You should never go back to the stipulations that you said in the beginning. You need to make sure that the target knows that what you offered is scarce, or this method is not going to work very well.

All of these principles can be effective ways for you to be able to use persuasion to manipulate your target. It is important to learn how to use them all and to do so in a covert way so that your target is not able to realize what you are doing. When you are successful with bringing all of this together, you are sure to get the results that you want each time.

The Importance Of Body Language

Dominance

Body language is a key part of displaying dominance, no matter the context. When a person enters the room, people consciously and subconsciously make judgments about that person based on what they see, how they hold themselves, and other subtle cues of nonverbal communication.

Katie enters a room, and her head is held high. She is not staring at the floor; she is making eye contact with the people she passes by and offering a slight nod and a grin as a greeting. Her posture is erect, with her shoulder back, and her stride is wide and confident. There is a slight sway to her hips that seems natural, and her arms swing freely at her sides. She has yet to actually speak to anyone, but you can form a pretty clear picture of what this person looks like as she enters the room. What is her body language communicating to you?

If you can form some kind of picture based on this description, there should be several adjectives that might come to mind describing her based on this nonverbal evidence. The first, as hinted at in the description, might be confidence. When someone holds themselves erect with their shoulders back, it tells people around her that she is not hiding from them and that she is confident enough to be on full display and to acknowledge and confront anyone she comes across, hence, the direct eye contact and brief greetings. And the higher the chin, the more the message moves across the confidence territory into the realm of dominance.

To assume and display dominance is to carry yourself in a way that does not connote fear or trepidation. The free swing of the arms and long strides suggests that she is not concerned with getting in anyone's way, and there is an unspoken expectation that people will get out of hers if need be.

Let us say Katie moves into one of the main offices, and there, she is awaited by a few powerful people who are meeting her for the first time. Now, we're ready for the handshake.

The handshake can actually say a lot more than most people know to look for, but it is common knowledge in the realm of power and money and politics that how you choose to shake someone's hand can be a strong signal to a person's attitude, as well as their perception of the person with whom they are shaking hands.

The way to signal a position of dominance involves shaking hands in a way that your hand is on top with the palm facing down. This places the other's hand in the subservient position or with the palm facing up. The grip and pressure which the person doing a handshake chooses to employ also send a message about dominance. Politicians who are constantly being photographed as they shake hands with other leaders and political figures might make special efforts to convey dominance by shaking hands in this position and making sure their hand is sending a strong signal to those who know what it means.

Katie chooses, however, to shake hands in a balanced way that does not assume dominance but instead orients the position of hands as to be equal with palms facing each other. This sends a non-threatening message of balance and a willingness to cooperate with another. It is smart to avoid intimidating or using aggressive behaviors in a situation where you want to form a working relationship based on trust and mutual benefit. Katie also is careful to smile and directly address the people she is meeting with eye contact and attentiveness. This should echo back to the first instances in which we examined how attentiveness, listening, and active engagement with a speaker sends the signal that you are interested and invested in what the subject is saying. From a broad point of view, we can say that Katie practices dominance and strong leadership when she is in front of her employees, and she likes to cultivate a balanced working relationship with higher-ups and colleagues of equal stature within the business.

There are certainly much more overt ways to assume dominance, such as outright aggression, and there are also very subtle, covert ways, such as in the instance of a young professional gradually taking over a room and winning the hearts of those whom he might later utilize to his advantage. The alpha then operates as the individual on top until another comes along who wants to take the position for himself, and the alpha is challenged.

Seduction

Seduction is another major category in which body language plays an especially vital role, both on the part of the person trying to seduce and his subject.

The reading of body language comes into play in this scenario as soon as the seducer makes his approach. From the moment the target acknowledges the seducer, she begins sending signals, which are both conscious and subconscious messages that will either reinforce the efficacy of the seducer's tactics or give him warning signs that his target is not as open to suggestion as he'd thought at first. Let's look at some examples.

The seducer approaches from behind the subject, who may be standing and listening to some music about to begin at a bar. When the approach happens, the target must turn her body to orient herself to the speaker if she is acknowledging the approach and willingness to engage. The seducer then examines how much of her body begins orienting toward him, and how much she is responding by keeping her orientation pointed away from the seducer. If she fully engages and turns to meet and look the seducer head-on, this is a strong signal that the lady is amenable to the interaction and is a strong positive sign that the seducer has chosen the right target for his intentions. On the other hand, if the target remains facing toward the stage and/or does not move to orient any part of her body toward the seducer, then she is sending a strong signal that she is completely uninterested in an interaction at that moment. This could be motivated by a variety of different reasons, but the seducer would usually abandon his approach and perhaps try again a little later; otherwise, he may simply move on to different target entirely.

The seducer pays attention to every movement and mannerism the target makes as he is engaging with her. The trick for successful interaction and seduction, however, is not to appear as if he is trying so hard to read her thoughts through her behaviors and nonverbal communication. An attempt at seduction, for example, which is accompanied by lots of staring at the target's body instead of her face, is certainly not going to go over well, as the seducer's intentions are all but being broadcast by his behavior and areas of attention.

The skilled seducer will be able to multitask as he listens to the target's words and pays attention to nonverbal cues as much as possible, without seeming like this is what he's doing. The seducer must come off as comfortable, friendly, and nonthreatening. The idea is to ignite some kind of attraction in whatever form he can. Once this is accomplished, he can begin playfully moving in as he exploits this newfound weakness. Positive body language cues that will often signal to the seducer that he is progressing well include smiling and giggling while keeping the body oriented toward the seducer. Women who are simply pretending to be comfortable and engage will often smile and giggle playfully, but the orientation of their bodies will give away their anxiety. The seducer would likely not move forward in this situation until he can inspire a little more comfort into the interaction. However, as the seducer persists, he also runs the risk of intensifying the anxiety, as the target may or may not be experiencing a gut instinct to stay away or get out of the situation. This can be a powerful tool on the part of the target if she is able to really pay attention and listen to her instincts when she feels something is a bit off.

As the seducer finds a target and is able to get some positive signals, he will use his own powers in the form of nonverbal communication to inspire attraction and interest. Flattery can be utilized in ways other than direct verbal communication. A seducer who wants to introduce just a bit of flirtation and sexual interest might let the target catch him looking briefly over her as he then quickly returns to face her. This tells her a lot of different things about the seducer, and if played correctly, it will work to the seducer's advantage if the signal comes off as playful and flirtatious without getting into creepy territory.

There is a balance to all of these behaviors and interaction, and the same methods may work differently based on the personality and demeanor of the target. This is why practiced seducers will zero in on specific types who more often respond positively to such advances.

Sociopathy

Psychopathy and sociopathy are 2 personality conditions typically connected to serial killers or lawbreakers. In truth, though, there is so much more to psychopaths and sociopaths than meets the eye. In this segment, you will discover the true nature of the condition and the people who have it.

By the end of this segment, you should have a clear grasp of what causes psychopathy and what are the clear indicators that a person is a psychopath. More importantly, this segment will teach you how to stop being manipulated by one

. What and Who Is a Psychopath?

Psychopaths have gotten a lot of attention over the years, but extremely little information today is accurate. Considered as a character disorder, psychopaths are often seen as cold-blooded serial killers or those who have the prospective to become serial killers. This is not unexpected, thinking about how among the most popular serial killers today, Ted Bundy, is called a psychopath. Still, others may argue that he is a sociopath instead.

Psychopaths versus Sociopaths.

These 2 terms are usually interchangeable, but there's actually a significant difference between these them. While the science is still not precise, studies have limited distinctions among the 2:

Regarding Cause.

It is normally accepted that psychopaths are born and not made. It is viewed as a hereditary quality, pursuant to a Minnesota Research study about the condition. On the other hand, sociopaths are made and not born. Sociopath propensities normally happen as a result of environmental factors that seriously affected an individual's frame of mind. It can be anything from the early loss of mom and dad to rejection by an enjoyed one.

Regarding Education.

While the condition is not a sign of intelligence, psychopaths typically have a pretty good career and are well-educated. In contrast, sociopaths are typically not able to hold down a stable job. It is also not likely that they have reached tertiary education. Of course, there are certain exceptions to this.

Regarding Conscience/Empathy.

Psychopaths are generally accepted to have no conscience and lack empathy. This is maybe the most defining attribute of a psychopath. On the other hand, a sociopath has little empathy. They have a conscience, but this is not exercised greatly. As a result, psychopaths form no attachments (although they may act a lot like they do) while sociopaths form little attachments to certain groups or individuals.

As to Conduct.

Psychopaths work out outstanding control in their own person and try to extend this to their surroundings. They are known to be highly manipulative as opposed to sociopaths that struggle with erratic behavior. Sociopaths are more likely to be aggressive and violent.

As to Criminal offense.

Keep in mind that being a psychopath/sociopath is not tantamount to be a criminal. Those who do fall into a life of criminal offense, though, tend to follow a general pattern for their acts. Psychopaths are careful and plans ahead, taking calculated risks and guaranteeing that the evidence is minimized, if not wiped tidy completely. Sociopaths are more out of control and tend to commit violent/physical crimes. Nowadays, psychopaths are more tailored toward organized crime, fraud plans, and the like.

Psychopath versus Narcissist.

Many individuals make the error of using these two terms interchangeably. There's actually a significant distinction between the 2 in that all psychopaths are narcissists but not all narcissists are psychopaths. Narcissism is a personality condition recognized by DSM (DMS-5) or the Diagnostic and Statistical Handbook of Mental Illness. It is defined by a grand sense of self-importance and a real need for extreme affection from other ones. Narcissists may also do not have empathy and believe that they are entitled to tons of things in life-- even if they do not necessarily work for the same. Narcissists often daydream about holding severe amounts of cash, power, control, charm, success, and so on. They believe that they are unique and thus should have to be looked up to by others.

A narcissist is not always a psychopath, since some of the qualities of the psychopath might not exist in a narcissist. Nevertheless, narcissism is a crucial attribute of a psychopath.

The 'degree' of narcissism also matters. Psychopaths typically fall within the extreme scale of self-grandiosity while some narcissists aren't as extreme in their belief of self-importance.

Psychopath versus Antisocial Personality Disorder.

Despite the obvious popularity of the terms psychopath and sociopath, it is fascinating to note that both character disorders aren't pointed out in the Diagnostic and Statistical Manual of Mental Illness. The acknowledged mental disorder that is closest to the definition of a psychopath is Antisocial Personality Condition. Regarding medical diagnosis nevertheless, psychiatrists do not identify an Antisocial Personality Disorder without a previous diagnosis of conduct condition. Thus, specialists usually make use of "Antisocial Character Disorder" instead of psychopath.

False Concepts About Psychopaths.

Since psychopaths are typically incorrect for serial killers, it's best to first get the myths out of the way. Here are some of the things you might have become aware of psychopaths but aren't entirely real:

Psychopaths Are Insane.

Psychopaths aren't insane. They work perfectly well within society's limits but are separated in their way of thinking. Many psychopaths are actually upstanding members of society or have managed to make a success out of their lives.

Psychopaths Are Wrongdoers.

A big part of psychopaths ends up as lawbreakers due to their inability to manage or effectively manage impulses and the consistent need for

stimulation. As you'll learn later, though, criminal offense as a profession is just one of the options a psychopath has for work. There are presently jobs available that naturally draw in a psychopath and a lot of these are perfectly acceptable and even celebrated within society.
You're Either a Psychopath or You Aren't.
Do not expect that all psychopaths are a lot like Hannibal or Ted Bundy. Psychopathy actually exists on a spectrum, which means that while some characteristics of a psychopath are strong, some might be weak and therefore easily managed. In fact, research studies have shown that a lot of the past United States presidents have a level of boldness and assertiveness comparable to that of psychopathy. It must be kept in mind that this assertiveness is a crucial factor in what made them presidents.
You Can Self Really Diagnose Psychopathy.
While there are definitely a ton of online tests to help identify psychopathy, none of these are legitimate. For a correct diagnosis, people will have to go through a legitimate physician for personality disorders. Usually, it takes more than just a survey to detect psychopathy. Nowadays, a brain scan can be made to better track the brain's response when asked questions.
Psychopaths are Dangerous.
While a lot of the psychopath traits are negative, this does not immediately make them unsafe or violent. Be aware, though, that your mental health might be at threat, since psychopaths can quickly break down a person's confidence and self-esteem. If you feel as though you're at risk when with a psychopath, it's usually best to just move from them.
Signs and Characteristics of a Psychopath
The reason that these two-character conditions are typically interchanged, is as the standard characteristics of the two are remarkably similar. However, there are certain attributes that are unique to the psychopath. We'll talk about the characteristics that are unique in psychopaths along with those common with sociopaths. There's typically a 20-point character basis that experts use to check--

but keep in mind that the best rating is not necessary for a medical diagnosis. Some validated psychopaths do not have some characteristics-- but there are some that are never ever gone from the list.

Lack of Empathy/Remorse/Guilt

This is the most defining characteristic of a psychopath. Thus, it can be said that ALL psychopaths lack compassion. Empathy is the ability to get in touch with people and put yourself in their position so that you can have compassion with them on an emotional level. Compassion is the reason that people donate food to the homeless, say sorry after a mistake, and feel bad for doing something very wrong. It is the ability to recognize real pain in somebody-- and psychopaths do not have this ability. For this reason, psychopaths are mainly incapable of connecting with people or creating relationships. Note, though, that this is an internal characteristic and most psychopaths are smart adequate to fake compassion.

Lying Pathologically

Psychopaths are also pathological phonies in that they have this compulsive need to lie in order to suit their own ends. Sometimes, there isn't even any great reason for the lie as long as they find it practical to provide. Psychopaths can be rather skilled in their lies, particularly when it is part of their grand scheme. Being careful, some of their lies are well-thought of and thus hard to identify.

Superficial Appeal

Of all the qualities of psychopaths, beauty is maybe the most unexpected among all. Psychopaths have the fantastic ability to coax people into their point of view, radiating an appeal that can be appealing for most people. While some psychopaths are not as achieved in faking the genuineness of their charm, there are those that are more than capable of fooling the public. Ted Bundy, infamous serial killer and psychopath was so skilled in exercising charm that ladies happily supported him during his trial for murder.

Manipulative

Together with charm is their capability to control people. Combine this with their lying capability and psychopaths can be exceptional puppet masters. In simple fact, studies show that there are tons of psychopaths in top-fields of business and politics, 2 professions that require a certain mix of appeal for success.

Promiscuous Conduct

Their lack of guilt or remorse makes it simple for psychopaths to exceed societal limits without thinking twice about it. This is why a lot of psychopaths have no issue remaining in some relationships at once-- even if they are already married. They are promiscuous and their manipulative character makes it simple for them to manage several relationships at one time.

Inflated Sense of Self Worth

They actually believe that they are better than other ones in practically every element, which is a conceited trait. Psychopaths need to be smarter than everyone else, stronger than everyone else, make more than everybody else, drive a better car, and so on. They are of the opinion that they are always right and will for that reason have a hard time accepting errors or criticisms.

Blaming Others

Since psychopaths really believe that they can never be really wrong, it makes a lot of sense for them that another person slipped up. They always blame other ones and never accept duties for mistakes or issues. On the flipside, if something good happens, they fast to take credit.

Continuous Need for Stimulation

Research studies have shown that psychopaths have a consistent need for stimulation. This can be connected to the fact that they do not have compassion and therefore do not feel the same low and high of emotions related to relationships. Psychopaths need a much different way in which to promote their senses. They have the tendency to lock down on a particular stimulation and pursue it till they are satisfied. An issue is that, much like a druggie, some psychopaths might need a larger fix each time for stimulation to happen. This is why psychopaths who are also killers typically reach this level by steps. Other criminal behavior happens right before they commit murder.

The Levels Of Consciousness

Freud's theory subdivides the human mind into three levels of consciousness. These levels play a major role in influencing people. The three levels are:

The conscious mind

The subconscious mind

The unconscious mind

Each of these three contributes a certain percentage to reality.

The conscious mind

Consciousness can be defined as the state of being aware of something. It refers to the ability to conceive something like an event or activity in the mind and recalling it after it has already taken place. From figure 1 above, it is estimated that only 10% of the human brain constitutes the conscious mind.

Some of the common functions of the conscious mind are to:

Control a person's focus or concentration for the short-term memory

Imagine things that are not real

Collect and process data

Identify and make a comparison between patterns

Respond to situations in a thoughtful way

Make decisions

Give orders

This segment of the mind works in the form of a scanner. It helps you to identify or understand events and activities trigger the reaction and store the occurrences related to the event in the subconscious or unconscious segment of the mind. People are always aware of every activity that goes on in their conscious mind.

The subconscious mind

This is the place where memories that you need to remember quickly are stored. Such memories may be things like your identity card or telephone number. It acts as a storage place for the information you use on a daily basis. This information is what forms your habits, behavioral patterns, and feelings.

The subconscious mind works the same way as a computer's random-access memory. It is where dreams come from as well as the knowledge required to do some of the things you are used to.

The unconscious mind

This is the level that holds all the past memories and experiences. It acts as a storage place for most of the memories that are no longer important, and those, which are almost being forgotten. These memories and experiences also contribute a great deal to a person's behaviors, habits, and beliefs.

The unconscious mind is directly connected to the subconscious mind. However, the unconscious mind is a collection of all the habits, memories and behaviors of a person. It is like a reservoir that contains all the emotions you have been collecting since birth.

The unconscious mind accounts for between 30 to 40 percent of the human brain. It plays a very essential role yet it is mostly inaccessible. As an individual, you may fail to understand what goes on at this level of the mind. The major roles of the unconscious mind are:

Performs most of the activities within the body – these include sleeping, breathing, heartbeat, controlling the temperature and many other activities that do not require your input

Protects you by keeping you to what you are familiar with and shielding you from carrying out some uncomfortable actions and decisions

Is the source of human emotions

It is also the source of creativity and imagination skills

It is the place where habits are made and controlled

Stores long-term memories

Besides these functions, the unconscious mind also takes instructions from the conscious mind. It triggers you to react towards threats. One characteristic of the unconscious mind that you should take note of is that it does not make any judgments. This means that you cannot depend on it when you need to make a choice between things that are good and those that are bad. It only accepts instructions from the conscious mind and causes the person to automatically behave, think and respond towards the instructions received.

Dimensions of the Human Mind

Basically, the human mind works in six major dimensions. These dimensions are:

Joy

Love

Fear

Boredom

Hatred

Sexuality

It is believed that these dimensions are present in the mind of all human beings. However, their intensity differs from one person to the other. It is actually impossible to eliminate any of these dimensions completely from the mind and those who try to do so only end up suppressing the way their brain performs.

For instance, many people who get misguiding spiritual teachings often try to suppress some dimensions from their mind and this result in some problems that may last for a lifetime. When you seek to understand how the mind operates, you will stop trying to suppress these dimensions and this will give you a better physical and psychological experience in life. Below is a more detailed explanation for each of these dimensions, and how they affect the mind.

1.Love

Love is one of the things that occur naturally in the mind. The human mind expresses this dimension through compassion, tenderness, empathy, charity, romance, service and devotion. Every mind is capable of releasing these expressions in one way or the other. In most cases, the mind triggers this dimension when the person feels secure around the person being loved. The level of love always diminishes when the person feels less secure.

When love occurs at the unconscious level of the mind, it can result in a state of disharmony and imbalance. For instance, when you are obsessed with a person, the mind can lead you into becoming insecure and over-possessive. This can result in over-indulgence in some not-so-good activities that may hurt or drive the one you love away from you. When passion is not controlled by some maturity or wisdom, it can make you a slave to the same thing that you love. This means that for love to work, the conscious mind should be involved.

2.Fear

This is also another nature of the mind. The human mind is, once in a while, controlled by fear. Some people are always more fearful than others. A person who is fearful is always resistant to change, growth and movement. Although this is considered to be a dark nature of the mind, it is impossible to suppress the feeling in the unconscious mind. However, as you become more aware of the feeling and how to control it, you will be able to identify what causes you fear and learn to live with it.

In most cases, when your mind is focused on the cause of fear, you will always have fear-based thoughts. However, when you become more conscious about what is fueling this kind of dimension, your fear will slowly become less intense and you will be able to overcome all your fears.

Fear is one of the several dimensions that awaken the mind. Some forms of fear that are common among people are anxiety, panic, worry, depression, horror, insecurity and nervousness. It is possible to control fear-related thoughts, but it is not possible to get rid of fear in totality. This is because fear is one dimension that is engraved deep in the human mind. The goal of those seeking to overcome fear is always not about getting the mind to stop generating fear, but arriving at an awareness or consciousness that they should not allow their behavior and activities to be influenced by the fear.

3.Boredom

This is another dark nature of the mind. Boredom refers to a state of the mind when you feel disinterested in the present moment. It is one of the most harmless dimensions although when prolonged it may result in depression. In most cases, when boredom occurs you will be triggered to move to more creative activities and environments which can help you develop new interests and desires. When you allow the feeling of boredom to mature, it may result in both mental and physical growth since you will be able to experience new spaces, ideas, and opportunities as you seek to kill the boredom.

Therefore, instead of suppressing the feeling of boredom, allow the mind to process this fully. The result of this will be several inspired actions that will lead you towards joy and fulfillment.

4. Joy

Joy is one of the positive natures of the mind. It refers to the state of being lively and energetic. Most people pursue this dimension because a joyful state makes the body to relax significantly. Some common expressions of joy include calmness, relaxation, enthusiasm, exhilaration, and excitement. Although all minds are able to experience this dimension, some experience it as relaxation while others experience more rigorous feelings like excitement and enthusiasm.

A good number of people always try to suppress this feeling because of other negative feelings existing in their minds like depression and sadness. However, it is advisable that you allow this dimension as much as you can so that you do not end up making some wrong mistakes from suppressing this feeling.

5. Hatred

Hatred is one of the ark natures of the mind. This dimension plays a vital role in identifying your likes and dislikes. Just like any other dimension, you can never get hatred completely out of the mind. Most people who tend to suppress the feeling of hate usually to end up bitter, and with a lot of negative energy. Such energy is highly destructive and toxic.

People express hatred in various ways. These include jealousy, resentment, dislike, stress, anger, impatience, suspicion, criticism, and anger. Once you become conscious of this aspect of the human mind, you will not suppress any feelings of hate. Instead, you will only learn not to personalize any activities and reactions related to this dimension.

When you become conscious about this trait, you will learn to allow the mind to process hate-based thoughts, but you will not waste your time on such. Trying to suppress thoughts that are related to hate only makes them worse since you may start judging yourself based on the negative feeling and it may not be possible to completely take such feelings off your mind.

6.Sexuality

This is a heavy dimension that can be seen either as positive or negative. When handled the wrong way, this dimension may lead to frustration, guilt, and depravity. It also manifests greatly in the physical realm since it involves reproduction. Sexuality also serves as a form of pleasure or entertainment. It is the only dimension that results from other dimensions like joy and love.

Since the energy emanating from this dimension can be so intense, suppressing it often results in disharmony and toxicity in relationships. Individuals who suppress this feeling always end up angry and full of hatred. Sexuality differs among all people. It is affected by several factors including a person's age as well as several dimensions of the mind. For instance, a person whose mind is full of fear often finds it hard to engage in sex. Boredom and hatred can also reduce a person's interest in sex. Love, joy, and peace always translate to a high sex drive. As long as the human mind is healthy and in good operation, it will often depict these six dimensions every day. Mostly, individuals embrace positive natures of the mind like joy and love but tend to ignore the dark natured dimensions such as hatred, boredom, and fear. Being emotionally mature gives you the freedom and ability to express these six dimensions in a way that does not influence others negatively.

Self-Protection

Know the Strategies

When you know what it takes to brainwash someone, it becomes a lot easier to identify when those strategies are being used on yourself. The more you practice brainwashing others, the easier you are going to be able to identify these unique mannerisms in conversations with other people. This will be important when it comes to protecting yourself against being subjected to mind control. They always say that knowledge is the best prevention, and this is also true when it comes to brainwashing. The more you know, the better.

Don't Buy into Fear

Fear is one of the most popular strategies to manipulate someone into doing whatever you want them to do. It is used by a large majority of the government, media, and general society. This is one of the most popular strategies to get people to do what you want them to do. It has been used to get people to vote for certain government officials, like or dislike certain groups of people, and otherwise behave virtually however someone wants them to behave.

When you notice scare tactics are being used, take the time to recognize it and do research to know whether or not what is being said holds any validity. This will help you know for sure whether or not you need to agree with the person attempting to brainwash you.

Fear works on the basis that it plays on people's emotions which, as you have learned, is one of the best ways to get people to agree with you. Instead of using logic, you simply use their emotions to get them to do what you want them to do. Make sure that you are not letting others use your emotions against you.

Learn to Consciously Recognize Subliminal Messaging

Subliminal messaging is everywhere in the modern world, and it is important that you do not allow yourself to be subjected to it. Not only is it present in mass media, mass advertising campaigns, and other major messages that are being shared with the world, but it also a part of other areas, too. Even entrepreneurs, independent marketers, and other people are using subliminal messages as an opportunity to get people to do what they want them to do. This is a common strategy that is being used by the average lay person, and it is important that you don't let this strategy be used against you.

Don't Follow the Herd

The herd tends to be guided by the mass media or government, which you have already learned tends to be responsible for brainwashing people. When you follow the herd, you are likely being brainwashed. This works on the basis of having proof: there is proof that "everyone else is doing it" which might make you feel like you should do it, too. Remember that this is an extremely popular method of mind control, and it can be very easy to be subjected to. We often don't want to be the odd one out or left on the sidelines while everyone else does something, such as buy into trends or believe a certain common belief that may not actually be true to begin with. If you take the time to do research and pay attention to the realistic truth, you will refrain from being brainwashed by anyone else.

Stay in Control of Conversations

Do not let others control conversations with you. When they do, you are more likely to be subjected to brainwashing strategies that will actually have an effect on you. You don't necessarily need to be leading the conversation, but you need to be prepared to actually control the conversation. Part of that may be allowing the other person to believe they are in control when they actually aren't. In doing so, you can actually witness the strategies they are attempting to use and see how they might succeed and where they are failing. This will give you the opportunity to identify where you can do better with your own practice. If you allow others to control conversations and you don't consciously tune into this, you may end up finding that you become subjected to brainwashing strategies by others, which will result in you potentially agreeing to something you don't actually want to agree with.

Trust Your Instinct

When all else fails, trust your instinct. If you practice listening to it, you are more likely to know when someone is trying to brainwash you or get you to think, believe or do things that are not what you actually want to do. Your instinct can almost always identify when someone has ulterior motives and is attempting to get you to do something you don't actually want to. You may get a general feeling that something is wrong, or you may be able to identify exactly where they are trying to manipulate or control you. This will help you prevent yourself from getting brainwashed. You can then either take over the conversation and get into control over the situation, or simply exit the situation altogether.

Reflection

If you find that you have been brainwashed, you should take some time to reflect on the situation. Try and identify what happened that caused for the situation to be effective, and why you were able to be brainwashed. Look for the strategies that were used by the other person and how they were able to work on you. Make sure that you identify the opportunity to use this as a learning curve so that you can prevent yourself from being brainwashed in the future. You should also try and uncover the exact strategies they used so that you can learn a lesson or two from them. After all, if they were able to brainwash you, they must be pretty good at what they do! This means that you will be able to use their techniques going forward to enhance your own abilities and have greater success with mind control going forward.

Once you become a master at mind control yourself, it will be nearly impossible for anyone to use your strategy against you. Really, the only way they can is if they are better than you at your practice. This is why you should aim to become the best. You don't only want to be able to use it to get what you want, but you want to master it to avoid getting what you don't want. The more you practice mastering mind control, the more success you are going to have with it and the less likely you are going to be controlled by anyone else.

Remember, knowledge is the best tool for prevention. If you really want to prevent yourself from becoming brainwashed by anyone else, arm yourself with knowledge of the various methods they could use to brainwash you so that you are less likely to be affected by it.

Additionally, if you find that you ever have been brainwashed, always look at it as an opportunity to learn more about the art. This will give you the chance to master your practice even more, and eventually become the most masterful mind control artist that exists. You will not be able to be brainwashed by anyone once you are fully aware of what it looks like and feels like to be under mind control.

This will also step up your own practice because you will be able to enforce the techniques of others in order to have total success with your own practice.

It is important that you always work towards learning how to prevent yourself from becoming subjected to mind control. You never want your own practice to be used against you, as this will really cripple your confidence and take away from your own success with mind control. Mistakes are bound to happen, but you always want to be aiming higher. Otherwise, you will never be able to have total success in getting your way and having success with mind control because you will be continually under the control of others. This is ineffective and will destroy your success. Do not let this happen.

All We Have Is A Dark Side

Have you ever thought yourself of creating a negative impact of this life? Sometimes people are engrossed with the right things or morals they have and forget their dark sides. Other scenarios are where one is prized highly even by parents that you value yourself of a higher standard than your counterparts. That feeling is sometimes unfortunate because you may think you are right in anything whereas other individuals see our weakness. That is why it is good to accept all corrections as one cannot identify their ills or wrongs unless you are told.

What about the dark side you have? You may be surprised to know that the dark side in you can be used as an advantage. Sometimes one is too proud to recognize the vices one has. Other people know their vices, and they feel pressured to control them, therefore generating a personality disorder. You may be that guy who is always viewed to be wicked; thus, everybody fears that character in you. You, therefore, feel isolated and think you cannot do anything to change their perception of you.

Another instance is that you may have been involved in a sorrowful ordeal. Your past tends to determine the life course one chooses. You feel that you cannot try a particular task because you failed once, and you believe you are a complete failure. Maybe at one time, you were short-tempered at the extent of injuring your friend or sibling with a machete. Therefore, you will grow with the attitude that there is a hidden darkness in you.

In some cases, this is the demonic part of you, and you should try to control it in every way. Many relationships have broken because the partners did not take time to know the evil of the other. All they shared is their bright linen, and they did not take time to understand the dirty linen of the other spouse. It would be hurting to know the prince charming or the queen you once believed can hart you in a way you never expected.

Therefore, it is suitable for everybody to recognize the demonic part of you and try to share it with anyone who can understand. Moreover, before getting into a relationship, dig in the background to identify the weakness of your beloved. Everybody has the evil spirit inside which you may know or do not. Do you ever think your enemies can ever tell you something positive? But consider asking them what they hate you for, you may realize they do not hate you but dislikes the vice in you. You may further be surprised that they want you to change for the better. It is essential to know who your real friends are because some are fake friends. They will relate with you to discover your weakness of which they will exploit you negatively.

Having that evil side is sometimes a positive thing because you will know your true nature. Sometimes you are afraid that your close friend will discover your dark side and laugh at you. At other times you like living alone because you feel the demon in you will harm the people you care. Such people experience low self-esteem and do not see any value in themselves. However, there is good news. do you know even the best of you may be the dark side to other people? You may be that bright guy in school or that star player, but do you know too much of anything is poisonous. You are used to being praised or celebrated by your colleagues; therefore you developed that arrogance attitude. Hence that is an evil nature in you.

How Can One Use the Evil Nature in You for Your Advantage?

You use that character one has to know who your real friends are. The worst betrayal is that which comes from close friends. That pal of yours may not even love you but as waiting at that moment you. Sometimes these friends are interested in the possessions or the richness you have, but when poverty strikes you, they will eclipse. Kings or queens are followed because of the influence, wealth, and authority they commission to that kingdom, but not out of the love the subjects have for them. Your dark nature in you will disconnect you from fake friends and connect you to real allies.

This feeling helps one to have an attitude of self-acceptance. Maybe you have done everything to stop these evils. However, your hustles are fruitless. You eventually feel that it is an epidemic that you cannot fight. However, by realizing your true nature, you will consequently learn that attitude to accept yourself. Therefore, you can face people confidentially as you feel you have the power to control that evilness you have.

Being weak and feeling disoriented in society is another negative impact of the dark side of you. However, if you learn to manage those feelings, you will have no more fear to face society. You will undoubtedly identify those people who are ready to support you and finish that distrust you possess. Sometimes you may have done wrong that you fear repeating such actions. Consequently, you even fear yourself, but if you do self-evaluation, you will stop that attitude.

Sometimes the evilness in you can help you to attain you want. You can be dictatorial in any way, but that attitude will command respect and obedient from your subordinates. They will fear you and will try to do everything right to please you. You always have a negative attitude in everything, but you will be a winner if your optimistic friend loses in an area he thought was achievable. If people fear that you will hurt them, they will allow you to do everything that pleases you.

Some scholars say that you can only 'solve evil with evil.' This ideology works when one wants to reduce the vices found in society. You are that saint whom everybody respects, but how can you fight those criminals who fight you if you do not know how they think. Therefore, if you have a Dark side, you will learn about it and recognize how to deal with it. Therefore, if your counterpart has the same element you will be in a position to manage him. That is why most people use reformed addicts or criminals to advise other individuals suffering under the same umbrella.

How Can One Use the Dark Side To Manipulate People?

Many are the cases people are conned, and they often say that the culprit manipulated them. This move can go to an extent where a person is coerced or brainwashed to do something of, not their wish. Manipulation in some people can be viewed as a vice that is not acceptable. It is usually a way of influencing, coercing or persuading a person to agree with what you want. In this case, you are the dominant force, and your counterpart is the less dominant person. Many of the manipulators use different approaches in eliciting you to do what they want. Some may be sweet-talking to influence you to do something that even you did not wish to. Others will forcefully blackmail you or corer you to do a favor,

Manipulation is an example of the dark side that you may possess. Being manipulated sometimes shows that you are gullible, and you can easily be fooled to do something that you never wished. Those particular people who influence others are mostly the emotional intelligent guys. Such personnel play around with your feelings and you sense danger you do not follow their instructions. One may ask how the dark nature in you is connected to manipulation. Remember that manipulation may be positive or negative, but in this case, consider manipulation on positive grounds. If you are a parent, you must show you wrong side so that the children can obey you. Imagine how you feared to do wrong when you were a kid because you were afraid of caning from parents. Therefore, the parents will manipulate you in doing something right by using such painful measures. Isn't that the right side of manipulation prompted by the dark side?

What are Yin and Yang

It is a Chinese philosophy that shows how contrary parties or opposite ones may intermingle, connect, and interdepend on each other. You will always feel oriented to mingle with another even if you do not share the same class. This principality is associated with the dark nature one has. Yin is expressed and marked as evil, wicked, feminist, and shadows. While Yang is marked as bright, masculinity, heaven, and eminence, these two groups of people usually relate to energize their colleague. Recognize that Yang is mostly associated with male and Yin is associated with females.

It has been found that both of these qualities very differently and are used in manipulation. A Yin person is characterized by being a listener, softy, coolness, surrender, and respectful. In Yang people, they are portrayed in being brave, authoritative, and strict. Therefore, in most cases, the Yang People Influences the Yin individuals

Dark Psychology Experts

When we talk about dark psychology, there are people that we encounter every day that are using it and using it on us. You may not consider them to be psychopaths or sociopaths, but when we break down their personality traits, they do possess all of the ones that put them in these categories. Here are a few examples of how they manipulate us in our daily lives.

Narcissists have come up quite a bit in this book so far. We aren't done yet, either! We see and deal with these people every day. They have a huge sense of self-worth and love. They try to get other people to validate them and their beliefs that they are better and more superior to everyone around them. They have dreams of being adored and even worshiped. They do show some dark personality traits and are star manipulators. They can easily persuade others to do anything that they want them to. Their actions are all leading up to how soon they will be worshiped by all who meet them.

Another group of people who are known for using dark psychology is those in politics. Politicians have been put in the realm of dark psychology even before it had a name. Many of them do use tactics that can persuade people to do anything that they want. Look back at Hitler, for example. Politicians want to do one thing: get the votes of the people to take office in a grand home. This is why many of them do use dark psychology.

Sociopaths are another group of people that we have mentioned quite frequently in this book. People that are sociopaths will appear charming to you at first. They will be very intelligent, but they act on their impulses quite a lot. They have problems showing their emotions to people, and they never feel remorse for anything that they do. They use all sorts of shady tactics to persuade people to do what they want them to do. They love to take advantage of people, and we may see these types of people every day in our day-to-day lives. We may even be living with one.

Attorneys are often put in the category of people who are psychopaths. Again, this does not mean that they are killers or crazed. Many of them have specific traits that make them fit into the psychopath category. Some attorneys will focus on a case so much that all they can think of is winning it. They can't imagine what their life is going to be like if they lose this case and they don't care what they have to do to win. Many of them will resort to dark psychology to get the exact thing that they want.

Being in sales is a very tough job that only a few types of people can do. When you are a salesperson, you have to be very focused on making a sale no matter what the customer is telling you. Generally, this could result in the customer feeling that the salesperson was too pushy. Salespeople are generally put in the category of psychopaths because of their focus to make the sale no matter what. Some salespeople will use dark psychology to get the sale even if it does mean lying to the customer.

Leaders are also put into the psychopath category. Not all leaders in the world are bad people, but many in history has shown us differently. We did discuss a few earlier on in this book. Some leaders used their darkest tactics to get what they wanted. They wanted votes, and they wanted their devoted followers to do anything that they were told. Charles Manson and Jim Jones are great examples of leaders who were also psychopaths.

Have you ever heard a public speaker and you were so blown away by what they said? Did you even remember what they said? Public speakers have a way with words, and they will often use shady tactics to reel people in. When they use dark tactics, their words and actions will cause the listeners to have some emotional change when they hear them. This is what makes people believe what the speaker is saying. They move their listeners with emotions and get everyone to buy what they are selling.

The last people on this list are selfish people. We all know them, and they are everywhere in our lives. You could even be one! Selfish people act on what they want, no matter who it hurts along the way. They have an agenda, and it is to take care of no one but themselves. They never meet anyone's needs but their own. This is what causes them to lose friends and loved ones in their lives.

Do you think that you could fit into one of these categories and you're scared to admit it? You can always ask yourself a string of questions to see if you're just paranoid. What is your goal for each interaction that you make? When you meet someone, do you focus on what they can do for you, or do you generally want to get to know them? Do you focus on how they benefit your life? Do you feel good when you leave a new interaction? When you are engaging in a talk with a new person or an old friend, do you feel good about what you are saying or what you are asking of them? Are you honest with them? Do you wonder if they are thinking of using you for benefits that you could give them? Do you ever think of using shady tactics to get more out of them? Think deeply about these questions and how you would answer them. You will soon realize if you do possess the ability to use dark tactics on those around you or if you do not.

Ways That You Can Predict Other's Minds

You are an expert in beginning psychology now! Since you know all the ways that others might have hurt you, it's now time to take this power and do something good with it. No matter what you might have thought about your brain and your abilities in the past, you understand now that you have so much power that you were just given since birth. These abilities are not easily used. Some people will struggle to ever figure out who they really are and what they want from this life. You might still not know that, and that's perfectly fine. You shouldn't keep yourself perfectly labeled in a box or else this is going to limit your thinking. Whatever others have made you feel in the past does not define who you are now. Learn from your past and don't forget who you are or where you came from. Let go of the hurt you have felt so that you can start healing and moving forward in a more positive direction.

Make sure that you really get to know people. Don't make assumptions. The better that you can really understand a person and who they are at their core, the easier it will be to have a more positive influence over them. Even when you are feeling like you have no idea what you're doing, you can always do some digging internally and externally to discover a greater, more meaningful truth. If you start to make too many assumptions and only allow people to be the labels that you have put on them, this is really going to limit your abilities to grow and understand the world better.

Communication is going to be how it all happens. It is always going to be better to just lay the truth out there and talk it out rather than trying to hold onto things so deeply. Though it might be really scary and challenging, it is going to make you feel so much better in the end when you can speak your truth and let others hear your opinions and feelings. Don't try to persuade in other ways besides communication. Don't withhold things from people, such as something they might need. You can manipulate others this way, but communication and talking things out is going to be more effective and have longer-term results.

The hurt that you have felt can be used for good now. All you have experienced has led you to right where you are in this moment. The darkest moments that you have gone through that you thought never would end are over now. The times when you wanted to run away and get rid of all of this have brought you to the person that you are now. Though you might never want to go back and do it over again, you should still learn to be grateful for these experiences, because without them, you wouldn't be able to be the positively influential person that you are about to become.

Getting to Know Them

Now it is time in the book to start to do the thing that you probably want to more than anything – persuade others! We live in a world where influence is essential. If you can't manage to persuade certain people, then it can keep you back from achieving the things that you really want in this life. The most important thing that you will want to do is get to know who you are trying to persuade. Whether you want to convince your husband that you're ready to have children, or you want to persuade your entire 100-member sales team that they need to push harder to drive sales, it all starts with really getting to know who they are and how they operate.

The first step in this process is to look at their background. How old are they? What gender do they identify as? Where do they live? What are their strengths? What are their weaknesses? What do they have already? What is it that they want? When you can answer these kinds of questions, it will become much easier to know how to come up with a plan of persuasion in order to suit your favor.

Certain kinds of differences will be important in this situation. For example, asking your 18-year-old boyfriend for $20 is going to be done in a different way than you would ask your 80-year-old grandmother for the same thing. In order to persuade people, you have to really understand the things that generically define them and then get into their deeper characteristics, such as things that create the personality that they have.

Next, you will want to determine what their likes are. What things make them happy? These should be easy to understand for people that you already know. When it comes to trying to analyze your customer base if you are trying to persuade sales, then think of basic things they'll like such as discounts, freebies, and other little rewards for being a consumer.

After you have managed to determine what it is that they might like, you should next try and figure out the things that they aren't as big of fans of. This might include things like long return times after purchasing something, having hidden fees, or not being able to customize their products. When you can identify both the things that they like and dislike, then it is easy to act accordingly. For everything that you might have that they will dislike, offer up a solution by providing something that they like. It seems so obvious, but a lot of people who try to influence others will completely disregard this.

Finally, make sure that you are highly aware of the way that they communicate. If you understand of this, it will be that much easier to make sure that you are expressing things with them in the same way. Always listen to the other person and ensure that you are giving them a platform to speak. Don't just look at the words they're saying but also their face as they start to share information with you. If someone feels as though they aren't being listened to, it will make them want to turn away from you and they will be far less likely to be persuaded in the end. The subsequent segment is going to discuss further the importance of communication and how you can better enable this kind of healthy interaction in your life.

Understanding the Importance of Communication

Communication isn't easy for everyone. It seems so simple to just open your mouth and start talking. We all do it, sometimes with others, often alone, and sometimes without even thinking before we do start chatting away. It's not uncommon to find that you are struggling to share what you are feeling through the use of your words, even though you are currently experiencing that kind of emotion. The better you are able to communicate, the easier your life is going to be, and the happier you will become in the end.

To start off by bettering your communication skills, remember that it is a practice. There is no pill you can take or a secret trick that you can start to do right now. You will have to make sure that you are practicing talking to other people in order to get better at it. If you're just starting, practice first by having small conversations. This might be with a barista at your local coffee shop or someone at the bus stop as you both are waiting. Don't bother other people, of course, but just look for ways that you can articulate your voice and try to say something beyond the basic "how are you?"

Make sure that you are effectively expressing your feelings to yourself. Sometimes when we are all alone, we still won't fully understand what our emotions mean. If you have to, start journaling your feelings every day. The more that you can work them out yourself and write down the emotions that you are feeling, the easier it will be to work through them on your own. How can you expect to effectively share these with others if you aren't sure how to share them with yourself?

When it comes to starting to persuade others, ensure that you are careful with your words. You never want to force anyone to do anything or put them in a place where they might feel as though they have little to know control. Avoid using phrases such as "You should do this." No one wants to be told what to do.

Talk about yourself first. It seems counterintuitive, but people will be more likely to respond by picking up on example rather than having you tell them what to do. For example, let's say that you want to persuade your spouse to start waking up earlier because you think it would help prevent the stress of being late every morning. Rather than saying something such as "You should start to wake up earlier," you can say something such as "I found that by waking up earlier, it's helped me to be a lot less stressed in the morning before work."

Let others believe that the idea is their own. They will want to believe that they were the ones to come up with this plan, not the other way around. Give them the chance to work through the plan on their own, and they can figure out their own positives and negatives. It will be a more effective persuasion when you are able to inspire it within other people rather than forcing them to believe something.

After this, ensure that you are careful of your own tone and body language. Create an atmosphere where they can be comfortable around you. The more calmness, love, and compassion that you can show to them, the easier it will be for them to relate to you. Sometimes we feel as though we need to be rigid and stern in order to get people to do what we want. This isn't the case at all! You should be kind and loving, and others will be much more receptive.

Last but not least, ensure that you are being very respectful of those that you are trying to persuade. You want to make sure that they feel comfortable with you, not as if they need to be ashamed or embarrassed around you. If someone says something stupid, no matter how dumb it sounds, don't make fun of them for it! Don't laugh at people or belittle them for their beliefs. Build others up and you will find that they have that same kind of respect in return.

Conclusion

Congratulations on making it throughout the book. You might still need some practice or have to do further research in specified areas, but you should still feel really proud of where you are now. There are so many people in this life that will blindly follow others. There are many individuals that will never look deep within themselves and really confront your thoughts. It's not easy to do so, but it's important that we really dive deep into our psyche in order to live a happier and healthier life.

Remember that it's still perfectly normal and healthy to let others influence you! Think of all the great leaders of the world and how they might be able to inspire positive passion and inspiration in those that follow them. You are not wrong for falling under the influence of others. The difference going forward is that it's going to be based around positive and uplifting inspiration rather than malicious-intentioned manipulation.

Always remember as you travel throughout your life that you need to use your brain power for good. Even though it might be hard sometimes, this is always going to be the better option. You might find yourself in a position one day where you have a very simple and reachable chance to manipulate someone else. Don't take advantage of this! The other person might be someone easily manipulated, and maybe on some level it is their own fault for not being more aware. Never assume this, however! Some individuals will have gone through things that really made it harder for them to break free from their thinking patterns and discover a healthier method of dealing with their thoughts and feelings.

Always help others, never hurt them. Even those that might have done the same to you in the past shouldn't be individuals that you target. You are an intelligent person who can use their powers for good. Make the world a better place with healthy influence and you will discover that this brings you everything that you have ever wanted.

This book was to prepare you for the world of dark psychology better. We are all part of the world that has tendencies to have some very dark people on it. It is important to look out for yourself when it comes to building new relationships and friendships. We have pretty much laid out how you should know if you are being manipulated and ways to get out of it. If you are still unsure if you are being manipulated, share some of your stories with friends or family members. You should even share it with a trusted doctor or therapist. With all of these people in your life, you should be able to see what your relationship is doing to your life finally. Just think about how much happier you will be when you make a good decision to get out of your abusive and manipulative relationship. You will be free of the negative energy in your life, and you will be able to begin again and move onto a much greener pasture in the end. Stick with your final decision to leave this abusive life and start a brand new one. Remember that you are completely worth it, and you will be able to find ways to make yourself happy without someone trying to control your entire life and making you incredibly unhappy. Just remember to look for the traits and signs of those who have manipulated in the past. You are well on your way to living a happier life once you finish this book.

PART TWO

Introduction

I n our modern world we rely mostly on the use of persuasive tactics or techniques. Their strength depends on our ability to evaluate a situation and to choose the right weapons. Different psychologists have given different lists of basic tactics: these ones are offered to help you get a clear view in order to plan your influence strategy.

1. Persuade Only Those Who Can Be Persuaded

We can all be influenced at one time or another provided the timing and the context is right. However, for some people, it can take a lot of persuading. Take a look at the politicians and their campaigns - they focus their money and their time almost exclusively on the small percentage of voters who are responsible for determining the outcome of an election. The very first step to successful persuasion is to identify and focus on the people who can, at that moment in time, be persuaded to follow you and your point of view. By doing this, a certain percentage of others, those who can't be persuaded at that moment in time

2. Get You're Timing and Content Right

These are the building blocks of persuasion. Context is what provides a standard for what is and isn't acceptable. For example, an experiment carried out on Stanford prisoners showed that students who overachieve could easily be molded into prison guards with a dictatorial nature. The timing is what dictates what we are looking for from other people and from life.

Often, when we marry, it is to someone very different to whom we may have been dating in our younger years, simply because what we want at any given time is subject to change.

3. Uninterested People Cannot Be Persuaded

You simply can't convince people to do something if they genuinely are not interested in what you have to say. In general, the human race is concerned primarily with their own individual selves and most of their time is spent thinking about three things – health, love, and money. The very first step to persuading someone is to learn to talk to that person about themselves. Appeal to their self-interest and you have their attention.

Continue to do it, and you will hold their attention long enough to persuade them.

4. Reciprocity is Compelling

Whether we like it or not, most of the time that someone does something for you, you feel innately compelled to return the favor. It's the way we are made, a survival instinct that goes back many millions of years. You can use that reciprocity to your advantage by giving someone something they want; you can then ask for something much more valuable back from them, and they will feel compelled to do it. The principle of reciprocation is more effective if you are the first one to give and if your gift is personal and unexpected.

5. Be Persistent but not Overbearing

If you are prepared to keep on asking for what you want, to continue demonstrating real value, you will ultimately succeed in the art of persuasion. Take a wander back through history and look at the vast numbers of figures who have persuaded people through persistence, in both message and endeavor.

Look at Abraham Lincoln; look at what he lost — three sons, his mother, his girlfriend, one of his sisters. He failed abysmally in business, and he also lost at no less than 8 elections.

Still, his persistence paid off when he was finally elected as President of the Unites States. He never gave up and neither should you.

6. Be Sincere in Your Compliments

Whether we admit it or not, compliments do have a positive effect on us, and we are much more likely to place our trust in a person who is sincere and who makes us feel good.

Try it — be sincere when you compliment a person, pay them compliments for something that they honestly wouldn't expect it to. Compliment them on something they had to work for: it can be something as simple as their clothing choice.

Don't compliment them on their beauty or on other things they were born with. It's quite easy once you learn how to do it, and it costs nothing. The rewards will speak for themselves.

7. Set Your Expectations

One of the biggest parts of persuasion is learning to manage the expectations of others when it comes to placing trust in you and your judgment. If a CEO were to promise his employees a pay increase of 20% and then give them 30%, he would be rewarded much more than the CEO who promised 20% and only delivered 10%.

Learn to understand what other people expect of you and then over deliver on it.

8. Never Assume

This is a bad mistake to make: to assume what people are looking for. Instead, offer them your value. Take the sales world; often products and services are held back because it is assumed that people simply don't have the money to purchase them, or they have no interest in them.

Be bold, get out there and say what you have to offer, say what you can do for them and leave the choice to them. Be persistent, and it will pay off.

9. Make Things Scarce

Virtually everything has a value these days, on a relative scale.

We need the bare necessities to survive, so they have a far higher value than something we don't need. Often, we want something because someone else has it. If you want to persuade people to want what you are offering, it may not be enough to point out the benefits of things or services we are offering. It could be much more effective if we would tell people about its uniqueness and what they could lose. That would create a scarcity feeling, and the less there is, the more people want it. The logic of scarcity is very simple: when something becomes scarce, people want it more.

10. Create a Sense of Urgency

One of the finer points of persuasion is being able to instill such a sense of urgency in people that they simply have to act straight away or miss out. If a person doesn't have any real motivation to want something now, they aren't likely to want.

It's down to you to persuade them that time is running out; persuade them now or lose them forever.

11. Images are Important

Most people respond better to something they can see. Quite simply if they can see it, then it's real; if you just talk about it, then it might not even exist. Images are potent, and pictures really do speak a thousand words. You don't actually have to use images; just learn how to paint that image in a person's mind.

12. Truth-Tell

Sometimes, hard though it may be, the easiest way to persuade a person to trust you is to tell them something that no one else will say something about themselves. Facing up to the truth is often the most meaningful thing any of us will go through.

Do it without any judgment and without an agenda and you will be surprised at how quickly that person responds favorably to you.

13. Build up a Rapport

The human race is a funny thing. We tend to like those who are more like us, and this often goes way beyond the conscious into the unconscious. By "copying" or matching your behaviors, regarding cadence, body language, patterns of language, etc. you will find that it is easier to build up a rapport with them and easier to persuade them to your way of thinking.

14. Be Flexible in Your Behavior

Have you considered why children are often so much more persuasive than adults are? It's because they are quite happy to work their way through a whole list of behaviors to get what they want – crying, being charming, pleading, trying to strike bargains, etc. The parent is stuck with just one response – No – which often turns to another – Yes.

The more different behaviors you have in your repertoire, the more likely you are to be persuasive.

15. Be Detached and Calm

If you are in a situation where emotion is running high, you will always be the most persuasive person if you are calm, show little to no emotion and remain detached from the situation.

In times of conflict, people will turn to you for help, and they will trust you to lead them in the right direction.

16. Use Anger in the Right Way

Most people really don't like conflict and if you are prepared to escalate a situation to a level of high tension and conflict, many of your adversaries will back down. Don't make a habit of doing this and never do it when you are in an emotional state or are on the verge of losing control. Do use anger in the right way to gain the advantage.

17. Be Confident, Be Certain

The most intoxicating and compelling quality is a certainty. If you are confident and full of certainty, you will have the edge in persuading people to follow you.

The Psychology Of Persuasion

Persuasion is the act of prevailing over another person to believe something by the use of various reasoning or arguments. There is ethical persuasion and dark persuasion. The difference between these two types of persuasions is the intent. An ethical persuader may try to convince another person to do something without giving much thought to certain tactics. They may do this without ulterior motive or real understanding of the person they are trying to persuade. This particular persuader may be concerned with creating good for many people like a diplomat negotiating against the war. This is the persuader known to be ethical.

On the other hand, there is a dark persuader. This particular individual is well aware of the bigger picture. He has a full understanding of the person he is trying to persuade, what motivates them, and to what extent they can go for their tactic to be successful. A dark persuader is not concerned with how moral their manipulation is doing the right thing is not their motivation. When a dark persuader identifies a thing they want, they devise a way to get it and do not care who gets hurt in the process. Their goal is to always get what benefits them no matter the cost.

When is Persuasion used?

Persuasion is used every day by every person in various ways. Children use persuasion to get their parents to do for them what they want or buy for them something. In intimate relationships, partners persuade each other in order to get what each wants. Persuasion in business is common. A business owner needs to persuade his or her customers to buy their services or products. Persuasion is common and can be ethical or unethical depending on the intent of the person doing the persuasion.

Different techniques are used to persuade individuals. These techniques can be used for both dark persuasion and ethical persuasion. The outcome of any form of persuasion is to get your opponent, partner or audience to do as you wish them to do so that you benefit. It becomes unethical persuasion when the only person that stands to gain is the one doing the persuasion. When it is only one person gaining, it means it is getting what a person wants at the expense of the other person.

Persuasive techniques used

Persuasion is used to convince a person about something they would not have considered otherwise. Advertisements are one-way persuasion techniques are employed. The same techniques used to sell a good thing can be used to manipulate a person. There are other ways a person can persuade you, these include:

Appealing to authority – if you are trying to persuade a person into doing something, using important people or experts to pass your point across is very convincing. When you reliably research, you can make your argument very convincing and sway your audience. For instance, a person can say:

Example - The former first lady Michele Obama has said the only way to eradicate obesity among children is getting rid of junk food from vending machines.

Example – according to a recent study, watching TV reduces stress causing a reduction in the risk of heart diseases.

Both these statements whether true or falsified can convince a person that what is being said is true because a person has appealed to authority. Dark persuasion can also appeal to authority in order to convince their victim to do as they wish for them to do.

Appeal to reason – people are easily convinced when a person uses logic to persuade them. For instance, a person would say:

A bar of chocolate contains 300 calories and 20 grams of sugar. That is not so bad! You can still enjoy your bar of chocolate every day because it is within your caloric limit.

Although that statement is not entirely true, a person that wants you to push their sales, yet they know it is not healthy for you will use it to persuade you. People tend to trust where there are figures believing the information to be authentic. This tactic is widely used to manipulate individuals to do as other wishes.

Empathize or appeal to emotion – making a person feel sad, angry or happy can help you persuade them. For instance:

A person may say to you that your donation is important because it may feed a hungry child for a day or

If you do not donate, a child will go hungry and die and you will be part of the reason.

Both those statements serve to persuade an individual to make a contribution. The first one appeals to the person to empathize with a situation while the second statement serves to guilt-trip the individual. Both statements are aimed at getting a contribution. However, one is used in an ethical way while the other is unethical or dark persuasion.

Appealing to Trust – if a person trusts and believes you, it becomes easier to persuade them. Most psychopaths make sure their victims trust them and that is how they are able to persuade them. It is almost impossible to persuade a person that doesn't trust you. Trust is important if one is to be convinced. For instance:

If a person seems to be doing well financially and tells you to invest in something, they may say to trust them that is how they began. They know you are desperate to have financial stability and because you may know their story, you will believe them.

If this person is genuine, then you are likely to have made a good investment. However, embezzlers, on the other hand, are people that are also trusted by those that invest with them. They convince their victims to invest in a certain thing because it pays. You trust them because they seem to have a good reputation and seem to know what they are doing. Unfortunately, this person is appealing to your trust to invest your hard-earned money, but they swindle you. This is dark persuasion in play. All the people that have had their funds embezzled trusted their embezzlers.

Plain folk – manipulators know to persuade their victims or audience; they must appear to be the average kind of a person. For instance, politicians use persuasion tactics to get voters. He or she may just say:

"I am an average person. I relate to the suffering we have endured under the current leadership and it is time we changed the narrative. I have grown up with you in this neighborhood, I have faced the same challenges and therefore I am the best candidate."

This kind of appeal is to show that a politician is an average person just like the voters. The politician wants the voters to believe he can relate with them because he is one of the – ordinary. Whether the information is true or not, whether the politician just wants votes and will do nothing or not, he will manage to convince the electorate through such statements.

Bandwagon – this is the presumption that everyone trusts it, so it must be good or true. This is very common in advertisements. For instance:

A company advertising its brand of toothpaste may claim that 2 out of every American household use this product. It has been trusted by families for generations to offer the best in cavity protection.

No one wants to have cavities. If you are convinced that that product is the number one bestseller and the majority of the people trust it, you will definitely buy it. It is important to remember that some of these statistics are not true. To push sales of a product regardless of if the product does perform as indicated, companies can come up with untruths.

Bandwagon is also a tactic used majorly on social media. If a person notices many likes regarding a particular product, they rush out to buy it. The assumption is that if many like it, it must be good. However, it is possible that it is the advertisement that was well crafted and not the product.

Rhetorical Question – when a person wants to persuade another one, they will use rhetorical questions. For instance, if a person is promoting a skin care regiment, they may ask their audience, "Who wouldn't like to have fair glowing skin?" the answer is obvious. It provokes the person to think and wish to have flawless skin and end up buying the product.

Another person may want to sell you shares knowing very well that the share value is likely to drop. They show you convincing figures and ask you, "wouldn't you want to make money?" Even the richest person in the world wants to make more money! This kind of tactic will end up convincing you to invest even though it could be a wrong investment.

What Is Manipulation

When coming from a psychological point of reference, manipulation is mostly about perception. How we perceive things or actions determines our laws, social formalities, and even our lives.

The manipulator changes these norms with tactics. The determination of the positive or negative connotation of these actions remains subjective. Psychological manipulation is often considered devious. With the subject of dark psychology, we can take into account that the manipulation practiced is often exploitative at the expense of others.

So, what is manipulation of the dark?

Sources tell us that it is concealment—hiding in the shadows knowing when to strike. It is also a false front, hiding true intentions. When we are talking about this level of deception, we are talking about hiding aggression. When we take, there is a certain level of aggressive behavior that happens. A small part of manipulation is hiding that aggressive behavior so that the victim sees only good nature.

This is accomplished in various ways and means, one being knowledge. When we allow another to know us, we display vulnerability along with strengths. The knowledge of these personal traits can give the manipulator the ability to maneuver around without any alarms going off.

The effectiveness of manipulating those strengths and vulnerabilities arrives when the practitioner of the dark knows what is vulnerable and what inspires pride.

A reoccurring ideology that drives us to war takes into consideration that war is more negative than positive. We want to avoid it. The

168

manipulation process sees the pride in all of us and plays to that pride. It is our strength. However, when used to drive an army to slaughter others, the intention of our pride has been manipulated to enforce the agendas of others.

There is ruthlessness when we talk about psychological manipulation. When dealing with someone other than the pure psychopath who feels little to nothing, ruthlessness can be measured. Often soft ruthless behavior can sneak up on its prey and snag it before it knows what is happening. This harm of the prey becomes less than even a momentary qualm in the mind of the manipulator.

Often the practitioners of dark psychology use aggression and fear to drive us. The less dark side still falls into the category of knowing what weakness is, and that weakness leaves the individual open to control.

How the manipulator uses that control determines the severity of manipulation. There is and are positive versions of manipulating others. Like convincing someone that they are not doing well and that they need to get help. We, however, are looking at the darker side of this. The manipulator uses their skills of control to get what they want—and the cost does not apply.

There are many ways to move another into a place of being controlled. From the positive to the negative, psychological manipulators utilize all tactics.

When positive reinforcement is used, charm is displayed. A forced smile or laughter can trigger laughter in all of us. As when we were infants, we copy what we see. When we see tears, we want them to stop. When we see a smile, we find ourselves smiling as well.

The manipulator using positive reinforcement can shower money, charm and gifts to get us to feel something. The usage of these things allows control of us on an instinctual level. We follow those who tell us what we want to hear.

Psychological manipulation can also implement negative reinforcement. This is a form of deflection. A substitution of one thing for another

Often, we have things we need or have to do and we do not really want to do them. The psychological manipulation of negative reinforcement uses that power of negativity to lure the subject from their original need, pushing them toward something they want done instead. The long game, a slow play of putting tasks into another's life and then controlling those tasks so that the manipulator can get what they want is an extremely effective and subdued tactic.

Sometimes only partial reinforcement is required to gain control. We are talking about elevating the fear or doubt regarding the tasks needed done. The partial is the long play. It knows that in the end, the victim will lose. It knows that by planting small seeds now, victory will eventually happen. It knows that we all have our weaknesses and that by planting even a small seed we can take someone to that weakness. An individual trying to work toward something they already were shaky on, or had doubts about, will listen to the lie and flow with that idea, and use it to their own destruction.

The partial manipulator only needs to put the thought in the mind, knowing the weakness is already there, and utilizing it will take their prey to a destructive end.

Psychological manipulators flat, outright punish. From an actual physical lashing to the passive aggressive playing of the victim, punishment is very effective when one wants to control another.

We skulk and cry and yell and nag and go completely silent. This is the blackmail of the manipulator. It inspires guilt in us. That "wanting to be the better person" rises to the front and we do what the manipulator wants.

When the manipulator sets free the crocodile tears, we have no idea if they are real or not. The degree of crying is not up to us to determine. Only the manipulator knows if the tears are legitimate or not.

In this case, the trap is often sprung from the victim's side. They walk up to the hurt individual to help, only to find that the manipulator is just lying in wait to strike.

One extreme version of manipulation is violence.

Violence triggers something inside us. We often do anything to avoid it. The manipulator knows that violence strategically applied can make us go into a state of avoidance. There incites the control. Physical violence can have mental scarring. The manipulator causes the scarring. It places violence in tactical places to get the result they want.

Some would say this is the darkest of the dark.

Taken to the individual, this can mentally damage them for a long period of time, if not permanently. Placed on a world stage, it can lead all the way up to the physical conflict of genocide.

The manipulation process in dark psychology is normally not a single move. It is a complex series of moves, often with the outcome only known by the manipulator. The motivations of manipulators are as convoluted as human nature.

Mostly it is about gain. Manipulators of the dark want to gain... something. When we speak about gain, we are talking about power and influence, control and manipulation over others. The trophy is up to the individual. This can be everything as to gaining affections, to money, and even to life itself.

It is about gaining for their personal reasons and gratifications. The taking of others and making the power and control their own Selfishness to the extreme. The mind of the dark practitioner sees the ultimate win as gain over others.

They have power. Superiority is the power over another and taking of someone else's power makes them feel superior. This is a huge driving force behind the manipulator. Often, in the case of immature individuals driving manipulations toward superiority, any is pushed aside for just the feeling of being superior.

In relationships, it is about control. The manipulation of power can put one in control. Although we have looked at the role of the vampire and power, and we know who really has control.

This feeling of control can be overwhelming to the mental state of the dark. Almost drug-like, it is a feeling of emotion that is most logical. Control is one of the easiest manipulation tactics to achieve with only logic to guide. It drives not only the victim, but the manipulator as well.

Psychological manipulation can also be about self-esteem. The self of the manipulator is always in question. This is one of the reasons they manipulate, to define themselves. How easily they are able to manipulate another can tell the dark that they are better than others. That weakness and strength can be measured in the tactical playing field of the hustle.

This defines who they are. Can they manipulate? Yes? They are stronger. No? They are weaker. It is a measuring device for self-esteem.

However, we are not saying it is the only device for measurement. Self-esteem can be measured by far fewer damaging means.

The mind gets bored. And what do we do when we get bored? We seek entertainment. How do we achieve entertainment? We manipulate.

We all do it.

Let us assume we are bored, and we want to remove or alleviate that boredom with something else. Do we just sit back and wait for something new to happen?

No. We actively search for something to replace boredom. Manipulation can take place on many different levels, as well as the severity of which they are applied. From picking up a crayon and coloring, to taking a mental absence, to massacring everyone around you.

The dark psychological manipulator is bored most of the time. More than most the psychological manipulator will often use manipulation to determine their own validity of feelings and emotions

What this boils down to is that manipulation applied in relations with others helps the manipulator to regulate reactions to validate or not validate their own emotions. The manipulator measures the self and their self-esteem by how others handle their personal self-questioning.

This happens when the practitioner does not have a grasp on what emotions are. They look at their own emotions as invalid and manipulate the situation in such a way as to validate them.

We are stuck with ourselves, and we cannot get away. Psychological manipulators validate or invalidate themselves by the tactical controlling of others. It is an interesting way of viewing life, although there is one form of manipulation that we all idolize.

The con

One common form of manipulation is the convincing of another to make their money yours.

This is a hidden agenda of the criminal. This form of mental manipulation preys mostly on the elderly and the rich. However, we all can fall to this form of manipulation. What we choose to spend on and what we do not is our response to a form of psychological manipulation.

Something happens when the buck is passed over. We go from manipulation into action. Something drives us. It is within us and it is outside forces that drive. What causes this drive and the drive itself is called...?

Persuasion

When And Why To Use Manipulation

Who Manipulates?

Manipulators come in several forms. Some are younger and simply have not learned how to interact with the world. Others still just happen to be manipulative by nature—they are intentionally using their abilities to get what they want with no regard for how it hurts other people. Ultimately, however, the manipulators tend to have several traits in common.

They are always the victim

It does not matter what has happened—the manipulator will always be the victim or not at fault in some way. The manipulator could pull out a gun and shoot you and would rationalize that he had no choice and insist that he was the victim as he holds the smoking gun in his hand. This is a common trait of manipulators as it makes them deserving of sympathy, which gives them the upper hand in many different situations. They will try to figure out how to get all of your friends and family on their side and will blame everything on you. The worst part is that since they are so skillful at doing exactly this, they can often convince other people to fall for it.

They regularly distort the truth

The manipulator will always twist reality. Skilled at weaving webs of lies, the manipulator will always have a way to rewrite history, change a situation, or otherwise make it, so their narrative is the correct one.

They are passive-aggressive

Manipulators tend to be passive-aggressive. A part of this is to make sure that you know your place around the manipulator—they use it to assert dominance and covertly exert their own influence and desire over you. For example, they will intentionally use passive-aggression to make you feel bad, and then be satisfied that they held power necessary to make you feel bad in the first place.

They will pressure you

The manipulator is convinced that he is always right no matter what, and with that in mind, he will not hesitate to pressure you in order to get whatever he wants from you at any given moment. He knows that his way is the right way, and he will force the point until you agree.

They will not work to solve a problem

If you find that there is a problem with the manipulator, good luck—they will not work to come to some sort of solution. Instead, they will continue on as if nothing is wrong, or at the very least, that nothing is wrong with them. They could not care more about your own problems, so long as they are not the manipulator's problems.

They will always keep the advantage

The manipulator has an uncanny way to always remain in control in nearly any situation. They will oftentimes find a way to ensure that they can find a way to stay in charge. They will always pick the restaurant that you go to, or they will always invite you out of your comfort zone and into theirs, all done intentionally to maintain power and control over the situation. When they do this, they effectively guarantee that they are able to stay in charge long enough to keep you off balance and make sure that they always have the upper hand.

They will always have excuses

When they do happen to make a mistake, manipulators typically will have some sort of excuse. There was a car accident on the way over, or they just got fired for no reason at all. It does not matter what the problem is; there will be some sort of excuse that will arise to take the blame away from the manipulator and push it onto someone else.

They will make you feel unconfident

Something about the manipulator will always leave you feeling incompetent and unable to do anything right. This means that you will constantly be feeling like you are the problem rather than seeing that the whole problem may have been resting firmly with the manipulator all along.

Why Manipulate?

Manipulators have all sorts of reasons to manipulate others, with some simply having no reason at all. When you begin to understand the motivation behind these drives, you may be more inclined to understand those techniques that the manipulators everywhere tend to use. This means then that you will be able to figure out how to fight back. You can defend yourself and others based on the knowledge that you have. Knowing why people manipulate others can be a critical skill to develop if you want to be successful in the world around you.

They want to advance in life

When you feel like you need to advance somehow, whether due to needing the money in order to get what you wanted or needed, manipulation is one way to get it. When you manipulate someone, you are usually using them as a sort of steppingstone for yourself in order to ensure that you can, in fact, withstand future struggles while also progressing the agenda that you have. Typically, this is the most selfish of the reasons on this list—these manipulators do so simply because they can.

They need power and superiority

Similar to the last reason for manipulation, oftentimes, manipulators need to feel like they are in power. They simply are only secure in themselves so long as they are in a position of power over other people. If they feel like their superiority will be questioned in any way, shape, or form, they will feel insecure. They will feel like the only way they can make themselves feel comfortable is if they exert and enforce their own superiority, which they give themselves through making a point to manipulate those around them.

They need control

When people are particularly controlling, they may find that manipulation is one of the easiest ways to get the results desired. When you are able to manipulate someone else into doing what they need to do, you are able to ensure that you maintain control in nearly any situation. You may have to find a way to covertly encourage the other person to do what you want, but as soon as you manage to do that, you can effectively maintain control, even if the other person does not realize that you are in control of the situation at hand. The need to be in control can be particularly motivating for people when it comes to deciding to manipulate.

They need to manipulate to better their own self-esteem

Some people, such as narcissists, tend to feel like they are only comfortable with themselves when other people are lavishing them with attention or admiration. These people tend to result in manipulation to get that attention, especially if they are not particularly outstanding or deserving of attention in the first place. In manipulating other people into giving them the craved attention, they are able to feel better about themselves.

They are bored

Some people simply enjoy watching the world burn and will make it a point to manipulate other people simply to get entertainment. They treat it like a game or a challenge, intentionally testing boundaries to see how far they can get with no real reason or motivation beyond being bored to guide them. These may be some of the more dangerous manipulators as they have no real goal in mind—they simply want to wreak havoc and spend some time messing with other people despite not getting anything other than their own satisfaction in return.

They have a hidden agenda

More often than not, the manipulator has some sort of reason to manipulate those around him or her. This is typically hidden from the target but can be figured out with enough time and information. Think about how some people will intentionally seek out vulnerable people with ulterior motives. They may marry in order to get their hands-on money, or intentionally volunteer as a caregiver for an elderly family member in order to steal money from them. No matter what the hidden agenda is, the manipulator has good cause to try to keep it hidden.

They do not properly identify with the emotions of others

Sometimes, the manipulation is unintentional and a side effect of simply being unable to identify with other people. Effectively, they lack empathy, and that lack of empathy is enough to make it so they cannot easily identify when they have done something that is manipulative, nor do they automatically recognize when what they have done is problematic. These are people who simply do not understand social norms for some reason or another. They may have a personality or other mental health disorder.

When Manipulation Occurs

No one wants to be on the receiving end of manipulation, and yet it seems to be all around us. The world is literally surrounded by different people and their attempts to manipulate. You can see it on television and in the media. You can see it in religion and politics. It happens in all kinds of relationships when they become unhealthy. There is no real way to truly avoid manipulation and that in and of it can be incredibly disheartening.

However, because manipulation is everywhere, it becomes prudent to understand what it looks like in a wide variety of situations and cases. You want to be able to notice when it is happening and figure out how best to fight back from it to ensure that you actually are able to protect yourself. When you are able to protect yourself from manipulation, you can guarantee that you, at the very least, are not regularly being used by other people simply because you refuse to allow yourself to be

We will take a look at manipulation in several different relationships and contexts for a brief overview of what to expect and why it happens.

In relationships

This is particularly referring to romantic relationships. Romantic relationships seem to attract manipulation frequently, especially if one member of the couple happens to be on the less confrontational side and is afraid of ever standing up for him or herself. When this happens, you may find that you have run into quite the conundrum—you need to figure out how best to leave a romantic relationship rife with manipulation, which can be difficult if the manipulator has done his job right.

In friendships

Manipulative friends may try to get on your good side as quickly as possible, but they will soon fall into the habit of always needing you but never being available when you need them. At first, you will assume it is a coincidence, but over time, you will realize that it is actually a pattern, leaving you stuck to decide whether you would like to leave the friendship altogether or if you would prefer to instead put up with the manipulator's lack of support and enjoy what you can.

In churches

Churches commonly also manipulate people, attempting to force them into situations and actions that they may not necessarily want. In particular, you will commonly see threats of damnation and punishment if they do not live by a very specific life, and that is a perfect example of manipulation. They use their authority to sort of force your hand and make you feel like you have no choice but to comply. This is what they count on—they assume that you will continue to donate, to serve, and to attend because they threaten you if you do not. While many people may not see it as a threat, being told that you may be excommunicated or that you will be damned for eternity are two ways to sort of scare someone into behaving a certain way.

.

Technics To Influence Other

All of us live different lives, and there may be those of you out in your own community who go into battle every day. Therefore, here is a list of all the known persuasive methods that masters use to manipulate and get what they want.

Nonetheless, please note that great responsibility comes with high energy. Always use your experience and not just your own for the good of everyone. You're having that, Spidey?

How to Cooperate with People

Humour-You makes people feel good if you can make them laugh. This allows you to build a relationship with them quickly.

Smile-First impressions last, and first impressions with a smile are a benefit. Try to smile at every person in the street.

Respect-We all know that it is appreciated and not hated. Firstly, however, you should always thank everyone you encounter. It's still convenient for someone who loves you to do a favor.

Create quick connections-people who can immediately make contact with someone have more friends and can build good relationships than people who can't.

Using body Language-Body language awareness is included in the program. Our regular contact is 55% body language. Although the people you talk with interpret the signals instinctively, learning how to identify such messages is an asset in the art of persuasion.

The Halo Effect–Generally, we classify people as good or generally evil. Any characteristic that you will show a person in the future can be influenced by what you teach today. Make sure anybody you meet today feels like you're usually right.

Similarity-Same feathered birds, don't they flock together? If you can always find a way to understand what is shared between you and the other person instantly, you can quickly build a connection. This relationship eventually becomes faith, which is always what people have to do for you.

Goodwill-Be genuine always if you show interest in others. Being frank about your concern for others will make them quicker like you.

Bonding–The names of people sound to their ears like jingle bells. Address people by name and they will pay more attention to you.

The methods of mirroring and matching Mirror your language– Mirroring is a technique used for neurological programming to create relationships with an individual unconsciously. Using the same language, the other person uses will help you build this relationship in no time.

Match your breathing–breathing alone can help you create a link that you are convinced to use. The effectiveness of this method is dependent on its disguise. Who will ever know that somebody is trying to copy their practice of breathing?

Match the Tone-Matching, the voice of a person, operates on an unconscious level as you see all the mirrored techniques here.

Mirror their moods–If your partner is in a bad mood, are you jokingly approaching them? Of course not of course not just assess the attitude of people until you do what you want.

Test your energy level–The energy level of a person can tell you how likely you are to make suggestions. If you can be as cheerful or as energetic as they are, you can lead them to your plans much faster.

Cognitive dissonance test

Create relationships–If you are able to get people to commit, this person will most likely do what you asked them to do. You will have a sense of uncomfortably that will last for some time if you don't.

Using written Obligations-Written promises are better than oral ones. It can also function as a bond between you and the other person.

Build public commitments-public commitments are even better than written promises. There will be not only a concern for the relationship but also the integrity of the individual.

Using external rewards-business, people always use their workers' incentives. Although the inspiration it provides lasts only for a short time, it still does the job.

Always make them say "Yes" –This is a kind of conditioning in which the response of the person is matched by the stimulus that you offer in this case.

Make a concerted effort–if you can get people to make an effort, they will more likely stick to your plans or execute their requests.

Create dissonance and offer a solution-just take care to provide a way out if you plan to make someone feel uncomfortable to get them to do as you like.

Create a sense of obligation

Present Giving-How do you feel about giving a gift to someone and you've got nothing to give back? Very bad, isn't it? You'll probably say, "Geez, don't you have anything. Just let me know if you need anything..."

Mutual compromise–Often, people will try to influence their minds, so that you may feel helpless when you know that you don't agree with what just happened. Don't worry! Don't worry! What the other person does not know is that when it is your turn to make him / her consent to your application, he or she is just as weak.

Give a favor, get it back-people do things for you sometimes, whether you like it or not. The problem is that it induces a need to reciprocate in the mind of the receiver. If you are a generous person who is happy to give favours to others without anything in return, simply make sure you let them know.

Sharing secrets-Share the secret to building a bond, a sense of duty, and a sense of trust Just note, the secrets that you share depend on the type of person with whom you share them.

Group power think

Build a team-The The more extensive the band, the better. Human beings have a substantial socializing need. People join groups to have a sense of belonging. If you want people to live up to your values, reinforce the community, and develop it.

Familiarize everyone-if you can get people to identify strongly with your party, it will be easier to influence their actions. Make sure everybody is the same as they think.

Set the values–companies typically have beliefs that they bring together in the form of mission and vision statements. Such costs need to be adhered to by people within the organization or group.

The Persuasion Language

Using repeated language-avoid using offensive words and replacing them with less offensive ones. For example: use mentally challenged rather than communication, idiot, propaganda, instead of torture, enhanced interrogation, etc.

Play with Numbers-Play with numbers while you illustrate something to convince. Seek anything like, "close to nine in ten" or "less than five in all..." 38. Using positive words— what you want is for people to feel comfortable and confident in what they want. So, when you try to communicate, use positive words.

Words with emotion–Words filled with emotions are incredibly helpful for people to behave. Only look at how the term "terrorism" was used by George W. Bush in his war against the enemies of America. Be quiet-the best thing to do after making a contract is to be silent. The person has already chosen, and you won't want to ruin the whole thing by giving the other man contradictory ideas by accident.

Painting images with Words-Isn't it nice to walk around the park with the beautiful trees all over the place, swinging back and forth to the fresh air? You can only feel the morning sun's rays hit your soft skin softly before you stand on a pile of dog poo (Hey! We just smash you. We're not even in the middle of the list)

Choose the right words-The the right words will make a big difference sometimes. Instead of uttering, "Sir, I'm very sure we will have difficulty convincing your staff." Try this, "Sir, I am sure the workers will appreciate it and will give you more support if we try other forms." Replace "you" with "let's"–more people will participate by replacing "let's" with "you." The term "let us" gives you a sense of engagement. So from now on, let's try using "let's."

Use simple statements-In simple, direct, and short statements; give your instructions. It's easier not only to remember but also to understand and absorb.

Use your everyday language-your listeners and/or readers will only be fooled by complicated language. You have an enormous vocabulary, definitely, but if you speak like an intellectually dexterous (geek) person all the time, you will be misinterpreted more likely.

Avoid vulgar words and curse words-try to prevent profanity in your comments (especially new acquaintances) as far as possible. Your reputation depends most of the time on the sort of terms you use.

Avoid jargon, and technical Language-There is no problem when the person you talk to works in the same field you are in. Nonetheless, you communicate with different people in most situations.

Keep phrases brief-A single phrase can stand as a whole in the early centuries. Today, we clearly live in a world where a single word like "party" is sufficient to say it all. This said, "Let's" "run."

Don't beat around the bush-say it clearly if you have something to say.

Using words-Words in speech are more likely to move people. Keep in mind that your words are conceived by the person with whom you speak. Thought takes precedence over motion.

Terms like Free, Easy, Earn Now, Sexy, And Guaranteed are just a few of the other attentiveness terms that you can use. Try to Experiment these words in your statements.

Highlight what you want-look at the last sentence above.

Pace-Research has shown that speaking faster is more persuasive than talking slowly and monotonously.

Avoid vocal Fillers-What does this mean... Uhm to make ...Uhm your thoughts accepted. When speaking, don't use these kinds of words.

Determine your pitch-it has been more effective for convincing speech to lower the pitch of your voice.

Change the Voice-Speak loud enough to listen to you. Check the sound system first if you speak to a crowd so that the audience doesn't end up being deaf during your speech.

Be more concise-concepts conveyed easily and regularly add credibility. People will most likely respond to your questions or orders if they can understand fully what you want to say.

Taking a while to take a break— emphasis does not mean that you should talk louder, more quickly, in a low voice, etc. Sometimes you have to pause so that people have time to digest what you just said.

Techniques Of Manipulation In Life

H ave you ever noticed that the most successful people are also the most persuasive? In the workplace, it is rarely the aggressive bossy people that rise to the top. Great leaders have a knack of making other people feel better about them and achieve better results. Use the following techniques to become a better manipulator both at work and at home.

- Inspire confidence

Do you give compliments regularly? Are you quick to praise people when they achieve their goals? If not, then why not? A few words can go a long way to boost someone's confidence. Make sure you tell people when they have done a good job and encourage them to greater things.

Once you master this technique and feel comfortable giving praise this will spill over into your personal life. If your partner looks sensational then tell them! If your kids have done well at school, then reward them with your praise.

Quick tip: Only give sincere compliments and do not use them to play people. If you are using manipulation to avoid tasks at work you will soon get a reputation for using people.

- Repetition

Many people believe that passion alone can make an idea stand out amid a sea of other ideas. This is not true and successful people realize that the key to standing out in societies information overload is repetition. We have all developed filters to protect us from the bombardment of information in this media led world and need to hear something multiple times before it sinks in. If you have a great idea and voice it to someone make sure you follow up with a written version.

- Deliver your message in context

Too often we are tempted to make ourselves look more intelligent by using technical jargon or abstract references. You will achieve much better results if you tune into your audience's frame of mind. Avoid terms that are non-specific. If you have an idea to make things "easier to use" or "better and quicker" then state how much easier or how much better and quicker

- Personalize your message

Statements of fact can often be bland and uninteresting. If you can personalize your speech you have a greater impact on your audience. This is a great tool at work, if you are approaching someone who is creative then tailor your speech to reflect this.

This technique will also help your social life. Whenever you are meeting new people try and do a bit of homework so you know more about them.

- Use your contacts

Everyone is more open to people who they believe have mutual associations. Your connections can help you progress and providing you don't abuse their influence they can aid your progress at work. Your credibility can rise with the relevance of your contacts and friends.

- Use visualization techniques

Have you noticed that the most successful sales pitches have a strong visual element? Picture Apples Steve Jobs and you can visualize the stage and the graphics that he used to get his message across. Even his clothes became part of the whole message that Apple was trying to convey.

Not everyone will be able to comprehend what you see in your mind's eye, especially if they have less knowledge in the domain you represent.

- Social media

Do you use social media to its full potential? Are you prepared to invest time and energy in your online connections? If not, then you are missing a huge opportunity. The potential to reach thousands of people who can help you in your career is invaluable.

Potential investors or customers are all waiting for you to tell your story or promote your product. Social media allows you to solicit ideas from a huge audience all with the click of a mouse. The power of a "like button" is not to be ignored! The evidence of thousands of positive affirmations will only serve to amplify your voice and make more people listen.

Your social life can also thrive online. Groups of like-minded people are all out there waiting for you to join them. Maybe you have a passion for sailing or extreme sports but aren't sure of the facilities near you. Facebook is a great place to start looking for groups in your area, reach out and connect. Use Twitter and Instagram to help your dating life if you are looking for love! Providing you take precautions and always meet for the first time in public you can meet some interesting people!

Quick tip: Social media can also be a brutal place and it is essential you monitor your settings. Before you join a group make sure they can only see the information you are comfortable with.

- Listen intently

If you want to get someone to like you the best way is to let them talk about themselves. Adopt a relaxed posture and allow them to tell you all about themselves. Show genuine interest and ask pertinent questions as you listen.

What is the common factor all these questions have?

"That is fascinating, how did you manage that?"

"Interesting, do you have any examples of what you mean?"

"Your knowledge about....... Is amazing, what do you think about...?"

They are all questions that elicit a response. This shows the speaker that you are not just listening, but you have a genuine interest in what they are saying. You are also allowing the speaker to expand the conversation and this creates a bond between the two of you. They will see you as an ally and a person they can trust.

Persuasion and manipulation are both powerful forces that can be used to make your life better. Ethical communications help others and make them a part of your team.

Emotional Manipulation Tactics

O nce a person understands the power of emotions, he/she can use it ethically or unethically. The last thing that we want is having someone manipulating our emotions, whether it is a friend, colleague, or politician. There are some ways through which a master manipulator can use emotional intelligence against you. Please note that not everyone who has the characteristics listed below and used the said skill has selfish intentions. Some people practice them with no intended harm. Nonetheless, having an increased awareness of these behaviors will empower you to deal with manipulators strategically and sharpen your intelligence quotient in the process.

1. Manipulators play on fear.

The majority of manipulators will overemphasis specific points and exaggerate facts in an effort to make you scared and have you acting as they want. The way to identify this play is by looking out for statements that imply you are not strong or courageous enough or that if you miss out on a particular thing, you are a loser.

2. Manipulators deceive

Everybody values honesty and transparency thus will avoid deceivers. Manipulators understand this concept and are very cunning when lying. They twist the facts or try to show you only the side of the story that benefits them. For instance, a work colleague can spread some unconfirmed rumor to gain an upper hand. To avoid being deceived, do not believe everything you hear. Instead, base your choices on credible sources and ask questions if the details are not clear.

3. Manipulators take advantage of your happiness

Have you noticed that you are more likely to say yes to anything when you are happy or in a good mood? When we are happy, we tend to jump on opportunities that look good even before we think things through. Master manipulators have this knowledge thus will take advantage of the moods. To manage this emotional opportunity and avoid manipulation, work to improve awareness of your emotions, both positive and negative. Strive to strike a balance between logic and emotions when making decisions.

4. Manipulators take advantage of reciprocity.

Do you know that feeling you get when you owe someone a favor especially if they helped you at one point? That feeling of debt makes one vulnerable. It is hard to say no to a manipulator if you owe them something. Most of the manipulators will attempt to butter and flatter you with small favors then ask for a big one in return. As much as giving brings more joy than receiving, it is more important to know your limits. Do not be afraid to say no when you have to even if you owe someone a favor.

5. Manipulators push for a home court advantage

It is very easy to convince a person when you are in a familiar place. As such, a manipulator will push you towards meeting you in a place he/she is familiar with while you are not. Ownership gives power and comfort thus a place like home or the office will give the manipulator some authority. You will have to make requests for meeting in a neutral place where familiarity and ownership are diluted so as to disarm the manipulator.

6. The manipulator will ask a lot of questions.

Naturally, it is easy to talk about oneself. Master manipulators know this thus they take advantage to ask some probing questions. Their agendas are hidden but basically, they seek to discover your weaknesses or other information they can hold against you. Of course, it would be unfair for you to assume that everyone has wrong motives because there are a few people who genuinely seek to know you better. However, it is okay to question people, especially those who reveal nothing about themselves.

7. The manipulator will speak quickly

In order to manipulate you through your emotions, the manipulator will speak quickly and sometimes use jargon and special vocabulary. This will give them an advantage because you will not have enough time to think. Fry you to counter this form of manipulation; do not feel afraid to ask for some time to process what the person said. Also, make a point of asking the person to repeat any unclear statements. To gain some control of a conversation, repeat the points the other person makes in your own words and let them sink.

8. The display of negative emotions

Some manipulators will use voice tones to control your emotions. The most commonly used tone and body language by manipulators are negative. For instance, basketball coaches (they use manipulation for positive purposes) are masters at raising their voices and using strong body language to manipulate the emotions of the players. To avoid such manipulation, you should practice pausing. It involves taking a break from the conversation or situation and having some time to think before reacting. In fact, you may walk away for some minutes to get a grip on your own emotions.

9. Manipulators limit your time to act

Basically, every manipulator wants to win. They may do this by ensuring that you do not have enough time to think. For instance, an individual may force you to make a serious decision in an unreasonably limited amount of time. He/she will try to steer your thoughts to their advantage. You will not have enough time to weigh the consequences. To avoid a situation where you give in without thought, do not be in a rush to submit. Ensure that the demand is reasonable. Take the pause, ask for some time, and if the person does not allow you to think, walk away. You will be happier looking for whatever you need elsewhere.

10. The silent treatment.

According to Preston Ni, a manipulator will presume power in a relationship by making you wait. For instance, when a person deliberately fails to respond to your reasonable messages, calls, emails, or other inquiries, he/she makes you wait and at the same time, places uncertainty and doubt in your mind. Some manipulators use silence as leverage. To avoid being a victim of manipulation through silent treatment, give people deadlines and do not allow them to intimidate you. For instance, after attempting to communicate to a reasonable degree, let go of the mater and let the other person reach out.

Manipulators will work to increase their emotional awareness so as to have an upper hand on others. In fact, a large number of people are learning how to be emotionally intelligent. You too should seek to sharpen your emotional intelligence levels, for your own protection.

Manipulation Games

You have heard of mind games. You have surely played them before and had them played on you. You can use mind games as an effective persuasion tool when you know what to do and when. There are numerous techniques that are effective, and they are not that difficult to learn. This means that once you know what they are, you can start utilizing mind games right away to start getting what you want.

Kick Me

This likely reminds you of that game when you were a kid where you put a sign on someone's back that read "kick me." This is similar. You want to make yourself look like someone that deserves pity. Once you get pity from someone, it is easier to get them to do what you want. You can use this for just about anything in life from getting someone to allow you to apologize to getting a boss to give you a promotion once you get really good at it.

Now That I've Got You

This is a game that you will use when you want to show a person you are winning and better. You can also use it when you are angry and want to justify it. For example, your friend had a party, but he neglected to invite you. So, you decide to host a party the following weekend with the intent to just not invite him. This game basically has you working to one up another person to get them to give in and give you what you want.

You Made Me Do It

This is another one you used during childhood and you likely did not even realize at the time that it was a type of mind game. This is a game that works to make another person feel guilty while simultaneously absolving you of any responsibility for your actions. For example, you want to be left alone. However, someone comes in the room to ask you a question. As a result, you are startled and drop your beverage. You tell that person that they made you drop your beverage.

If It Weren't for You

This is another mind game that is used to absolve yourself of any guilt for something you might have done. With this type of game, you essentially create a scenario that allows you to put guilt onto someone. This gives you an array of advantages. When a person is feeling guilty about something, they are more vulnerable to suggestion. For example, you are unable to go to work for whatever reason. You find a way to blame your spouse for this and make them feel guilty. As a result, you are able to coerce your spouse into making you a meal or buying you something.

Let You Both Fight

The purpose of this mind game is to share blame, control other people and even make you seem like a good friend. In most cases, this is a mind game that women will play, but it is becoming more common among men. For example, a person knows that two people are attracted to them. This person then talks both of the interested parties into fighting with one another to basically win their heart. This is basically a type of transaction; however, at the end of the game, both interested parties are usually left without anyone.

RAPO

This mind game can be a major ego boost, give a sense of satisfaction and increase how desirable you see yourself to be. It is a type of social game in which you essentially convince a person to pursue you. You convince them in a way that is not obvious to them, so they do not even know what is happening. How you choose to convince them is flexible and really dependent on your preferences and what it takes to get into the subconscious of the person you are seeking to lure. What is good about this game is that it generally does not take long to put into practice.

Perversion

The purpose of this game is to avoid responsibility and garner sympathy. Basically, this mind game is used to seduce another person. You cause them to feel guilty if they are not fulfilling your romantic needs. You talk about a bad past relationship, whether it was real or not, to first get sympathy from them. Then, once they essentially soften to the idea of fulfilling your desires, you go in and take what you want. If they are still resistant, you cause them to feel guilty to ultimately get what you want.

Clever Me

This one improves your identity, social capital, attention and ego. You do something to show someone what you are great at and you want the entire world to know that you are awesome at this specific thing. You manipulate the situation to make sure that someone will learn about your skill. You get attention from them and they tell others. Before you know it, your skill or talent is being spread around and a lot of people are coming to you to pay you a compliment.

Wooden Leg

This is a game people play for sympathy, as a plea of insanity or to avoid responsibility. You have likely heard the saying that you can only expect so much from a person who has a wooden leg. This game is built upon this saying. Basically, you use a perceived shortfall or disability to gain sympathy and make your actions seem justified. For example, you just cheated on your spouse and he or she found out. You would say something like, "well, my parents had a bad marriage, so what do you expect of me?" They then start to give you sympathy and you are absolved of your guilt.

The Double Request

This is a common mind game among those who want something big but know that they will not get it just asking for it. For example, you ask for a new expensive watch, but you really want a new jacket that tends to be less expensive. You mention both items, but you make it seem like the watch is what you truly desire. In the end, the friend you are talking to remembers that the jacket was cheaper and also something that you wanted, so they buy it. You end up getting the jacket you wanted from the start.

You're a Good Person

This is a common mind game to play when you want to get something out of someone that they are not normally asked. When you start the conversation by telling them that they are a good person, they are getting recognition and an ego boost from you. This already softens them and makes them more prone to give you exactly what you want. Once you see that their body language is softer or even just neutral, you want to go in and ask for what you want.

Understand The Various Dark Personalities

Both world history and regular day to day existence are brimming with instances of individuals acting heartlessly, malignantly, or childishly. In psychology just as in ordinary language, we have different names for the different dark inclinations human may have, most conspicuously psychopathy (absence of sympathy), narcissism (over the top self-assimilation), and Machiavellianism (the conviction that whatever it takes to get the job done, so be it), the alleged 'dark group of three,' alongside numerous others, for example, selfishness, perversion, or anger.

Even though from the outset there give off an impression of being critical contrasts between these characteristics - and it might appear to be progressively 'worthy' to be a self-seeker than a mental case - new research shows that every dark part of human character is firmly connected and depends on a similar inclination. That is, most dark qualities can be comprehended as enhanced appearances of a solitary typical essential aura: The dark center of the character. By and by, this suggests if you tend to show one of these mysterious character qualities, you are likewise bound to have a robust inclination to show at least one of the others.

As the new research uncovers, the shared factor of every dark attribute, the D-factor, can be characterized as the general propensity to expand one's utility - ignoring, tolerating, or maliciously inciting disutility for other people -, and joined by convictions that fill in as avocations.

As it was, all dark attributes can be followed back to the general propensity of setting one's objectives and interests over those of others even to the degree of enjoying harming other's - alongside a large group of convictions that fill in as legitimizations and therefore forestall sentiments of blame, disgrace, or something like that. The examination shows that dark attributes when all is said in done can be comprehended as examples of this standard center - even though they may vary in which viewpoints are dominating (e.g., the defenses angle is excellent in narcissism though the part of malignantly inciting disutility is the principle highlight of twistedness). This shared factor is available in nine of the most customarily contemplated dark character characteristics:

• Egoism: an excessive distraction with one's bit of leeway to the detriment of others and the network

• Machiavellianism: a manipulative, hard disposition and a conviction that whatever it takes to get the job done, so is it

• Moral withdrawal: subjective handling style that permits carrying on deceptively without feeling trouble

• Narcissism: unnecessary self-retention, a feeling of predominance, and an extraordinary requirement for consideration from others

• Psychological qualification: a shared conviction that one is superior to other people and merits better treatment

• Psychopathy: the absence of compassion and poise, joined with hasty conduct

• Sadism: a craving to incur mental or physical mischief on others for one's pleasure or to profit oneself

• Self-intrigue: a craving to further and feature one's own social and money related status

• Spitefulness: damaging tendency and readiness to make hurt others, regardless of whether one damage oneself all the while

In a progression of studies with more than 2,500 individuals, the analysts asked to what degree individuals concurred or couldn't help contradicting proclamations, for example, "It is difficult to excel without compromising to a great extent.," "It is at times worth a touch of enduring on my part to see others get the discipline they merit.," or "I realize that I am unique since everybody continues letting me know so." what's more, they considered other self-announced inclinations and practices, for example, hatred or impulsivity and target proportions of narrow-minded and dishonest conduct.

Dark Psychology is both a human awareness development and investigation of the human condition as it identifies with the mental idea of individuals to go after others inspired by psychopathic, freak, or psychopathological criminal drives that need a reason and general suppositions of instinctual drives, developmental science, and sociologies hypothesis. All of humankind has the probability of defrauding people and other living animals. While many control or sublimate this propensity, some follow up on these driving forces. Dark Psychology investigates criminal, freak, and cybercriminal minds.

Dark Psychology is the investigation of the human condition as it identifies with the mental idea of individuals to go after others. All of humanity can mislead different people and living animals. While many control or sublimate this inclination, some follow up on these driving forces. Dark Psychology tries to comprehend those musings, emotions, and discernments that lead to savage human conduct. Dark Psychology expects that this creation is purposive and has some objective, objective arranged inspiration 99.99% of the time. The staying .01%, under Dark Psychology, is the severe exploitation of others without a purposive goal or sensibly characterized by developmental science or a strict authoritative opinion.

Inside the following century, predators and their demonstrations of robbery, viciousness, and misuse will turn into a worldwide wonder and cultural plague if not squashed. Sections of predators incorporate digital stalkers, cyber bullies, digital psychological oppressors, digital lawbreakers, online sexual stalkers, and political/strict devotees occupied with digital fighting. Similarly, as Dark Psychology sees all crook/immoral conduct on a continuum of seriousness and purposive aim, the hypothesis of predator follows a similar structure, yet includes misuse, attack, and online exploitation utilizing Information and Communications Technology. The meaning of iPredator is as per the following:

iPredator

iPredator: An individual, gathering, or country who, legitimately or by implication, participates in misuse, exploitation, pressure, stalking, robbery, or demonization of others utilizing Information and Communications Technology [ICT]. Predators are driven by freak dreams, wants for force and control, revenge, strict enthusiasm, political retaliation, mental disease, perceptual mutilations, peer acknowledgment, or individual and monetary benefit. predators can be any age or sexual orientation and are not bound by financial status, race, religion, or national legacy. iPredator is a common term used to recognize any individual who takes part in criminal, coercive, immoral, or harsh practices utilizing ICT. Key to the development is the reason that Information Age lawbreakers, freaks, and the savagely upset are psychopathological arrangements new to humanity.

Regardless of whether the guilty party is a cyberstalker, digital harasser, cybercriminal, online sexual stalker, web troll, digital fear monger, cyber bully, online kid sex entertainment purchaser/wholesaler, or occupied with web maligning or loathsome online double-dealing, they fall inside the extent of iPredator. The three criteria used to characterize an iPredator include:

• Mindfulness of making hurt others, straightforwardly or in a roundabout way, utilizing ICT.

• The utilization of ICT to get, trade, and convey destructive data.

• A general comprehension of Cyber stealth used to participate in criminal or immoral exercises or to profile, recognize, find, stalk, and draw in an objective.

Not at all like human predators preceding the Information Age, have predators depended upon a large number of advantages offered by Information and Communications Technology [ICT]. These help incorporate trade of data over long separations, rate of data traded, and the interminable access to information accessible. Malignant in aim, predators constantly hoodwink others utilizing ICT in theory and fake electronic universe known as the internet. In this way, as the web offers all ICT clients obscurity, typically, if they choose, predators effectively structure online profiles and diversionary strategies to stay undetected and untraceable.

Arsonist

The Arsonist is an individual with a burning distraction with a fire setting. These people frequently have formative accounts loaded up with sexual and physical maltreatment. Regular among sequential fire playing criminals is the proclivity to be hermits, have scarcely any companions, and captivated by fire and fire setting. Sequential torches are profoundly formal and will, in general, a show designed practices as to their approach for setting fires.

Engrossed by fire setting, Arsonists regularly fantasize and focus upon how to design their fire setting scenes. When their objective is set on fire, a few fire playing criminals experience sexual excitement and continue with masturbation while viewing. Regardless of their obsessive and formal examples, the sequential light playing criminal feels pride in his activities.

Necrophilia

Thanatophobia, Necrophilia, and Necrologies all characterize a similar kind of confused individual. These are individuals, and they do exist, who have a sexual appreciation for bodies. A paraphilia is a biomedical term used to portray an individual's sexual excitement and distraction with items, circumstances, or people that are not part of regulating incitement and may cause trouble or significant issues for the individual. Subsequently, a Necrophile's paraphilia is sexual excitement by an article, a perished individual.

Specialists who have incorporated profiles of Necrophiles demonstrate they have colossal trouble encountering a limit concerning getting physically involved with others. For these individuals, sexual closeness with the dead has a sense of security and security instead of sexual closeness with a living human. Necrophiles have uncovered in interviews feeling an extraordinary feeling of control when in the organization of a corpse. A sense of association gets auxiliary to the essential requirement for saw control.

Police Manipulation Techniques

Allffective actions have the same structure—a sequence of
stages—the absence of any of which dramatically (sometimes
to zero) reduces the likelihood of success. The impact, built
clearly on this structure, is triggered with the greatest possible
probability—true, not one hundred percent. The impact, I repeat,
refers to any and in any field—in politics, in business, in personal
relationships, in sports, in war, in religion. If the effect worked, you are
very likely to find a familiar structure in it.

This miracle is called a single impact structure. A single impact
structure can be described in two languages, each of which is useful:

- Background lines

- Stages of exposure

Background Lines

So, whatever our goals, if we want to influence another person (or
group of people) successfully, we must build three lines of
communication:

- Contact line

- Line of distraction

- Line of exposure

Contact Line

Contact is an opportunity for mutual exchange of information. Contact is a desire to perceive each other. Contact is the assumption that communication is more beneficial than ignoring. If there's no contact, nothing—therefore, the mainline is the line of contact. It begins earlier than all; it ends later than all.

Since it is precisely we who are interested in establishing contact, we are doing everything to make it appear and be present throughout the communication. We find time for a meeting, we call up, we try to be noticed, and we dress and talk so that we are agreed to be distinguished from the general background—and even when a person "escapes" from communication, he thinks, "Is it not that I run too fast?"

Any advertisement should contain "contact information," the one on which the proposed product or service can be found—at least, with the help of a search engine.

If the advertisement is new-fangled and contact information has not yet been offered, it means that the seller prefers to keep in touch with you through his advertising media. A telephone and address will be offered later. This also corresponds to the structure.

Conversely, when a person is afraid that the impact of the other side will be more effective than his, he can just break the contact—so debtors avoid meeting with creditors, so passers-by try to get around street vendors and gypsies, so many business people refuse to watch TV, so children run away from home to not be invited to dinner, so weak fighters try to escape from the enemy, running around the edge of the tatami.

However, contact is not only important for this. Through the contact line, we receive information about the interlocutor's reaction to our influences: feedback. And based on this information, we correct our behaviour. Actually, this is one of the main differences between a literate communicator and an ordinary communicator—a literate one notices when he is mistaken and quickly fixes what needs to be fixed.

What the interlocutor likes, what he agrees with, what worries him, what he hides—he will tell us everything—not a word, so a body. Generally speaking, our line of contact pertains to the line of influence of the interlocutor on us. The words of the interlocutor give us the key to how to communicate with him—appearance, emotional reactions, the appearance or disappearance of signs of trance, changes in his posture and breathing—*open only your eyes and ears!*

Distraction Line

A man is designed so that his first involuntary reaction to a direct offer or request is a refusal—anyway, any new information. Outwardly, he may not give a look, but he is internally tense. (Track, by the way, your reaction to these allegations) Did you agree at once?) Then, after thinking and weighing the pros and cons, he can make a positive decision—but inexperienced communicators by this time May already leave upset.

We all unconsciously strive for the same thing—to maintain the status quo, so that nothing changes, to make everything familiar, and so that there were guarantees that tomorrow would be like yesterday— because we are already used to what we have. Let us live in a swamp, but it is ours and is familiar to the last bump. Here, we can easily get rid of any enemy—but we won't fight back, so we'll hide in a pre-prepared assortment. Therefore, the reaction to change is appropriate—*wary.*

And all this goes by the mind—involuntarily—that is, quite reasonable, logical, profitable ideas and suggestions pass by. In the sense of being eliminated, it is rejected at distant approaches. And few are able, having thought it all over again, to return to what he himself had sifted out. Therefore, even when we offer a person a truly valuable transaction, point of view, or information, we have to introduce a line of distraction.

In other words, in order to act effectively, it is necessary to distract the "internal controller" of the interlocutor. Well, about the same as if you wanted to get into a guarded building—you first have to deal with his guard. Say the password, show the pass, arrange for him a "call from above," sell to pity, bribe him, shy away with a baton, or blow up an explosion packet at a neighbouring entrance, finally. In a word, it is reliable to neutralize until we finish all the machinations we need.

How do you distract the "controller"? For example, the interlocutor's consciousness goes on a mental journey through the past or future, which we will arrange for him. Do you remember the charm of the words, "Do you remember," and the stories of, "Beautiful far away?" Likewise, let the "controller" get carried away with the struggle with the flow of information, fall into an emotional whirlwind, live in a fabulous reality, and listen to our explanations. (All this and much more are ways of inducing a conversational trance.) Let him be distracted. Because while he is watching, we cannot do anything worthwhile In the meantime, the "controller" is resting—we will work—and keep in touch with this!

Line of Exposure

When there is contact or when the interlocutor's consciousness is reliably distracted, a line of influence may appear—fragmentarily, imperceptibly, and always ready to hide even more reliably. On this line, we inspire—throw ideas, form the necessary attitude, suggest suitable interpretations motivate, awaken desires—*the main work is on-going.*

It is clear that the vast majority of suggestions are indirect. Yes, we are not impudent. We act just where we are not resisted. We do not suggest, "Give us all the money." We explain, "It's not just a cactus but a big-money cactus," and therefore, this cactus costs "only five thousand American dollars." We are not saying that the person needs to obey everything; we only make it clear that in the prevailing— *terrible!*

And I remind you: the line of action is fragmented. Most of our words are either reliable or unverifiable in the current conditions. However, our suggestions are forwarded: there is a not quite logical combination, and there is not a completely substantiated statement. Here, we say "possible," and after a couple of sentences, "only possible." Here, the word in one sense; there, in another. Likewise, for example, you can create a mood with one story, and then transfer it (there are special methods) to another—and all this briefly, forwarding, no pauses, continuing to speak, without stopping the speech flow, taking away attention away from "slippery places."

The second feature—all forwarding work for the same purpose, inspire the same thoughts—let the wording be different, but their essence is one. Thus, an outwardly ordinary conversation with all the usual paraphernalia turns out to be filled with a dense stream of suggestions that work for a given purpose.

At this moment, all three lines are simultaneously involved: impact, distraction, and contact—but *that* is the essence of a single impact structure.

Stages of Exposure

If you need to know about the three lines of communication necessary for success in order to understand the essence of a single impact structure, for practical use, it is useful to consider it as a sequence of stages, each of which is necessary and sufficient in its place.

How to move from lines to stages? It's very simple. If you project the background lines on top of each other, it turns out that there are five key segments in a single impact structure:

- Fixation of attention

- Depotentialization of control

- Intervention

- Latent period

- Synchronization

The presence of each of them is mandatory. The absence of any of them can ruin the effect on the root—and it is clear that, without finishing the previous one, it is impossible to move on soon enough. However, now, the difficult task of holding two or three background lines at the same time turns into a clear step-by-step scheme, from which it is clear what to do and why.

Fixation of Attention

Attraction and retention of attention—without it, no impact on a person is possible. For if you did not attract his attention, you, for him, are not—and nothing can affect. Therefore, the first active step in any manipulation algorithm is to fix attention.

Hence, the goal of the stage is to attract and capture the attention of a potential interlocutor so that it turns from potential into reality. To begin with, you provide yourself with the opportunity to be seen and heard. In order to do this, you can:

- Be in plain sight;

- Appear in a personal area (approximately 1.5 meters from the body);

- Say hello;

- Contact by name;

- Offer to talk;

- Offer to look at what you show;

- Ask for a moment of attention;

- Sometimes, touch;

- And so on.

However, it is not enough to attract attention—it is also necessary to *keep it*.

The attraction of attention is similar to wrestling capture—after it, reception is possible—and experienced fighters, by the way, are fighting precisely for the seizure, as the rest is a matter of technology. Then, you can make a trance, "powder your brain," and offer the interpretations we need. There is attention; they listen to you.

Attention must be attracted—and attracted attention must be retained (and in case of distraction, returned). In other words, to be effective, you must be able to attract attention constantly, over a given period of time, and then let go, and become invisible—you need to be able to do this, too.

Covert Emotional Manipulation

N ow you are probably thinking is that different from Emotional Manipulation and if so, how. The answer is Emotional Manipulation occurs within the realms of your consciousness, so you are aware that someone is trying to appeal to a more generous side of you to get what they want. Think about the time when your parents wanted you to visit them for the summer but you had a different probably more exciting summer plans with your friends or a special someone and your parents insisted you visit them instead or take some extra time off to make the visit. You tried to convince them that you would visit for Thanksgiving and your calendar is booked solid and they might have retorted with statements like "we are old and we wouldn't be around for so long, you need to make us your priority" or "we haven't seen you in forever and we miss you, come over to visit your loving parents". During this conversation you are completely aware that your parents are attempting to change how you feel about your summer plans in their favor. This is a classic and harmless case of Emotional Manipulation. On the other hand, Covert Emotional Manipulation is carried out by individuals who are trying to gain influence over your thought process and feelings, with the means of subtle underhanded tactics that go undetected by the person being manipulated.

By definition Covert Emotional Manipulation goes undetected and leaves you acting like a pawn in the hands of the manipulator, which makes this a manifestation of Dark Psychology. The dictionary definition of the word covert is "not openly shown or engaged in"; therefore, it presents a stark difference from all other Emotional Manipulation techniques. The victims of Covert Emotional Manipulation are unable to understand the intent or motivation of the manipulator and the way they are being manipulation and even just the fact that they are being manipulated. Think of Covert Emotional Manipulation as a bomber with impeccable stealth, one that can tip toe in your subconscious without being detected, leaving you with no defense what so ever. Our emotions primarily dictate all other aspects of our personality and thus they also dictate our reality. Someone attempting to manipulate your emotions is equivalent to them cutting open your jugular vein making you lose control over yourself and your reality.

Let's have a brief look at some of the more frequently observed forms of dark manipulation.

Gas lighting

The tactic used by manipulators aimed at making their victim doubt their own thoughts and feelings is called Gas lighting. This term is often used by mental health professionals to describe the manipulative behavior to convince the victim into thinking their thoughts and feelings are off base and not in alignment with the situation at hand.

Passive-Aggressive behavior

Manipulators can adopt this duplicitous behavior to criticize, change behavior of their victim without making direct requests or aggressive gestures. Some of these traits include: sulking or giving the silent treatment, portraying them as a victim or intentionally cryptic speech.

Withholding information

There is no such thing as a white lie but manipulators often provide selective information to their victim, so as to guide them into their web of deception.

Isolation

The dark manipulator is always aiming to gain control and authority on their victim. In order to succeed they will create an increasingly isolated environment for their victim and prevent them from contacting their friends and family.

The many differences between Persuasion and Manipulation

1. Motive/Intent

As we have established people with active dark psychological traits including manipulators, aim to establish control and authority on their prey and exploit their victims to serve their own interests. On the other hand, persuaders are concerned about the wellbeing of their audience and attempt to convince them to change their attitude or behavior in a free environment.

2. Method of Delivery

Manipulators create an inviting environment for their victim, who is often an unwilling prey and primed emotionally and psychologically to act in ways that benefit their predators and threatens their own health or well-being. Whereas, persuaders only hope that their audience will respond to their influence and the suggestions. Ultimately the individual is free to decide whether or not they want to accept the suggestions made by their persuader and alter their thoughts, feelings and/or behaviors.

3. Impact on the social interaction

Dark manipulators will always aim to isolate their prey from the rest of the world and prevent any contact from their loved ones. The victim of dark manipulation like brainwashing, develops extreme views and may commit heinous acts of antisocial behavior. Unlike manipulation, acts of persuasion are never lethal for the audience and society. It could be as harmless as your brother's admiration for Nike shoes leading you to buy a pair of your own or the ads from McDonalds inviting you to enjoy a quick meal with your family.

4. Final outcome

Persuasion usually results in one of these three possible scenarios: Benefit to both the persuaded and the persuader, commonly known as a win-win situation; Benefit only to the persuaded; Benefit to the persuaded and a third party. However, dark manipulation always has a singular benefactor that is the manipulator. The manipulated individual is at grave disadvantage and will act against their self-interest.

How To Master The Basics Of Psychology

If everyone around you is using tactics to get what they want, you may be tempted to want to do it at least once. But then, do you know how? Some of the tactics are things we may occasionally do but doing it deliberately and calculatedly can help us gain some amount of control over other people. Let us look at some of the ways that manipulators can apply dark tactics.

1. Hiding intentions

One form of manipulation that has been around since the beginning of time is lying. Manipulators usually use this tactic when they are faced with a responsibility that they want to flee from or when they feel that saying the truth will not benefit them. Many of them even go ahead to lie when they have no reason at all to do so and it makes them feel good to know that they are causing trouble and playing with others' feelings. When you come in contact with a skilled manipulator, they could make you believe in a lie until you're neck-deep in it. They may do this because they want to take advantage of someone else or they might just be using the lie as a smokescreen to cover their true intentions. Or they may be using it to prevent you from seeing that they want to keep being steps ahead of you.

For example, a friend who is looking for the same thing as you will hide any information that will make you get it before them.

2. Attention Seeking

Drama queen Drama King. We've probably had to use these words on people who are always being dramatic. It's not bad for one to have drama once in a while because life doesn't have to be too serious but manipulators thrive on frequent drama. They normally create it intentionally because they want to be the center of attention and massage their ego.

For instance, in a group of three friends, one of them may try to cause conflict between friends A and B by peddling stories of each of them to the other party. This will make friends A and B to have misunderstandings and normally they will turn to the manipulator to lay their grievances and seek comfort. Because of this, the manipulator feels needed and important. One partner in a relationship can keep bringing up fights so that their partner will keep their attention on them.

3. Giving Off Unnecessary Emotions

Manipulators could be people who show emotions a lot, do dramatic stuff and have loud outbursts when they want to get their way. They are often loud, melodramatic and will go all emotional even at the slightest incitement and usually, they display their attitude in appropriate environments.

For instance, one partner may resort to raising their voice and arguing loudly in a restaurant because their partner is not giving in to their demands because they feel that their partner will be embarrassed by the scene and give in to what they want. This is a subtle and very effective manipulation tactic.

4. Crying Foul and Playing the Victim

There are people who love it when people feel sorry for them always. They are always making people feel that they have the worst of luck. They are the ones who will even make you feel guilty for complaining about your problems because they always have worse problems than yours. Of course, we all have bad moments but a manipulator knows how to make them look like the victim of all victims and draw lots of attention to themselves. Tell them you have a fever and they'll narrate to you how they've had to deal with migraines every day for the past month. Say you forgot your coffee cup and they'll tell you how their expensive coffee maker got destroyed. They just look for ways to solicit pity from people just so they can get attention and people's concentration.

5. Claiming Undue Credit

Manipulators do not see anything wrong in getting someone else to make an effort involved in something and then coming in, later on, to take credit for the work as if they have done a major part of the job. This kind of manipulation can be seen in a professional setting where people will be delegated to do jobs as a group but end up prancing around, being busy without actually doing anything and when the job is done, they come in to take credit for it.

6. They Want You to Depend On Them

Manipulators want to feel needed and they want you to need them. They want to see you agree that you cannot exist without them. In every social setting, you see them as the famous ones that attract and magnets others and it makes you feel like you should really be a part of them. That's what they thrive on.

A manipulative person in a relationship will always want to remind their partners that they are nothing without them and they cannot survive without them. They will do you a favor at your needy moment and create that feeling of indebtedness in you so that they will later come and ask you to return the favor. You cannot get a free favor from a manipulator.

Manipulators have built a fantasy that you need them in your life because as you continue to depend on them, their control over you grows and that is the main motive behind whatever help they are rendering to you. They come when you're vulnerable and they become indispensable and continue to enjoy the status that they have given themselves in your life. The more support they give you, the more their chances of leeching on to your emotions and taking advantage of you.

7. Selective Honesty

You may have experienced a complete betrayal from someone who seemed so generous and then after realizing that you didn't even know half of what was taking place, you felt awful. When a manipulator is feeding you with information, they will tell you only what they want you to know and intentionally hold back the rest and that is why you will feel terrible when you find out.

Using selective honesty to disarm unsuspecting people is a manipulative tactic that most professional settings make use of. If there is a promotion to compete for in a workplace, a manipulative colleague may keep feeding you information on the state of affairs. You might be thinking they care so much as to let you in on the inside info that they get without knowing that they are not telling you everything.

They may keep the juicy tip and hand to you whatever information they want to tell you while making you feel gratitude for their generosity.

8. Faux friendship

Some people could pretend to be friendly to you just because of their sinister motive. They could be acting like your friends while they are underground collecting every kind of information that they can about you. Although some people may be trying to be your friends but you should be careful if you are being asked personal questions especially when you are just meeting.

This tactic is often used in professional settings. Among friends too, there can be a friend who really tries to control the conversation without making it obvious. The conversation will be based on what they want; things will be done at their own pace. They could even manipulate you into taking impromptu decisions and that matter too.

9. Commitment issues

They have a lot of problems trying to commit to something. It doesn't even matter if you have asked for their support to do something important and urgent. They will find a way to hold back the response to your plea especially if it puts them in a place of power where they can turn the situation for their own benefit.

They only care about themselves and so you cannot see them commit to anything unless they do it so they can have something to control you with.

10. Playing Dumb

You may see someone feigning innocence over something that is happening. Sometimes, they know more than they let on and they act as though they don't. People often overlook this manipulative tactic but it is mostly used in professional settings. In an office, an employee who may know something in full details may lie that they are not sure of what they know. The work will then be reassigned to someone else. Think about the times you have had misunderstandings in your group of friends. It is possible that the person who acts as though they know nothing about what led to the misunderstanding will get away with the fact that nobody knows how much information that have about why the disagreement happened.

11. Pointing a finger at others

You will never find a manipulator with dirt on their record. They strive to make sure nothing is found on them by keeping their hands clean

They do this by staying away from all forms of responsibility and also by accusing someone whenever there is a problem, so they can easily wriggle out of whatever it is. You will notice this especially when the issue is something that can tear their reputation apart and make people see them for their lies and deceit. A manipulator is the person around you that blames everybody else for a problem but themselves. To them, they are never a problem and will often want someone else to be their scapegoat.

12. Saying what you want to hear

When you're being flattered, you feel good. It's difficult to not feel flattered and you will start making conscious effort to like the person that is saying the things that you always want to hear. Of course, we will be drawn towards being with these people who are always saying what will be pleasant to our hearing. Despite how good you feel about hearing those things, it doesn't show that you're with a good friend. Besides, they could just be massaging your ego and soliciting your love for when they will want a bigger favor and you will be tempted to grant it to them because you feel that they have been so good to you.

13. Controlling decisions

You can see manipulation in a romantic relationship when one partner tries to control the other party's decision.

It is very normal for someone in a relationship to want to make their decisions based on their partner but the motive behind it is what matters. Is the decision made to truly make them delighted or are you trying to avoid their wrath?

In a relationship, there is just a thin line between making a partner happy and manipulation.

When you find yourself canceling many plans too often because of the way your partner feels or you stop putting on some outfits that you like, or cut your hair or do something's just because of your partner. Then there is a possibility that they are controlling your life on a low key. It may start off with innocent and harmful suggestions but in the long run, you will find out that you're only living to please and you're doing only little to make yourself happy.

The Art Of Lying

Let's face it; if you want to tap into people's psyche, you need to lie at one point or another. Lying is an art; there are good liars and bad liars. Some people are so good you'd never even know they were lying despite using polygraph tests or putting them under psychological scrutiny until you see the truth right in front of you, and you finally realize that there was something off with what they were saying.

Lying is important to manipulating people. There are a lot of mistakes that people make when trying to learn how to lay 'properly.' We're going to cover what lets a person know that you're lying so that you can avoid any of those pitfalls.

The first and most obvious pitfall is the renowned 'web of lies.' Getting caught in a web of lies is terribly embarrassing, but it's easier than you think. If you tell a lie, make sure you make careful note of exactly what you're saying, so that you can come back to it later. If you feel that you need to lie, think about it ahead of time so that you can poke any holes in it and patch them up before your 'audition.'

This leads naturally to the second biggest issue, something that a lot of people do when they try to lie is to make it sound like it was rehearsed. If you ever listen to somebody speaking naturally, it doesn't flow perfectly as if they were reading from a script. In fact, it tends to flow rather awkwardly, even among the best-spoken people. This is because the brain and the rest of you tend to become essentially detached when you're speaking off the cuff. It takes a second to think, process, and then say your thoughts. If you have a long train of thoughts, this becomes even more difficult. Sound as natural as you possibly can. Practice your lie and your intonations and be sure that they sound like your genuine voice. You know the saying, "It takes a long time to look like you just woke up?" The same applies here; it takes a lot of rehearsal to sound unrehearsed.

Another thing that a lot of people do is that they use excessive or insufficient body language. For example, a lot of people know that old gem of knowledge that people who are lying will touch their face or avoid eye contact or look up at the sky. Because of this, they'll start to overcompensate with extremely awkward facial and head language. For example, somebody who is trying to seem like they aren't lying will often make too much eye contact. While it's worse to avoid eye contact, doing too much can be quite bad in and of itself. Be careful not to go overboard in the pursuit of telling a lie.

Lying, ultimately, is not very difficult. There is a methodology to it. The first thing that you need to do is, think ahead of your lie, if possible. When you have the time to consider all of the possibilities that stem from the lie, you can start to revise your lie before you ever need it. This makes it less likely that you've got a paper-thin lie.

When it comes to lying, you need to relax. Do whatever you can to relax, in fact. Take deep breaths before you need to lie, think about something else, and do whatever you can to get your mind off of your lie. Or, more importantly, take your mind off the fact that you're lying. You might even spend some time before you lie trying to convince yourself the lie actually happened, that way it comes out as truth. Of course, your subconscious mind will know that the lie didn't happen, but if you can have your conscious thought processes acting as though it did, that should be enough to at least clear through the lie.

One of the things you must never do if your lie starts being questioned is to get defensive. Defensiveness is the number one reason that people get caught for their lies. Regardless, getting defensive over a lie will make people trust you a lot less than they would otherwise. The best thing to do if your lie is questioned is to stick to your guns but do so in a rational way. Explain yourself further, but you need to be careful that you don't explain too much. If you have to give more than 2 sentences after being questioned just to explain yourself, you've messed up critically somewhere.

The real trick is to just think of yourself as though you were telling the truth. If you were telling the truth and asked to defend yourself, what would you do? You would still tell only the truth. Let's say, for example, that your boss asked you if you finished a report. You actually had, and you put it on his desk. So, you say "Yes sir, I put it on your desk," and he says "No, it's not there. Did you finish it?"

What would you say? What you wouldn't say is something like "Yes sir, I was up all night working on it, and I put a huge amount of work into it. It's a great presentation, and I have no clue why it isn't there. Do you think that maybe somebody else has it? Or the cleaning lady picked it up by accident?"

You'd say something along the lines of "Yes sir, I put it on your desk, I'm not sure why it's not there. Could somebody have gotten ahold of it?" That's all the explaining that you would actually do. Don't put pressure on yourself to do anything more when you're lying. It becomes terribly transparent.

When the lie is finished, you, unfortunately, will have to keep track of it. This is one of the most difficult parts of lying in general. You'll have to maintain the lie for the duration of time that the lie will directly affect anybody. You may genuinely want to consider keeping an encrypted lie journal on your computer if you intend to lie often or have a particularly hairy lie that could easily get out of hand.

In the end, though, lying is relatively simple. It's an important part of your repertoire if you want to influence people. Lying is like manipulation, it isn't inherently bad as long as it doesn't hurt anybody. While you can definitely consider it as taking advantage of people, as long as nobody is getting hurt then that isn't an explicitly bad thing. Morality is ultimately very vague, and the ends will often justify the means. This is no exception.

Normal Female Dating Signals And Gestures

B

e that as it may, here's a mystery you should know ladies stress over dismissal and embarrassment the same amount of as men do – all the more in this way, by and large, the same number of men respond seriously to being drawn nearer. Thus, ladies will as often as possible give unobtrusive, non-verbal markers that they'd like you – truly, you – to go converse with them. By watching out for these signs – otherwise called "approach solicitations" – you can ensure that the individual you're moving toward needs to converse with you.

Approach Invitation #1: She Plays Eye Games

One of the most widely recognized methodology solicitations is additionally one of the subtlest: she'll utilize her eyes. Eye to eye connection is unbelievably incredible and private; actually, thinks about have discovered that delayed eye to eye connection can trigger sentiments of adoration and enthusiasm in individuals. This is one motivation behind why intentional eye to eye connection is frequently utilized as a methodology greeting; we seldom look at individuals we don't care for. Indeed, purposely evading eye to eye connection is one of the manners in which people endeavor to abstain from getting brought into a discussion with other individuals.

So in case you're pondering whether somebody is keen on you, watch her eyes. In addition to the fact that you should try to look at ladies, you should look for the ladies who're attempting to get your attention. Somebody who's effectively attempting to look is bound to be available to a methodology. More often than not when we look at somebody, we take around 3 or so seconds to analyze their face. On the off chance that the individual takes longer – four or five seconds, state – at that point that is a truly solid marker that they're keen on you; there is something in particular about you that captivates them.

Obviously, somebody simply giving you the shaggy eyeball may be intrigued... or she may be attempting to make sense of why you help her to remember that companion she hasn't found in years, particularly if she has the "I'm attempting to do complex math" look rather than a grin.

A lady who's keen on you will regularly meet your eyes, turn away (as a rule down or to the side), and at that point think back once more, ordinarily with a grin. This can be a simple greeting to botch; all things considered, looking away can be viewed as a "gracious god, don't give them a chance to think I was intrigued" move. A great many people will in general accept that the eye to eye connection was inadvertent and proceed onward. It's the "think back" part that is significant; it's an inconspicuous and regularly coy method for verifying whether despite everything you're intrigued

Approach Invitation #2: She Checks You Out

Obviously, while there're ladies who get bothered when they're discovered seeing individuals they're keen on, there are additionally those who're extensively progressively open about passing on their advantage.

Since sex jobs are a thing, numerous self-assured ladies still want to be the drawn nearer as opposed to the approacher. Now and then this is on the grounds that they need somebody with the certainty to really come say "howdy". Now and again this is on the grounds that they value feeling wanted and having somebody approach them approves that feeling. Once in a while she has enough fearlessness at the time to be clearly coy however insufficient to pull the trigger herself. Different times it may be the case that she's as apprehensive about dismissal as men are and are happy to leave a little conceivable deniability; in the event that he doesn't react, it's simpler to play it off than an immediate dismissal.

So what do these increasingly clear approach solicitations resemble? The most immediate – and forward – rendition is the great "lift look". A lady may meet your eyes, find you and down (giving her eyes a chance to follow your middle), before looking at you back without flinching again and grinning. She may likewise give you "clingy eyes", distinctly maintaining eye contact with you with an intriguing grin. They may try looking before checking out the room, at that point meeting your look once more; a sign that they've looked at the challenge and still incline toward you. They may toss a discrete wink or utilize the triangle look – looking from your eye to your lip and back to your eyes. They may likewise plan something to focus on their mouth – contacting their lip with a finger or gnawing their lip.

Approach Invitation #3: The Body Language Cues

Different indications of intrigue – and markers that they'd welcome you making a methodology – are practically oblivious motions. Individuals, people both, will in general make little, unpretentious changes in accordance with their non-verbal communication when they see somebody they're pulled in to. One of the most well-known models with ladies are what are known as "trimming" motions – making little changes in accordance with her attire and hair, so as to introduce herself at her best. The most widely recognized case of dressing conduct in ladies is playing with their hair – smoothing it down, twining it around their finger or brushing it gradually away from their faces. They additionally may begin scouring their neck or wrists; self-contacting is another indication of enthusiasm, as it draws the eye towards those parts.

Another basic indication of intrigue – one that every now and again goes before other approach solicitations – includes her middle. To begin with, somebody who's available to be drawn nearer will have progressively "open" non-verbal communication. She'll be confronting outwards towards the room, as opposed to confronting the bar or her companions. Her arms will be calculated away from her middle; crossed arms are a protective, cut off sign that says "leave". At that point, on the off chance that she sees somebody she likes, she'll alter her body somewhat. One normal sign is that she'll fix up and square herself off; it's a method for improving her stance and showing herself to a superior advantage. She'll additionally as often as possible point her middle towards you. People will in general be objective situated and point themselves at the things they're keen on. On the off chance that you get somebody's attention and they open up towards you, they're unquestionably intrigued.

You may likewise observe some reflecting; if you make a motion when you grab her attention – a wave or an eyebrow-streak – at that point that is an indication of intrigue and a marker that you ought to go over and present yourself.

Simply recollect: one signal can be luck and two might be fortuitous event. Rather than searching for one marker, you should search for bunches of motions that happen either all the while or close on the impact points of different indications of intrigue.

Approach Invitation #4: Proximity and Lingering

Another basic approach greeting that ladies will offer is to utilize nearness. They'll situate themselves to be in your quick circle. They may post up close to you as you're remaining near – not directly by you however close enough that it's anything but difficult to make casual chitchat. They may try in every case simply happening to be in your region on various events while you're both there. You may understand that you're continually observing her out of the side of your eye, she generally appears to wind up in a similar column of the book shop as you or that you both simply happen to continue chancing upon one another, figuratively. It gives a degree of conceivable deniability to her attempting to become more acquainted with you; if you're not intrigued, at that point she's ready to proceed onward rapidly without managing the humiliation of immediate dismissal.

Another regular type of closeness is the "incidental" knock – she tries brushing past you or "unintentionally" crashing into you in a spot where there is very room. When there's a lot of room at the bar, say, the lady who unintentionally bumps your arm or crushes past you and touches against you likely could be attempting to get you to pivot and begin a discussion.

Two or three expressions of caution: first, in the event that you're some spot swarmed, at that point impacts are practically inescapable. This is particularly valid on move floors; somebody chancing upon you on the move floor isn't really an encouragement to move toward them except if you have different signs that she's attempting to stand out enough to be noticed. The other is that closeness and waiting for work for ladies; when folks do it, it will in general be frightening. Credit it to the more serious hazard ladies face from men than men face from ladies and don't drift.

Approach Invitation #5: The Plausible Denial Conversation Starter

This happens more regularly than you'd understand, especially when you're out on the town during the day. Have you at any point had somebody who plunks down by you and mentions some remark or objective fact – to what extent it's taking for her to get her espresso, the issues with the Wi-Fi, why the transport is so off-plan, something? This will in general be a conceivably deniable method for beginning a discussion; she's basically hurling out a low-venture greeting to talk (frequently called an observational opener in a virus approach) so that she can wave it off as her simply conversing with herself.

It feels less scary to hurl those out there in light of the fact that it doesn't feel as explicit as "hello, you appear as though you're intriguing" way to deal with meeting someone.

Stop Being Manipulated & Defence

As you have read so far, you can probably see how easy it is to become part of someone's manipulations. You don't have to give into them though. There are many ways that you can stop the cycle of emotional abuse and manipulation. We need to know how manipulators work to be able to avoid them altogether.

Manipulators are looking for something from you that they may not be getting from life or even from themselves. Many of them are not happy with their life, and they have very low self-esteem. They want to make problems for others to make themselves feel better. They love the idea of someone else feeling the pain that they are feeling. If they can inflict this pain on others, they are no longer worried about their feelings.

Some manipulators love the feeling of having power in any situation. They will find those that they consider weak and persuade them to do what they want. The victims in these situations are generally bullied and will feel as if they have been dominated by doing things that they never thought they would. In general, manipulators aren't all that bad. Some of them want very small things from people, while others will take anything that they can. Psychologists find them to be misguided and inconsiderate. So what are the best ways that we can stay away from manipulators? We have quite a few that can help you out.

Staying Away from the Manipulators

Think about it: the easiest way to avoid being manipulated is just by staying away from them. Why does this seem to be so complicated, though? There are plenty of reasons that we allow ourselves to stay close to those who manipulate us. Manipulators, after all, learn how to control us in many ways. Most psychologists think it is learned behavior on their part. They have probably been a victim of it, and it could have started as early as their childhood.

So if you cannot stay away from someone who is manipulating you, be very firm in your communication with them. Many of them will ask you questions over and over again until they get the answer that they want. When you say yes to them, it means yes, but sometimes saying no to them could also mean yes to them. By being firm with them and saying the answer more than once to them, they should be able to get the full picture. If they do continue to think you are saying yes to them, it could be time to get away from them and not think twice about it.

Ever hear that everyone has an inner child? Well, manipulators have an inner child, but it does not play and joke around as yours might. Most of the time, manipulators will only listen to that inner child to make their decisions. If that inner child is telling them all of the ideas of what to get out of people, they will turn into a manipulator to get everything that they want.

Manipulators do have goals in mind when they begin to push you to do anything that they want. Generally, these goals are to make you feel as if you are always doing something wrong. They also want to see just what they can get you to do for them. This is when the firm words you use can help you. If they are not getting the point of your words, use your actions to show them that you are tired of them using and manipulating you.

It may surprise you, but manipulators can change. They have to unlearn the behaviors that they have been using on people, though. This can take them quite a long time, but it is possible. Yes, they may be able to change, but if you cannot take the emotional abuse anymore, now is the time to get out. Perhaps you can give them a second chance when you have seen the changes, but that is up to you.

This brings us back to why people can't leave abusive relationships. It is very easy for those of us who see manipulation, to tell our peers to leave their relationship. It isn't always the easiest thing to do, though. For one, our society has some strange ways of accepting unhealthy behavior and manipulations. The victim may not even be aware that anything is wrong in their relationship. If the victim has always been in these types of relationships, they may think it is the normal way that relationships work. If they think this is normal, they may look at you like you're crazy when you even suggest that they leave.

Manipulation and emotional abuse are pretty crippling when it comes to our self-esteem. If you are being manipulated and want to leave, you may feel like you can't because you think that you can never find anyone else. If the victim is always feeling worthless, and they want to get out of the relationship, it can be quite difficult. They think of where they will go and who can they stay with. Sometimes this makes it nearly impossible for them to get out of the relationship.

If the manipulation has gotten to the point of physical abuse, it may be very dangerous for the victim to feel that they can leave the relationship. Chances are the manipulator is now threatening them, and they could be afraid that they will hurt them even more if they do leave. Many victims have been killed after leaving physically abusive relationships, and this is terrifying for those who are in these types of relationships.

Lastly, our society makes it sound like no matter what we feel, we must stay with our partner forever. We must ride it out and think that it will all get better. We do know that some manipulators can change, but not all of them will. It is up to the victim to get away from them before it becomes too late for them.

Avoiding the Manipulators

It is easy to say avoid these predators, but it is not that easy. First, you need to see that they are manipulating you. Once you have decided this, you have to be careful about what you do. To acknowledge them, you will have to keep in mind that most of them do have specific traits. They know exactly how to find your weaknesses and what makes you weak. When they figure out what your weakness is, they will use it to their advantage and use it against you. They will try to get you to give up the things that you love. For example, many predators and manipulators will try to get your family to go against you. This will leave them there to be your shoulder to cry on when they don't want to see you or talk to you anymore. They will also try to get you to give up on your hobbies and other things that you love.

You do not have to put up with any of this, though. You can choose to ignore them and hope that they will go away and stop trying to get closer to you. Once you have noticed that they are trying to manipulate you, say no to them. You don't have to do everything that they ask of you. This is where many people have trouble. They want to be kind and polite and not hurt anyone's feelings. You can say no to people without doing so. If they are trying to manipulate you, they will more than likely become furious when you tell them not to things, but this will give you a sure sign that they are trying to manipulate you.

When you have discovered that they are manipulating you, keep your distance. In different situations, you may notice the manipulator acting a lot different. This is a sure-fire way to know that they are trying to manipulate you. Sometimes they may act polite to you, but so rude to anyone who tries to befriend you. Once you notice this, give them the space that they need. You will see how they react, and this will also help you to determine just how much they are trying to manipulate you.

It is important that if you do fall victim to a manipulator, please do not blame yourself. They know what they are doing when they choose you to be the one that they manipulate. They know your weaknesses, and they want you to blame yourself for it. You will be able to figure out if they are manipulating you by seeking the answer to the question of are you being treated with respect by them? If you answer no immediately, you are the victim, and it is time to get out of this situation.

It will throw them off when you start turning the tables on them. Ask them some questions that will make them think you know what they are doing to you. Find out why they think their demands are reasonable and how this situation will benefit you. When you turn the tables on them, they may do the running away from you. Always trust your judgment when it comes to asking these questions. They may be a very good liar, so ask a few questions that will get them to think about what they are doing to you.

Many victims of manipulators have to reinvent themselves not to let it happen to them again. How do you do this? Part of reinventing yourself is to learn how to say no when these manipulators start to ask you to do things for them. They have already seen your vulnerable side, and now they want to attack it. If you put up emotional walls and make it so that they cannot see your vulnerability, you will be able to stop them in their tracks! You also need to stop compromising when they want you to. Just keep telling them that you don't want to do something. Eventually, they should get the point, but if they don't, it is time to walk away.

Respecting yourself is another way to make sure that they stop manipulating you. Once again, they will be able to see this when you are confident and self-aware. They may even feel threatened by your new sense of self. This will act in your favor when they finally decide to call it quits with their manipulation.

How To Sneakily Get What You Want

The power of persuasion is one way to get what you want. And it's not that evil to persuade people to do things is it?

Advertisements are powerful persuasions. Everyone uses ads to get what they want. Politicians use them, and companies use them. So how bad can it be, really?

When used for positive purposes, this power isn't anything bad. But when used for bad things, persuasion can get people into real trouble.

The Power of Positive Persuasion

When a friend has found something new, they really like and want you to join them.

"We went on a trip to the river last summer, Gail. I think you'd love it. You should come with us this year."

"I don't care for water."

"What do you mean, you don't care for water? Everyone loves water. And then there're these gorgeous sunrises and sunsets. You love those."

"I do love those. But the cost is probably much too high for me."

"Is free too high, Gail? I said you could come with us. And there's lots of fun to be had while floating down the river."

"Floating? Oh, no. It sounds dangerous."

"Donny is only five and can't even swim, and he floated down it with us. I think you'll find it safe, fun, and relaxing. Plus, we barbeque each night you love Allen's ribs, don't you remember?"

"I do love his ribs. How long are we talking about?"

"A week"

"Oh, no I can't be gone that long. What about my dog, Pookie? What would I do with her while we're gone?"

"She can come too. It's pet-friendly."

"Well, it seems you've persuaded me to go. Thanks, it sounds like it'll be lots of fun."

The Power of Manipulative Persuasion

"Folks, we've got some great deals for you. Step right up and let me tell you all about these steak knives we've got on sale now."

"I have a set already, thanks though."

"No, wait. You don't have these knives. These knives are a must for every household. You don't want to be the only guy on your block with cruddy steak knives, now do you?"

"Well, no. But mine are just fine."

"As fine as these. Just look at how they shine. And boy can they cut too. Just look at them slice through this thick steak

"Well, that's pretty good. They are shiny. But I've got some. See ya."

"Wait. What if I told you that these are the same type of knives they use in the White House? They're good enough for our president and his family and the visitors that go eat with them. So, why aren't they good enough for you?"

"They are good enough for me. I just have some already."

"Why pass up this special offer? You don't know if you'll ever get this chance again. I'm only here for one day. I can't promise you that you'll ever get this chance again. It's the same knives as the White House uses. Don't you want to be a proud American?"

"Oh, heck Give me a set."

The Power of Helpful Persuasion

"You should totally try this blush, Peggy. It'll look so good on you."

"Um, I haven't ever worn any makeup. I'm not sure how to put it on. I'll just make myself look like a clown if I try to wear any. Thanks though."

"Nonsense, you'd look great with makeup on as long as you don't use too much. I can help you if you want."

"I don't know. I've got this red hair, and my skin is so pale. I've never been able to find anything to match my skin tone."

"You have alabaster skin. It's like God's gift, Peggy. Come on, we can go to the store and I can help you pick out all the right things. For about a hundred bucks, I can get you all set up. And I promise to help you put it on and teach you how to do it so you can do it yourself. What do you say? You want to let me help you be a better you?"

"Well, when you put it that way, how can I refuse? Thanks."

The Power of Gentle Persuasion

"Good afternoon, Jimmy. How was school today?"

"It was school." He tosses his school books onto the coffee table.

Mom looks at them. "So, do you have homework today?"

"Always," he huffs as he tries to leave the room.

But Mom has something to entice him into doing his homework now, instead of leaving it to the last minute, like he's always done. "I've got some cookies I've just baked. How about I get a plate of them and some nice cold milk and you and I can tackle your homework together? You know, get it out of your way?"

"Not now."

"You don't want any cookies?"

"What? Cookies you said something about cookies?"

She gets up to go to the kitchen. "Yes, I'm going to get a plate of my freshly baked chocolate chip cookies and a couple of glasses of ice-cold milk. Why don't you take a moment to freshen up, splash some water on your face? I'll take the cookies and milk to the living room while you do that."

"That sounds nice, Mom."

Moments later they meet in the living room. Mom puts the things on the coffee table and picks up one of the books as Jimmy digs into the cookies and milk. "Oh, you have an assignment in biology today?"

"Yeah it sucks."

"I used to love that class. Care if I take a look at the assignment?"

"Go ahead. Why should I care?"

Flipping to the marked page, she sees the assignment. "Whales, huh would you look at this? They live to be over a hundred years old. Can you imagine that?"

"Really He sits after to her, looking at the book with her. "How do they know how old a whale can get? Not many people live to be that old."

With Mom's gentle persuasion, Jimmy got his homework done.

The Power of Sexual Persuasion

"I really should be going now."

"Why right now? We've got plenty of time."

"My laundry needs doing."

He gently caresses her cheek. "Laundry I think you'll have time for that tomorrow, won't you? I thought we could open a bottle of wine and sit on the sofa and watch a movie together, just the two of us."

"Well, that does sound nice. But I really should be going. It's getting late."

"My bed has plenty of room if you'd like to stay over." He trails a line of kisses up one side of her neck. "I won't kick you in my sleep, I promise."

"Fluffy probably needs to be let out."

"Don't you have a litter box for your cat?" He snuggles closer to her. "I'm sure she'll be fine in the morning. And it's snowing outside. You really should stay. It wouldn't be hospitable of me at all if I sent you out in this kind of weather."

"I think I'll be fine."

"I can light the fireplace." Another trail of kisses flows over her face. "You'll be nice and warm here, in my arms, in my bed."

"Oh, boy, do you know how to persuade a woman!"

The Power of Bad Persuasion

"I started my diet last night."

"Good for you. Marsha. I wish I could find the self-discipline to start a diet too." Tatum picks up a donut from the box near the coffee pot at work.

Marsha stares at the gooey treat as her friend takes a large bite. "Yeah, I barely have had any cravings at all. So far

"Wow, how great is that?" The donut drips some red jelly down Tatum's chin. "Oops."

Marsha hands her a napkin. "Here yak go, Tatum."

"Thanks." Tatum wipes her chin. "For lunch, I and some of the other girls from the office are all going to pitch in for pizza. Want to join in on the pizza party?" She puts her hand to her mouth as she raises her brows. "Oh, sorry I forgot."

"Yeah, my diet doesn't allow pizza." Marsha holds up a brown paper bag. "I brought a salad and some celery sticks from home. Thanks for inviting me though."

Walking to her desk, she pulls a soda out of the drawer as Marsha makes herself a small cup of straight black coffee. "I can't stand that tasteless coffee. I've got to have my soda. I've got an extra can of it in here if you'd like it."

Looking forlornly at the can of soda Tatum shows her, Marsha slowly shakes her head. "It's not on my diet."

"What is on that diet anyway, Marsha? Twigs and berries?"

"Berries? I wish." Marsha sighs heavily. "I should get to work."

A few hours, Tatum shows up in Marsha's office with one piece of pizza. "I saved you a slice. Come on, one slice of pizza won't hurt you, girl."

"I am starving." Marsha holds out her hand and takes the slice of pizza. "Thanks, Tatum."

Tatum looks at the bottle of water on Marsha's desk. "Here, girl. Have a soda too." She pops it open. "You only live once, right?"

And now Marsha's diet is a thing of the past, just that easily, thanks to Tatum's help and power of persuasion.

The Power of Evil Persuasion

"Look, Joe, everyone is doing it."

"Yeah, but I still don't think I should. My wife and I have a lot of trust in each other."

"She's out of town, Joe. What she doesn't know won't hurt her. You know what I'm saying? And that girl hasn't stopped looking at you since we came into this bar."

"Yeah, I shouldn't even still be here. I told my wife I'd get one drink with you guys from work then I'd get home and feed the dog. Butch is probably starving by now. I really should go."

"I am not trying to be a buttinsky, Joe, but I've seen your wife. She's nice and all, but a little on the plump side and not so easy on the eyes."

"Hey, that's my wife you're talking about!"

"I don't mean any harm, Joe. I'm just saying that you and your wife got married right out of high school, right?"

"Yeah, we were high school sweethearts. She's been the only girl for me."

"Yeah, that's what I'm saying. She's been your only girl. You've got no one to compare her to. And don't even get me started on how boring life would be if all you ever got to eat was vanilla pudding, Joe. And there's a nice cream pie that's just standing there, looking at you, waiting to be tasted. I'm not saying to eat the whole pie, Joe. I'm just saying that you should take a taste of it – of her. What your wife doesn't know won't hurt her, right? Here, have another cocktail to help you get those pesky morals out of your way, Joe."

"Another drink? When did you order this?"

"Just a little while ago. Now that drink cost me five bucks, Joe. I expect you not to waste it. Oh, would you look here? She and she equally as tasty friend are heading our way. I tell you what, Joe. Just to make it easier for you, I'll take her friend. That way you won't be all alone in this. We'll both be doing it. No one will ever know, Joe. No one."

"I'll know."

"Not if I buy you a few more drinks, you won't."

What To Do If You're Discovered — Regaining Favor

S o, let's say the worst has happened. You've been caught out in a
lie or, worse, somebody has realized that you're trying to actively
manipulate them. What can you do in this situation? How do
you get back into a position where the person can trust you?

Well, from here, there are two possibilities. The first is that the bridge
will be burned entirely from their end. In that case, there's not a lot
that you can do to redeem it, unfortunately. Even if they still talk to
you, they will in one sense or another be completely shut off to any
sort of emotional connection with you. The only possible way around
this is if they catch you in a moment of true vulnerability at a later
point and then start to come around on you again, but even then the
process will be terribly slow-going to the point that it's hard to really
say if it would be worth it.

Now, let's consider the other possibilities: they're gullible, or the
transgression wasn't bad enough that they'd try to burn bridges with
you at least. In this case, there's a procedure that you should likely
follow. You can tailor it to whatever situation has popped up; but in
general, the best method probably is to follow a relatively similar
approach.

The first thing that you need to do is accept all the blame they will
throw at you. Don't send it back at them; this will only start to make
them dislike you. In these cases, you really just need to soak up
whatever they do.

Then, give it a few days before you talk again to this person.
Depending on how close you two were and how serious the offense

was, you may need more than a few weeks or a few months. However, the chances are good that for most small conflicts, a little less than a week will be an appropriate amount of time to wait.

After your self-imposed exile, you need to try talking to them. By that, we mean, genuinely talking to them. Don't try to reach out to them through email or text, because the chances are likely that they won't respond. However, a short email expressing your interest is much more useful instead of speaking to them face-to-face.

Really, both techniques have their own respective perks. If you speak to them face-to-face and you're good at showing whatever emotion you want to show, you can easily convince them that you're genuinely sorry for what you've done. If you keep the interaction relatively brief and then sheepishly walk away, you can make it come off as though you actually feel bad about what happened.

On the other hand, the email presents a lot less of an initial obstacle for them to overcome. While they may not respond at all, this may be what you need; an email gives them the opportunity to respond when they feel they should respond if they feel they should respond. It doesn't put them on the spot as a face-to-face confrontation would.

Really, which one would work best will depend upon your specific circumstances. However, most of the time, the first one will be your best option.

Let's assume that you proceed with the first option. What do you do after you apologize? The thing to do afterward is to give it a few more days to let the apology sink in. If they accept your apology and they seem genuine about it (use the emotional reading skills we've developed to tell!), then try to set up a drinking session with them and some mutual friends. This can be a great opportunity for the two of you to have a 'moment of truth' where you confess how badly you feel about what happened. Be sure there are other people there, though, so that no bad blood occurs between the two of you, especially if they're a rowdy drunk and may still be harboring some anger. Here, though, you can finally bury the hatchet and hopefully go back to being good friends. I'd recommend after this that you not manipulate the person any longer, as you really only get one chance to patch things up with people when you manipulate them. They don't fall for it a second time.

If they accepted your apology but didn't seem genuine about it, your best course of action is to wait a bit longer and then start some discourse with them that's unrelated to anything professional or academic. Don't, for example, find a reason to ask them about the test that's coming up. Do send them something that reminded you of them, though. Maybe even just send them a message out of the blue that says, "Hey, how are you?" It's not very intimidating and gives them the freedom to respond whenever, but it also shows that you're serious about rekindling the friendship that you had with this person.

If they strictly don't accept your apology, then it's alright. They will either come around or see themselves as the jerk for not accepting your apology when you were being genuine about it (If you came across as being genuine about it, that is. They may reject it because you're clearly being fake), or they may leave the bridge burned, never to be fixed. The first is a far better position to be in than the second, so hope for the second.

All in all, it's not too difficult to get back to square one from wherever you are. Really, it's just a matter of knowing who you're working with and the exact situation that you're in. I'd like to say one more time that you really shouldn't be putting yourself in situations where you're negatively manipulating someone. If you're just using people as thoroughfares and treating them like people in the meantime, then you shouldn't really have any huge issues aside from being caught in a lie, especially if you're being smart about your tactics.

Seduction Using Dark Psychology

S eduction and sexual conquest are sometimes common features of dark psychology. This is an important topic to discuss because all of us have been or know someone who has been seduced by someone else who used these dark psychological principles.

The human sex drive can be a very powerful urge and not being able to fulfill it can sometimes lead to unhappiness, worry, and stress in the person's life. On the other side of things, some of the most famous historical figures are known for their frequent and full fulfillment of sexual urges. For example, emperors and kings have often been afforded the finest women as their reward just because of their status.

One example that is very famous is the powerful seducer King Henry the 8th from England. His appetite for women was so strong that he decided to create a new religion in his country so that he could change his wife and marry any woman that he chose. He also exercised utter control over all the wives he had, and many of them were beheaded when they didn't satisfy his needs or help him meet his goals any longer.

This begs the question: Is all seduction a form of dark psychological seduction? Of course not! Yes, all seduction is going to involve the perusal of the other person. Those who don't have the skills of dark manipulation will do this in a clumsy manner. This is shown in some of the popular romantic comedies that come out, where the clumsy guy keeps making mistakes when they try to pursue the girl.

But a dark seducer is going to be someone who knows what they want and they know how to get it. They will go after the other person in order to fulfill their own personal needs, and often they don't really care how the other person feels about it. They can be charming and they are not going to be clumsy at all, and they always know the right thing to say and do.

Why Do People Choose Dark Psychological Seduction?

One question that people will have is: Why would someone want to choose this path for attraction? Is it not a better idea to go on some dates and court someone in an honest manner?

A dark seducer doesn't really want to get into a relationship, at least not into the boring stuff with it. They want to just get certain things out of the area of romance. They don't really care about the other person because they know they can use the techniques of dark psychology to find another partner later on if this one goes south later on. This allows them to approach life, and the relationship, with a non-needy and carefree mindset. If the seducer does decide to settle down with someone later on, they are going to be able to do it without feeling like they rushed or settled into the first relationship to get what they want.

So, how is a dark seducer have so much success and influence within the world of dating? It is because they understand the dark psychology principles and they have the right skills in order to execute these principles.

One of the key advantages that the users of dark psychology will have over their rivals, especially in the world of dating, is that they understand the human mind, almost like a secret weapon. While others may feel like the human mind is impossible to understand, the dark seducer is able to read it like a book and get the information that they want from it.

Someone who works on the principles behind dark psychology in the dating world may find that it is really going to change their dating experiences when compared to their past efforts. They will have a feeling of confidence and control, rather than feeling doubtful, needy, and insecure.

Sure, it may seem kind of mean. The dark seducer is able to jump from one partner to another, using each one in the manner that matters most to the seducer. And there are people who are harmed in this process, especially the ones who are looking for more of a long-term relationship, or those who are looking for more out of it.

But a dark seducer is only interested in what matters to them and nothing else. They can read the mind of their victim and be the exact person that victim wants. But they only do this to get their foot in the door and get what they want. As soon as the victim isn't meeting the needs of the seducer, then the seducer will move on.

Where Does Dark Seduction Begin?

Now that we have an idea of the basics of dark seduction, it is time to move into some of the steps of how this seduction can work. Most dark seducers are going to have a guiding approach that is going to motivate their efforts. They will also have tactics that are going to come from their philosophy. Let's take a look at some of the different philosophies that are there that a dark seducer may choose to use.

One approach is the deployment of a process that is rigid and structured. These seducers feel that they have mapped out how the sequence of attraction should be in great detail and they may have a process that seems like it is from a flowchart. They want their seduction process to be replicable and predictable. These systems not only work for the dark seducer but can work for others who understand these systems and learn how to implement them in the proper manner.

These seducers are going to use a series of stages in their process. They will try to get the target to go through a range of emotions. This range is designed by the seducer to fit their needs. They will move them through emotions such as interest, attraction, and then excitement. These seducers will see the whole process as a series of checkpoints that they need to pass through to help them reach their goals.

The strength of this method is that it gives the dark seducer a feeling of certainty because they know the exact steps to take each time. They won't have any surprises that come up during the seduction, and it kind of becomes routine and habitual for the seducer. The biggest problem with this is that it doesn't take into account that sometimes people are going to be unpredictable and won't go along with the structured emotional program that the seducer planned out.

Another option is the natural approach. This approach is going to involve the dark seducer cultivating a genuine emotional state internal to the seducer and then expressing them freely to the one they are working to seduce. An example of this is when a person who uses this is likely to spend some time trying to understand their own emotions and then try to perfect these. They are then going to express these to others. The philosophy behind this one is that "I can't make others feel good until I can feel good."

You can also work with hypnotic and Neuro-Linguistic Programming (NLP) seduction. NLP is a combination of neurological processes, language, and behavior. This is kind of a subset of dark seduction. Unlike the structured seduction that we talked about before or even the natural version, NLP and hypnotic seduction are going to involve triggering specific emotional states in the victim and then linking these back to the seducer.

Let's look at an example of this. The NLP approach to seduction is going to involve allowing a person to explore their own intense positive emotions. The seducer may even try to get more of those emotions out. Then, they will work to anchor these to the seducer. That way, when the victim sees the seducer, they will naturally feel intense physical pleasure, even though they may not know why that happens.

Hypnotic seduction is another option to work with, but it can be a difficult one to work with on a regular basis. This is because few things are going to make someone suspicious about a seducer than the odd techniques that come with NLP. The other seduction types are going to seem somewhat normal to the victim, but hypnotic seduction doesn't seem this way. However, there are some who will respond to it.

Dark seduction can allow the seducer the ability to get exactly what they want out of the relationship. It can sometimes be used by those who are not looking to take advantage of others, but who are open about what they are doing and just use the techniques to give them more confidence and avoid a boring relationship. But there are plenty of dark seducers who use it as a way to use the other person, with no care about how it is going to affect the other person at all. Either way, it is still important to be on the lookout for this kind of behavior so that you don't end up getting into a relationship that is bad for you or isn't what you are looking for from the other person.

Understanding Narcissists' Manipulation Schemes

N arcissism is a psychological condition that is demonstrated by extreme regard to oneself and the disregard of others. Because narcissistic individuals typically think that they're superior to others, they usually hurt them. The narcissistic disorder has existed from ancient times. A notable example of a narcissistic character is one found in Greek mythology called Narcissus. Because of his beauty, Narcissus used to love himself so much. This inflated self-regard was so extreme that the character used to scoff at those who loved him. Due to this strange behavior, the supernatural powers punished him by making him obsessed with his reflection in the river until he committed suicide. Many fields of study have drawn lessons from ancient Narcissus to help them understand the behavior of a narcissistic individual. These fields include psychiatry, psychology, and counseling. The objectives of this piece are to highlight and explain some of the traits of narcissistic individuals. Additionally, the article will focus on how narcissists can harm you and how to relate safely with them.

Traits of Narcissistic People

Narcissistic individuals are incredibly obsessed with their self-esteem and disregard the respect of others. In psychology, narcissism is a disorder that has various characteristics

1. Self-Absorption – People suffering from narcissistic disorder are so much preoccupied with their sense of self-importance. They always want to be the center of interest and cannot offer others an opportunity to contribute to a dialogue. Furthermore, they don't recognize or appreciate the input of other people during a discussion.

2. Harshness – Narcissistic individuals are fierce and may not sustain a healthy relationship. Their harshness and extreme regard to themselves makes them not to recognize other individuals in a relationship. The narcissistic individuals lack the empathetic skills that are core in establishing and maintaining a healthy and robust relationship. Empathy demands that you attentively listen to the other party and relate to their tales and experiences. It's an essential ingredient in a successful relationship.

3. Sense of Superiority – People suffering from narcissism think highly of them and view others as being inferior. Their knowledge of superiority is highly inflated and may not offer you the time to express your views. They usually don't value other people's opinions and points of view.

4. The Demand a Lot from Others – In case narcissistic individuals occupy positions of power; they usually come up with challenging goals to achieve. Their primary interest is to see you fail so that they can have a reason for punishing or hurting you.

5. Exaggeration of Attainments – Narcissistic individuals, talks highly about their achievements and may not focus their attention on any failures. In case they failed, they may explain that that failure may have been caused by someone else. They may select a few areas that they've succeeded and keep on talking about them in every conversation.

6. Highly Sensitive – Also, narcissistic individuals are sensitive to any criticism leveled against them. They think highly about themselves and regard themselves as beyond any mistakes or reproach.

7. They Always Want to Be Admired – Due to their exaggerated sense of importance; the narcissistic individuals crave to be admired all the time. They see themselves as perfect and still yearn for attention.

8. They See Themselves as Being Influential – They have a false belief that they are influential and essential in decision making. They always want you to pass or consult them when you need something.

9. Inflate Their Abilities and Talents – They tend to believe that they have extraordinary talents and skills that must be recognized and celebrated. However, when you observe the way they do things, you'll realize that they don't have any extraordinary talents.

10.   They exploit others – The narcissistic individuals may exploit other people to achieve their goals. When they're in positions of leadership, they may come up with unrealistic goals and ensure that you attain them after much exploitation. They may also assign you many tasks that are beyond your pay.

11.   Lack of Empathy – Empathy makes you put yourself in other people's situations and appreciate their experiences. An empathetic person listens actively to other people, offers them the attention they deserve, and starts recognizing their situations. The narcissistic individual lacks empathy and is generally disinterested in other people's stories.

12.   Always Blaming You – A narcissistic individual wants to blame you always because they have an exaggerated sense of themselves. They still want to show you that you're wrong and blameworthy, and they're always perfect.

13.   Show Off – The narcissistic individual always wants to show off about what they've. They may post their possessions about what they've so that they annoy others. Their aim is to show off and hurt other people.

14.   All Knowing – The narcissistic individual may portray themselves as all-knowing individuals. They want to show that they know everything and represent other people as incapable. They may intrude into conversations where they're not invited and start

Emotional Intelligence 2.0

interrupting others. Their aim is to criticize and righting some of your viewpoints.

15.   Violation of Boundaries – Due to manipulation tactics, narcissistic individuals, may overstep the boundaries that you have set. They may apply coercive tactics in forcing you do want you don't want.

16.   Unreasonably Difficult – Some narcissistic individuals may be complicated and keep nagging you. They may understand that you don't want their antics but decide to be difficult because they want to be a thorn in your flesh.

17.   Use of Specific Phrases upon Hurting You – The narcissistic individual may sometimes use certain expressions when they have damaged you. For instance, they may say, 'I didn't mean to hurt' when they have discovered that they've hurt you. The narcissist's intention is to keep you around as they keep hurting you.

18.   They lie – They may use complementary expressions occasionally, but their aim is to ensure that you keep them company as they keep hurting you. Phrases like 'you're smartly dressed' may once in a while come from their mouths, but they use them ironically.

19.   They May Apply Convincing Language at First- When they want to penetrate into your life, the narcissistic individuals may use sweet expressions like, 'this is the best relationship that I have encountered.'

258

Difference Between Persuasion And Negotiation

What is Negotiation?

Negotiation is a way of resolving differences. It is a mechanism through which consensus or agreement is achieved while disagreements and conflicts are avoided.

In any conflict, people understandably try to accomplish the best result (or perhaps an entity they represent) for their status. However, the foundations for a successful result are the core values of fairness, mutual benefit, and maintenance of a relationship.

In many situations, specific types of negotiation are being used: in international affairs, law, administration, industrial disputes, or intra-regional relations. But in a variety of activities, overall negotiation skills could be managed to learn and applied. Negotiation experience can help solve the conflicts between you and anyone.

Negotiation phases

A formal negotiation strategy can be beneficial in securing a favorable outcome. In a job situation, for instance, it may be appropriate to schedule a conference where all the parties concerned will interact.

The negotiation process contains the following phases:

Preparedness

Talk of the matter.

Objectives clarity

Negotiate for the Win-Win results.

Agreement

A course of action to be followed

1. Preparedness.

A decision must be made before any discussions about when and where to discuss the issue and who will be involved. It is also beneficial to establish a limited time period to avoid more conflicts. This phase involves making sure all the applicable facts are known to explain your position. In the above example, the knowledge of your organization's "rules" for which assistance is given is included when aid is not deemed appropriate and the reasons for such refusals. The rules you can adhere to in preparing talks may be in the organization. While addressing the dispute, planning can help prevent future disagreements and unintentionally waste time during the session.

2. Talk of the matter.

Individuals or representatives of each side put the case as they choose, i.e., their awareness of the situation, forward during this stage. In this step, key skills involve interviewing, listening, and explanation. It is sometimes helpful to note all points rose during the debate stage if further clarification is necessary. Listening is extremely important; as it is simple to make the error that you talk too much and listen too little when there is conflict. Each hand should have the same chance of presenting its case.

3. Objectives clarity.

The aims, interests, and views of the two fronts of the dispute must be clarified from the discussion. Such considerations should be identified as objectives. Through this explanation, certain mutual respect can often be found or created. Clarification is an integral part of the negotiation phase. Unless it is overlooked, difficulties and challenges to obtaining a positive outcome can occur.

4. Discuss the Win-Win results.

In this phase, what is called a win-win in outcome is focused on where the two parties feel their views are considered. This phase concentrates on what is called a win-win output. Generally, the best result is a win-win outcome. It may not always be feasible, but this should be the final goal through mediation. Various strategies and sacrifices suggestions need to be considered here. Commitments are often positive choices, which are often more beneficial than holding the initial positions for all concerned.

5. Agreement.

Accord can be established after attention has been extended to recognizing the opinions and desires of both parties. In order to reach an acceptable outcome, it is necessary that everyone concerned remain open-minded. Any contract must be made absolutely clear so that the decisions have been taken on both sides.

6. A course of action to be followed.

The intervention plan must be followed to carry out the determination under the Agreement.

Non-agreement

If the negotiation process breaks down, and no agreement is reached, another meeting is expected. It prohibits both sides from engulfing themselves in warm debates or disputes that not only bother wasting time but can also affect future interactions. The negotiation phases should always be repeated at the next meeting. Some new ideas or desires must be addressed, and the condition revisited. It could also be useful at this point to look at alternatives and/or to mediate in another individual.

Informal discussions

Sometimes, more unofficially, it is necessary to negotiate. In those cases, it might be difficult or necessary to take the above steps officially if there is a disagreement. However, in a variety of casual settings, it can be very helpful to remember the main points in the stage of formal negotiations.

The following three components are important and will likely affect the final outcome of negotiations in any talks:

Attitudes

Awareness

Interpersonal competencies

1. Attitudes

The attitudes to the system itself, for instance, attitudes towards problems and individuals involved with the individual case or attitudes aligned with social acknowledgment requirements, have strongly influenced all discussions. Know always that: mediation is not a place for personal successes to be accomplished. The need to bargain with the government can be resentful. Through bargaining, characteristics may affect the actions of a human, such as that of individuals.

2. Awareness.

The more awareness you have of the issues concerned, the greater your involvement in the negotiation process. Well-preparedness is essential, in other words.

Gain as much knowledge about your assignments as possible about the issues. Therefore, it is essential to understand how things are resolved because mediation in various situations can require different approaches.

3. Interpersonal competencies.

To successful talks, both informal settings and in non-formal or less formal or one-to-one meetings, strong interpersonal skills are important.

Such competencies include:

Successful verbal contact

Hearing

Project study

Solving question

I am deciding.

Stability

Tackling difficult circumstances

Are negotiation and persuasion the same?

Negotiation is defined as two, or even more, people interact to reach an agreement on one or more issues and also to talk with another person to arrive at an agreement.

Persuasion can be described as the act or method of manipulating, or of moving to a new opinion, place, or course of action–through argument or intercession. It's the key to all discussions to transfer somebody to a new post or action path. Throughout immobilization negotiations, two parties try to find a compromise. This is particularly the case. While anyone may try to negotiate, an efficient and persuasive negotiator typically works more successfully.

Bringing up persuasion as a strategy of negotiation means looking at the various types of conviction values that relate to property transactions there are six different opportunities for self-interest, individuality, comparison, swap, sameness, and logical sense in property negotiations.

In a perfect world, everybody would agree with you, and you would still be correct. About 99 percent of the time is not like that. What are you doing? Frequently people use manipulation to manipulate their stance on the other side. Persuasion is perfect if it succeeds because it does not cost you much but often does not succeed so that you may have to bargain. So, what the distinction between persuasion and bargaining is.

It is best to switch to a dictionary to describe persuasion, and the meaning' to persuade' of Merriam-Webster is' to compel (somebody) to do something by questioning, debating and/or giving reasons.'

A brilliant short book called "Eristic Dialectic, the Art of Being Wrong" has been published by Arthur Schopenhauer and is still one of the popular rhetoric's of the day. Its 38 stratagems educate you about using logical errors, false proposals, generalization, and other handy instruments. In both processes, there are some important differences: the point of persuasion is to say, and trade is a negotiation. Strategies of persuasion are to explain, to promote, to manipulate, to inspire, to argue, to advise, and to contest.

Negotiation implies, on the other hand, that concerns, desires, shortcomings, motivations, and goals can be discussed, so that a better understanding can be made available from both sides. There is not strictly exclusive convincing and mediation either.

Both could be close to their results or goal. All strategies are very successful, and citizens are often persuaded that they prefer their own reasoning and beliefs above compromise. The other party's reasoning and views tend to us not to be particularly interested. The individual may find it difficult to change his position, but we still choose it as persuading is which we've developed with since childhood and used again. Negotiation is challenging because we really must be attentive to the other party's views, values, and reasoning and therefore considers ways of dealing with them.

If we speak about compromise, there is some uncertainty about whether we say mediation or coercion. Negotiations, in their very essence, warrant a rapprochement between the two sides to reach a compromise. Convincing or manipulating, though, is the process of making the other party do what they want.

The art of convincing is often termed negotiation.

Good negotiation leverage you will learn when and how to use convincing skills to be a good negotiator. This is probably happening at times when you seem unable to agree on negotiations. In these cases, it is also necessary to understand how and when to persuade efficiently.

Use of queries to help persuade others to compromise

Comments are high as they speak to the other arm. Yet reacting to what is being said is the real art of interrogation. This doesn't mean that you hang on each word. "The detection, selection, and interpretation of keywords that turn information into intelligence," is the definition of Mullender's listening. His conceptual model is' information you use for your benefit.'

In sale's situations, implied and explicit requirements are the keywords that a customer of our SPIN ® Selling Skills model would listen to. An effective sales representative is someone who can turn that information in the form of profit statements into intelligence.

The profit statement requires that sellers dive into issues or perceived concerns, which is precisely the same as that recommended by Mullender to "steer anxiety" in circumstances of recovery. You will define the specific desires (what other side wants to do about this) and render helpful suggestions only by finding the real source of the pain.

Unsurprisingly, in these cases, Mullender points to SPIN ® as a "stunningly clever" template.

Ultimately, while talks can be seen as a separate part of a process and a different ability to sell/persuade, a successful leader must still be willing in a negotiating scenario to execute suitable persuasive techniques. They recommend that negotiators develop strong selling strategies and negotiation skills to help them produce win-win outcomes. This is why they support

What should I select?

Seek first to convince and see whether it fits for you. I'm positive, though, we were all on the other hand of someone who told us constantly that we just don't approve. It can be quite annoying. Although persuading and bargaining, know when you hit an impasse.

The Influence of sound is always stronger than the power of language. When you have the point of no-return, substitute the tone to be more convincing or switch your bargaining dialog — you are much more likely to get a response. The Influence of sound is always better than the influence of words.

Conclusion

E veryone uses manipulative tactics sometimes to get the things that we want. People don't do this often but when it happens there is usually some self-centered reason behind it. Dark psychology focuses on the human mind and reactions to it. Everyone analyzes people to try and find ways to work them for their needs. Like Bundy, Blanchard and Manson, all used their manipulative nature to make those who they felt were weak do as they commanded.

These are extreme cases, but the man focus is to notice how normal each of them appeared to the ones the manipulated. A manipulator would have no qualms about using someone to their benefit and would treat people as commodities.

Once the person loses their worth, they lose their purpose and become worthless to the narcissist/manipulator in question. They won't worry about the victim's goals, dreams or even their social life.

They would focus all their energy on the control that have over the victim. It would be hard for them to conceal their true intentions after a while. The cracks on the surface would be important to analyze when considering the person that qualifies as a narcissist.

They would try their best to hide it, but it would come out in small details. It would be in the way they react to people knowing too much about them; it would be in the way they react to something not going their way; it would be in the random fits of anger that may occur as a result of not being able to control what they're doing. Every choice that is made by a manipulator is calculated and planned, down to the even the tiny losses of control. They will find ways to regain it but if it is lost completely, the manipulator will break.

Paying close attention to what the manipulator/narcissist does when they lose control is crucial. They may start to use ultimatums or leave because they don't want to stay with the person. They might even start to show more aggressive and violent behaviors. The dark triad dictates that people who rank high on this scale aren't capable of feeling remorse or morally guilty for the choices they made.

These choices are primarily focused on what the manipulator feels they lack in their lives. Bundy needed the two women who were devoted to him because he needed to feel powerful. Those women made him feel like he was high on the pyramid. He didn't see anything wrong in his violent acts and would never feel guilty for what he did. Manson felt he was wronged by the people that were killed by his cult. They rejected him and he pinned the blame of his unhappiness on those that didn't comply with his rules and control. And when they didn't comply, Manson would punish those with violent and often abusive behavior.

Many manipulators, like domestic abusers and emotional abusers, need fear. Fear is what many domestic terrorists use to get the desired result that they want. The focus is on what they can achieve with the power they got from their victims.

They have analyzed and discovered what they can get from each victim and they know what to do to achieve their goal. Many don't even know what they want until they discover the victim. The women that Bundy killed were unfortunately the personality types that wish to help those in need. That's why his broken arm or leg ruse would work.

In an episode of Criminal Minds, a serial killer would use his sick dog to lure his victims to the van. And a common ruse that's used to kidnap children is a kind adult that is bringing them to their parents that might be injured in some undisclosed location and they sent their friend to pick them up.

The manipulation ploy is the most important part of the ruse. They must use something that would persuade the victim to follow along. Its important recognize when something is a ruse or just being used to manipulate a person. When an abuser manipulates, they will use threats and often validate them with harsh remarks or even physical pain. The manipulator doesn't see this as pain or abuse. They want something from their manipulative con and would make sure that they get it.

The dark persuasion techniques are meant to psychologically manipulate the victims into following the manipulator without them knowing that they are manipulating someone.

These techniques are used mostly by people with more to lose if it is discovered what they are doing. They would use these techniques to get into the subconscious of their victims and work them without having to do more than say a few words or even ask the right questions.

Using dark persuasion means that the manipulator believes they are smarter than the people they surround themselves with. They would feel the need to be better than the ones they are manipulating. Manson's cult was a long con that he started when he first got out of jail. During his time outside, he began to spread the word that he was the second coming of Jesus. That fueled the people who followed him blindly into doing the drugs he did and following his teachings.

Eventually he would get violent after beginning this cult to "spread peace". Manson's end goal was to make money, even his first crimes before the murders were petty theft and robbery. Manson had a man killed because he denied him money. The one thing Manson wanted most from his victims was their money. A long con usually involves money and/or something or material value. Sometimes these cons even come from the manipulator just wanting the victim to finance a lifestyle. They don't always end as violently and tragically but in Manson's case, his long con was manipulated by his drug use.

A manipulator that people don't often think of is also drug manipulation. Drug induced hallucinations can cause self-inflicted manipulation of the subconscious. A narcissist would be greatly affected by drug use, as would a psychopath and a person with a mental health issue. The drug use would exacerbate any underlying issues and would even cause psychosis.

Like with Manson, his use of drugs would cause him to believe that he was Jesus and he would take this belief out into the world. The people who followed him did the same drugs and would believe his hallucination. They would humor his delusions which would lead to him feeling mighty.

These feelings of being godlike would lead him to believe that he was, and it incited different manipulative tactics to come from Manson. He would rile his followers up to commit the violent murders The Manson Family is known for, feeling personally responsible for the chosen few that were lucky enough to receive his blessing. Many manipulators feel this way and would do what they want to those that are unlucky enough to fall for their acts. The acts committed by a manipulator or narcissist rely solely on those who follow them.

The victims are the most important part of any manipulation technique. The manipulator can't be one without the people they manipulate. They primarily will rely on weak victims that are less likely to fight back. The important quality they look for is passive complacency.

An ideal victim would not be able to see through their methods. The manipulator would be able to control the situation, the whole relationship and the people around them that are unaware of their manipulative tendencies. The victims are often coworkers, close friends, romantic partners or even family members. As seen with the Blanchard case, Dee manipulated her daughter and their neighbors. No one would believe the horror show that Gypsy detailed occurred in that house.

Usually when manipulators are described by their victims, they are spun in such positive light and it is often hard to believe that they are even somehow involved.

They see no issues with it, and they would do anything to protect their plans and manipulation. Covering the tracks is important, as this can be seen with Dee Dee consistently moving around to avoid being detected by doctors and caregivers that encountered her daughter.

Dee Dee knew that the wrong doctor would find out that her daughter wasn't sick, and she could come under fire for all the benefits that she reaped from people believing her child was terminally ill. She tricked people into getting her new equipment for the child, a new accessible home and money to take care of her. They went on numerous news circuits, gaining traction and mass media attention. Everyone wanted to know more about the Blanchard family.

Even when it ended in tragedy, people still want to know more. Dee Dee wanted to be famous and known for efforts to take care of her sick child, the story has even been made into a limited series on Hulu to discuss the manipulation, abuse and fear that Gypsy lived in every day with her mom. The slow decline of their relationship began with Gypsy started questioning her mother's intentions.

Confrontation is the scariest part of breaking down the manipulation. Because as a possible victim you aren't aware of how the narcissist would react to their confrontation. It's important to remain calm, but also assert dominance. It's not ideal to do this alone. But it's also not ideal to do this when the manipulator is concentrated on using fear to incite the victims.

They could abuse them because they need to break them to get what they want. If they confront them, it is likely that this could escalate any violent behavior or also cause a panic which would equally be just as bad. As with Blanchard, she abused her daughter and kept her a prisoner when she was starting to exhibit behaviors that would mean possibly losing control of the situation that she created to benefit herself from. Dee Dee wanted attention and many narcissists only crave having people spend time focusing on them. Gypsy could've gotten sick once before in the past and the attention that Dee Dee got was more than she could handle, and it sent her off into a spiral.

If Gypsy was old enough and able to identify her manipulation, she could've calmly talked about what happened but instead she most likely handled it as a child would. Children are more likely to be manipulated because of their young age and naivety. They also wouldn't handle a confrontation well which is why they are more likely to accept things as they are and internalize them.

Most manipulators do come from troubled pasts and it is very likely are the children of manipulators themselves. Whether it is due to conditioning or abuse, there is no excuse for being an abusive manipulator but there is also no reason to ignore the factors that can lead to manipulation.

PART THREE

Introduction

Have you anytime looked at someone and thought you had them understood just from that look? Is it exact to state that you were right? Or then again would you say you were stirred up about some piece of their character? Despite whether you were right or wrong, you essentially tried getting someone, which is an ability that most of us would love to have. Everything considered, in case you can tell when your chief is feeling incredible, you understand when to demand a raise, right? When you understand your people are feeling awful you know, it is anything but a chance to unveil to them you scratched the vehicle. It is connected to appreciating what understanding people means and how its capacities.

What Is Reading People'?

When you look at someone and feel like you can condemn whether they are feeling extraordinary or a horrendous one, paying little heed to whether they are a wonderful individual or a mean one or whatever else using any and all means, you are getting them. At the point when all is said in done, understanding someone means researching them and it does not just should be a speedy look, and knowing something about them without them saying anything in any way shape or form. It is a tendency you get from looking and from viewing the way in which they stand, the way wherein they look around, the way where they move. There some different features that could play into your inclination and cognizance of them, yet the most critical thing is that they did not explicitly uncover to you whatever that thing is.

By and by, various people investigate someone and acknowledge they know something. You mull over inside 'charitable, they look sincere' or 'astonishing, they look upset.' These are instinctual suppositions and thoughts that we have when we see a person. As we speak with them, we may achieve new goals or even as we watch them over the room. Maybe you never banter with that individual, anyway you have examinations and considerations in regard to the kind of person that they rely upon what you have seen of them. You are getting them, and whether you are right or wrong is an assistant point.

For What Reason is Reading People Important?

For what reason would it be a smart thought for you to essentially disturb getting people? Everything considered, there are a couple of special reasons this can be a better than average capacity. In any case, at a most fundamental level, it reveals to you how you should approach someone. If they look neighborly, you might also be prepared to approach with a smile and a very much arranged welcome. If they look down and out, you might undoubtedly approach with a reason rather than basically stopping to make appropriate associates. If a friend looks upset, you may ask them what's going on or what happened. Understanding what they feel like just from a quick look can empower you to imagine whatever is going on essentially like that, and the better you get with the mastery, the better you'll be at talking with people.

In case you do not have the foggiest thought about how to scrutinize people in any way shape or form, you could wrap up interpreting something that they do or an action or an outward appearance mistakenly, and you may start to expect things about a person that is not correct. Maybe you see their face and accept that they are a perturbed person when they're basically furious with a condition. Maybe you think they look threatening, anyway they're basically perplexed with something that is going on around them. By making sense of how to scrutinize better, you'll have the alternative to push your life from numerous perspectives.

Understanding people can empower you to acknowledge who to approach with that unprecedented new idea (and when to approach) and who you ought to stay away from. It is like manner discloses to you how to familiarize something with them, paying little mind to whether from a precise perspective or dynamically fun and creative one. Before you know it, understanding people will be normal to you if you practice it routinely enough. Additionally, what's shockingly better is that you have no doubt been doing it for as long as you can remember and not despite contemplating it. That is in light of the fact that it is something that even kids will give a shot every so often, without acknowledging how huge it is.

Dark Psychology Secrets

Manipulators, narcissists, and other adepts in dark psychology have their own treasure trove of secrets that allow them to read people and bend them to their will. Narcissists are particularly skillful at reading others, poising them to seek romantic partners based on their perception that they can control them. Below is a list of some of the dark psychology secrets that can serve you in your attempts at reading people more skillfully.

Be conscious of clues that suggest the other person is trying to establish rapport with you, such as mimicking your gestures and words.

This is really about paying attention. Most people do not notice the things that others do to try and establish a connection with them. In truth, the only people who usually notice this are those who have been manipulated before or the manipulators themselves. Although it is true that those who truly want to be our friend can show signs of closeness, this tactic is often used by those whose goal is to manipulate or harm.

Others are trying to read you too, so be guarded in the information that you share.

You are not the only one out there trying to read the nonverbal and verbal cues of others. Other people are trying to read you too, potentially using that information against you. At the same time that you are reading others, you may want to be a little guarded yourself.

Be aware of when you are engaging in actions that seem not to benefit yourself.

This secret comes from the victims of narcissists. Although this book has generally approached the subject of reading people with the goal of potentially influencing them later, it is also important to recognize signs that you yourself are a potential target of someone else. Engaging in actions that benefit the other party frequently occurs in narcissistic relationships, even brief ones such as coworkers in an office, so pay attention to your own actions in interactions and think about where they are coming from.

Instead of taking words at face value, always question what the motives of others are.

Although no one wants to suspect everyone they meet as being a liar and manipulator, the reality is that the world is in some respects a different place than it was fifty years ago. We do not live in communities where we share the same goals as those around us, and we knew everyone's name. Now, we have to be on guard for those who may wish to control us. Always think in the back of your head what the intentions of the other person are. This is important in verbal communication as well as nonverbal communication.

The use of vague or nonspecific language can be indicative of an attempt at mind control.

Be wary of when the person you are reading uses vague language. This can either be a sign that they are attempting to weasel themselves out of a lie, or it can be a clue that they are engaging in a mind control tactic. As we have seen, suggestive words can be buried in otherwise innocuous or meaningless sentences, so be on the lookout for vague or confusing language.

Touching is a sign that someone wants to establish rapport with you or control you.

Touching and what it represents is an aspect of reading others that everyone should know. When someone is touching you, it always indicates something. A manipulator will touch you during a conversation because they have designs regarding you and need to first establish rapport. But someone who likes you or who is your friend also may touch you. Use this body language cue in conjunction with others to get a sense of what is really going on.

Learning to read micro expressions will improve your reading abilities considerably.

Micro expressions are facial expressions that last less than half a second. That means they appear on the face and leave very quickly. But if you learn to recognize these, you will gain an insight into others that very few have. Learn to notice when someone's expression seems to change very quickly. Pay special attention to the eyes.

A sudden pause or looking away can be a sign that someone is lying.

A pause gives the other person to stall, giving them a chance to think of what to say. This can be a sign that the other person is lying. Think about it. When we are intoxicated, we speak honestly because we are not thinking about what we are saying beforehand. When someone is taking time to think about their words, it can often indicate deception.

Use your intuition.

It is not always easy to use this particular tidbit of advice because intuition develops over time. If you are not used to analyzing others, you will likely lack the intuition about people. Let us face it; men often do not use their intuition when it comes to reading others because they tend to focus on verbal communication rather than nonverbal communication. Start to read the body language of others and develop a sense of what it means. Your judgments will be honed through a process of trial and error. Then, in the future, use your intuition to guide you.

Learn the clues that indicate how someone thinks.

When we say how someone thinks, we mean how they process information. NLP manipulators learn what side of the brain of their target is dominant and use eye movements to gain information about how the brain processes information. This is not easy, but it is a valuable skill that can be developed over time. Watch the eyes and learn to make a connection between eye movement and how the other person thinks.

The Basics Of Analyze People

As explored, there are many stimuli that trigger human responses and lead to decision-making, and researchers have developed extensive methods to measure these outcomes, whether using biometrics, surveys, or focus groups. However, these research methods may not be at your disposal on a daily basis. Below are methods techniques you can use in everyday interactions to analyze the cognitive and behavioral processes of individuals around you.

Observe Body Language

Research found that body language accounts for 55% of how we communicate, while words only account for 7%. The tone of voice represents the rest. People can tend to be over-analytical when reading human behavior and it may seem counterintuitive, but in order to be objective in analyzing people, observe naturally and try not to over-analyze.

Appearance

One of the first things that speak the loudest is the appearance of an individual. Take notice of a person's dressing. Is he or she dressed sharply in a suit, traditional clothing, or casual style? Does he or she look particularly conscious about the choice of clothing or hairstyle? The way a person dresses can determine his or her level of self-esteem.

Posture

When reading people's posture, observe if they hold their head high or slouch. Do they walk indecisively or walk with a confident chest? How do they esteem themselves? Posture also reveals confidence levels or a person's physical pain points.

Movements

People generally lean towards things they like, and away from things they do not. Crossed arms and legs suggest self-protection, anger, or defensiveness. When people cross their legs, their toes point to the person they are most comfortable with, or away from those they are not. When hands are placed in pockets, laps, or behind the back, it is an indication that the person is hiding something. Nervousness can also be revealed through lip-biting or cuticle-picking. Some people do that to soothe themselves under pressure or in awkward situations.

Facial Expressions

Aforementioned, emotions may not be visible unless expressed. Frown lines indicate over-thinking or worry, while crow's feet evidence joyfulness. Tension, anger, or bitterness can be seen on pursed lips or clenched jaws. Facial expressions can be one of the most evident ways to read human behavior towards specific things, places, or people.

How to analyze people effectively and efficiently

So, you want to learn how to analyze people effectively and efficiently. Well, you came to the right place! I will teach you everything you need to know about reading others. I will even teach you how to understand yourself. We need to talk about a few things before we get into the meat of the matter, however.

So, as you can see, there are many reasons to unravel the techniques of analyzation. Scanning people for warning signs or just for information about them puts you ahead of the pack. There is nothing more beneficial to your life, your relationships, and your protection. Spot narcissists before they have a chance to victimize you. Understand your boss's motives and learn how to nail down what they want from you, without even hearing them say it.

Here are some jobs which actively employ analyzing others:

•Politicians

•Lawyers

•Criminal investigators

•Military officials

•Psych professionals

•Forensic experts

As you can see, it truly is a universal tool. Many different people have to analyze others daily in their day-to-day lives.

I hope that these are the skills you want to learn. They are invaluable, and it is my pleasure to help you improve your life, one impression at a time.

There are, of course, incredible benefits to consuming the knowledge I am offering to you today. First off, you will find that you can communicate your needs to other people far more effectively. Being able to tell how they are reacting and changing your approach accordingly is more than helpful. Communication is the most important skill that we can hone, quite frankly. It helps ease tension, earn the confidence of others, and put us in a positive light. Emotional intelligence goes hand in hand with communication as well.

This is another skill that will be furthered when paired with the power to analyze others. Your emotional intelligence greatly relies on your ability to understand others. The goal is always to meet people where they are: understanding what they need and being able to tell how they need to be handled. Whether you lead a team, need to help your children through their struggles, or are feeling the tension in your love life, I am here to help.

Strong relationships are the glue of society and, more importantly, of families. We need to know how to handle our spouses, children, and anybody else directly related to us. Strained relationships lead to strained relations, and none of us want to be caught up in a family feud. Learning how people tick and how to handle tough situations is the key. You will also learn how to watch for red flags with your children. Knowing how to read their body language and pick up on their verbal cues do wonders for seeing warning signs well in advance.

If you are a parent, this will be a key book in taking your parenting to the following level.

As for another skill, leadership, you will soon be at the front of the crowd. You will find that people not only listen to you but that they actively want to listen to you. Becoming a strong leader means being able to tell who a person is just by carefully observing them. True leaders understand the absolute power that body language holds. After all, it is the oldest form of communication among them all.

I would like to get you started with a few rules. As you can imagine, there is a baseline to start when it comes to analyzing others. You can remember some steps to help you begin which are not hard and fast but excellent for helping you to understand the process. Practice makes perfect, so make sure you pay close attention to this list.

These rules are as follows:

1. Understand What Their Baseline Is: Everybody is just a tad bit different from the rest. It is almost like how parents can tell their twins apart, but nobody else can. Learning how to analyze others means you can tell them apart on a much different level. Understand that you can only tell their "baseline" after knowing them for a while.

You can watch for signs that they are nervous. Perhaps ask probing questions you know will elicit the emotion you want to pin down. If they tend to become physical restless under duress, you know what sort of body language to watch for.

This is the first rule for many reasons. Most importantly, it reminds us that we need to see the whole person. Cold reading is great.

2. Notice the Changes: Take into account the entire picture of the person. This builds off of the first rule. Understand that any gesture can mean something, but you need to put several clues together to really solve the mystery that is a person.

This will also build off of noticing what signs of nervousness you may be looking for. We are using nervousness for these examples, but it goes for any emotion. Anger, unease, discomfort—they are all negative emotions you can begin to pinpoint.

3. Watch for Warning Signs. When certain behaviors are brought into the light and therefore meaning in your eyes, you can start to piece it together. If you have noticed that they shift their eyes around when nervous, and their eyes tighten up when they are angry, you will know when you are treading on dangerous territory.

There are several different clusters of behaviors that can be seen across the board. As mentioned, humans are pack animals in nature. This means that we have learned how to communicate with each other whether we like it or not. Certain tip-offs are pretty well-known. However, a lot more will be missed to the untrained eye. That is why you are reading this!

4. Compare Behavior Changes: The following rule in this line-up is to always make sure you watch how they behave with others as well. It is a popular belief that you do not watch the person who is speaking—you watch the reaction of the person you want to impress. Making sure you are taking note of your boss's body language while listening to co-workers, for example.

Notice the changes between them talking to you and them talking to others. This will help cue you into their true emotions about you as well as how they feel about others. Are their arms crossing when they talk to their friends? Is their body still turned towards you even while engaged in conversation elsewhere?

5. Watch Yourself. One of the most powerful things you can do is be aware of your body language. We do not just need to understand others but also ourselves. We influence others with our facial expressions without even knowing what it looks like. That is not what you want to be doing. To control a situation or a conversation, or even influence it, you need to practice expressions.

The best way to do this is to do it in the mirror.

6. Listen to Others Talk. Identify the strongest person in the room. You will notice them right away, most likely. Sometimes, however, it takes a little time. Look for open body language being used purposefully but elegantly. A big smile, a voice that commands attention and self-confidence are all ways of saying "I am the boss in this situation." They do not need the approval of others and they often hold the most sway in the situation.

Even if somebody is technically the boss, that does not mean they are completely in control. A confident, strong person will make an impression and quickly become somebody whose opinion the "head honcho" deeply trusts. Knowing which strings to pull will push you further and further toward getting what you want out of a situation.

7. Watch Them Move. Looking at body language while they talk to you, especially sitting or standing still, is one thing. You also need to watch their general state of being while moving around. You can tell quite a bit about a person just by the way they walk and how they move. Confident people tend to stand

tall, with their shoulders back and chest pushed a little out. They walk with purpose, as though they always have somewhere important to be.

On the other hand, somebody who is unsure of themselves embodies the exact opposite traits. They try to make themselves look small, perhaps hunching over a little, keeping their head low.

8. Listen to Speech Patterns. Another rule is to listen closely to how they talk and what they are saying, both about the topic at hand and about themselves. How a person speaks tells you so much about them, both literally and figuratively! When you can identify how they speak when they are being truthful and genuine, you can figure out when they are being the opposite.

There are several different ways to go about this. However, looking for "action words" is one of the best. A lot of ex-agents talk about how looking for these words, especially strong verbs; it helps you figure out how their brain works. These words do not just convey their thoughts, but they convey the patterns of their thoughts as well.

9. Key into Their Personality. The last rule is to always put all of this information together. You cannot use one of these rules without following up with the others. These are the cardinal tenets off of which all analyzation of others is built. Once you put together their verbal communication, their body language, and understand them as a whole, you have won half the battle.

Ethical Consideration Of Manipulation

Deception

One example of a Challenging place, ethically, is deception. For a few, all types of lying are incorrect. Including white lies and partial truths - If you're among these individuals, it is possible to still utilize the hints in this book, but it's likely to alter how that you approach manipulation. Especially, your strategy will prevent using deception and concentrate, rather, on Power and persuasion.

For everybody else, you may want to choose just how much and what kinds of disturbance you're feeling comfy.

To begin with, think about the problems with deception. Deceiving others may lead others to activities which behave against or without fostering their particular interests. A negative effect of hauling them to behaving on your own - Deceiving others might also be of advantage for them, tricking them to activities that will boost their wellbeing or livelihood in the very long run, but that they weren't capable of doing.

Telling a Kid, their favorite superhero loves vegetables, is a good instance of this. The deceit is meant to enhance the child's diet plan, which might benefit their long-term wellbeing.

Deception may also have unintended effects. Typically, telling this type of lie into a kid is not likely to end in tragedy, but it is not possible that a kid may detect the ruse, also create uncertainty involving the deceiver. This may damage them from hardening their susceptibility to prospective manipulation within their pursuits, or it might promote lying trends in the kid. There's not any knowledge, for sure, the best effect of a certain action.

Consider, too, the situation in which Deception occurs. It is possibly expected behavior to test and totally fool your counterpart, even regarding your aims, at a game of chess or checkers, warfare, or perhaps in contract discussion. But a lot of individuals would think it immoral to maintain even the tiniest untruth out of a prospective partner.

You will possibly take the position that parting, and some other behavior, is a crime if you get caught. It is a possibly cynical world perspective, but there is an argument to state that it is a dog-eat-dog planet, and in case you are not inclined to be callous, somebody else will do the exact same for you.

It is not the location of the Book to pick in which you draw your own lines from the sand. But some guidance is to set any moral boundaries, for example, "no lies whom I've reason to think will lead to injury to another." You may come across this overly strict or too cynical, therefore specify your personal borders and in the event, the moment arises in which you realize an opportunity to break that border, to your very own possible profit, at the least you are going to have the chance to face your own book, if you choose to proceed or not.

Abuse

Together with the reminder, This Book Isn't telling you the way to align with your ideology, it's necessary, nevertheless, to say that the majority of men and women believe abuse is a poor thing. The matter is how to identify misuse.

You've probably heard the term "misuse of power" Consider something which the majority of individuals would set at the bottom end of this spectrum, like the sexual abuse of emotionally handicapped minors. Its misuse on several levels since the small has quite a few vulnerabilities. Notably, parents and guardians of those folks are in a place of confidence, to guard those folks. They have very little defense against and lack the decision to comprehend the methods by which sexual abuse may affect their psychology. It is a poor, sobering notion to set up the intense end of this misuse spectrum.

In the other end of the spectrum, then there may be Nuanced or contentious cases of what some people today call misuse, like ordering an excess part of fries after charging a meal into the business accounts. It is an unnecessary affair that makes it possible for the "abuser" to gain too from the hope they've been given.

Taking this further, it is possible to draw into question the essence of business associations. You may think about the notion of somebody "sleeping their way into the very best" to become dismissive. But how can it be feasible to reconcile private relationships where one individual obviously has power over another, for instance, a supervisor and an employee, together with thoughts of this misuse of power? Are these relationships potential without components of misuse?

Someone may naturally be attracted to their own boss as a Result of power that they hold, as was established. At precisely the exact same time, it might not be possible for a manager to input a non-abusive connection, given that the inherent vulnerability of the worker.

Maybe it is totally possible to separate function and enjoyment; however, these scenarios are tacky, to say the very least.

More relevant to those times, it's likely to draw Comparisons into the function of a casting director for Hollywood films. A lot of individuals have stated it is inherently wrong for somebody who has authority over the others, i.e., they could aid their progress towards accomplishing their objectives, to enter into an intimate connection. Is not it true that, in a few of those cases, aspiring celebrities are throwing themselves in people in places of power? The implication, then, is that power brings responsibility. Surely, that conveys an element of fact in the opinion of several people and a lot of their media.

Once More, You'll Need to determine what Constitutes abuse on your own eyes. This could possibly be characterized by the possible victims of your own actions, in which case you may not see a large business because of especially tragic casualty, so that additional basket of chips. Extra food for consideration is to think about what makes someone "vulnerable," and whether it is really possible to determine that an individual is "not exposed "Should you manipulate a different individual then, certainly, to a level, they're exposed -- if just to your own adorable.

Honor

Assessing all of these moral Problems can, to a level, induce you to rely upon a code of honor. This may be ordered by means of a civilization, or even a creed. It could possibly be made on your own or your coworkers. It might even be a part of a commitment designed to maintain a specific degree of ethics -- as is normal among trusted media outlets.

This can allow you to make moral decisions, from placing bounds for you. But it is rare that, if push comes to shove, a hint of honor will really block you from taking a task out its boundaries. That's you up alone.

The Ends vs. the Means

One option to setting clear ethical Boundaries would be to judge every case entirely on its own merits. In this example, there's more flexibility. Specifically, you might decide that any activity could be justified, even if the outcome is favorable sufficient to outweigh the way of reaching it.

There is a further problem, which the most elastic moral gymnasts should look at. Even if the ends justify the way, can these ends be attained less wrongdoing?

Once More, It isn't the area of this Book to enforce a particular ethical code. But even if your strategy to integrity, in Manipulation, is elastic, would you eliminate anything by specifying bounds anyhow? In that circumstance, you can realize when you cross these borders, and it provides you a prompt to speech and justify your motives for doing this.

Intent and Unscrupulousness

This Book has partly addressed the problem of Intent in Manipulation. Think about the kid who cries; young kids make a great deal of decisions based on instinct and emotion. The purpose might be to control; however, the manipulation remains present.

In Case you have spent time around kids, You Might understand that, when a kid hurts themselves, there's a pause until their response. Oftentimes, they'll look to your own parent. In the event the parent's response is shock, then they might become restless and begin to cry; when your parent's response would be to stay calm, frequently, the child will stay calm.

They're Learning How to navigate the planet and their Influence inside. It's hard to assign blame for your kid to get manipulative behavior, even if you'd discover this behavior to be undesirable within a grownup.

On the Topic Of adults, you might also distinguish between unscrupulousness (willful disregard for rules or morals which stand in the manner of somebody's aims) and also a complete absence of comprehension of these bounds. Though both are possibly moral breaches, the latter suggests a lack of obligation, although the former is still an intense type of egoism -- complete self-interest.

In training, this should not be an option you are able to create. Successful manipulation must demand an investigation of your activities and, in the minimum, a fair estimate of the outcomes. That means you'll have the tell

Also, making ethical decisions, according to data and attention, will permit you to rest in the knowledge that you just took responsibility for your choice and knowingly understood the results. It might keep you from creating a choice you live to repent.

The Law

Under no circumstances will it be advisable for you to violate the law enforcement and, in case you suspect that you're participating in criminal activity, such as fraud or a different kind of prohibited deception-based manipulation, then you're advised to inquire into the law thoroughly and then prevent any wrongdoing.

Ending up in prison is almost surely not a means to attain your own targets, and the perfect approach to steer clear of jail would always be to not violate the law.

Verbal Vs Non-Verbal Communication

Verbal Communication

Whenever messages or data is traded or imparted through words is called verbal correspondence. Verbal correspondence might be two sorts: composed and oral correspondence. Verbal correspondence happens through up close and personal discussions, bunch talks, advising, talk with, radio, TV, calls, updates, letters, reports, notes, email and so forth.

Whenever messages or data is traded or imparted without utilizing any verbally expressed or composed word is known as nonverbal correspondence. Non-verbal correspondence (NVC) is generally comprehended as the procedure of correspondence through sending and accepting silent messages. Non-verbal correspondence is an incredible munitions stockpile in the up close and personal correspondence experiences, communicated intentionally within sight of others and saw either deliberately or unwittingly. Quite a bit of non-verbal correspondence is accidental individuals are not in any case mindful that they are sending messages. Non-verbal correspondence happens through signals, outward appearances, eye-to-eye connection, physical closeness, contacting and so forth.

Non-verbal communication

Is anything that does not have to do with your speech, when you communicate non-verbally, you are doing so with your body language. Non-verbal communication is older than history. It is the most primitive type of communication around. Animals may not have a complex language to go off of like we do, but they are still very much able to communicate with other people. This is why non-verbal communication will be where we start. You need a good handle on what people say with their bodies before you get into the much trickier topic of what they are trying to say with their voice.

Body language is a much better indicator of a person's true feelings towards an event that is taking place or toward the people in the room. You can pretty easily hide your true feelings with your voice and say the right words to brush it all away. However, there will always be tip-offs related to how you are moving your body.

Movement is the biggest part of communication. You need to keep an eye on everything from the person's hands to their eyes, feet, up to their chest. It can feel a little overwhelming. This is a lot of information to take in and not a whole lot of time to master it. If you feel like you are a little overwhelmed, just keep in mind that you already have a solid background in this. You have been communicating with others and reading their communications, both verbally and non-verbally, your entire life.

Keying into non-verbal communication allows you to read people silently. Even if the person is not speaking to you or you cannot hear them, you can still figure out what their general disposition is. Being able to silently read people is an incredible talent.

These are all things you know subconsciously. You just need to bring that all to the surface and begin to understand the inner workings of these things. Do not feel discouraged by all of the information. You bought this book so that you could not only read it but also keep it as a reference as you make your way through the world of analyzing people. None of this information is going to stick with you immediately.

Knowing your audience is a huge part of making friends and making sure they stay as your friends. It is also a large part of keeping people, even those you do not happen to know, interested and engaged with what you are saying. If you are going to address a crowd, for example, you need to know how to read the room and figure out how to tackle your speech or toast.

It is vastly easier to do once you have a solid handle on cold and speed reading.

We all know how nerve-wracking it can be to have to face groups of people. Nobody wants to put themselves in a situation where they are in front of a large crowd of other human beings who are all just waiting for them to slip up. That is how it feels, anyway.

However, there is a certain kind of stress being one-on-one with somebody can bring. Reading a room is great, but knowing your audience is not just about rooms of people. It is also about being able to figure out whether you are aiming to please the person you are talking to, or whether they are not going to like or pick up on your message. This is why you need to understand non-verbal communication–it helps you to key in on the person's needs.

Everybody needs something different. Depending on our personality types, whether you are looking at the Myer-Briggs or a different form of categorization, there will be different styles on how you tackle conversation. Some people will be receptive to you joking around with them and adding humor to your approach. Others will be better suited to a serious conversation with a point-blank premise laid out clearly before them. It depends on the person; that is why reading them is so necessary.

Understanding The Self - What Does My Behavior Display

S elf-understanding or self-perception/awareness is critical to the analysis of personal behavior. If all forms of non-verbal communication must be interpreted in the light of the personalities and behaviors of the communicators, then it is important to understand the self and to be aware of our peculiar tendencies and baseline behaviors.

Many people are guilty of sending the wrong signals, or signals that do not necessarily align with their immediate intentions, and this boils down to a lack of understanding of themselves and what their behavior displays every time. For instance, under normal circumstances, a man who expresses love and interest in a particular lady would want to 'pursue' her until she yields. Even if the lady likes him from the onset, she will likely be inclined to hide her feelings and play 'hard-to-get' for a period, before eventually reciprocating the affection. Therefore, her eventual yielding and the associated behaviors are exhibited as a matter of choice and satisfaction, and not unconsciously. This is the typical progression, but there are exceptions. This standard is only exhibited by those who understand themselves and thus keep their behaviors in check to avoid letting off signals of love or affection too early, in order to keep the pursuer busy. However, females who are yet to come to a proper understanding of their peculiar nature may begin reciprocating the show of affection and interest too early, thus undermining the sweetness and effectiveness of the chase, and by the time they discover that they reciprocated too early, it may be too late to retract.

Instances like this and many more only serve to underscore the importance of understanding the self, and while some people are born with an innate ability to understand themselves and define their personalities, other people aren't, but can learn how to.

There are six major keys that can be used to understand the self. These keys are specific pointers to your innermost peculiarities and baseline tendencies. Note that the process of understanding the self is a protracted one, so there is no easy 'one-click' solution to it. Nonetheless, exploring these six keys could give you a great head-start down the path of understanding yourself.

Your values

What are your values? Your value system defines basically everything you do and also how you do it. Your values are also greatly reflected in your behavior and disposition towards others. Ninety percent of the time (if not a hundred percent), your values are directly or indirectly reflected in your non-verbal communication approaches.

Your values are what make you tick. They are the foundation of your behavior and personality. When you do thorough introspection and discover exactly what makes up your value system, you have discovered a critical part of yourself that was perhaps unknown to you. This way, you can have a firmer handle on your behaviors and be aware of the role they play in shaping your future.

Your temperament

Since Hippocrates's theory on the four temperaments emerged several decades ago, there has been a lot of speculation about the purported effect of temperament on human behavior, and whether all humans can really be classed into either of the four temperament types. However, following extensive studies on Hippocrates' work and experiments with people, it has finally been accepted that human temperament influences several key aspects of our existence, especially our behaviors, responses, careers, and relationships with other people.

To a large extent, every behavior we exhibit is linked to our temperament, and so are our baseline tendencies. Your temperament is basically a description of your innate preferences and tendencies, and many people struggle in life like fish on land, because they are trying to function in a zone or area that is foreign to the natural preferences of their temperament type.

Your interests

What are your interests? They basically include anything and everything that has the potential to 'catch' your attention and sustain it for a period of time. Discovering and understanding your interests is the key to understanding yourself and what your behaviors may indicate. We behave differently towards things that we are interested in and things that we aren't.

The things we are interested in are things that can move us when we least feel compelled to do so. They drive our curiosity and keep us concerned and focused. They keep our brains firing impulses, and because they are a vital part of our being, they also influence our behaviors. Understanding our interests helps us know more about our behaviors and how to be more in control of them by essentially directing their expression and intensity to suit the occasion.

Your strengths and weaknesses

Your strengths and weaknesses are an important aspect of yourself and understanding them is critical to self-understanding. Your strengths include your natural abilities, inclinations, talents, character strengths like persistence, patience, loyalty and integrity, and a few others. They form your make-up and give you a sense of identity and self-confidence. Your weaknesses could also include a lack of tenacity in seeing things through to completion, or a habit of reacting impulsively to situations and circumstances.

Ignoring your strengths and weaknesses robs you of the opportunity to understand yourself and define your behaviors. When you know your strengths, you can leverage them for better results in life and in your career, and when you know your weaknesses, you can work on them to become a better person.

Your life goals

What do you want to become in the future? Why? What factors have influenced your decisions to pursue that line of career or profession? In many cases, your life goals are a direct reflection of who you really are!

The kinds of experiences that have shaped you also matter greatly. The things that matter to you matter because they have found a strong affinity within your soul, on which they anchor themselves. So, identifying what matters to you most, the experiences that have changed your life, and the things that you hold dear will offer you key insight into the real you.

Your biorhythm

This is another subtle element that defines a lot about each individual. Some people feel an energy rush when they wake up in the morning, so they work best in the early morning, while others are at their best in the late evenings or even at midnight.

Understanding this key characteristic can give you key insight into your true nature.

These six factors are the most important aspects of SELF, which must be explored and considered well for adequate self-understanding to be achieved.

Benefits of Understanding Oneself:

Some of the advantages of understanding yourself may already be obvious, but there's more!

Happiness and fulfillment: When you understand yourself, you are more likely to feel happier, more content, and more fulfilled than those who do not understand their uniqueness.

Better life outcomes: When self-understanding is achieved, you are better aware of what makes you 'tick' and what doesn't; thus, you can direct your energies, accordingly, conserving and maximizing resources at your disposal.

Immunity against negative pressure and influences: To a great extent, self-understanding helps one against the effects of negative pressure and influences from peers, society, and work. When you understand yourself, your values and your goals, you're more equipped to say 'yes' to situations and opportunities that are in alignment with your peculiarities; and to say 'no' to those that are against your values and preferences.

How To Have Hypnotic Body Language

3 Non-verbal keys for Hypnotic communication: 1-true smile and real laughter-he can remember when he was as a child when his parents invited friends for supper, when his mother always told him to make sure that he was smiling and to show his teeth when the guests were arriving (I was never cheeky enough to grow, although the man was tempted). His mother knew that smiles produced positive reactions from people on an intuitive level.

This man speaks here of a real, genuine smile. A smile from the center of your body, which reflects joy, a natural smile makes the eyes and face wrinkle; insincere people smile with their mouths alone. Genuine smiles are often from the unconscious mind; people can feel, see, and feel real. A real smile means you smile all over your face-your muscles move, your cheeks rise, your eyes shrink, and your eyebrows slightly go down.

Smile more, then. However, smile happily, fun, and joyfully. Smile in the future.

The explanation of why a photographer uses 'cheese' is because it's a term that helps you to relax your face muscles-but often it gives an insincere smile. How many photos did you see that the smiles are cheese-powered and not authentic?

Professor Ruth Campbell, University College London, says that in the brain there is a "mirror neuron" which triggers the neurology responsible for the acknowledgment of face expressions and causes an immediate, unconscious mirroring response. The world smiles at you when you smile. In other words, know it or not, very often the facial expressions we see are unintentionally expressed.

So, if you smile more often than not-people around you smile more sincerely-it means they feel better about you. You build for yourself and others around you a better immediate environment. How would you feel if you walk down the street and seeing someone with such an unhappy or cross face? Science has shown that the more you smile the more positive reactions people give you.

Would you smile more if you watch a funny movie with friends? Robert Provine found that Laughter in people in social situations was more than 30 times more likely than alone. He found that Laughter has less to do with jokes and funny storytelling and more to do with relationship building. Laughter creates a connection.

If you smile (a real smile) at another man, they almost always return the smile with a genuine smile that gives both of you and you genuinely positive feelings, because of cause and effect. This creates a cycle of comfort: you smile, and you feel the good smile, and feel good, etc.

Studies show that most meetings run smoother, last longer, have better results and improve relationships dramatically if you make a point of regularly smiling and laughing until it becomes a custom. He guesses you already knew all this-yet you really smile a lot. Recent research shows that as a kid, we smile 400% more-how often do you really smile at the world today?

2-Confidence–something that the person was obviously missing when he was younger, answering the receptionist in an embarrassing way.

I remember watching a documentary about a schoolgirl murdered in Great Britain. The girl's parents gave a press conference calling for help in the apprehension of the killer. It was the fall of the murderers. The way the father behaved at this press conference prompted the police to suspect him and to show him that he killed his own daughter at last.

Many criminals are caught not because they have clues but because they are responsible, conscious of themselves, and lack trust. These feelings are sufficiently communicated to create suspicions.

When we are emotionally congruent and trustworthy, our body language is positive and expresses it to the world.

Psychologists advise us that by modifying our physical actions, we can alter our attitudes. Thus, adopting the physiology of trust can help you appear and become more trustworthy. When you are confident and hold your body that way more often—cause and effect mean holding your body that way will lead to you feeling confident too.

I recall reading a book a little while ago, and it taught you three great ways to build confidence with your body alone: first, he suggested that you be a' front seater.' Wherever you go to movies, classrooms, meetings, and presentations, the back lines appear to fill up fastest, aren't they? Many people go back so that they aren't too visible. This often shows a lack of confidence in him. Start sitting up today, relaxed with other people's eyes, and build confidence.

Furthermore, making direct contact with the eyes tells you a lot about confidence. If someone avoids contact with the eye, we might start wondering what's wrong with them or what they must hide. Lack of eye contact may indicate that you feel weak or that you are, in some way, afraid. Conquer this and let the person in the eye look—you don't have to stare hard! Just look in your eyes to tell them that you believe you are honest, open, confident, and comfortable.

If you seem confident and think of yourself, the other person tends unconsciously to agree that there is something worth knowing about you-why should anybody else be, if you aren't confident or feel good about yourself? This is implicitly conveyed beyond conscious minds, often with these sages' good feelings. David Schwartz gave the other great tip to walk 25% faster. This man knows that his father always told him to slow down when he was taken to football to see his beloved Nottingham Forest as a boy because he was enthused and enthusiastic about their destination.

Psychologists link Slovenian stances and slowness to disagreeable attitudes towards oneself, work, and the people around us. But psychologists also tell us that by changing your posture and movement speed, you can change your attitudes. Body action is the result of mental action-and vice versa-as this man already said; cause and effect! The person with low morality is shuffling with little confidence and literally stumbles through life. Likewise, average people are on average. You can see it, and you can hear it.

Confident people travel purposefully, they have to go somewhere important, and when they get there, they will succeed. Open your chest, throw your shoulders back, lift up your head, be proud of yourself, move a little faster, and feel that your trust will grow. It doesn't have to be dramatic; just keep your body safe.

The right-hand sides of the brain-most people are right-handed, and as such, their thoughts and lives are processed on the right-hand side of their brain, and motor reactions and functional brain use reside on their brain's left-hand side.

This is debated by evolutionary psychologists; most of them think we all have six basic emotions. All else is derived from these. Those six emotions are central: Happiness, Surprise, Disgust, Fear, Rage, Anger, and Sadness.

It's worth noting here that only two of them are really good. If we are real, only one is guaranteed to be great to ourselves, isn't that? Following April's foolish day, he is reminded how much he enjoys' his surprise!

The vast majority of our thoughts in our minds are somehow negative. It is true, and bad things tend to stand out much more than the good things in our minds.

So if you respond to the right brain of anybody, you may unconsciously associate yourself in the right brain with all those emotions. You don't want to do it.

If you first meet someone to use this knowledge in life instead, put yourself, so they have to look slightly right to look at you. See your right eye when you shake your hands. He believes that this picture is so much on his website's right-hand side, that in his rooms, the man places his chair so that his customers need to look correct when we communicate, and so on.

There are three powerful things to remember when improving your success and performance without opening your mouth.

Note that if you really smile and smile with enthusiasm, if you behave with faith and connect with the right brain pieces, you start resonating far more gradually with the whole world.

How To Persuade People

D o you want to know how you can persuade people so that you can get whatever you want? Well, let's answer this question first: what makes people do exactly what YOU want?

Persuasion is motivation

Usually, the one thing that separates a successful persuasive person from everyone else is the power of influence. The following are some of the tactics that have great potential in helping you to increase your persuasive powers. These tactics are not plucked out of thin air; they have been proven through psychological research.

Instead of a thousand words

Often, when dealing with people we do and serve our interlocutors many subtle and very large signals. These gestures are perceived by our counterpart unconsciously and are fraught with a lot of limiting information. Interpreting this information will be possible after mastering body language.

Understanding nonverbal communication when communicating allows you to "read" your opponent, understand how the other person took heard, and know what his opinion is even before it is made public. With expertise in the field of the human subconscious, you can just adjust their behavior to achieve the desired outcome when dealing with other people.

Common facial expressions and gestures

The key communicative gestures and facial expressions, as a person, do not vary a lot in different countries. Someone that is happy –

smiling; someone in grief – frowning. A man in a fit of rage and anger, too, has his own distinctive facial expression. A very clear example of a universally valid, universally accepted gesture is a shrug. It is very clear for all people and means misunderstanding.

Nonverbal signs perfectly reflect the position of a person in the society, the level of education and occupation. Given the above, you must know and use the sign language so you can always put yourself at a greater advantage.

For important communications, it is required that you reduce your rate of gesture. You can use only the most basic and universal movements that accompany the phrases used when meeting or communicating with the secular.

How to persuade a skeptic - be confident and talk fast

The very best way to persuade your audience, especially if they are not agreeing with you, is to speed up your pace of talking. Listen to someone who is talking fast; don't you find it distracting? Can you hear or pick out any flaws in the argument? I thought not. The opposite is also true; when you are talking with an audience that is on your side, slow down your speech, let them hear exactly what you are saying and give them the time they need to agree with you a little bit more.

Talking with confidence is also a great way to boost your persuasive power. In fact, it has been proven beyond a doubt that confidence is even better than accuracy when it comes to earning trust from other people. Most people prefer to take advice and learn from someone who is confident, even going so far as to forgive and forget about a poor track record in someone who exudes confidence. Unfortunately, in a competitive situation, this can result in some people who offer advice, who want people to follow them, exaggerating just how confident they are.

It is a natural thing to associate confidence and expertise. If you truly know your product or service, if you are confident of the facts about the benefits, and you truly believe that it does what it says, you will be naturally confident. To successfully persuade others, you need to be able to communicate your confidence, well, confidently.

Swearing can persuade your audience

If you go overboard and litter your words with profanity, you will lose all of your credibility and any respect your audience may have had for you. Recently, researchers gathered 88 participants and split them into three groups. Each group was to watch one of three speeches, each slightly different. The only real difference was that one of the speeches included a mild swear word at the beginning of it. The second speech had the mild swear word at the end of it, and the third had none at all.

When the researchers measured the attitudes of each group of participants, they found that they were influenced the most by the speeches that included the curse word, in this case, the words used were "damn it." The use of the word "damn" resulted in the audience taking more notice of the intensity of the speech, and that resulted in an increase in persuasion. None of the three groups changed the way they perceived the speaker's credibility, just the speech they were giving, proving that a little mild swearing can do wonders for your power of persuasion.

Get them to agree with you about something

If you want to persuade someone to do what you want them to do, begin by giving them something that they can agree with.

When you attempt to sell something, be it a service, a product, or an idea, come up with a statement or a view that your audience can agree with and get it out there in the open right from the start, even if it has nothing to do with the idea you are selling.

A balanced argument is more persuasive

If what you are saying or selling is likely to inspire criticism, do not, under any circumstances, cover up the weakness or flaws in your arguments.

On the whole, people aren't stupid. Knowing how to persuade means that you are acknowledging that they know how to think if you omit to mention the other side of the argument, your audience will know that, and they are less likely to believe in what you are saying. If necessary, mention the downsides or the shortfalls in your product or service on your website.

Frame the Positive

When you emphasize the positives in your message, you will find that they are far more positive than pointing out any negative. 29 different studies were carried out on a total number of 6738 people, and the findings were that there was a slightly more persuasive advantage in giving a positively framed message than there was in a negative one.

These studies were to do with the way the participants related to the prevention of disease. The ideas promoted included encouraging people to use more sunscreen and eating a healthier diet, but the ideas behind it could be used for a much wider appeal. The researchers came up with the thought that the reasoning behind it is that people do not like to feel they are being bullied into changing the way they live or behave, so framing the message in a positive way would have more effect than banging on about the negatives.

Try it for yourself, frame your message in a more positive way and see how much difference it makes.

The Strange Paradox of Choice

Think about it – the more you have to offer the less likely people are to take you up on things. A study was carried out in a jam tasting stall, set up inside an upmarket Californian supermarket. Occasionally just 6 flavors of jam were offered while at others there were 24. Tasters were then given a voucher to go and buy some jam at a discount price.

More choice of jams attracted far more customers, but most of them only looked; very few bought any jam. The stall that offered the limited number of tastings made more sales – significantly more.

Mind Reading

The logic of many living things is quite simple. If there were no incidents, then there would be no subjects to talk about. That is, if people could not read each other's thoughts, then no one would know of such a thing as telepathy. You do not necessarily have to possess special skills to read thoughts. Many of us were already able to do so, except that it happened without us knowing, and we never realized. Remember how in some stressful situations, or there is a man with superpowers, and people start to run twice as fast to overcome fear or started to hear voices? All these examples prove once again that man has great potential. The most important thing is for this ability to manifest itself in us.

Body Language

In today's world, body language and facial expression are important but not compared to how important verbal communication is. Therefore, a great importance is attached to their interpretation. The use of a variety of gestures and facial expressions when communicating is called "nonverbal communication." It involves distinct movements, which are gestures used by man with the help of various items. Expert psychologists believe that 7% of the information is passed through speech, while 59% of the information is passed through body language. Obviously, how a person talks is a lot more important than what he says.

Often, people do not care about the expression on their faces and the gestures they make. In fact, these are not just a reflection of our perception of incoming information but can also have an impact on the interlocutor. For these reasons, the idea of body language was so widespread among politicians and big businesspersons.

Mimicry, reading "a person."

Even if a person happens to lie with words, then completely controlling his or her body language is something none of us can do.

Facial expressions - a mirror of the feelings and thoughts of humankind, through a person's face you can understand everything that is going on in the person's mind. Understanding facial expressions will help you achieve mutual understanding when communicating with one another.

Thus, wide eyes, raised eyebrows and drooping corners of the mouth are a sign that a person is surprised. Frowning brow, frowning eyebrows, narrowed eyes and tightly closed lips is a clear sign that your opponent is angry. Grief and sadness are shown by "closing" the eyes, the eyebrows coming together, with the mouth drooping to the corners. If the eyes are lit with a serene expression and barely perceptible smile at the corners of the lip, then this is a clear indication that people are currently satisfied and happy.

Understand Human Behavior Psychology & Analysis

As suggested, studying people is not reserved for psychiatrists but any other person even though psychiatrists are best positioned to analyze people. Analyzing people requires understanding their verbal and nonverbal cues. When studying people, you should try to remain objective and open to new information. Nearly each one of us has some form of personal biases and stereotypes that blocks our ability to understand another person correctly. When reading an individual, it is crucial to reconcile that information against the profession and cultural demands on the target person. Some environments may force an individual to exhibit particular behavior that is not necessarily part of their real one. For instance, working as a call center agent may force one to sound composed and patient when in real life, the person acts the contrary.

Start by analyzing the body language cues of the target person you are trying to read. Body language provides the most authoritative emotional and physiological status of an individual. It is difficult to rehearse all forms of body language, and this makes body language critical in understanding a person. Verbal communication can be faked through rehearsal and experience, and this can give misleading stand. When examining body language, analyze the different types of body language as a set. For instance, analyze facial expressions, body posture, pitch, tonal variation, touch and eye contact, as a related but different manifestation of communication and emotional status. Additionally, it would be best if you lent attention to appearance

Furthermore, observe the physical movements in terms of distance and gestures. The distance between you and the target individual is communicating communicates about the level of respect and assurance that the individual perceives. A social distance is the safest bet when communicating, and it suggests high levels of professionalism or respect between the participants. Human beings tend to be territorial as exhibited by the manner that they guard their distance. Any invasion of the personal distance will make the individual defensive and unease with the interaction.

For this reason, when an individual shows discomfort when the distance between communicators is regarded as social or public, then the individual may have other issues bothering him or her. Social and public distances should make one feel fully comfortable. Allowing a person close enough or into the personal distance suggests that the individual feels secure and familiar with the other person. Through reading, the distance between the communicators will give a hint on the respect, security, and familiarity between the individuals as well the likely profession of the individuals.

Correspondingly, then try to read facial expressions as deep frown lines indicate worry or over-thinking. Facial expressions are among the visible and critical forms of body language and tell more about the true emotional status of an individual. For instance, twitching the mouth suggests that an individual is not listening and is showing disdain to the speaker. A frozen face indicates that the person is shell-shocked, and this can happen when making a presentation of health and diseases or when releasing the results of an examination. A smiling face with the smile not being prolonged communicates that one is happy and following the conversation. A prolonged smile suggests sarcasm. If one continually licks, the lips may indicate that one is lying or that one is feeling disconnected from the conversation.

Relatedly, try to create a baseline for what merits as normal behavior. As you will discover, people have distinct mannerisms that may be misleading to analyze them as part of the communication process. For instance, some individuals will start a conversation by looking down or at the wall before turning to the audience.

Mildly, mannerisms are like a ritual that one must activate before they make a delivery. Additionally, each person uniquely expresses the possible spectra of body language. By establishing a baseline of what is normal behavior, one gets to identify and analyze deviations from the standardized normal behavior accurately. Against this understanding, one will not erratically score a speaker that shuffles first if that is part of his behavior when speaking to an audience.

Furthermore, pay attention to inconsistencies between the established baseline that you have created and the individual's gestures and words. Once you have created a baseline, then examine for any deviations from this baseline. For instance, if one speaks in a high-pitched voice that is uncharacteristically of the individual, then the person may be feeling irritated. If one normally walks across the stage when speaking but the individual chooses to speak from a fixed position during the current speech, then the person is exhibiting a deviation that may suggest that the individual is having self-awareness or is feeling unease with the current audience. If an individual speaks fast, but usually the person speaks with a natural flow, then the person is in a hurry or has not prepared for the task.

Correspondingly, view gestures as clusters to elicit a meaning of what the person is communicating or trying to hide. When speaking a person, will express different gestures and dwelling on the current gesture may make you arrive at a misleading conclusion. Instead, one should view the gestures as clusters and interpret what they imply. For instance, if a speaker throws the hands randomly in the air, raises one of their feet, stamps the floor and shakes his or her hands, then all of these could suggest a speaker that is feeling irked and disappointed by the audience or the message. As such, different aspects of body language should be interpreted as a unit rather than in isolation.

Then compare and contrast. For one to fully read the target person, try comparing the body language of the person against the entire group or audience. For instance, if one appears bored and other people appear bored, then you should conclude the tiredness of the person is largely

315

due to the actions of the speaker for speaking longer than necessary. In other terms, the body language of the target person is not isolated. However, if you make a comparison, and it happens that the target person's body language deviated from the rest, then you should profile the actions of the individual accordingly. Making a comparison and contrast helps arrive at a fair judgment of the target person.

By the same measure, try to make the individual react to your intentional communication. Another way of managing to read a person is to initiate communication and watch their reaction. For instance, establishing eye contact and evaluating the reciprocation of the target person can help tell more about their confidence and activeness in participating in the interaction. When an individual ignores your attempts to initiate communication, the person could be concentrating on other things, or the person feels insecure. Initiating communication is critical where it is difficult to profile a person, and one wants to convincingly read the person.

Go further and try to identify the strong voice. A strong voice suggests the confidence and authority of the speaker. If the speaker lacks a strong voice, then he or she is new to what is being presented or has stage fright. However, having a strong voice that is not natural suggests a spirited attempt to appear in charge and confident. A strong voice should be natural if the individual is feeling composed and confident in what he or she is talking about.

Relatedly, observe how the individual walks. When speaking to a target person, he or she will walk across the stage or make movements around the site where the conversation is happening. From the manner of walking, we can read a lot about the individual. Frequently walking up and down while speaking to an audience may indicate panic or spirited attempt to appear in control Speaking while walking slowly across the stage from one end to the other end indicates that one is comfortable speaking to the audience. If a member of the audience poses a question, and one walks towards the individual, then it suggests interest in clarifying what the individual is asking.

It might be necessary to scout for personality cues. Fortunately, all people have identifiable personalities, but these can be difficult to read for a person not trained in a psychologist. However, through observation, one will get cues on the personality of the individual. For instance, an outgoing person is likely to show a warm smile and laugh at jokes. A socially warm person is likely to want to make personal connections when speaking, such as mentioning a particular person in the audience. Reserved individuals are likely to use fewer words in their communication and appear scared or frozen on stage when speaking.

Additionally, one should listen to intuition, as it is often valid. Gut feelings are often correct, and when reading a person, you should give credence to your gut feeling about the person. When reading a person and you get a feeling that the person is socially warm, you should entertain this profiling while analyzing the body language of the person. While considering gut feeling, you should classify it under subjective analysis, as it is not based on observable traits and behaviors but an inner feeling.

Expectedly, watch the eye contact. Creating eye contact suggests eagerness and confidence in engaging the audience. Avoiding eye contact suggests stage fright and shyness as well as lack confidence in what one is talking about. A sustained look is a stare, and it is intended to intimidate, or it may suggest absentmindedness of the individual. If one continuously blinks eyes while looking at a target person suggests a flirting behavior. An eye contact that gradually drops to the chest and thigh of the individual suggests a deviation of thoughts from the conversation.

Additionally, pay attention to touch. The way a person shakes hands speaks a lot about their confidence and formality. A firm handshake that is brief indicates confidence and professionalism. A weak handshake that is brief indicates that one is feeling unease. On the other hand, a prolonged handshake, whether weak or strong, suggests that the person is trying to flirt with you, especially if it is between opposite sexes. Touching someone on the head may suggest rudeness and should be avoided.

Finally, listen to the tone of voice and laughter. Laughing may suggest happiness or sarcasm. Americans are good at manifesting sarcastic laughter, and it is attained by varying the tones of the laughter. The tone of the voice tells if the person is feeling confident and authoritative or not. Overall, a tonal variation implies that the individual is speaking naturally and convincingly. A flat tone indicates a lack of self-confidence and unfamiliarity with the conversation or audience and should be avoided.

Controlling Your Body Language To Send Out The Right Message

The thing that we need to focus on now that we know a bit more about body language and how to read it in your own target is how to use these same techniques for your own. If you are able to master your own body language and use it in the proper manner, you will be able to send out the right message to the target every time and will ensure that you will be able to get the target to feel comfortable with you and ready to do what you ask.

Even though the target is not going to necessarily realize they are reading your body language, there are certain things that you can do and say in order to get them to follow you, and your body language is something that you can control to make this happen. There are a few different parts of your body language that you are able to focus on, and these include:

Watch your eye contact. The first thing that you want to focus on when it comes to your own body language is eye contact. You want to pick out eye contact patterns that show you are interested in the other person, and that they have all of your attention, but not so intense that you are staring them down and making them feel uncomfortable.

What this means is that the individual will need to focus their attention mostly on the target, but an occasional glance away and a steady amount of blinking can help. This will ensure that you are able to show the target that you are interested in them, without overdoing it and scaring the target away because the eye contact is too intense.

Pay attention to your tone of voice. Your tone of voice is going to depend on the message that you want to get across. If you are trying to be somber and serious the voice is going to be a little bit softer and lower. If you want to be aggressive, then the voice tone is going to be a bit louder and kind of harsh. If you are really excited about an opportunity that you are talking about with your target, then you will want to have a louder but pleasant voice to help get this point across.

Before you give off any message to your target, think about the tone of voice that is going to be the most appropriate for the situation. Then practice a bit to make sure that your tone of voice is going to shine through, and get the message across, so you are more likely to manipulate the target when you are trying to work with the target.

Keep that smile out. Nothing is going to help grow your connection with the target and get them to trust you more than working on that smile. A true and genuine smile is going to make a world of difference in how much the other person likes you. This can take some time though. There is a difference between a real smile and a fake smile, and while not everyone is going to be able to tell the difference, there are going to be some people who can tell, and you want to make sure that your smile is attracting your target, rather than turning them off.

A real smile is going to use the whole face. It turns up the corners of the mouth, adds in little crinkle lines by the eyes and mouth, and even the eyes seem to smile. A fake smile is not going to look the same, and when you get a chance to compare them both, you will start to see the difference. You want to make sure that you are always showing off that real smile, rather than the fake one, and see what a difference this is going to make. Practice for a bit each day in front of a mirror to help you get this done.

Use a firm handshake. Any time that you meet someone who is your target, or someone who is a potential target, make sure that you greet them with a nice handshake. You can tell a lot about a person based on their handshake and you want your target to feel like you are strong, friendly, and confident someone they can really trust. If you have struggled with this one in the past, then do a bit of practice before you work on manipulation.

Use gestures, but not too much. Gestures are going to be your best friend when it comes to manipulation. Using just the right amount is going to help you to really get your point across and will ensure that you are able to add something to the conversation. You don't want to go too crazy with this though. If you add in too many gestures, gestures that are too big and grand, you will end up making it too much and bring into question some of the things that you are saying to them. You want to use these gestures sin a way that helps you to really get your point across and to draw the target in, so use them at the right times. If you can't figure out the right balance, it is often better not to use them at all.

Consider the direction your body is facing. Another part of body language that we need to focus on is the direction our bodies are facing. If our bodies are facing towards our target, it is going to help show that you are confident, that you are caring, and can show your target that you are actively taking an interest in them and that you want to hear more from them. When the target feels like you are paying attention, rather than focusing on the thoughts in your own head or giving in to all of those distractions, you will find that the connection you need can be formed in no time at all.

What happens though when you turn your body slightly away from the target? This can have the opposite effect. The direction that your body is facing is going to be a clue to what holds your attention. If the body is faced with the door for example, then this is a sign that you are impatient and ready to go.

We obviously don't want that to happen, so it is better to pay attention to the direction of your body. This means that your body, including your torso and your toes, needs to be facing right to the target. This will help you to show your full attention to the target and will make sure they know they are valuable to you. While you are at it, make sure that your posture is upright and confident, and you are well on your way to getting the target to form that important connection with you.

Dress nicely. Even the clothes that you wear when you meet with the target will matter. People are going to take a look at your appearance and what you are wearing and what you look like. And if you want your target to be more likely to do what you want and go along with what you are asking, then you need to make sure that you are wearing an outfit that will impress.

The outfit that you are going to choose will depend on the target, the situation where you meet the target and more. If you are coworkers who are going out for the night for a bit, a nice pair of jeans and a nice shirt is probably enough. But if you are going to a big party then it is probably better to wear something that is a little dressier. Make sure that you never look like you have just gotten out of bed or have holes and stains and other issues with the clothes you wear. This is often enough to take the authority out of your words and can make it harder for the target to build up trust and a good connection with you.

How To Understand If A Person Is Lying

Y ou can't expect to effectively manipulate people if you can't tell when they are lying. When you try to manipulate someone, who gives you the wrong idea about themselves, you are not actually manipulating them. You are manipulating a false version of themselves.

A strategic liar thinks carefully about every lie they tell. They carefully plan each movement they make to exhibit body language; they painstakingly consider every person they interact with and what version of the truth they crafted for them. They have a map in their minds of what frames they have given to what people.

Most people aren't capable of this level of lying. It gives people too many things to pay attention to, and they simply can't keep up with it. You still have to watch out for strategic liars, because they are certainly out there.

These kinds of liars often can't be objective about their evidence. They may swear as soon as they talk or have certain giveaways for when they lie. Most of us don't recognize these people as liars, despite the fact that they are so common. We don't recognize it because to us, they just seem to be happy, positive people.

Don't misunderstand us — it's not that all bubbly, positive people are liars. Of course, not we are just making the point that this is the personality that a compulsive liar takes on. It provides a cover for their schemes.

There is a distinction between strategic and compulsive liars because they are so fundamentally different. The first group tends to be more introverted and cunning: they know exactly when to tell the truth and when to lie so that nobody catches. The second group — the compulsive liars — are basically the opposite. They may have been strategic liars at first, so they could gain some social advantage.

But they don't fit this description anymore. Most people who start as strategic liars can't keep it up because of the unending and gigantic cognitive load that it requires: the successful strategic liar must keep track of what frames they gave to which people while simultaneously giving off the appearance of an ordinary, truthful person. This simply isn't an act that your average person can get away with.

Therefore, they turn into compulsive liars. Compulsive liars compensate for their inability to keep up with every lie they have told by displaying exaggerated, confident body language. They use the techniques we have used here, except they take it too far and lose all sense of moderation. Their lies do not stop, and neither do their overwhelmingly bubbly and sanguine personalities.

They are called "compulsive" because their lies have become part of their personalities. They don't even lie to try to gain social power anymore. It is just something they can't help but do anymore. Since they no longer have control over it, they also feel the need to overcompensate for all the lies they know they are telling with their exaggeratedly confident body language.

With this important distinction in mind, it is time to get into the signs that you can use to determine whether someone you know is lying to you.

First of all, here is a useful fact you may not be expecting: research has shown that a good indicator of whether someone is lying is whether they drink coffee!

You read that right. This British study showed that people who drank coffee were more likely to be identified as liars. Of course, this could be interpreted in a variety of ways. Many people drink coffee, so we think that a fair way to interpret this is that everyone is a liar to some extent. It's no secret that each and every one of us is a liar at some level. It is almost impossible to go through life without telling some lies. That's why we start this list of "tells" for liars by saying this: you have probably told lies yourself, so start paying attention to the behaviors that you exhibit when you are lying.

Do you sound different on recording when you lie? Do you stand or sit differently? Ask yourself these questions, and it will help you figure out what other people are doing as their "tells" when they lie. This is a useful tool for you, because people are not so different from one another, and what you do as a "tell" when you lie may be a good path to figuring out what tells other people are giving.

After you know about these "tells" in more detail, take a little time and spend some time listening to other people talk. Talks to people you do not know much about, and you'll get a feel for what they are saying, and how their words sound to you.

One quicker thing for giving you these tells: there is no such thing as a 100% accurate tell for whether someone is lying. We can closely monitor someone's actions to figure out if they are lying, and we even have some good, reliable tells that usually tell us someone is lying. But that doesn't mean they are accurate every time, and this is an important thing to remember. There are some signs that are pretty huge indicators that someone is telling lies, and those are the ones we focus on here.

We said perceptual sharpness is crucial to telling liars, and that's because our unconscious minds are better at knowing than our conscious minds. This bears out in the research: when people listen to what their guts tell them — when they listen to their brain's cryptic language — they are actually great at knowing when people are lying. It's when they overthink their determination that they get bad at it. So as we give you the list, this is something you need to keep in mind.

The first one we give you, like all of them, actually needs to be taken with some conscious judgment. Behaviors like finger-pointing and embellishing can sometimes be indicative that someone is lying.

But this is why it still requires some conscious judgment: there are people who exhibit these behaviors when they are not lying. Therefore, this person might just be telling the truth while exhibiting the same behaviors they always do. However, we still consider this among our list of indicators for lying because of people who don't normally do it.

If you are talking with someone who does not normally point their fingers and add insignificant details to their stories, you are probably talking to a liar. As long as you remember the difference between these two situations, this is a good indicator of a liar.

Also, remember that someone who doesn't do these two big indicators may still be lying. Like we said, most people who are lying are compulsive liars who are not this skilled, but there are liars who have gotten so good at it that they have stopped giving so many tells that they are lying.

If the person you are watching seems to start to do one thing, but then does another, this is hesitation. This is oscillation, and it is a good indicator that the person may be a skilled, strategic liar. They are hesitating because they are about to do one thing, but they get scared that they will give away that they are lying, so they start to do another.

Here is a good example of this. The person may be talking about something, but they suddenly stop. In a split second, they are talking about something else. In most cases, you might not even pick this up as suspicious. They try to start up the new topic so quickly that you don't even realize what they are doing. But the truth is most people who are telling the truth don't do something like this. People who tell the truth don't care about what topic they are talking about. They will just talk without thinking about it, because they don't have to keep track of whether they are lying or not.

This is not the case for strategic liars. They are very much aware of what lies they are telling and how to tell them in an effective way. Sometimes they start a conversation topic but realize suddenly that this topic might make something sensitive come up that could reveal them as a liar — so they start talking about something else. There aren't many tells for strategic liars, but this is a very good one.

Strategic liars start conversations or engage in open discussion with their target a couple of times, and when they finally make the decision that they are not going to tell the truth. There is a "bounce back" period where they get energized from the excitement of the initial attraction. When you catch them in the "bounce back" period, this is where you caught those changing topics. You have caught the hardest liar to catch if you do this successfully.

The rest of these tells are more focused on the compulsive liars who are less careful and easier to spot. This one is simple: if someone is turning their head a lot and if they're doing it quickly, that is a sign they are probably lying. Compulsive liars do this because they are highly alert, not wanting to be caught,

You should also watch out for how quickly someone is breathing. People who breathe quickly are likely to be liars. They do this for a similar reason as to why they jerk their heads quickly — they are nervous and alert. When people are nervous about being caught in a lie, they need more oxygen, so they need to breathe more heavily.

This tells is especially useful because people can't control it. You can't control how much air you need, so it is not something you can simply choose to cover up. Breathing is unconscious, so if you need more air, you will just breathe more heavily without being able to control it.

A change in breathing itself may be hard to notice since it is pretty quiet even when it gets deeper. But you can still pay attention to things like whether the potential liar is raising their shoulders more or if their voice sounds different. It can be obvious sometimes if someone is running out of breath in the middle of a sentence. This isn't something that normally happens with someone who is telling the truth. If someone is running out of breath while they speak, this is a pretty good indicator that they are laying.

Someone who keeps saying the same thing might be making a bold attempt to make you believe something is true. It is actually an effective strategy from an NLP perspective since repetition will get something into someone's mind, whether they like it or not. However, it is pretty sloppy if done incorrectly, because people can tell when you keep saying the same thing.

As a psychology manipulator yourself, you know this: if someone keeps repeating themselves, they are trying a little too hard to make you believe something. They are trying very hard to make you accept their frame. It could be a method for them to stall for a while they try coming up with a new technique for mind controlling you.

All About The Mind

Use your left index finger to point to your brain. Easy, right, now, point to your mind using the same finger. You probably hesitated because you never realized there is a difference between the brain and the mind. While it is quite easy to pinpoint the physical location of the brain, it is rather difficult to understand where the mind exists. Understandably, all those who don't have a degree in neurobiology would use the terms brain and mind synonymously. You talk about feeling, thinking, remembering, and dreaming but when using these terms, you are not referring to your brain. When using the mind to describe something, you might say, "I recognized my babysitter in a crowd last week because she was wearing a long necklace, which is so weird that I remember it now."

You would not say, "A stream of photons appeared on my retina, triggering the optic nerve to carry an electrical signal with it to the lateral geniculate body and then the primary visual cortex. These signals were sent to my striate cortex, where the color and orientation of the image were determined. Then this signal was sent to my inner temporal and prefrontal cortex where the object was recognized from my memories, causing me to recognize my babysitter." Now, this is an instance of brain talk. There certainly exists an interconnection between the brain and the mind. The mind is believed to be identical to one's feelings, beliefs, thoughts, memories, and behaviors. It is not made of any physical materials, but it is incredibly powerful.

The brain is made of soft tissue, weighing about 3 pounds, and is present within the skull. It is the physical source of the mind. If you have a specific thought or feel an emotion, it is because your brain has relayed an electrical signal along a string of neurons, and these neurons provide certain neurochemicals to cause the specific thought or emotion. It is almost the way a runner in a relay race hands over the baton to the next runner.

Computer needs hardware to work, and hardware requires software to function. The hardware will be rendered useless without the software, and the software cannot work without the hardware, etc. So, in this scenario the mind is the software and the brain the hardware. However, the difference between these two concepts is more complicated than that comparison and these terms have overlapping meanings.

You might have come across stories about the unbelievable powers of the mind, from miraculous remissions of chronic illnesses via mind and body interactions to Herculean feats of strength during a moment of panic and showing incredible perseverance during hardships. It is also responsible for significant insights and epiphanies that seem to appear out of the blue with new creative and inventive ideas. Therefore, it is not surprising that in quiet moments, we often think about the meaning of life and our place in the universe. Any thoughts about how wonderful certain food tastes to how beautiful nature looks are questions that often lead to a deeper one - what is the mind and what power does it have? Philosophers and great thinkers throughout history, as well as scientists in the modern era, have been trying to answer these questions. It is an orthodox belief in the scientific community that the mind or consciousness is a byproduct of all the electrochemical activity taking place in the brain. Now, this is just a belief and hasn't been proven yet but there is plenty of debate in the scientific community. Rupert Sheldrake, a visionary biologist, thought that the mind being present in the brain is a principle that people accepted without question. Sir Julian Huxley, a popular biologist during the 1900s, was asked whether the brain was a good way to describe the mind. He answered that the brain is not the only thing responsible for the mind. Even though it is the precursor for its manifestation, he believed that when the brain is isolated, it is merely a biological organ that is rendered meaningless the way an isolated individual is.

There is no doubt the brain is important for the proper functioning of certain aspects of the mind. For instance, any damage to the brain, injury, or illness, can affect one's ability to remember, reason, think logically, and so on. However, there are frontier scientists who believe the mind is not entirely dependent on the brain for its existence. The mind seems to exist beyond the brain, and even outside the physical body. After all, the concept of collective and global conscience does exist. Frontier science believes the mind must be considered to be a form of energy and information that is not only spread through every single cell in the human body but beyond the body and connects to the entire universe and everything present within.

So, this belief tells us the brain, and, through extension, the mind is not just restricted to the skull. These days, the paradigms of biology are slowly changing, especially about the different chemicals released by the brain. Depending upon the way you think and feel the brain produces certain biochemical. This biochemical are known as neuropeptides and often dubbed as molecules of emotion. They're essentially messenger molecules, and how your thoughts transform themselves into these molecules affect your entire body.

For instance, whenever you feel anxious, your body produces its own type of Valium to calm you down. When you feel exhilarated, it produces a molecule known as interleukin 2. The levels of interleukin-2 reduce whenever you feel stressed. Why does all this matter? Well, interleukin-2 is an immune system booster and is believed to have certain anti-cancer properties. Stress tends to reduce the levels of this helpful chemical and thereby compromises your immune system. It certainly is a good reason to maintain a more positive attitude in your life and take less stress.

At least on the molecular level, your mood directly affects your immune system.

Every thought or emotion has a biochemical counterpart to it. So, your body has different chemicals designed for anger, love, happiness, lust, guilt, and so on. At one point, it was believed that these molecules of emotion were manufactured only by the nervous system and the brain. However, ongoing research in this field shows other systems in the body influence every cell present within and not just the nervous system.

So, it is safe to say that the mind, in a literal sense, describes an overall body phenomenon. One can also conclude that the physical body is merely an extension of the subconscious mind. Instead of thinking of the brain as the commander and chief of the body, our emotions, perceptions, and thoughts guide the brain to produce the required molecules. Therefore, the mind works through the brain to organize and coordinate different metabolic functions required for survival. If you think of the brain as the guitar, then the mind is the guitarist playing the music reverberating throughout your body.

The Conscious and the Unconscious Mind

Low self-worth, restricting beliefs, perfectionism, procrastination, or failing to achieve are issues associated with the mindset. However, before you can learn how to do this, it helps to get a better understanding of what is going on within your head.

Let us move a little further with the hardware and software analogy. If you have a computer in your head, then the brain is the housing, whereas your mind controls this hardware. Your brain has all the wiring, processing power, connections, memory, and storage you require to function. Whereas your mind is the operating system that helps gather, store, and manage all the data using the processing resources present in the brain. The brain and the mind are two integral aspects of the same entity, and you cannot effectively operate without either of them.

The human brain contains billions of neurons, which creates the central nervous system. All these nerve cells help transmit and receive electrochemical signals that essentially form your actions, thoughts, emotions, and other automatic functions of your body. To put things in perspective, 100 billion sand grains can fill 5,000,000 teaspoons and weigh about two metric tons. Even though it is packed with over 100 billion neurons, the brain is roughly the size of a cauliflower. The thoughts produced by your mind depend on your brain software. It is believed that there are different levels of consciousness in your mind, and they are the conscious mind and the unconscious mind.

The Conscious Mind

The conscious mind accounts for less than 10 percent of the total operational power of your mind. It is responsible for the following functions:

- Gathering information

- Assessing and processing the data you collect

- Creating and noticing patterns while making comparisons

- Decision-making skills

- Enabling thoughtful responses to situations instead of reactions

- regulating short-term memory

Whenever something is present in your conscious mind, it is often deliberate, and you are always aware of it.

The Unconscious Mind

The other 90% of software your brain requires to function is your unconscious mind. It might feel a little inaccessible since you're not consciously aware of whatever goes on in there, but it is incredibly powerful. Most of the body functions are controlled by the unconscious mind like digestion, breathing, heart rate, temperature, sleeping, blinking, and so on. All these functions carry on regardless of whether you are aware of it consciously or not. You don't have to lift a finger to start any of these functions, and they go on until your last breath. The unconscious mind tries to maintain the status quo, and it is the reason why you feel uncomfortable while dealing with change. Your mind tries to steer you back to all that it is familiar with, and safe. Your unconscious mind is the center of all your emotions, creativity, and imagination.

All the habits you create and maintain are also a resultant action of this unconscious mind. However, the subconscious can be influenced by any commands given by the conscious mind. The unconscious mind also helps to store and retrieve any long-term memories. Unlike the conscious mind, which is the seat of rationalism, the unconscious is seldom rational. Your decisions and judgments don't stem from here; it merely accepts what it is told as the truth, regardless of the credibility. Once your mind accepts something to be true, all your thoughts, emotions, and behaviors will be consistent with that truth.

So, why should you feel the need to understand how the mind works? Because knowledge is power, the more knowledge you have the more control you will have over your conscious and unconscious mind. When you understand how it works, will you be able to change yourself and affect another person's train of thought. Only by learning to combine and harness the true potential of your conscious and unconscious mind, you can make things happen.

The mind is merely the manifestation of your perceptions, thoughts, memories, imagination, and determination. All of this takes place within its physical housing unit - the brain. Your mind has an awareness of consciousness that you know the ability to control what you do and know your reasons for doing the same. It gives you the ability to understand. Animals can interpret their environment but cannot understand it.

Female Dating Signs

Awoman is full of contradictions. She could show or say that she likes you, but every now and then she pulls away and her interest lessens. This is probably because she wants to know if you are interested in her beyond sexual reasons. Because many women long for a serious and long-term relationship, they don't want to appear easy. They know that if she plays hard-to-get, you will pursue her more. If not, then it only reveals that you are interested in a fling or a short-term thing. Hence, if a woman doesn't want a mere one-night stand, anticipate that her signals will be conflicting. Women also need reassurance. The reason why they are not sure if they like you is because they don't know if you will stick around. They are also concerned and afraid of expressing their feelings.

Conflicting signals mean that she shows both gestures of interest and disinterest. She can express interest with direct eye contact and lean towards you, but at the same time cross her arms. These mixed signals are very confusing and baffling. When combined, they don't form a new meaning. Rather, what you should do is analyze them independently and weigh if there are more counts of signals of interest than disinterest. If it is half and half, then you should know how to adjust the results in your favor. She usually combines body gestures because she is not sure if you are interested in her too. So reaffirm her by also showing gestures of interest.

A woman is like a book. You should read her from start to finish. Take note of her body language before she approaches, when you start talking, and when you finish. Her signals could be positive at the beginning, and then take a negative turn somewhere in the middle. If you don't take the necessary measures, there will be no happy ending. This means that she doesn't really connect with you and she can't really relate to the topic that you've chosen. Maybe you talk too much about yourself rather than talking to her. However, if she maintains the positive gestures all throughout, or lets them become even more pronounced, then the two of you are clicking and your date might even have a sequel.

The reason is that women are creatures that need emotional stimulation. She has to be able to feel something more with you for her to want to deal with you on a long-term level. She has to be stimulated with different emotions to fall for a guy.

Now the disadvantages of having just charisma are as followed. First, yes, you can sleep with women of higher sexual market value than you, but this leads to more insecurity on your part. Humans are not stupid, and we know when we are dating someone of higher or lower sexual market value than us. So, when a man dates a woman out of his league, he tries to overcompensate by giving her more attention, or by buying her gifts. It forces the woman to lose respect for him because he is acting like he is below her, and she starts to believe that he is actually below her.

The woman will now subconsciously start treating the man terribly, and in response, the man not knowing what is wrong will chase more. Now the relationship is on a downward spiral, and you end up losing the girl anyways.

If you are a guy who is naturally charismatic but lacking in the looks area, and you attract a dime, never try to overcompensate. Remain confident in yourself and treat her like any other woman, not a queen; in turn, she will stay attracted to you for longer.

Secondly, yes, women will date a man longer term that has charisma, but remember that women are also fickle creatures who love status. You must always maintain a masculine and seductive frame with a woman who thinks she is hotter than you because, in the back of her head, she is always telling herself, "I can do better."

It is not just with women, but with men also. Imagine you reading this, that you started dating a woman who was two points lower than you on a sexual scale, no matter how good she treats you, you will always say to yourself that "I can do better."

Now let's talk about looks, and its advantages. First, if a woman finds you really attractive, she will sleep with you without caring about building an emotional connection first. All you have to do is get her comfortable and don't talk your way out of sex. I firmly believe this because I deal with it regularly. I invite women straight over, and within twenty minutes of them being at my place, we are having sex.

I do this with really attractive women, not ugly women. For those of you who have been following me long enough, you have seen the quality of women I post on my Instagram. I don't believe these women are doing this with every guy, and I believe that they only do this with guys who they find really attractive. You can bet every dollar you have that every woman in your life past or present has slept with a guy on the first date before.

Secondly, with looks, women tend to shit test you less. A shit test is a test a woman throws at you to test your value. For example, let's say you are on a date with a woman, and she might say something like "those shoes you have on look funny." Now a guy who feels lucky just to be on a date with her might lose confidence and get bothered by her comment. When in fact, she might actually like your shoes but wants to see you defend yourself and stay confident.

A great way to respond to shit tests from women is to agree and amplify. If she says, "those shoes you have on look funny," you respond, "yea these are my favorite shoes, I have five pairs." Her comment to you was rude and childish, so you want to agree and amplify her statement. When you respond with "yea, these are my favorite, I have five pairs," you show her that you are not bothered by what she says and that you are confident in who you are.

The point I want to make is that when a woman finds you really attractive, she doesn't make these stupid remarks or shit test because she feels as though she is lucky to be on a date with you because she thinks you are of higher sexual market value than her.

The disadvantages of just having looks are crucial. First, yes, women will sleep with you without caring about building an emotional connection first, but the relationship has no substance. I mentioned earlier that women need to be emotionally stimulated to fall for a man, well if the guy only has looked, she will never fall for him and all the relationship will always be about just sex.

Secondly, although women will shit test you less, you can easily never see her again. I deal with this also, I have lots of one-night stands, but sometimes all the women want is just sex, and she doesn't really care to see me again. This is why she doesn't even test because she just wants dick. Crazy as it sounds, but yes guys, women sometimes just want sex and nothing more.

Personally, this doesn't bother me since I'm a guy who is not looking for a relationship, but if you are a guy who is interested in long term relationships; this is something you might have to deal with.

Now the verdict, drum roll, please... I believe in 2020 as a man; you need more looks than charisma. I'm going to be completely honest with you, gone are the days when women were pushing for relationships. Unless you have been hibernating for the last five years, I'm sure you have noticed this also. Women in 2020 just want to sleep with whoever they want, whenever they want.

So this means more women are looking for flings, not a relationship. So unless you have insane charisma, where you light up a whole room with your charm, then a woman really doesn't care. She wants the guy that gets her rocks off sexually. So if you are not an incredibly good looking guy in 2020 and you want to still sleep with plenty of beautiful women and have your pickings without paying for play, you must do this.

Facial Expressions

Your face is only one small part of your body, but it has a massive impact on what people will be able to pick up from you. While your face might be smaller than something like your stomach or the rest of your body as a whole, it's still an important part that can express a lot of very crucial signals to the person that you're communicating with. People will often look at your face more than anything. They want to look in your eyes, at your mouth and get a better understanding of what you're trying to share. Let's take a look at all the ways that your facial expressions can share greater truth about you in yourself.

Importance of Eyes

We say that the eyes are a window into the soul. That's pretty true; our eyes give a ton of information away about us. Most animals will communicate through eye contact. Our eyes are the one thing that we use to see what's around us and how we pick up on different situations. Let's first discuss what looking up might mean.

How many times have you simply looked up, but somebody else accused you of rolling your eyes? This can be a sign of discomfort. Our eyes will look for the things that are the most interesting around us. When a person looks up, it can often be because they're only looking for more information. They're looking around themselves, trying to either escape the situation by picking up on something to change the subject, or they're searching their brain for more knowledge to include in this interaction.

Looking up can also indicate that we might be trying to recall different types of information. Looking to the left or right could give a signal to the other person that we're lying.

The squinting of the eyes means that we might be trying to focus on something a little more precisely. You'll have to look at the gaze and how long it might be so that people can better understand what the

---

intention of that glare might be. Frequently, we are just like kids are like animals where if we see something shiny or pretty out of the corner of our eyes, we're going to look. It's just a natural human instinct to want to see things that are around us. To use positive eye movements on other people, you can try to notice glances. You might glance at something across the room that you want them to look at as well. Our eyes do a lot of talking to the other person without us even realizing it. If you look at something across the room, then they might be more likely to look at it as well. Alternatively, think about how somebody else might look across the room, and then you also look in that same direction. It's merely a way of our minds thinking that there's something more attractive now than when you got in the room. Even subtle glances that are less than a second can be an indication that somebody is thinking about something else. For example, if you're having a conversation with somebody and they glance rather quickly right at the front door, then it could be a sign that they're getting bored and that they want to leave. They might look at a clock because they're feeling as though time is passing too slowly. They might glance down with their hands because they're not interested in what you're talking about and are trying to distract themselves.

While eye contact is important, remember that too stiff of eye contact can also mean that they're trying too hard to show you that they're paying attention. Eye contact is still essential, but it's also difficult for those with anxiety. They might shift their eyes around simply because they aren't sure what they want to look at. In the same instance, we can also cover our eyes when there might be things that we don't want to see. If somebody is giving you bad news or shocking information, you might cover your eyes as an indication that you're not interested in seeing the truth of the situation.

Pay attention to how people use their eyes, but also consider where they're looking in the context of the location so you can better understand the intention of their eyes.

Micro expressions

micro expressions are tiny little features within our face that give us a better indication of what somebody else might be thinking or wanting to do. Whether it's a small wrinkle in their forehead or the way that they move their mouth, we can start to pick up on these tiny micro expressions to better understand what somebody is really thinking inside their head.

There are seven different emotions that we can pick up through micro expressions. These include anger, fear, disgust, sadness, content, happiness, and surprise.

These micro expressions will show people in different ways. However, there are specific indications that we can use, which will help us better understand what somebody might be feeling.

Let's first discuss anger. Anger is something that we can pick up on by the way that a person uses their eyebrows and their mouth.

If eyebrows are pointed down and inwards towards the nose, then this is a sign of anger. The lower lid might also become raised up and closing over their eyes, in a way that makes their lives look a little bit more squinted. They'll often keep their lips sucked in and tight around their mouths.

They might have a frown in the way that their cheeks are tense, and their mouths are pointing downwards. Let's move on then to discuss something that we do when something might smell bad, or if we simply don't like the information that somebody is telling us.

We can show disgust in the same kind of way that we do anger in terms of eyebrow usage. Disgust will often leave the person with their mouth hanging open a little bit more. They'll have tense cheeks and a wrinkled nose. Their face is basically recoiling away from the disgusting thing that they're hearing.

Fear is going to have similar eyebrow movements as well. However, they'll be raised extremely high and flat.

If somebody's forehead is wrinkled, and their mouth is slightly open, then this can also tell us that they are feeling fear. Look at the rest of their body to indicate if it's fear, or if it's just surprise. Surprise looks a lot like fear but a little bit more positively. When somebody is surprised, they'll have curved eyebrows versus flat eyebrows as when they're fearful. They'll have their mouth open, but they might have the corners of their mouth turned up a little bit as well.

Even when we receive bad news, we can still sometimes have a smile. The smile might manifest simply because we're trying to work through that emotion in our brain. Sadness is like anger turned downwards. You'll have those arched eyebrows; except they'll be hanging a little bit looser and closer to your eyes.

A more relaxed cheek is seen in sadness, but the corners of their mouth will also be turned down. Content is sort of like complacency. You're satisfied with the moment, but you're not necessarily happy. You feel comfortable, and you're not really angry or anything likes that. Content is when we keep our mouths flat. You might have one side or the other rose. Not in a smile just sort of half expression.

This is because we don't have that much emotion at the moment, but we're trying to show the other person what that emotion might be in our face.

And finally, let's discuss happiness. This is undoubtedly one of the easiest micro expressions we can pick up on. Somebody who's smiling is going to be a happy person. The bigger the smile, the easier it is to understand how they might be feeling. Let's take a more in-depth look into what smiling can tell us about another person.

The Influence of Smiles

Fake smiling is frequent because it's a way to make the other person know that we're okay with what's going on, but we might not necessarily fully be feeling that emotion.

You can tell somebody is fake smiling by what their eyes look like. Somebody who is fake smiling is not going to have any wrinkles in their eyes, and their eyebrows are going to be completely normal. Somebody who is genuinely smiling will have slightly raised eyebrows and lines in the corners of their eyes.

While their mouth might look the exact same, it's the top of their face that you can use to determine whether somebody's smile is genuine or not.

There are some studies that show that smiling can make you look younger, thinner, and generally like a more exciting person. Those who smile more might actually live longer. We need to conduct more research to really determine if this is the truth or if it's just coincidence. However, some research has helped us realize that people do tend to have longer lifespans based on how much more they might be smiling. When somebody is smiling, and their mouth is slightly open, then you know that they're thrilled. However, if they're smiling and their mouth is free, and they are genuinely using their eyes, it could be a sign of fear or anxiety. They might be feeling comfortable, but they're using a smile to try to suit the situation. What we have to understand about smiles more than anything else, is that the other person might not be actually that happy but they're at least letting us know that they're feeling generally good. A smile can be a potent tool so you should learn all the ways you can show one. Practice smiling in the mirror to make it look more genuine. Fake smiling isn't always the greatest if you're in a personal relationship. However, a smile can really help in a business and professional setting, it makes everybody feel better, more relaxed, calmer, and more collected (Selig, 2016).

Clues To Revealing True Intentions

When children are being evaluated for neurological challenges, one of the main observable points is their ability to maintain good eye contact. Although an intricate detail, the ability to lock eyes with someone else during conversation speaks wonders to the child's level of function. If a child is able to maintain direct eye contact throughout the course of their assessments, they are deemed high on the social spectrum. However, the inability to maintain eye contact could be a sign of autism or even social anxiety. The eyes reveal small truths to the inner workings of our biology.

Typically, what is the first thing you look at when meeting someone? Usually, their eyes reveal aspects of beauty that are attractive to first encounters. Many even remember people because of the shape, color, and size of the eyes. We are neurotically programmed to be visual creatures that make associations through what we see. Generally, these associations are labeled by what we give off. Since every aspect of the body works in conjunction with the brain, how do our eyes communicate with certain receptors?

The Eye Meets the Brain

The retina is like the gatekeeper of the eye. Everything we see, through the exchange of light, passes through the retina and is then transferred to two different aspects of the eye: rods which manage our ability to see at night, and cones which handle our daily vision activities such as color translation, reading, writing, and scanning. Various neurons travel throughout the eye and communicate with different functions within the eye to carry unique signals. These signals are then carried through the optic nerve into the cerebral cortex. The cerebral cortex is like the movie theatre of the brain. It controls our visual receptors that are responsible for perception, memory, and thoughts. When our eye sees something pleasurable, researchers have discovered that the pupil actually expands. This phenomenon proves that what we see is how we think. Through this, we can formulate opinions, draw conclusions, and even interpret body movements.

There are certain concrete directions carried out by the eyes that indicate true intentions:

Right glance: This is used to remember something, maybe a name, face, song, or book.

Left glance: This is used to remember physical features such as color, shape, texture, and other visual stimulants.

Glancing downward in a right position: This controls our imagination and what we believe something to be like.

Glancing downward towards the left: Inner communication, the conversations we have with the self.

The way our eyes work with the brain and perception is key to understanding body language. Since we use every aspect of our body to communicate, it is only natural that the eyes play a major role in this form of communication. Sure, the eyes may seem one dimensional to the untrained individual. However, their slight movements can indicate everything you need to know about a person. Let's consider a few examples.

Direct Eye Contact

Direct eye contact can mean a caveat of emotions. Surely, self-confidence is one of the primary indicators of locking eyes. When vetting for a job, recruiters will often instruct their interviewees to look the interviewer in the eye in order to display awareness. This shows the interviewer that you aren't intimidated and can take on any task. Similarly, animals utilize eye contact when interpreting dominance. For example, a trainer will often look at a dog in the eye that he is training in order to establish dominance. By the trainer locking eyes and refusing to move, the dog will know to listen to his commands. Humans also communicate via dominant signals. Direct eye contact trumps fear. It shows that you are comfortable with the conversation, and it even indicates interest.

In addition, balance is the key to everything. Too much direct eye contact could prove to be intimidating to the receiving individual. This intense stare could cause others to feel uncomfortable, with them maybe even questioning your overall sanity. Imagine engaging in a conversation with someone who never stopped looking into your eyes. Even when you looked away, their eyes were still locked on yours. Surely, you would chalk them up to be extremely strange. It's always important to be cognizant of what your eyes are doing as staring, in some cultures, could be viewed as rude.

Looking Away

When a person avoids eye contact, this is typically a sign of low self-confidence. The person may be uncomfortable with the conversation, person, or environment they are in. In addition, anxiety surrounding social settings can make a person apprehensive about locking eyes with someone they don't know. Avoiding eye contact also signals inner conflict. Perhaps they are fighting against subconscious urges of attraction; therefore, they avoid making eye contact; or maybe they are hiding something that heightens their anxiety. This doesn't indicate that a person is devious or even untrustworthy. They may suffer from debilitating self-consciousness that overwhelms their disposition.

Dilated Pupils

The pupils generate intricate signals that identify even the smallest of changes within the body. Studies have shown that when people are presented with a challenging question, their pupils grow larger. When the brain is forced to think beyond its capabilities, the pupils actually become narrow, according to a 1973 study. The pupils are also key indicators of stress on the brain. Health care professionals will shine a small flashlight into the eyes of their patients in order to check the normality of their pupils. If the pupils are balanced in size and react to the shining light, the brain isn't experiencing distress. However, any imbalance could indicate a serious brain injury.

As mentioned earlier, dilated pupils express extreme interest, even agreement. When you see or hear something that sparks your attention, your pupils will dilate almost immediately. The same occurs when a person is shown a representation of something they agree with. In 1969, a revered researcher sought to prove the notion that the pupils' dilation can reveal political affiliations. By showing participants pictures of political figures they admired, the participants' eyes dilated. However, when shown an opposing photo, the pupils grew narrow; often snake-like.

What Our Visual Directions Indicate

The positioning of our eyes and what we choose to focus on during a conversation can speak volumes. For instance, glancing downward could indicate shame, even submission. When children are being reprimanded, they are often looking down to show their personal disdain for their behavior. In ancient Chinese culture, one typically looked down in a submissive form to show respect to those in authority, on the contrary, glaring upward indicated traits of haughtiness. It is often associated with being bored or not wanting to engage in the activity at hand, in addition, looking up signal's uncertainty. Movies and television shows may depict a teenager taking a test and looking up because they are unaware of the answer.

Sideways glances are often cueing for internal irritation. For example, when a co-worker you dislike walks into the room, you may inadvertently look at them sideways, simply because they are the bane of your existence. This can also occur when engaging with individuals who annoy you. The takeaway from the sideways stare is discontentment. When you see something that just isn't right, or even a sneaky individual, you may give them the side-eye. This demonstrates total repulsion for their attitude, reputation, or even their expressions.

Many would attribute squinting to being unable to see. While true, a squint can also mimic signs of disbelief or confusion. One may hear something and want more information. Thus, they squint their eyes while listening; it's almost as if they are saying, "I don't believe you...I need more answers!"

Stress can induce quick blinking which causes a person to go into frenzy. You may notice a person rapidly blinking while moving frantically to finish a task. This could be accompanied by sweat or trembling. On the contrary, excessive blinking could be a subtle sign of arrogance. A boss, for example, may blink rapidly while speaking to an employee in an attempt to dismiss their conversation. This fast action blinking essentially blinds the boss from the employee for less than a second, indicating that they would rather be engaging in something else.

A direct gaze paired with a lowered lid and head indicates extreme attraction. It's almost likened to a "come hither" invitation between mates. This gaze is heightened through sexual attraction and may even induce pupil dilation.

Inability to Focus and Attention Deficit

An eye nystagmus identifies how long it takes the body to focus on one point after undergoing extreme movement. If a person has a nystagmus lasting longer than 14 seconds, they may have challenges with keeping focused. One academic facility tests the accuracy of a child's nystagmus by spinning them a number of times and having them glance up towards the ceiling. The eyes then move rapidly, sometimes dilating, then narrowing. The longer it takes the child to stabilize is documented. They further engage in this spinning activity weekly with the hopes of strengthening their ability to remain focused on one thing despite many distractions. As they continue to grow a tolerance, their eyes will stabilize in a lower amount of time. The goal is to strengthen their ability to dismiss outward distractions which will help with attention deficit disorder. The movement of the eyes tells trained professionals exactly how much assistance a child will need and in what specific area. Aren't the eyes magnificent?

Our eyes open the door to many revelations of the self. You are able to gain a psychological perspective on how you perceive yourself and others by a simple glance! Irritation, lust, attraction, and even doubt can be detected by paying close attention. Since the eyes have a direct pathway to the brain, it is only natural that they are the gatekeepers of the soul. By implementing these quick tips into your social life, you will have the grand ability to analyze a person in a complex manner. Of course, the eyes are also home to detecting deceit. As we continue to travel through our body language adventure, we will soon learn how the eyes can reveal the trustworthiness of an individual.

Types Of Personality

Types of Personalities You May Come Across

The Architect

The Architects are often hailed as bookworms pretty early in their lives. They have ambitions but often choose to pursue them in private. They are dreamers yet know how to add a dash of practicality to the same. They are curious about everything they come across and leave no stone unturned to gain knowledge whenever it is made available.

The Logician

Fiercely competitive and amazingly creative, the Logicians are known to be good human lie detectors. They can make a guess when the person talking to them is not sure of what he's saying. The Logicians usually use their friends as guinea pigs to test their half-formed theories. They are constantly trying to spot patterns in places that offer none.

The Commander

Among all, this is the person who will take a stand, put his foot down and lead the pack back home. He/she is the lone beacon of hope in a stormy night. This individual is strong-willed, intelligent, and willing to make bold decisions when the situation so requires. They love a good challenge and do not back off when adversities pile on. They can often come across as too loud and dominating, and perhaps even obnoxious. However, when allowed to become the leader of the group, they can take charge of the front.

The Debater

The Debaters are the most analytical sorts. They would not take an issue lying down. The pros and cons of a subject are well assessed and processed through their mental faculties before they formulate an argument. If you tell them a fact, they won't accept it right away. They will do a fair amount of research and attempt to disapprove an already established and recognized postulate.

The Advocate

The Advocates are the most argumentative type of the lot. Much like the debaters, they won't accept a fact for what it is. They have solid opinions about issues they connect with on an emotional level. They are the ones who are ready to make a bold decision and stick to it throughout.

The Mediator

Out of all the personality types, this is the most helpful one. They are always engrossed in their daydreams while at the same time being aware of what's going on around them. They may not come across as observational due to their delusional selves, but they are always watching. They have a tendency to reduce their keen observations into writing, which also explains why many of this personality type end up becoming poets and authors.

The Protagonist

The talker of the group, the Protagonist, leads from the front and hogs the limelight of a room right away. The best way to describe this personality type is the phrase "speak before you think." Often, Protagonists may end up making fools themselves, but that does not prevent them from being blunt about their opinions.

The Campaigner

These are the socially aware people in the group. They will keep their peers updated about what's happening in society while vehemently taking a cause seriously. They are always eager to help those who are in dire need. They care about their causes a lot and hence can be seen marching in parades and protests.

The Logistician

This group of individuals is all about facts. They rely more on statistics than emotions. They won't mind throwing an algorithm book in your face if you try to gain higher ground in an argument by citing humanitarian reasons. They keep a group grounded by sticking to scientific empirical evidence and numbers.

The Defender

They are the folks who stay very much connected to their loved ones. They do not care whether the people they love are wrong. If they are in trouble, the Defenders will risk everything to bail them out. It does not matter to a Defender whether the people they care about have been defaulters. The emotion of care is strong with this group.

The Executive

Some people are just good at managing things and people. These are the Executives. They may not be the most intelligent bunch of the lot, but when it comes to organizational skills, no one can beat them. They know how to handle things and create a smooth pathway for them to run. Being a natural at management skills, it is their pleasure when they are asked to look after stuff like gatherings, events, and meetings. Their strengths lie in coordinating dynamics, logistics management, and allocating resources.

The Consul

If there exists a trait that distinguishes people from this group, it is Popularity. These folks comprise the cheerleading teams and the basketball players. They have a social influence that is unparalleled. They may not initiate or continue an intellectual conversation, but they are amazing at encouraging people to do the same. You won't find such people being sarcastic, witty or quick to provide a retort. They are simple folks who just want to grab the limelight.

The Virtuoso

People belonging to this group can often be seen playing with things. The engineers, musicians, mechanics, and builders all belong to this type. These groups of people are usually talented in the fine arts, music, and playing instruments, etc. If they do not like the make and build of a structure, they will want to make it better by dismantling it and putting it back together, except in a better way this time around. They take the risk of being different by defying the set standards of beauty and arrangement. They experiment with what has always been there.

The Adventurer

You cannot put these folks in a box. You can never find them working in a cubicle job. They feel suffocated sitting at a desk, trying to draft an agreement that they don't even have an interest in. They want to explore the world and see places. They want to experiment with society and defy all the conventions. There is an element of spontaneity in them, and that is what makes them quick on their feet. They are the first ones to raise hands for a trekking trip with friends.

The Entrepreneur

You can spot them at parties, a self-made mindset, walking from one group of friends to another. They can never stay in one place to listen to the latest political news. They would rather talk about things that are artsy, flamboyant and superfluous. They have traits of a leader and desire independence and believe in working for themselves and providing services as opposed to work for an employer.

The Entertainer

The life of the party, in its true sense, is the Entertainer. They are full of energy as they talk, sing, dance, and gossip their way around the group. They do not give a damn about who is listening to them. Their sole purpose of the day is to please and interact with as many people as possible.

The Diplomats

The personality of the Diplomat will be a little less pushy than that of the analyzer. These are people who are likely to do more listening, but you will notice that they are reserved and tend not to speak when they don't need to. Happy and practical, these folks are the ones who know who they are. They tend to sit quietly in the limelight but are not afraid to come up with solutions when these are needed and are likely to be the kind of people who can compromise to please others. They might also have their own agendas and will cheerfully lead you toward their aims without being pushy about it.

The Sentinels

When you meet characters like this, you are in no doubt at all about who is in control. The sentinels are smart, sharp and know what they are talking about. They yield authority. These are people who can delegate without a pause because they are in the know and will always choose those most capable of doing what is being requested of them. If you meet one of these, you will definitely get the impression that you are in the presence of someone in authority and their body language will be such that no one will doubt that authority. They have the ability to make people around them feel comfortable and will not misuse their authority. Thus, they emit the feeling that they can be trusted and mean what they say.

The Exploratory Character

You can usually tell this kind of character from a distance. These are people who may not conform to the usual approach. Their characteristics will be bold and noticeable but not in the same way as the sentinels. They are happy to experiment and to try new things. Examples of characters that would fit into this personality profile would be entrepreneurs who are willing to take chances. They are flamboyant, and you will notice they are likely to be surrounded by people who are enthused by them.

The first impression that you have of anyone depends upon your background as well as theirs. You have certain expectations of people and not everyone is going to fit the mold. The wider you travel, the easier it is to distinguish the different characters that pass through your life, since you will have been exposed to many kinds and may not have taken much notice in the past.

Dark Seduction

eople with negative personalities are also in need of love. But thanks to their personality traits, they hardly approach it the right way. People with negative personalities use a number of sneaky tactics to warm their way into a person's heart. But the success of their dark seduction tactics boils down to the person that they decide to pursue. A perfect victim is a person who appears empty and isolated, or who can be easily isolated. The negative individual is likely to fail when they go for someone who's stacked with confidence and has their feet on the ground and sustains many relationships with different people.

The following are some of the dark tactics that predators use in seduction:

The art of indirect approach

Most people who have a hard time in seduction go into it pretty fast. They make everything clear in rapid succession. But Narcissists, Psychopaths, and Machiavellians understand the power of starting humbly. So, their approach is to start by befriending the victim and seem non-threatening at all. The victim drops their guards and believes them for a friend. However, as time progresses, the predator will start portraying themselves as a potential suitor. Initially, they give small hints, and then they become bold about it. In such a case, the victim is already so emotionally invested that it is hard for them to turn back, and they succumb to the seduction of the predator.

Giving mixed signals

When we appear in someone's life, they are obviously going to have a question mark about our intentions. Most of us fail by making our intentions too obvious. For a Machiavellian, they are masters at the game of manipulation, and they will send mixed signals, sometimes appearing soft, other times hard, sometimes appearing interested, and other times disinterested, sometimes posing as a lover, and other times posing as a friend. It's a form of psychological manipulation that makes the victim feel helpless. And once they successfully manage to confuse their victim, they now take the bold step of claiming them as their lover.

Boosting their appeal artificially

The fact is that human relationships are often based on shallow standards. A man who seems to be shunned by society will have a hard time attracting a mate as opposed to a man who seems to be pulling a lot of female attention. Since the Machiavellians and Narcissists are aware of this, they will try to pass themselves off as hot property, and this endears them to their object of interest. They achieve this by putting themselves in a class that they are not and living a fake life. But once they manage to capture the heart of their victim, the nasty truth soon comes out that they lead a fake life.

Planting the seeds of uncertainty and anxiety

It's not easy to ensnare the heart of an emotionally secure person using dark tactics. People with negative personalities know this too well and that's precisely why they try to seed uncertainty and anxiety in their victims before proceeding. The predator makes their victim feel inadequate, and at the same time, portrays themselves as the solution to their problems. Eventually, the victim gravitates toward the predator in hopes of receiving help, and then the predator will take advantage of the situation. Most people lack sufficient emotional security, and when a little pressure is applied, they always cave, and this is what makes it easy for the predator to succeed once they make their victim feel inadequate.

The art of insinuation

This is another tactic that Machiavellians and Psychopaths use to win the hearts of their targets. They understand that making open actions can easily backfire and so they focus on planting ideas on the minds of their target. Thus, they are excellent at making ambiguous remarks, retracting statements and leaving their targets in suspense. By putting a person in a continuous state of suspense through mastery of insinuation, they make them desperate, and thus they can take a bold of claiming their victim's heart. Through insinuation, they plant ideas on the victim's mind, effectively hooking them on fantasies, making it far easy to accomplish their aim.

Taking an interest in their activities

Everyone loves it when other people take an interest in what we are about and what makes us tick. So people with negative personalities know too well that by entering their victim's spirit, by making it seem as though they are interested in what they are up, their hobbies, and interests, they can easily win that person's approval and then go ahead to claim their heart. Of course, the interest that a predator shows toward the victim is fake, but since they are such good actors, it is hard for the victim to make sense of what's happening, until, of course, when it's too late.

Using temptation

We are not as strong as we might always think. Sometimes, all it takes for us to drop our standards and dignity is a temptation. Predators know too well that everyone yearns for a particular kind of life. Thus, they take it upon themselves to investigate the desires that a person holds, and they craft their temptation based off of those desires. For instance, they might walk up to their victim and say something along the lines of, "if you get into a relationship with me, I will help you build your own seven-figure business." If the person given that promise is a struggling middle-income earner, the promise of a seven-figure income is enough to tempt them into compliance.

Using unpredictability

Being unpredictable is simply being unable to guess your next move. People who are unpredictable tend to be very alluring because you hardly know what they are going to do next. Predators employ this technique too. They love to keep their victims in the dark about what action they are going to take next. Creating this scenario repeatedly makes the other person get drawn toward them. Being unpredictable creates suspense, and it allows the other person's mind to go on overdrive as they try to make sense of what's happening, and the predator has a better chance of winning their victim's heart.

Flattery

At any time, there's a lot of things happening in a person's life, thus when you approach them with boring talk, they can easily tune out. But when you say loaded phrases, get them to imagine that they are the best thing in this world, you make them have a pleasant attitude toward you, and they will accept you into their lives. This is the same tactic that a predator uses to win the affection of their victim. They tell them what they want to hear. As the victim basks in the flattering words they have been told, the predator now makes clear their intentions.

Becoming a mystery

There's nothing that pique's our attention more than a good old mystery. It makes our imagination run wild. When we meet someone and they immediately tell us the story of their lives from when they born up to now, we tend to consider them to be a bit boring. This is because we already know what they are about. But when we meet someone and we can't seem to figure them out, we are instantly hooked. Our mind keeps wondering what this person is about and we come up with various lines of thoughts as we try to analyze what this person is like. It is a bit hard to remain a mystery in this age considering the presence of social media where everybody feels compelled to post every little detail of their life. But predators have perfected the art of curating their life so that only a little bit of their life goes out. So, they end up becoming some sort of a mystery to the people they are in contact with, which can be endearing.

Vulnerability

Behavioral scientists say that we are more likely to get along with a person when we start with asking them a favor. By asking a favor from someone, you activate their empathy, and it becomes much easier to win their heart. Thus, Psychopaths and Narcissists are very good at acting vulnerable, and it makes their victims empathize with them, but since they are users, they take that as an invitation to go for whatever they want. Predators are pretty skilled at using vulnerability as a springboard to claim their victim's heart.

Isolating the victim

When someone is isolated, they are usually weak, and cannot engage their critical thinking skills quite effectively. A predator is aware of this fact and they aim to isolate their victims as it makes them agreeable. It's the main reason predators target people who seem empty. They know it is far easier to take such people into a corner and coerce them into accepting their proposals.

Analyzing People Through Their Handwriting

Every person's handwriting is known to be as unique as their personality. You can make an in-depth analysis about everything from their behavior to personality to thought process. Graphology is the science of studying an individual's personality through how they write. Handwriting goes beyond putting a few characters on paper. It is about glimpsing into an individual's mind to decipher what they are thinking and how they are feeling based on their handwriting.

Here are some little-known secrets about speed reading a person through their handwriting.

Analyzing Individual Letters of the Alphabet

The manner in which a person writes his or her letters offers a huge bank of information about their personality, subconscious thoughts and behavioral characteristics. There are several ways of writing a single letter, and every person has their own distinct way of constructing it.

For example, putting a dot on the lower case "I" is an indication of an independent-spirited personality, originality and creative thinking. These folks are organized, meticulous and focused on details. If the dot is represented by an entire circle, there are pretty good chances of the person being more childlike and thinking outside the box. The manner in which a person constructs their upper case "I" reveals a lot about how they perceive themselves. Does their "I" feature the same size as the other letters or is it bigger/smaller compared to other letters?

A person who constructs a large "I" is often egoistic, self-centered, overconfident and even slightly cocky. If the "I" is the size of other letters or even smaller than other letters, the person is more self-assured, positive and happy by disposition.

Similarly, how people write their lower case "t" offers important clues into their personality. If the "t" is crossed with a long line, it can be an indication of determination, energy, passion, zest and enthusiasm. On the other hand, a brief line across the "t" reveals lack of empathy, low interest, and determination. The person doesn't have very strong views about anything and is generally apathetic. If a person crosses their "t" really high, they possess an increased sense of self-worth and generally have ambitious objectives.

Similarly, people who cross their "t" low may suffer from low self-esteem, low confidence and lack of ambition. A person who narrows the loop in lower case "e" is likelier to be uncertain, suspicious and doubtful of people. There is an amount of skepticism involved that prevents them from being trustful of people. These people tend to have a guarded, stoic, withdrawn and reticent personality. A wider loop demonstrates a more inclusive and accepting personality. They are open to different experiences, ideas and perspectives.

If an individual writes their "o" to form a wide circle, they are most likely people who very articulate, expressive, and won't hesitate to share secrets with everyone. Their life is like an open book. On the contrary, a closed "o" reveals that the person has a more private personality and is reticent by nature.

Cursive Letters

Cursive writing gives us clues about people that we may otherwise miss through regular writing. It may offer us more comprehensive and in-depth analysis of an individual's personality.

How does a person construct their lower-case cursive "l?" If it has a narrow loop, the person is mostly feeling stressed, nervous and anxiety. Again, a wider loop can be a sign that the individual doesn't believe in going by the rule book. There is a tendency to rewrite the rules. They are laidback, low on ambition and easy going.

Again, consider the way a person writes cursive "y" to gain more information about their personality. The length and breadth of letter "y" can be extremely telling. A thinner and slimmer "y" can be an indication of a person who is more selective about their friend circle. On the other hand, a thicker "y" reveals a tendency to get along with different kinds of people. These are social beings who like surrounding themselves with plenty of friends.

A long "y" is an indication for travel, adventure, thrills and adventures. On the other hand, a brief cursive "y" reflects a need to seek comfort in the familiar. They are most comfortable in their homes and other known territories. A more rounded "s" is a signal of wanting to keep their near and dear ones happy. They'll always want their loved ones to be positive and cheerful.

They will seldom get into confrontations and strive to maintain a more balanced personality. A more tapering "s" indicates a hard-working, curious and hard-working personality. They are driven by ideas and concepts. Notice how cursive "s" broadens at the lower tip. This can be a strong indication of the person being dissatisfied with their job, interpersonal relationships or life in general. They may not pursue their heart true desires.

Letter Size

This is a primary observation that is used for analyzing a person through their handwriting. Big letters reveal that the person is outgoing, affable, gregarious and extrovert. They are more social by nature and operate with a mistaken sense of pride. There is a tendency to pretend to be something they aren't. On the contrary, tiny letters can indicate a timid, reticent, introvert and shy personality. It can indicate deep concentration and diligence. Midsized letters mean that an individual is flexible, adjusting, adaptable and self-assured.

Gap between Texts

People who leave a little gap in between letters and words demonstrate a fear of leading a solitary life. These people always like to be surrounded by other folks, and often fail to respect the privacy and personal space of other people. People who space out their words/letters are original thinkers and fiercely independent. For them, they place a high premium on freedom and independence. There is little tendency for being overwhelmed by other people's ideas, opinions and values.

Letter Shape

Look at the shape of an individual's letters while decoding their personality. If the writing is more rounded and in a looped manner, the person tends to be high on inventiveness and imagination! Pointed letters demonstrate that a person is more aggressive and intelligent. The person is analytical, rational and a profound thinker. Similarly, if the letters of an alphabet are woven together, the individual is methodical, systematic and orderly. They will rarely work or live in chaos.

Page Margins

If you thought it's only about writing, think again. Even the amount of space people leave near the edge of the margin determines their personality. Someone who leaves a big gap on the right side of the margin is known to be nervous and apprehensive about the future. People who write all over the page are known to have a mind full of ideas, concepts and thoughts. They are itching to do several things at once and are constantly buzzing with ideas.

Slant Writing

Some people show a marked tendency for writing with a clear right or left slant, while other people write impeccably straight letters. When a person's letters slant towards the right, he or she may be affable, easy going, good natured and generally positive. These people are flexible, open to change and always keen on building new social connections.

Similarly, people who write slanting letters that lean towards the left are mostly introverts who enjoy their time alone. They aren't very comfortable being in the spotlight and are happy to let others hog the limelight. A straight handwriting indicates rational, levelheaded and balanced thinking. The person is more even-tempered, grounded and ambivalent.

There is a tiny pointer here to avoid reading people accurately. For left-handed people, the analysis is the opposite. When left-handed people have their letters slanting to the right, they are shy, introverted and reserved. However, if their letters slant to the left, they may be outgoing, gregarious and social extroverts.

Writing Pressure

The intensity with which an individual write is also an indicator of their personality. If the handwriting is too intense and full of pressure (there is indentation), the individual may be fiery, aggressive, obstinate and volatile. They aren't very open to other people's ideas, beliefs and opinions. There is a tendency to be rigid about their views.

On the contrary, if a person writes with little pressure or intensity, they are likely to be empathetic, sensitive and considerate towards other people's needs. These people tend to be kind, enthusiastic, passionate, lively and intense.

Signature

A person's signature reveals plenty about an individual's personality. If it isn't comprehensible, it is a sign that he or she doesn't share too many details about themselves. They fiercely guard their private space and are reticent by nature. On the contrary, a more conspicuous and legible signature is an indication of a self-assured, flexible, transparent, assured, confident and satisfied personality. They are generally content with what they've accomplished and display a more positive outlook towards life.

Some people scrawl their signature quickly, which can be an indication of them being impatient, restless, perpetually in a hurry and desiring to do multiple things at one time. A carefully written and neatly organized signature is an indication of the person being diligent, well-organized and precision-oriented.

Signatures that finish in an upward stroke demonstrate a more confident, fun loving, ambitious and goal-oriented personality. These people thrive on challenges, aren't afraid of chasing these dreams. Similarly, signatures that finish with a downward stroke are an indication of a personality that is marked by low self-esteem, lack of self-confidence, low ambition and a more inhibited personality. These folks are likelier to be bogged down by challenges and may not be too goal oriented.

Stand Out Writing

If a particular piece of writing stands out from the other text, look at it carefully to understand an individual's personality.

For example, if the text is generally written in a more spread out and huge writing, with only some parts of the text stuck together, the person may most likely to be an uncertain, dishonest or mistrustful individual, who is trying to conceal some important information.

Concluding

Though studying an individual's handwriting can offer you accurate insights about his or her personality, it isn't completely fool proof. There are several other factors that are to be taken into consideration to analyze a person accurately. It has its own shortcomings and flaws. At times, people may write in a hurried manner, which can impact their writing. Similarly, the way people construct their resume or application letter may dramatically vary from the manner in which they may write a to-do list or love letter.

If you want an accurate reading of someone's personality, consider different personality analysis methods like reading verbal and non-verbal communication techniques. Various techniques may offer you a highly in-depth, insightful, precise and comprehensive method of understanding a person's inherent personality.

The Effects Of Dark Psychology

Kleptocracy

This is the process where government leaders (kleptocrats) take advantage of their powerful positions to exploit their subjects and natural resources within their area of jurisdiction to extend their gains politically and financially. These kinds of individuals depict narcissistic behavior, whereby the feeling of superiority gives them a sense of entitlement over their subjects. While considering those, it is doubtless that kleptocrats use dark psychology as a tool to receive noteworthy favors, and they bribe by using state resources to benefit themselves, their associates, or kin at the expense of their subjects.

Also, they bypass the rule of law by using their political might to pass laws that benefit them and their close constituents.

Brainwashing

Brainwashing is commonly termed as thought reform is categorized under the social influence sphere, which is generally a set of ways in which people can use mind manipulation to alter other people's behaviors, viewpoints, and attitudes. Brainwashers take advantage of their subjects by using three crucial processes—compliance, persuasion, and propaganda to change the behaviors, viewpoint, and attitude. For instance, propaganda is used to influence individuals who have no belief in the knowledge being imparted on them by trying to alter the individual's beliefs by promoting the idea that suggests, "I am doing this because it is the right thing to do."

Brainwashing is categorized as an extremely severe and dangerous method of social influence because it integrates all of the approaches named above to revamp how an individual does think without the person giving his consent or fully opting to take part.

The brainwasher needs to have total control over the individual so that the brainwasher controls the day-to-day activities like sleeping, praying, and eating of this individual. This explains why brainwashing mostly happens in prisons or insurgent's camps because the persons being brainwashed are isolated and entirely depend on the brainwasher.

Workplace Bullying

Dark psychology tactics like Machiavellianism can be used in workplaces by some employees to exploit others in a bid to advance their agendas and maintain control over others. These kinds of people tend to work under the belief that arrogance is way more efficacious when dealing with others that ethics and moral conduct are for the weak that it's better to have people fear you than love you, and that humility is a trait that should not be shown. They fail to share crucial information with others, consequently landing those that are uninformed into problems with management. They come up with unrecognizable ways of making other workers look bad to the boss. They rarely meet their obligations and are known to spread rumors that defame other people.

Lying/Exaggeration

Machiavellians tend to be at ease and more experienced at lying and are less likely, to be honest when interacting with others. These lies are essential to the liar because they give him control; they create an impression that will make you like them, and in some cases, when the liar miserably wants the lie to be true.

Usually, humans tend to treat people according to the first impression they make. Therefore, people will lie to create a favorable first impression to attract you to them and consequently make you like them. Any revelation of the truth will doubtlessly make us have a change of mind about them; hence, they use other lies to cover their first lie. Consequently, we end up falling for their lies, and before we know it, we are damaged beyond repair. This explains why some job interviewers end up giving the job to an unqualified person because they fell for his lies.

Secondly, lying is crucial to mind manipulators because they are people who fancy the idea of being in control of situations. This kind of control puts them in a position to get the type of reaction they expect from other people and consequently help them in influencing the decision of those people.

Manipulators who use propaganda know that the message they are passing across is partly or entirely not true but because they are overwhelmed by the desire to make their lies true, they lie about it. They are hopeful that repeating the lie over and over again will somehow make it true.

In other cases, people simply lie to be malevolent and cause harm to others. These kinds of people often come out at as likable and friendly but deep down, beyond our naked eyes, they harbor a lack of remorse because their primary goal is to cause harm to others.

Withdrawal

People undergoing withdrawal usually feel hopeless, doomed, or lack self-worth; they may cry from time to time and may find eating and sleeping difficult. After being subjected to obscure mind control and exploitation using clandestine techniques, people realize they have been used, and the hope and expectations they had were nothing but a short-lived dream. This feeling of betrayal drives them to blame themselves for trusting the manipulators easily and not looking beyond the manipulator's deceit.

This depression that people go through during withdrawal is often recounted as way bitter as the usual day-to-day sadness. The people who face the effects of manipulation in some instances recount those moments as an empty and desperate state, which is an entirely different feeling from what they felt before being manipulated and exploited.

It can also be characterized by a lack of energy or zeal to go on with life, especially if the manipulation affected a central part of their lives. In addition, there is a natural feeling of being let down, disenchantment, and the loss that is felt by people when a good feeling or moment turns bitter all of a sudden.

Such feelings may take a toll on the victim and drive them into taking severe measures like suicide to avoid the pain; therefore, it is vital for them to talk to a psychologist who will help them carry the burden of depression because psychologists understand your feelings and how to handle them.

Conclusion

Mind control can be carried out only when the understanding of the mind's internal operations is obtained. This can be done by providing a subject with detailed information about themselves and/or by allowing psychologists to carry out in-depth examinations. This sort of heart and mind analysis is required to understand the criteria that regulate processes that govern the actions of a particular subject. You cannot start developing any system that drives a person until you fully understand how external stimuli stimulate them.

There are tools designed to control people or specific aspects of human behavior. A single device alone is not enough for the tasks required for mental control. Several phones must be used. The growing system will concentrate on a specific parameter type. These are not limited to emotional awareness and perception. Using these instruments, one can analyze how certain stimuli are responded to, record the results of the performance of the subjects, and use them to establish control specifications. The control spec is accurate only if the issue is in the same state as the spec. The stimuli produce different outputs as the only state changes.

If the subject is aware of the study, it will not be easy to collect data. A willing question may not perform very well, even if they want to cooperate. This is evident when you measure consciousness. This is clear. To obtain an accurate result from a subject, it must be in a grounded state or an average awareness level, indicating that the examinations are unaware of them. The output can only then be used to determine control requirements. There is no way to get a subject's agreement unless they know what they agree to. It can be possible to understand theoretically what the experiment is, but it undermines the validity of the study.

During the time mind control was developed, the technology needed for such experiments was not available without the subject, today, particularly in the world of digital technology, several ways to pry an individual's heart and mind without their permission. The same innovation has also made it possible to create more powerful and effective intelligent control devices. Mind control devices should not be confused with traditional methods that people use every day. Mind control devices consist of different types of components, some of which are made from human hardware, others are social components that have specific functions that fit a particular subject, and chemicals are also standard components of these devices. A group of these components can be combined to work on a specific subject parameter. These are ideal tools not always connected by physical materials but by intent and collaboration. Many of these intelligent control devices can be created to submit certain input types of data that incite the subject to generate control specifications. These are carefully developed and maintained because they are costly and time-consuming.

When stimulated, each type of control parameter produces a different effect. The stimulation can be deliberate (performed by a human agency) or a result of relatively unintentional natural events. In most instances, certain external circumstances dominate. What we want here is the power that a human entity initiates. The switch of one type of control influences the other and causes a dynamic change of state. A person of full consciousness attracts many external stimuli. Given the possible conditions, awareness of fully human consciousness may be almost impossible.

There are interferences to be addressed to gain reliable control over the mind. Natural phenomena often present problems during the mental inspection of adverse state changes. It is essential to filter this interference. Acquired control specifications obtained by the experimentation in a grounded state can only serve as the basis of the calculation of the deviation from the grounded state performance. Filtering can be achieved by manipulating the interpretation so that the subject is grounded. Measuring improvements make it more difficult for developmental control devices. Dynamic change in control parameters involves several qualified members or multifunctional members who can manage many changes in the system.

Mind control tests with individual subjects are not isolated. Small and large classes of humans, people, pets, plants, insects, other conscious objects which can be influenced by stimulants may be subjects used in these studies. For cases involving human subjects, the inherent respect for human life or freedom of choice is to be diminished. Those who finance behavioral health programs appear to be wealthy or have access to large amounts of money and see it as a valuable resource investment. A carnal desire for power lacks reverence in hearts for others, and the alien force of covetousness takes over. As a result, human rights are grossly violated, and all individuals, women, children, and other conscious creations in the world are affected.

The violation of privacy is at the heart of the practices involved in the development of intellectual power. Privacy infringement is an essential component required to obtain control specifications because a subject cannot be aware of the experiments. Projects relating to intelligent control will be postponed, canceled, or suspended as a result of information leaked concerning privacy violations. Those who announce preparations for human rights violations are regarded as dealers or dissidents. The power or authority to breach privacy is typically extracted from a global or national crisis. Such problems are being funded by people to make progress in command practices. Sometimes even disasters are created by members of their societies to strengthen human rights. The fight to violate human rights stems from those who raise society's awareness by disseminating information, as the mysterious agendas of mentally corrupt people begin to be seen in powerful positions, the chance of mind control decreases gradually.

PART FOUR

Introduction

Manipulation is a sort of influence that intends to alter others' behavior or perception via indirect strategies. By enhancing the interests of this manipulator, these processes might consider deceitful and exploitative. The social effect or influence is not essentially negative. For instance, individuals like family friends and physicians can attempt to convince to modify these behaviors and actions. The social effect caused by this is regarded as harmless when it respects the right of those affected to reject it or to take it. In such instances, it isn't unduly coercive. Based on the context and motivations, manipulation may be constituted by social influence.

Theories on Effective Manipulation

According to psychology writer George K. Simon Psychological, manipulation primarily requires the manipulator:

·   Concealing behaviors and motives that might be aggressive and being affable.

·   Knowing the victim's vulnerabilities to determine which approaches are very likely to be the best.

·   Possessing a degree of ruthlessness to have no qualms about causing injury to the victim

·   The manipulation is very likely to accomplish through competitive and covert ways to hide the aggression.

According to Braiker

Harriet B. Braiker (2004) identified the following manners that manipulators restrain their victims:

· Positive reinforcement: This comprises of compliments, superficial charm, shallow sympathy (crocodile tears), extreme apologizing, cash, acceptance, presents, and focus, facial expressions like a forced laugh or grin, and public awareness.

· Negative reinforcement: This entails removing one out of a negative situation for a reward, e.g., "You won't need to do your homework if you let me do so to you."

· Partial or irregular reinforcement: This includes intermittent or partial reinforcement, which can make a productive climate of uncertainty and anxiety. Occasional reinforcement may cause the sufferer to persist -- such as in different types of gambling, the gambler is very likely to win repeatedly but still drop money.

· Contains yelling, nagging intimidation, threats, swearing the guilt trip, playing with the victim, yelling, and sulking

· Traumatic studying: Manipulating with explosive anger, abuse, or other similar behavior Even one episode of behavior can train or condition victims to prevent facing, bothering, or contradicting the manipulator.

Based on Simon

Simon recognized the Subsequent manipulative methods:

· Lying (by commission): It is tough to tell if someone is lying in the time, they take action. Frequently, the fact becomes evident later when it is too late. One method to lessen the odds of being lied to is to comprehend that some character types (especially psychopaths) are experts in the art of cheating and lying, doing it regularly, and in many subtle ways.

· Lying by omission: That is a subtle kind of lying using a substantial quantity reality

· Denial: Manipulator will not acknowledge they have done something wrong

· Rationalization: A justification produced by the manipulator for improper behavior. Rationalization is associated with spin.

· Minimization: This is a kind of denial combined with rationalization. The manipulator claims that their behavior is not reckless or dangerous as others suggested, for instance, stating that insult or a taunt was a joke.

· Selective inattention or discerning attention: Manipulator will not focus on anything, which may distract their schedule, stating things such as "I do not wish to hear it."

· Diversion: Manipulator prefers not giving a direct answer to a question and rather than being diversionary by steering the dialogue towards other topics.

· Evasion: Much like recreation but providing immaterial, rambling weasel words, vague answers

· Covert intimidation: Manipulators throwing the victim on the defensive by using veiled (subtle, indirect, or suggested) threats.

· Trip: A sort of intimidation strategy a manipulator indicates this to the victim that they are too greedy, do not care, or have it simple. This results in the sufferer feeling awful, keeping them at a place.

· Shaming: Manipulator uses put-downs and sarcasm to improve self-doubt and anxiety from the sufferer. Manipulators utilize this strategy to defer them and so to make others feel unworthy. Shaming approaches can be subtle rhetorical remarks, like a look or a glance tone of voice sarcasm. Manipulators will make one feel embarrassed to challenge them. It is an efficient means to foster an awareness of inadequacy.

· Vilifying the sufferer: More than another, this strategy is a strong way of placing the victim on the defensive while hiding the competitive intent of this manipulator although the manipulator falsely accuses the sufferer like being an abuser in reaction once the victim stands up for or defends their standing.

· Playing with the victim function: Manipulator portrays himself or the behavior of others to get something or to obtain sympathy pity or wreak havoc. People, who are conscientious and caring, can stand to see anybody suffering along with the manipulator finds it effortless to perform to acquire collaboration.

· Playing with the servant function: Cloaking a self-indulgent schedule in the guise of an agency to a noble cause, such as stating they are behaving in a specific way to become "obedient" to or at "support" into an authority figure or "just doing their job"

· Seduction: Manipulator utilizes compliments, charm, flattery, or supporting others to make them lower their defenses and provide their confidence and devotion. They will provide help to add accessibility and confidence.

· Projecting the attribute (blaming others): Manipulator find scapegoats in frequently subtle, hard-to-detect manners Many times, their thinking will endeavor the victim. Manipulators would assert that the sufferer is the person who is responsible for thinking lies that they had been conned into thinking if the manipulator was compelled, they play the blame game to get their work done in the manner they like. Their behavior employed as a way of management and manipulation. Manipulators lie about dishonesty only to re-manipulate the first, less believable narrative to a "more suitable" fact that the sufferer will think possible. This is another way of manipulation and control projecting lies. Manipulators like to accuse the victim as "worthy of being treated like that." They assert that the sufferer is violent or crazy, particularly when there is proof contrary to the manipulator.

· Feigning innocence: Manipulator attempts to indicate they did not do something they were accused of or that any injury was accidental. The manipulator may wear a look of anger or surprise. This strategy makes the sufferer question their sanity and their judgment.

· Feigning confusion: Manipulator attempts to play stupid or perplexed about a problem by pretending they do not understand what the sufferer is talking about this sufferer confuses the sufferer to doubt their precision of perception. They start focusing on the components that the manipulator contained there's uncertainty in. Manipulators will have utilized cohorts to help back up their own stories.

· Brandishing anger: This includes anger to jolt the victim. Manipulator uses anger to brandish sufficient intensity. The manipulator is not mad, but they just put on an act. They simply want what they need and get "mad" once denied. Anger frequently employed to hide intent or to prevent confrontation, avoid telling the truth. There are threats utilized by the manipulator of reporting abuses. The manipulator works this way to frighten or intimidate the victim for going to the authorities. Other problems and blackmail dangers of exposure are different kinds of manipulation. Anger, particularly when the victim refuses suggestions or requests. Anger can also be employed as a defense; therefore, the manipulator can prevent telling truths at conditions or times. It is frequently employed as a shield or an instrument to ward off distress or queries. The sufferer becomes more concentrated on the anger rather than the manipulation strategy.

· Bandwagon result: Manipulator conveniences the victim to submission by asserting (whether false or true) that lots of men and women have done something and the sufferer should do it too.

These include phrases like "Lots of people like you..." or "Everybody does this." Manipulation could see in peer pressure situations, occurring in situations into believing drugs or other materials, prey.

Nlp And History

In the 1970s, psychological researcher John Grinder coined the term Neuro-Linguistic Programming (NLP) for a mind controlling method to change our conscious thoughts and behaviors as desired. Neuro (mind/information) Linguistic (language/words) Programming (learning/control), simply put it's the art of learning the language of your mind to generate satisfying results. NLP is a lot like a User Manual for the brain, to help you communicate the goals and desires of the unconscious mind to the conscious self. Imagine you are in foreign country and craving chicken wings, so you go to a restaurant to order the same but when the food shows up, it ends up being liver stew because of a failed communication. Humans often fail to recognize and acknowledge their unconscious thoughts and desires because a lot of it gets lost in translation to the conscious self. NLP enthusiasts often exclaim: "the conscious mind is the goal setter, and the unconscious mind is the goal getter". The idea of being your unconscious mind wants you to achieve everything that you actually desire but if your conscious mind fails to receive the message, you will never set the goal to achieve those dreams.

NLP was developed using excellent therapists and communicators who had achieved great success as role models. It's a set of tools and techniques to help your master communication, both with yourself and others. NLP is study of human mind combining thoughts and actions with perception to fulfill their deepest desires. Our mind employs complex neural networks to process information and use language or auditory signals to give it meaning while storing these signals in patterns to generate and store new memories. We can voluntarily use and apply certain tools and techniques to alter our thoughts and actions in achieving our goals. These techniques can be perceptual, behavioral and communicative and used control our own mind as well as that of others.

One of the central ideas of NLP is that our conscious mind has a bias towards a specific sensory system called the "Preferred Representational System (PRS)". Phrases like "I hear you" or "Sounds good" signal an auditory PRS, whereas, phrase like "I see you" may signal a visual PRS. A certified therapist can identify a person's PRS and model their therapeutic treatment around it. This therapeutic framework often involves rapport building, goal setting and information gathering among other activities. NLP is increasingly used by individuals to promote self enhancement, such as self-reflection and confidence as well as for social skill development, primarily communication.

NLP therapy or training can be delivered in the form of language and sensory based interventions, using behavior modification techniques customized for individuals to better their social communication and improved confidence and self-awareness. NLP therapists or trainers strive to make their client understand that their view and perception of the world is directly associated with how they operate in it, and the first step toward a better future is keen understanding of their conscious self and contact with their unconscious mind. It's paramount to first analysis and subsequently changes our thoughts and behaviors that are counterproductive and block our success and healing. NLP has been successfully used in the treatment of various mental health conditions like anxiety, phobias, stress and even post-traumatic stress disorder. An increasing number of practitioners are commercially applying NLP to promise improved productivity and achievement of work-oriented goals that ultimately lead to job progression.

Now, let's look at how NLP works. John Grinder, in association with his student Richard Bandler, conducted a research study on techniques used by Fritz Perls (founder of Gestalt therapy), Virginia Satir (Family therapist) and Milton Erickson (renowned Hypnotherapist). They subsequently analyzed and streamlined these therapy techniques to create a behavioral model for mass application in order to achieve sand to reproduce excellence in any field. Bandler, a computer science major, helped develop a "psychological programming language" for human beings. On the basis of how our mind processes information or perceives the external world, it generates an internal "NLP map" of what is going on outside. This internal map is created based on the feedback provided by our sense organs, like the pictures we take in, sounds we hear, the taste in our mount, sensations we feel on our skin and what we can smell. However, with this massive influx of information, our mind selectively deletes and generalizes a ton of information. This selection is unique to every person and is determined by what our mind deems relevant to our situation. As a result, we often miss out on a whole lot of information that can be immediately noticed by someone else right off the bat and we end up with a tiny and skewed version of what is really occurring. For example, take a moment and process this statement: "Person A killed person B", now depending on our circumstances and experiences we will all have our own version of that story. Some might think "a man killed a woman", or "a lion killed a man" or "a terrorist killed a baby" or "John Doe killed Kennedy" and so on and so forth. Now, there's a method to this madness, whatever story you came up with, realize there is way you got to that story which was driven by our own life experience. Our mind creates an internal map of the situation at hand and then we compare that map with other internal maps from our past that we have stored in our mind. Every person has their own internal "library" based on what is important or relevant to them in accordance with their personality. Once the mind settles with a preexisting mental map that is comparable to the new one, it starts adding meaning to what is happening and decides how you feel about it and ultimately your response to it. Your physical and mental state has a significant impact on the meaning that your mind makes from moment to moment. Whether you are physically sick, or emotionally stressed or even happy and relaxed can alter how you add meaning to the situations. For instance, the physical sensations of terror and excitement are the same, like increased heart rate, high blood pressure and even palpitations, so the meaning that our mind adds to these sensations decides whether we are just ecstatic or terrorized. It always comes down to the story that you write in your mind.

"The laws that apply to mechanical, nonliving systems are not the same laws that apply to the interaction of biological, living systems." – John Grinder

Did you ever feel that once your conscious mind makes you aware of what you want to do or gain, suddenly the universe seems to be propping up signs that could help you find your way to get what you want? For example, one day you wake up thinking I need to take my family on a vacation. You go on with your day the same way as you have been for days or weeks, but you suddenly notice a poster on an exciting trip to Florida on your way to work, that you later learnt from your coworker has been up for over a month now. You suddenly see that close to that same Starbucks you visit every day, there is a big travel agency that you had never paid attention to. When browsing the Internet, you will suddenly see travel ads all over your Facebook or ads from Airbnb popping up on your YouTube videos. Now all these may come across as coincidences, but the matter of the fact is those things or signs had been there all along, but your mind deleted that information or perception because they were not relevant to you. So, as your conscious mind starts connecting the dots between your wishes and the reality of the world, you start picking up on new information that may have already been in plain sight, but you are only tuned into now.

Your personality profile also plays a major role in what information your mind chooses to exclude and what is processed. People who are more focused on security, they are constantly assessing their situation to determine whether it's safe for you or not. On the other hand, people who are more freedom oriented, they tend to think of their situation in terms of options and limitation with no focus on safety at all. Your personality determines what and how you update your mental library and ultimately the meaning you add to these internal maps. For example, a kid looking at a roller coaster is thinking only about the fun of traveling through open space in a cool looking ride and given the opportunity will easily and fearlessly jump on the ride, because his personality is not security oriented. But an adult who is able to focus not only on the fun and excitement of the ride but also its safety and potential hazards, will think twice before making that same decision.

Psychology Of Persuasion

Becoming more persuasive can help our many walks of life, from making us more efficient at our jobs or helping us attract an amazing partner to successfully debating and influencing others. The ability to persuade means we have changed someone's perception of something, which otherwise would have stayed the same. This shows just how powerful this art is. We can make people think or behave in the way we want them to - now that's magic.

Throughout history the most powerful leaders and trail blazers seemingly possessed a quality which made others believe in them and subsequently follow them. These influential people mastered the art of persuasion. They had a way of communicating which made others pay attention. Most of us have met people who have a natural sense of charm and they somehow seem to easily gain the trust of others. I believe all of us are born with this natural charisma, however due to the struggles of life we lose touch with it.

To understand what makes people persuadable we have to learn what makes them tick first. We do this of course by looking under the hood at human psychology. Changing the way people think involves altering their attitudes, values, beliefs and goals which then impacts what action they take in the future.

Persuasion is made-up of 6 main aspects -

Intent – Persuasion should come across quite naturally but with intention. We want people to see our perspective on things. The 'hard sell' or aggressive tactics rarely work in this modern day and age. Most positive interactions will lead to a change in perception in both parties.

Force - This is when a persuasive act gains compliance from the other, so they follow the behavior you requested. However, it doesn't change their internal beliefs. It may actually strengthen their beliefs in the opposite direction. This occurs when people are forced or made to do something against their will.

Context - A new behavior may only be relevant within a certain context. For instance, someone may be pressured into arriving at work on time. But will continue to be late for every other appointment they have outside of work. Their inner beliefs around punctuation haven't shifted.

Plurality - This means being able to persuade a number of people at one time.

Presence - When we persuade in person, it is deemed maximum communication since we are present physically. We can also persuade through different means such as e-mail, telephone, social media, letters etc. These methods aren't as influential as physical presence.

Our internal programming is usually formed as a network of beliefs. The art of persuasion involves breaking and redirecting some of these connections to create a new belief. Sometimes we may have to alter a number of interconnected beliefs before we can change a deep core belief.

Basic Human Needs

From a psychological understanding we know that humans have fundamental needs. This has been defined in many texts none more so than Abraham Maslow's hierarchy of needs. Using these major model corporations and advertising agencies have been able to determine what appeals to the most basic of human needs, so they can increase interest in or sell a particular product. The main emotions these companies focus upon are Safety, Belonging and Esteem (well-being). Since these are basic needs it makes them powerful motivators for advertisers to use. These three emotions are ranked highly in most people's personal value structure. In fact, the more these needs are fulfilled the more happiness and peace we experience in life.

So, by creating a sense of safety, belonging or making people feel important, we open the doors to influencing and persuasion. Here are three simple phrases which help change the way we see things -

1) 'What if' - This phrase takes ego out of the equation and allows people to feel comfortable in creating a safe environment where they can explore deeper feelings and curiosities. 'What if' is a magical phrase and we often hear it from children when they allow their imaginations to run wild. Used wisely it can be leveraged to open people's minds to new ideas and possibilities. Try asking someone, 'what if you had a million dollars?' they'll tell you more about their real desires and interests than you may have known prior.

2) 'Can you help please?' - This phrase intentionally hands the power to the opposite party. Humans naturally want to help others. By using this statement consciously, we can rely on people's good nature to get us what we want.

3) 'Would it help if' - Similar to example 1, such a statement shifts the focus from a problem to a solution. At the same time using the word 'if', allows the interaction or suggestion to maintain some flexibility. Most of us don't like doing things another person's way but by using the word 'if' we can gradually get others to accept our proposal.

Dale Carnegie the famous author of the book 'How to Win Friends & Influence People' discussed the art of influencing others at great depth. Here is a snippet of some of his main points to winning people over.

1 - The only way to win an argument is to avoid it.

2 - Respect other people's opinions. Be opening minded and never say, 'You're wrong.'

3 - If however, you're wrong, don't be afraid of admitting it quickly and emphatically.

4 - Always start an interaction in a friendly way.

5-Get the opposite party agreeing with you immediately by getting them saying "yes, yes, yes"

6 - Listen intently. Let the other person do most of the talking.

7 - Allow the other person to feel that an idea or suggestion comes from them.

8 - Use empathy to see things from the other person's standpoint. Acknowledging this perspective, gives us greater power.

9 - Show understanding and sympathy for the other people's ideas and needs.

10 - Make things easier by appealing to people's values and motives.

11 - Set challenges for others. Competitive people naturally welcome challenges. Use this to your advantage.

Social - Being Liked

Sociality has a huge impact upon how easily people are influenced. Social proof means how well we are accepted by people and groups, whether personal or professional. How we are influenced in social situations is through three main factors - authority, likability and social proof. We are influenced by authority figures, by the people we like and those who provide us with social proof. For instance, a teenager at school would gain 'social proof' if they were seen mingling with the popular crowd.

Since humans are social creatures, we want to feel connected to one another and as though we're part of something bigger. For this reason, we're more likely to do something simply because we see others doing it. For instance, in a sales negotiation, a company may show a potential new client all the other businesses in the area they deal with. Or in a one-to-one situation we can influence someone by explaining Mr. Popular from another department agreed to it. Knowing others have taken some action before us helps to naturally reduce resistance.

Authority

We're naturally more influenced by those we deem to be above us in some respect. You're more likely to follow directions when they come from management at your place of work rather than if they came from a fellow colleague. We look up too and respect those who are an expert within a certain area or subject, we see these people as an authority.

Something as simple as informing an audience or an individual of your credentials prior to an interaction can help swings the odds into your favor when looking to persuade or influence. This technique can also be effective when emailing, by simply stating at the beginning about any skills you possess in relation to the subject can help make the other person more susceptible to your influence. If for example, you were contacting someone about the possibility of speaking at their event and you had previous experience of speaking at big events, the mere mention of the biggest events you've spoken at would have an impact on the way the recipient would view your application. We can use this too our advantage and maybe even exaggerate our accomplishments.

Consistency

This is another means of getting people to buy-in to us and is often used as a sales tactic. In this method we ask the target to admit their goals and priorities first and then align our request with their desires. This makes it difficult for them to say no too. Use the information they originally provided and offer them a solution based upon it.

People like to remain consistent and don't like being seen as dishonest, which is why it makes it harder for them to reject a request which matches their needs. When a target shares their goals first, they are invested, once they're invested, we can offer the right solutions for them.

Here are a few further strategies which can be used to influence.

This method is named Disrupt and Reframe - This process involves mixing up the words, behaviors or visuals a person is used too and then reframing our pitch/request while they're still trying to figure out the disruption. This method was put to the test by researchers who sold a product giving customers two different options.

The first choice offered - $3 for 8 apples

The second option offered - 300 pennies for 8 apples

The second choice was the clear winner, selling almost twice as many apples as option 1.

This technique works because the target has less resistance to the reframe (option 2) as the brain is thrown off by the initial disruption of the unusual wording.

Storytelling

Another method of getting people onside is through story telling. This enables others to identify with us and the various aspects of our story, which helps build trust. It is important however our story contains the right plot. The three main plots for an influential story are -

1. Challenge Plot - This is the story of the underdog, the rags to riches, and the person who made it through some adversity on sheer willpower.

2. Connection Plot - Another common plot, where people build a relationship which bridges a certain gap. This can be racial, cultural, class, ethnic etc.

3. Creative Plot - This is a story where someone achieves a breakthrough of some sort. Whether solving a long-lasting problem or overcoming an issue in a brand new or innovative way.

If you have any personal stories which you can make meet any of the above criteria, you should find it easier to hook people in.

2. Paradoxical Intervention

This term is simply another way of saying 'Reverse Psychology'. This is a term most of us are familiar with and has been used for years.

Reverse Psychology is a persuasion method that many of us tend to use unconsciously. It involves getting someone to do something we want by suggesting the opposite. This tactic tends to work better when our target is stressed and is making emotional decisions as opposed to thinking things through.

A simple form of reverse psychology is telling someone 'not to do X', by suggesting this we are implanting this very idea into their mind. As we know, children naturally want to do whatever they've been forbidden to do. We can take this further also. If someone commits to something, we can ensure they follow through by expressing doubt over what they have promised. This will make them assert themselves by completing the action in a bid to prove us wrong.

NLP Mind Tools

Humans spend countless hours seeking new ways to work just about anything. Through endless hours of research, they pour over books and journals looking for the message that will tell them the secret to harnessing mind power. Many never realize that the most powerful mind power tool is already on board and just aching to be used. It is the human brain, the mind itself.

Every time a person practices a new habit or thinks a new thought, they make a new pathway in the brain. Every time the habit is used, or the idea is thought, the nerve pathway becomes even stronger. The human brain is wired at birth to be an efficient machine and it is ready, from birth, to make an ever-increasing amount of nerve pathways and to strengthen the pathways that are used the most.

Sometimes thoughts and habits need to be changed for the improvement of the person. When people decide that they would like to make a change in their lives, there will be a period of adjustment. This is true whether the change is mental, emotional, or physical. During this period of adjustment, there will be some level of discomfort. When a habit or a thought is already formed, it has made its own path in the brain. When a stimulus is seen or heard, the message travels along the preset nerve pathway to the spot in the brain that controls that thought or habit. In order to change a thought or a habit, it is necessary for the nerve path to be changed. Until the nerve path is changed, the old nerve path will remain in the brain. The discomfort comes from the brain trying to automatically access the old pathway and the new pathway at the same time. This is painful for the brain to do.

It is easy to become frustrated when the brain goes back to its old patterns of thought and habit. Never fall into the habit of placing blame on a lack of willpower. Willpower has nothing to do with it. It is a very difficult thing to override preset pathways in the brain. The brain is a very powerful tool. When will power fails and mistakes happen, remember to use kindness and compassion in dealing with the failure? The brain is very efficient at doing what it does. The only way to change the pathways in the brain is to keep working on new pathways that will eventually obliterate the old, undesirable ones.

The brain needs a clear understanding that changes are about to take place and new pathways are about to be laid down. Remind the brain that new habits and new thoughts will be replacing the old ones. Blaming failure on a lack of will power is a self-defeating statement. The process of making new nerve paths in the brain takes hard work and time. It will help to keep reminding oneself of the impending change. By doing this over and over, it makes the process no longer about possible character flaws. The focus is now put on the habit of thought that is being built.

Is it possible to build new nerve pathways in the brain? Yes, it is possible, and it can be done. If more proof is needed, just compare the adult brain to the baby's brain. Every current habit and thought a person has is the direct result of having spent time practicing them over and over until they created a pathway in the brain. New pathways can be created. Think of it this way: they already have. The baby's brain has no idea of anything. It has no thoughts or habits. Every nerve path currently in the brain was practiced until it became a part of the brain. Think of the baby. The baby lies around day after day and does baby things. Then one day the baby notices the shiny rattle that mommy is waving in front of its little face. The baby wants the rattle. As the baby is waving its tiny arms around, the mommy puts the rattle close enough so the baby can touch it with its wavering hand. After a few of these sessions, the baby gets the idea that if the arm is in the air it can touch the rattle. A nerve pathway is beginning to grow. So the baby decides to lift its arm to actively reach for the rattle. The baby will be unsuccessful at first because the arms will wave wildly and will not connect with the rattle. One day, the baby will actually grab the rattle, and the nerve pathway is then complete.

While this may seem like a very simple example, it is exactly how nerve pathways are created in the brain. Every action, thought, or habit has its own nerve pathway. All pathways must be created. No one was born knowing to sit in front of the television and mindlessly eat dip with chips. No one was born lamenting the excess pounds they carry in strange places. No one was born hating their body. All behaviors are learned, good and bad. And the bad ones can be replaced with good ones.

So, if the ability to program negative thoughts into the brain exists, then the ability to disrupt those negative thoughts with positive thoughts also exists. The brain can be reprogrammed. It is a powerful tool, and its main function is to turn thoughts into reality. The brain is always working, so why not use the power of the brain to benefit rather than harm? Just because a particular habit or thought has been around all forever does not mean it needs to stay. Use the power of the brain to choose new habits and thoughts to focus on and replace the old, negative thought pathways in the brain.

The new thought needs to be believable; the new habit needs to be doable. It does not really good to try to stick to a habit that is impossible to accomplish or to try to believe a thought that is unbelievable. After years of seeing the reality of an obese body, it would be nearly impossible to suddenly believe that the image in the mirror is that of a skinny person. But the brain will likely accept something that mentions learning to take care of the body or learning to accept the body in order to correct its flaws. The brain will turn a belief in reality. Believing a positive thought will lead to quite a different result than the ending where only negative thoughts are present.

Be prepared to repeat and repeat some more. The primary key to being able to make a new habit stay is repeating it constantly. The more a new, desirable habit is practiced, the more the brain begins to accept it. The nerve path becomes stronger every day. With constant practice, this new nerve path will become the path the brain will prefer to use, and the old one will cease to exist.

In any case, be sure to allow enough time to effectively create a change. Accept the starting point and constantly visualize the ending point. Accept the fact that the path to the goal of a new habit or thought will not be easy or perfect. The path will almost never travel in a straight line. Sometimes people fall completely off the path, and that is okay too. Just get back up and get back on. Do not get sidetracked by the idea that this journey will be easy and carefree because it will not be. Just keep thinking of the new nerve pathway that will be created by the new thought or habit and it will eventually become a reality.

Most of the pathways in the brain are stored in the subconscious mind. This is the part of the mind that is always working without always being thought of. Think of learned skills like tying shoes, zipping a coat, and pouring milk into a glass. These were all learned behavior whose nerve pathways are firmly set in the subconscious part of the mind. This part of the brain is the bank of data for all life functions.

The communication between the conscious mind and the unconscious mind works in both directions. Whenever a person has a memory, and emotion, or an idea, it is rooted in the subconscious mind and translated to the conscious mind through mind power. The subconscious has the power to control just about anything a human regularly does.

For example, during meditation steady, deep breathing is usually practiced. The control of the breath is brought from the subconscious mind and given to the conscious mind to tell it to control the breathing. Once a pattern of deep steady breathing is begun by the conscious mind, the subconscious mind takes over and keeps the set rhythm going until it is told to stop. This is done by a conscious end to the deep breathing or an encounter with an outside stimulus like stress. The subconscious mind also processes the great wealth of information received daily and only passes along to the conscious mind those things that are necessary for the brain to remember.

When sending thoughts from the conscious mind to the subconscious mind, the brain will only send those thoughts that are attached to great emotion. The only thoughts that remain in the subconscious are those that are kept there with strong emotions. Unfortunately, the brain does not know the difference between positive emotions and negative emotions. Any strong emotion will work. Both negative emotions and positive emotions can be quite strong. Also, unfortunately, negative emotions tend to be stronger than positive emotions.

Step one in learning to use the power of the subconscious part of the mind will be to eliminate any thoughts that come with negative emotions. Also, negative mental comments will also need to cease. Fears will usually come true, specifically because they are drowning in negative emotions. This is why negative ideas need to be eliminated because they can be very harmful roadblocks on the road to harnessing brain power.

One best practice to use to get rid of negative thoughts is to counter them with positive thoughts. This will take time and practice, but it is a very powerful and useful technique. Whenever a negative thought pops in the conscious mind, immediately counter it with a positive thought that is dripping with strong emotion. The actual truth will come out somewhere in between the two thoughts.

Another way to counter negative emotions is to delete them, just like using a remote control. When a negative thought comes into the conscious mind, imagine destroying it. Imagine writing that thought on paper and burning it. Imagine pointing a remote control at the thought and pressing a huge delete button. Whatever form used to imagine deleting the thought, the important thing is to get rid of it before it can take hold in the subconscious mind.

Find something energizing and use it to reach a goal. Those things that are found to be energizing bring boundless energy to positive thoughts. It is often necessary to invent motivation, at least in the beginning, to learn to create new habits and thoughts. But with a bit of practice and a lot of positive thought, new positive habits will soon be burned into the subconscious mind and the old negative thoughts and habit will fade away.

Nlp Techniques

NLP or Neuro Linguistic Programming has become the new buzzword in the sphere of learning, influencing, training and mind control techniques. Trainers, coaches and mind control experts all over the world are waking up to this phenomenon called NLP to condition and lead people's subconscious mind to do what they want them to. The sheer power of training and guiding the mind in a particular direction is what makes NLP such a fascinating subject.

Neuro Linguistic Programming Decoded

Neuro Linguistic Programming or NLP in simplest terms is the programming language of your mind. We've all had experiences where we tried to convey something to someone who doesn't speak our language. The result? They failed to comprehend what we were trying to say.

You go to a café aboard and ask for a fancy preparation but end up receiving tasteless food owing to the misinterpretation of language, expressions, and codes.

This is exactly what the challenge is when we try to convey through our subconscious mind. We simply believe we are ordering it to give us more fulfilling relationships, more income, a stable job, and other such things. However, if that does not show up, something somewhere isn't right. Our subconscious mind has the ability to assist us in achieving our goals only when we utilize codes and expressions it identifies and understands.

If you are asking your subconscious mind for steak and getting soup, it is time to bring a shift in the language. Think of NLP as a manual for the mind. Those who master NLP become fluent in the language of the subconscious mind, which is highly effective when it comes to re-programming people's thoughts, attitudes, ideas, actions and beliefs. This gives certain people the power to influence and persuade others, and on the flipside, even manipulate.

Neuro Linguistic Programming is a bunch of techniques, methods, and tools for improving communication within several layers of our brain. It is an approach that merges personal development, psychotherapy, psychology, and communication. Its founders (John Grinder and Richard Bandler) claim that there is a very strong connection between language, metaphors, expressions, behavior patterns, and neurological processes, which can be used for boosting learning, mind control, and personal development.

Here are a few expert techniques NLPers use to manipulate people or control their minds.

1. They Observe Eye Movements

NLPers will always closely observe their subject's eye movements to determine what part of the brain is being used, and how the subject stores/uses information. They give the impression that they are keenly interested in what the other person is saying and actually care about knowing their thoughts when in reality they are simply analyzing how a person access information from different parts of his or her brain.

Within a few minutes, practitioners of NLP can tell if a person is lying or telling the truth. The subject will almost end up believing that the manipulator has some psychic abilities or telepathic superpowers. NLPers carefully calibrate eye movements to know and conclude which parts of a brain are most active in a person, and how they process information.

2. Use the Power of Touch

NLPers use the power of touch effectively to induce certain feelings and emotions in their subjects without the subject even realizing it. Let

Emotional Intelligence 2.0

us say for instance that the subject is in a particular state of emotion such as happy, angry, upset, sad, etc., NLP practitioners will use touch (light tap on the subject's shoulder or touch their arm) and anchor that particular form of touch by linking it to a specific emotion.

Each time you want to invoke that specific emotion in a person to fulfill your intent, simply use the particular touch that you did when the subject was experiencing the same emotion earlier.

3. Use Vague Words and Phrases

One of the fundamental methods of NLP is generous use of vague verbiage for inducing a sort of hypnotic trance on the subject. NLPers believe that the more ambiguous and vaguer your language, the less likely is you're subject to oppose your ideas or disagree with you, thus making it easier to lead them into the trance state. You are basically limiting their ability to react to what you are saying.

Did you notice how effectively former United States of America president Barrack Obama used this technique during the famous "change campaign?" It was a word wrought in complete ambiguity. Anyone could interpret it in a way they wanted.

4. Relaxed and Permissive Words

Expert NLP hypnotists never start by telling their subjects what they want them to do outright. The commands follow more permissive and relaxed issuances such as "please feel free to de-stress or relax" or "you can have this for as long as you like" or "you're welcome to test this product." The subject is sort of given a loose rope, and the impression that the NLPer really wants to relax and enjoy without restrictions.

The language use is more relaxing and permissive. Skilled hypnotists realize that this is more effective when it comes to driving the subject into a state of trance over immediately commanding them into it.

404

When you begin with, "please feel free to let your hair down and relax completely", they are likelier to go into a trance gradually.

5. Layered Language

Skilled NLPers will always use language that is deeply layered or has hidden meaning/connotations attached to it. They'll use widely believed facts and slowly slip in their agenda into to manipulate the subject's subconscious mind into thinking in a particular way. For example, "food, sleep and going outdoors with me are the formula for a healthy life."

On the surface of it, the subject's subconscious mind tends to agree with it because everyone has been conditioned to believe that food, sleep and getting fresh air is good for their health. They will tend to agree with it without giving it much thought. However, the layered message here is – going outdoors with me. And boy did you just get someone to agree to that on a subconscious level? This is an extremely subtle yet powerful NLP technique that is harnessed to the hilt by experienced NLP practitioners.

You also follow up one question with another to create what can be termed as a conditioning by association. For example, you ask someone, "How many fingers are there on the human hands?" followed quickly by, how many on ten hands?"

The answer to the first will be ten, while the answer to the second question most likely will be 100.

The first is, of course, right, while the second is wrong. The answer to the second is 50. As an NLPer, you are creating a trap for getting your subject to think the way you want to through careful conditioning through association.

In NLP, you essentially build anchors or baselines that you can lead your subjects to whenever you want. It can come to anyone with a little bit of training and practice.

Talking about the power of association, it is widely used by advertisers to manipulate consumers into associating certain products with specific attributes and lifestyles. For instance, Coca-Cola always has these fancy advertisements about beautiful young people gulping glasses of bottles of the aerated beverage. They are hot (or cool if you please), rich, in gorgeous settings and look extremely cheerful. What are your impressions as you consume those images? That drinking Coca-Cola gives you access to the good life. The idea and associations are deeply installed and embedded in the subconscious mind and leads you to make a rather quick decision when it comes to purchasing.

6. Get them to Agree

If you can get your subjects to answer in the affirmative to several questions in a row, it will be tough for them to refuse your final request. NLPers know this only too well and use it liberally on their subjects to get them to do what they want.

This is one of the many clever manipulation and persuasion strategies used by sales and marketing folks. They will launch into a series of questions, the answer of which will rarely ever be in negative. After getting consecutive positive replies from their subjects, they will go for the kill and lead them into making impulsive and emotionally driven decisions. The entire technique is designed for engineering spur of the moment decisions by switching off the subject's ability to make logical decisions.

For example, an insurance salesperson will ask his client questions such as

"Wouldn't you like to financially secure the future of your loved ones?" Yes. "Wouldn't you like to use a policy that offers hassle free claims?" Yes. "Wouldn't you want to protect your family's dream for a low as $123/month?" Yes. "Wouldn't you want your children's education and future dreams taken care of even when you aren't around?" Yes. "Wouldn't you want coverage for the immediate family under one policy at a single rate?" Yes.

"Then you should not waste any more time because you never know what happens in another moment. Sign up for the policy immediately while it is available for a low monthly premium for a limited period."

See how a person is led into making a decision using the power of affirmatives or gets someone to agree to a series of questions before finally getting them to agree to the main thing. This can be as effective when you're asking someone out on a date.

When a person replies in the affirmative to a series of mostly emotional questions posed by the NLPer, it is hard for the subject to refuse the final offer.

7. Use Gibberish

NLP practitioners' resort to using a lot of gibberish mumbo-jumbo with the intention of attempting to program the subjects' internal emotions and leading them into where the manipulator wants them to go. As an NLPer, you can't afford to be specific or explain precisely what you meant. You have to utilize trance invoking ambiguous language that throws the subject off gear and allows you to take complete control of their feelings and emotions.

Phrases such as, "As you let go of this emotion slowly, you will see yourself transitioning into a state of alignment with the aura of your success" It doesn't make any sense in the logical scheme of things, but your subject is befuddled into doing exactly what you want him or her to. Since it cannot be comprehended immediately, they'll be less prone to rejecting it in a state of confusion. When you don't know what to do or can't think for yourself, you are more susceptible to blindly following the instructions of the person who is guiding or leading you.

The Secrets Of The Human Brain And How To Exploit Them

O ur brains are a fascinating thing to study, but they are not just fascinating: understanding our own brains helps us get into someone else's. The coming pages explore your brain and the mechanisms that make it work.

We have to get into some scientific detail, but the focus is not on the insignificant facts about the brain, but how we can use these facts to our advantage in psychological manipulation. The sooner you learn these facts, the sooner you will wish you had learned them soon — so don't dread the science, because you will find yourself constantly applying it later.

Our first lesson is about something called mirror neurons. We have not known about these special kinds of neurons for very long — they have been discovered relatively recently. They were discovered on accident while looking at the brains of chimps.

There were two chimps in the study: one chimp was holding a banana, and the other was watching that chimp. The scientists paid attention to the brain of the chimp holding the banana and noticed a special kind of neuron firing as it committed this action.

What happened with the other chimp was where things really got interesting. The scientists compared the special neuron that fired in the brain of the chimp holding the banana with another special neuron that fired in the brain of the chimp watching him. These scientists found that they were both the same kind of neurons.

The neuroscience community later called this special neuron the mirror neuron. You may have picked up this from the study, but these neurons fire both when we are doing an action and when we are imaging an action. That's why the mirror neuron fired for the chimp holding the banana, but the mirror neuron also fired in the chimp, watching the other chimp that was holding the banana.

In a sense, you could say this means that, to our brains, actually doing a behavior is very similar to imaging doing it. The implications of mirror neurons are great, but in the context of psychological manipulation, they are still great.

For one thing, we already know how hard it is to remain calm when we are spending time with someone who is trying to influence our emotions. The skill of state control is so crucial to learn because of this. But now we know the scientific reason state control is so hard: because when we watch someone who is sad, for instance, it makes us a little sad, too. The mirror neurons of the person we are talking to are firing a connection, and our mirror neurons are firing a similar connection. When you only want to display emotions that are useful to your psychology manipulation, this can make it especially hard to do so.

Another vital thing to learn about our brains is about a neurotransmitter called oxytocin. Oxytocin as a neurotransmitter has a wide variety of purposes, but in the context of psychological manipulation, you can look at it as the chemical that makes us feel attached.

Attachments are a powerful thing for human beings. They are the biological manifestation of the social bonds we form in our lives — and the way oxytocin is formed is so simple. As long as that person feels comfortable, you make oxytocin flow through their body simply by touching them.

This probably doesn't surprise you. We are all aware of the power of being touched by someone and how much it can affect us emotionally.

You know how huge emotions are as a tool for getting people to change. We told you how the purpose of memory activation is not to evoke the actual memory, but the emotions that go along with it. Any time you can get the subject to experience intense, positive emotions, this is a good thing to do, and it will help you mind control and manipulate them.

Touching can be a good way to promote relaxation and happiness; like with other emotions, touching feels better when it is done by someone you are close to. And being close to someone can feel wonderful if you care about them enough. People you are close to might feel annoyed by you sometimes, but quickly touching them in an innocent way will remind them that you are close, and they will be much more receptive to your psychology manipulation. It doesn't have to be exclusively used with people you know, but we will get into that in a moment.

Oxytocin is the most emotional brain chemical out there, and all it takes is touching someone. Now, of course, it is not always a good time to touch someone. It often is not a good time, in fact, and with many people you want to manipulate, you may not think you should touch them at all.

But if you feel that you don't want to touch someone at all, you may want to rethink how you view touching overall. If you touch someone, it does not have to be particularly intimate or close. It can be as simple as a split-second tap on the shoulder. In fact, this is the only one that you will have to depend on most of the time. As long as you do it quickly and with a mean-no-harm smile on your face, no one is going to be taken aback by it.

In fact, a quick tap on the shoulder can help you tremendously in getting into someone's mind. Without their realizing it, they feel a little closer to you because of this brief physical touch. This makes them more susceptible to manipulation and mind control. The touch itself won't do all the work for you, but if someone is on the borderline of cooperating with your NLP, physical touch and oxytocin can push them over the edge.

The cells in your brains are called neurons. Your neurons are constantly making connections with one another called synapses. Every little thing you do changes this arrangement of connections between your neurons.

When they form new connections, you are forming new memories, and this is called synaptic firing. But the formation of new synapses needs old synapses to be let go of to have room, and letting go of connections, or forgetting, is called synaptic pruning.

Neurolinguistic programming is learning how to communicate with someone's brain on the unconscious level. Since our brains need to pack in a ton of data into a small amount of space, the information in there is mostly not fully fleshed-out; it is a cluster of more vague understandings and gut feelings. This makes the language of our brain nonverbal and constantly evolving.

Thankfully, since our brains are constantly evolving in this process of neuroplasticity that means we can directly speak with people's brains to change them as we see fit. We speak the language of the human brain by imitating the unconscious cues of communication that people display these include the subject's eye contact, voice, body language, posture, and so on. When combined with the fundamental skills of NLP like perceptual sharpness and state control, paying attention to these cues is a sure path to manipulating someone or changing their beliefs.

The main thing is to make sure you couple the use of the techniques in this book with the theoretical principles that make up neurolinguistic programming. This is the essence of psychology manipulation: combining this book's techniques with the basics of psychology.

Understanding Psychopaths

Psychopaths have three parts of the dark triad; they are easily at the top of the list for whom to look out for, especially if you yourself are not one. However, the first interesting thing to note is that while all psychopaths are narcissistic, narcissists are not necessarily going to be psychopathic. Knowing this may be one of the weaknesses that may allow you to spot a psychopath if you find yourself crossing paths with one.

Psychopathy is identified as Antisocial Personality Disorder (APD). It has a lot of characteristics that, similar to narcissism, tend to be misconstrued by the public. This is often due to ignorance or misinformation, like that of the psychotic serial killer one sees in Hollywood movies. While this image isn't entirely untrue, largely due to the fact that these people are the most likely within the dark triad to become abusers and serial killers, many psychopaths are actually very good at blending into society. In fact, psychopaths are often well educated and intelligent.

Regardless of how well they blend into society, there is a way to help unearth the truth about them. Firstly, they will often have the same grandiose sense of self mixed in with compulsive lying and highly manipulative behavior that shows no regard for morality or the wellbeing of others. For one thing, research shows that they tend to be born the way they are. This means that your average psychopath educated or not, will probably show a history of bad behavior from an early age. They may even have a criminal record.

Examples of psychopaths from the history

Brain scans carried out on psychopaths show that the parts of the brain that are activated when most people feel stress, guilt, or empathy remain inactive when they are given stimuli that are meant to trigger these kinds of feelings (MedCircle, 2018). Their very autonomic system (which is largely responsible for reflective responses like the fight or flight and the immune system etc.) are wired differently from most peoples. Depending on the kind of psychopath, you will find that they often excel and be found in higher concentrations in occupations such as lawyers, stockbrokers, assassins, salespeople, surgeons and (quite surprisingly) chefs.

What how do they operate?

High functioning- while people think that the term psychopathy is monolithic, it actually has two subcategories that are important to understand if one is to know what to look out for. The first of these being the high functioning psychopath

These people are just more controlled and calculating. They are far less likely to become serial killers and rather channel that energy into something else, like their careers. In fact, these kinds of psychopaths are far more likely to be seen occupying high power jobs like CEOs of companies.

Don't think this makes them anything like the rest of society. These people are still vicious predators who will eliminate anyone in their way with a ruthlessness most people are not capable of. They aren't afraid to go as far as commit murder or ruin a business at the cost of countless people losing their livelihoods. They are incapable of remorse or shame and will not lose any sleep over their actions.

Low functioning- these are more the types we see in the slasher movies in theatres. The low functioning psychopath usually has a much more difficult time managing their instincts and emotions, so they are far more likely to become serial killers. However, they just don't operate the way most people would imagine.

They are more likely to draw their victims in with charm, or glibness. This is when they prepare to ruin their target's life. They are still calculating, but don't have the ability to redirect those instincts the way their high functioning counterparts do.

They still tend to be very good at concealing their true selves under a veil of normalcy. They are great liars, so leading a double life is not difficult for them. They are typically also well educated, so hiding their actions is no great feat since psychopaths generally seem to be intelligent people. So, don't count on them giving themselves away so easily.

What can we learn from them?

Now as dangerous as the psychopath might be, regardless of their specific brand of crazy, they are not to be ignored. They have a lot to teach, especially for those who are looking for upward mobility in life. These skilled predators among us are good to study for multiple reasons, the most obvious one probably being one's own safety.

While they only make up about 1% of any given population, you will find that it still makes a lot of people when you consider how many people there are on planet earth. This means that there is a very good chance that everyone will meet at least one psychopath in their life. So, it probably for the best that you know how to identify them and act accordingly for your own best interest and for that of those close to you.

One of the best things we can learn from psychopaths is their ability to detach their emotions from any action. While this cannot be mastered to the same degree by most people, it can be adopted to a certain extent. Finding detachment from the things and people around us can be a great end in itself. One does not need to become cold to everything and everyone they know and love. It is good enough that one simply learns to embrace solitude so that they can focus more on their own self-interest.

Psychopaths are not easily affected by stress. This gives them the ability to calmly assess any given situation and act accordingly. What's more, they are not as likely to suffer from paralysis by analysis. Their autonomic systems are a big part of the reason they are so unmoved by taking risks.

Nlp As A Tool Of Persuasion

N LP mainly focuses on helping people eliminate negative emotions, bad habits, mental blocks, internal conflict, or more. Yet, another part of NLP exists, in which the focus is on ethically influencing and persuading others.

Hypnosis

Hypnosis involves using language patterns to persuade another. Robert Dilts referred to hypnosis as "sleight of mouth," building on the concept of sleight of hand-the magician's ability to make things appear or disappear and yet that may seem like an impossibility. One of the best hypnotists ever known was Milton H. Erickson, a psychiatrist that had studied in-depth the subconscious mind through hypnosis. Erickson became so good at his art that he could speak to the subconscious of people without necessarily needing to hypnotize them. He could cleverly hypnotize people anytime, anywhere, even when a bland, everyday conversation was going on, earning this technique the term "conversational hypnosis." Over time, hypnosis has become a tool that not only influences and persuades other people but can help them overcome fear, limiting beliefs, and more even when they are not consciously aware. The technique can especially be essential when trying to overcome resistance. Below, we expound on conversational hypnosis.

Conversational hypnosis does not feature a slick man gazing upon you as you slide into a trance. That may be what Hollywood has taught you. Hypnosis, in reality, happens even in the most unexpected ways and times. For example, did you know that you can go into a trance several times in a day, for instance, when you lose track of time, forget why you came into a room, forget where you placed something or drive to a place and not really remember driving there? It gets even more interesting because even when you talk to yourself, you are technically in a trance. The only difference between this type of hypnosis and conversational hypnosis is that the latter happens during a conversation. So how does it work?

Conscious and Unconscious Control

Humans go into trances when they connect to their subconscious minds. Even when we dream, it is always in a trance, which is the automatic pilot mode of the body. However, this type of hypnosis is not as scary as understanding that someone can simply control your thoughts using speech. It should be a little comforting to understand that the whole of your childhood has been a series of hypnotic episodes as you learned the world and beliefs were instilled into you. Therefore, as long as you have control over your conscious mind, being hypnotized or hypnotizing another may not be such a terrible idea after all.

The real secret behind conversational hypnosis is the same as the basis for traditional hypnosis. In order to hypnotize someone in a conversation, you simply have to prevent information from reaching their conscious minds and encourage it to reach them at a subconscious level. So, how do you do that?

- Through the use of keywords which help to disengage the mind: Interestingly, there are some words which are like keys to the subconscious. A word like imagine acts as a direct command to the subconscious and the subconscious even begins to act on them even before the conscious mind can filter them. Visualization is the key to this type of hypnosis, and that is why such words are used. Let us take an example.

Timothy wants to convince John that taking their business beyond borders will be beneficial for them. However, John does not want the same, and he has reasons that are legitimate. Timothy tries to persuade John for a week, but he does not appear to be budging. His next resort is hypnosis. Timothy says to him:

"Imagine if we actualized this dream and expand internationally. There is a chance that we will be noticed by other multinational companies. Our reputation will grow and our profits will sky-rocket as we shall earn thrice as much as we earn now. This is our gateway to a better life."

There are chances that John has planted a seed of doubt in John's mind, and hence, he will begin to see the possibilities of future success in his head. In the end, John is likely to succumb to the temptation and forget the reasons that initially compelled him to dismiss Timothy in the first place. This only proves that the power of the subconscious mind exceeds that of the conscious one by afar.

- Through the use of vagueness and ambiguity: It is common to hear citizens of different countries complaining that the same ineffective leaders are chosen every election. Now, with the rate of literacy of many individuals in the world, you would think that we are more inclined as a race to make more rational decisions. This makes sense, but what you do not realize is that vagueness and ambiguity are the dirty little secret of most of the world's politicians. In fact, these people are nothing more than a bunch of skilled orators. Take note of the language, specifically, the words that these politicians use to gain the sympathy of voters and garner votes. You will come to the realization that their speeches usually lack logic and are full of ambiguous slogans and are ambiguous, serving no real purposes rather than to play with the emotions of the crowd. If a leader intends to use clear, unambiguous speech has a lower probability of winning because often, they cannot whet the emotions of the crowd.

You may wonder how vague and ambiguous language works. It is simple;

If someone talks to you in a logical sequence or tells you sentences that make sense, your mind will get to work and begin to decode what the speaker is saying. In the event of doing this, the mind will also be looking for loopholes while trying to decode. If on the other hand, I use ambiguous phrases and words, there is a probability that it will have a tremendous effect on the mind of the masses. While the voter is still trying to decode what the speaker is saying, the speaker is already bombarding them with vaguer information that will override their need to make logical decisions and just voting for them.

For example, a politician may ask the people of a particular city to rise up to the challenge and embrace the coming change. Further, he would tell them that the time is now and that they can do it.

There is a probability that a voter in the crowd will begin to wonder what challenge is being addressed, what change is needed and what time it is when the politician bombards them with the suggestion to vote for him. The subconscious mind processes the suggestion before any information from the conscious is processed.

Creating Rapport

Naturally, many of us tend to fear rats. Imagine getting into a room and finding it full of rats squeaking. Your natural reaction would probably be to shut the door and bolt off or simply get away from that scene. This is the case not because rats will harm you, but more because we as humans are fundamentally different from rats. When we see ourselves as different from a creature, we inherently begin to fear. The same case applies to us within ourselves. We often find that when a person is different from ourselves, we will be afraid of them. For instance, we are afraid of people we are not familiar with, people of a different religion or we find other cultures and their people strange. This is not a coincidence, as usually, we do not want to cross paths with the unfamiliar. This is the point of creating rapport through techniques like mirroring. These techniques help us make ourselves more familiar and similar to the next person, such that any feelings of fear or awareness created as a result of being different are eliminated.

Rapport involves creating a feeling of confidence and trust. Creating rapport can be quite easy. However, what is most interesting is that through using this technique, you have the power to get along with almost everyone as it teaches you to relate better with people while creating stronger relationships. These skills are, however, double-edged and they can be used for both good and bad. We believe that as our reader, you will choose to use these techniques for the better.

Mirroring

One effective way of creating rapport is by mirroring. When you mirror, you mimic subtle behaviors when communicating with the next person. Through mirroring, you will feel in connection with one another. Even with little knowledge of each other, you will feel as if you have known each other for eternity. Basically, you will need to mirror someone's movements. Take the example of when you look at yourself in the mirror. When you raise your left eyebrow, the right one reflects the same in the mirror. This method of creating rapport is so basic and yet so understandable that even chimps use it in their interactions. The same technique applies here, as there are some things you can mirror to gain rapport. They include:

- Gestures
- Posture
- Breathing pattern
- Volume and speed of speech
- Tone of voice
- Language

Basically, rapport makes your voices and bodies match in a special way. In fact, communication is usually largely about the mixture of body language and voice tonality than about the message being portrayed. If therefore, you learn to control your body language, you will highly improve how other people perceive you. But just like any other skill, mirroring may need time, and there are different levels of mirroring that you can achieve.

However, breathing is the most important thing you can mirror because as a component of physiology, it is unconscious yet the easiest to notice. You can watch the shoulders for an idea of the mirror's breathing pattern, especially if she is female. Other parts you can look at include stomach and chest. While trying to mirror reactions, remember that you should do it so subtly that it looks almost effortless and subconscious. It may seem unnatural to you, but over time, you will find it easy to mimic. When the skill becomes part of you, you will do it naturally without even being conscious of the efforts you will be making towards that end.

Effective Techniques Used In Nlp To Control Other

NLP training is conducted in a pyramid-like structure, with sophisticated techniques reserved for high-end seminars. It is a complex subject (whoever said anything related to the human mind would be easy?). However, to simplify a complicated concept, NLPers, or people who practice NLP, pay keen attention to people they work with. They watch everything from eye movements to skin flushes to pupil dilation in order to determine what type of information people are processing.

Through observation, NLPers can tell which side of the brain is dominant in a person. Similarly, they can tell what sense is the most active within the person's brain. The eye movements can determine how their brain stores and uses information. It is also easy to decipher whether the person is stating facts (telling the truth) or making up facts (lying) by looking at his/her eye movements.

After gathering this invaluable information, NLP manipulators will subtly mirror and mimic their victims (including speech, body language, mannerisms, verbal linguistic patterns and more) to give a feeling of being 'one among them.'

NLPers will fake social clues to lead their victims into dropping their guard and entering a more open, receptive and suggestible state of mind, where they become ready to absorb whatever information their mind is fed. Manipulators will cleverly use language that focuses on a person's predominant senses.

For example, if a person is focused on his/her visual sense, the NLP manipulator will most likely use it to his/her advantage optimally by saying something like, "Do you see where I am coming from?" "Can you see what I am trying to tell you?" or "See it this way?" Similarly, if a person is a predominantly auditory person, the manipulator will speak to them using auditory metaphors like, "Just hear me out once, Tim" or "I hear you."

By mirroring their victim's body language and verbal linguistic patterns, NLP experts, or NLPer manipulators, attempt to accomplish a clear objective – building rapport. Once the manipulator uses NLP to build rapport and get the victim to let down his guard through clever use of body language and verbal patterns, the victim becomes more open and suggestible. Fake social cues are fed to the victim to make their minds more malleable.

Once they build a rapport, NLPers will begin to lead the victim into increased interaction in a sublime manner. After having mirrored the victim and establishing in the victim's subconscious mind that he/she (the manipulator) is one among them (the victim), the manipulator increases his/her chances of getting the victim to do whatever the manipulator wants. They will subtly change their behavior and language to influence their victim's actions.

The techniques can include leading questions, sublime language patterns and a host of other NLP techniques to maneuver the person's mind wherever they want. The victim, on the other hand, often doesn't realize what is happening. In their view, everything is occurring naturally/organically or according to their consent.

Of course, manipulators (however skilled) may not be able to use NLP to get people to behave in a manner that is completely out of character. However, it can be used to steer people's responses in the desired direction. For instance, you can't convince a fundamentally ethical and truthful person to act in a dishonest manner. However, you can use it to get a person to think in a specific direction or line of thought. Manipulators use NLP to engineer specific responses from a person.

NLP attempts accomplish two ends, eliciting and anchoring. Eliciting occurs when NLPers use language and leading to draw their victims into an emotional state. Once the desired state is accomplished, the NLPer will then anchor the emotion with a specific physical clue - for example, tapping on their shoulder. This simply means that an NLPer can invoke the same emotion in you by tapping your shoulder.

For example, let us say the NLP manipulator makes you feel depressed or unworthy using language, leading and other NLP techniques. This is followed by tapping the back of your hands in a specific manner to create anchoring. Thus, each time they want to create an emotion of being disillusioned, depressed and unworthy in you, they will tap the back of your palm. It is nothing but conditioning you to feel in a certain way with linked physical clues.

Now that you have a fair idea of what NLP is or how manipulators can use it for submission, what can you do to guard yourself against NLP manipulators?

Here are some tips to prevent NLPers from pulling their remarkably smart yet sneaky tricks on you:

1. be wary of people mirroring your body language. Agreed, you didn't know this until now, but people imitating or copying your body language is one of the biggest red flags of them trying to manipulate, influence or persuade you to act in a desired manner. I really enjoy testing these NLP experts using subtle hand gestures and leg movements to gauge if they are indeed mirroring my body language to establish a rapport.

If they follow suit, that's my clue to flee! Experienced NLPers have mastered the art of subtle mirroring, which means you may not even realize they are imitating your actions. NLP beginners will instantly imitate the exact same movement in their eagerness to establish a feeling of oneness. Good way for you to call their bluff!

2. Confuse with eye movements. Another fantastic way to call an NLP manipulator's bluff is to notice if they are paying very close attention to your eyes or eye movements. NLP users often examine their target or victim's very carefully. The eye movements are scrutinized to gauge how you access and store information.

In effect, they want to determine what parts of the brain you are utilizing to gather clues about your thoughts and feelings. I say beat this by darting your eyes all around the place randomly. Move them upwards and downwards or from side to side in no clear pattern. You are throwing your NLP manipulator off course. Make it appear natural. Their calibration will go down the wayside.

3. Beware of people's touch. One of the techniques NLPers use is anchoring. If you know a person practices NLP, and you are in an especially heightened or intense emotional condition, do not allow them to touch you in any manner. Just throw them off course by suddenly laughing hard or flying into a fit of rage. Basically, you are confusing them about the emotion they need to anchor. Even if they attempt to establish a physical clue to invoke certain emotions, they'll be left with a mixed bag of crazy laughter, rage and whatever else you did.

4. Watch out for permissive language. Typical language used by NLPers includes "be relaxed," "relax and enjoy this," and other similar statements. Beware of this NLP, hypnotist style language that induces you into a state of deep relaxation or trance to get you to think or act in a specific manner. Skilled or covert manipulators rarely command in a straightforward manner.

They will cleverly seek your permission to give you the impression that you are doing what they want you to do out of your own free will (one of their many sinister tricks). If you observe experienced hypnotists, they will never outright command you to do anything but seek your permission to make it appear as if it is being done organically, with your consent.

5. Guard Against Gibberish. Watch out for mumbo jumbo that just doesn't make any logical sense or twisted/complicated statements that mean little. For example, "As you free the feeling of being held by your thoughts, you will find yourself in alignment with the voice of your success." Does this make any sense? NLP manipulators won't say anything purposeful, but rather, they will program your emotional state to lead it where they want to.

One of the best ways to guard against this sort of hypnotism-NLP induced manipulation is to urge the manipulator to be more specific. "Can you be clearer about this?" "Can you specify exactly what you mean by that?" It won't just interrupt their cleverly set technique but will also force the interaction into precise language, thus breaking the trance brought about through ambiguous words and phrases.

6. Don't quickly agree to anything. If you find yourself being compelled to make an instant decision about something important, and it feels like you are steered in a specific direction, escape the situation. Wait a day to make a decision. Do not be swept or led into making a decision that you do not want to make on an impulse. Sales professionals are adept at manipulating buyers into purchasing something they don't need using sneaky manipulation and NLP tactics. When someone rushes you into a decision, it should be a warning signal to back off and hold on until you've thought more about the situation.

Dark Psychology And Nlp In Comparison

Dark Psychology is an investigation of the human condition comparable to the mental idea of people to go after others. In lay terms, Dark Psychology investigates that part of human instinct that permits us intentionally and persistently takes activities that carry damage to our kindred people. Mind you, the utilization of prey right now not really convert into the physical hurting of an individual despite the fact that, there is a part of Dark Psychology that is committed altogether to this. In consequent sections, we will contact quickly on those territories to show signs of improvement comprehension of the subject.

In films or books, you may have gone over words or expressions implying darkness inside". Indeed, even probably the most well-known savants made references to this. The venerated book of the Christians discusses how "the core of man is urgently devilish". We have all experienced that one person who we have portrayed as extraordinarily quiet or saved in social settings just for this equivalent individual to execute a demonstration so naughty that we think that it's hard to connect that demonstration with this person being referred to. In some cases, we are those people. As amazing as it might appear, it isn't altogether stunning.

Those cases are simply activated reactions to outer circumstances. The pot was blended so to talk and those dark feelings that stowed away underneath stewed to the surface. Normally they retreat once control is applied. Everybody has an inactive propensity to be somewhat shrewd or simply out and out underhandedness if the right "catches" is pushed. Some others then again are completely in charge of these dark feelings. They support them, feed them and when it fills their own needs, they stubbornly release them to the detriment of someone else.

Once in a while, these feelings are prepped since the beginning. A youngster discovers that in the event that the person cries with a specific goal in mind, the grown-ups in their lives race to do their offering. In the event that the guardians don't dazzle on the kid early enough the misleading quality of this, the kid grows up deduction individuals in their lives can be controlled into doing their offering. The crying would stop to be a weapon as they develop however, they would proceed in their manipulative manners. Where they don't utilize tears, they use feelings to coerce their unfortunate casualties. In this way, what began as a blameless infantile conduct turns into a dark need to control.

The lengths that this individual would go to apply their control would characterize the power of their activities. Dark Psychology is tied in with examining the point of view of an individual like this. It looks to comprehend the intention behind these activities, the examples displayed from before these demonstrations are done to after and illuminates how an individual can adamantly observe those activities to end knowing the hurt and torment it may cause to another person. Dark Psychology lights up the clouded side of human instinct.

NLP or Neuro-Linguistic Programming is a method that changes a person's way of thinking and behaving, with the promise of helping people to achieve more in life. Richard Bandier and John Grinder developed this technique and quickly became popular in different marketing, political, and other movements beginning in the 1970s. Today, NLP continues to be used as a treatment aimed at changing people's thinking and behavioral patterns for a variety of reasons, including the treatment of certain types of anxiety and phobias. This program or series of techniques is often promoted with the promise of improving communication, performance at home, work, and overall better enjoyment of life.

In order to understand the topic easily and clearly, there is a need to know what the acronym NLP means its full meaning, the benefits, the uses, and also any pros and cons. The meaning of the acronym NLP is Neuro-Linguistic Programming. It also involves three different components.

In simple terms, Neuro-Linguistic Programming is broken down into:

Neuro: This means the neurological part

Linguistic: It is the language that is used

Programming: Refers to the language used for the neural functions.

Neuro

Neurology is the study and treatment of the nervous system, which includes the brain and spinal cord. Every day, our senses work together to pick up different stimuli from our surroundings, including odors we smell, sounds we hear, textures we feel, and sights we see they then relay these stimuli to the brain, which generates an apt response.

The human mind consists of two parts—the conscious mind and the subconscious mind. The conscious mind governs your senses and helps you make decisions. The subconscious mind is like an autopilot mode, operating outside of consciousness. Your body is just going through the motions, seemingly without the involvement of your mind and absent of thought. Even if your subconscious mind helps you perform certain tasks automatically, you still need to consult your conscious mind daily.

What if you can reduce some of the load on your conscious mind? What if you can empower your subconscious mind to make more decisions? It will certainly make your life easier, won't it? NLP helps your conscious mind converge with your subconscious mind.

Your mind will be able to relate and respond faster to similarities. It will collect and sort information from your brain into specific folders for safekeeping. Then, you will only need to extrapolate and apply that information to different situations that arise.

Linguistic

Linguistics refers to the study of languages. You cannot communicate effectively without adequate language skills. If others cannot understand you, or you cannot understand them, then how can you progress? We call these issues language barriers. Human beings are wired for expression, so it is unfortunate to be unable to effectively convey our thoughts and feelings. To get your point across, you need to improve the way you speak. You need to put effort into establishing better communication skills.

At the same time, internal communication is also critical, because immediate action requires clear thought and expression. If your mind tells you one thing and you do another, then you will not be able to accomplish your goals.

Programming

Programming involves the bifurcation and transportation of information to different folders in your brain. You need to program yourself in a manner that is conducive to productivity and makes the most of your skillset. When we are young, our minds are fresh, impressionable, and capable of capturing a lot of information. Not just that, but we can also remember things for longer. However, with age, this changes, and it becomes difficult to process and store information. You can fix this problem with NLP. NLP will help you not only acquire information, but also divide and store it in your memory.

In short, Neuro-Linguistic Programming means the language used to understand the mind. A simple example will help us understand better. Have you ever had to communicate with another person, and you do not get to understand each other? One of the reasons could be a language barrier. This mostly happens when you are from different regions.

This happens when you visit a new and foreign country; you get hungry and decide to look for a restaurant. You get the menu and decide to get a steak, only to be disappointed later when lamb chops are offered. This is because of the typical relationship that a person has with their unconscious mind. Every human being loves a positive life, healthier relationship, having peace with the member of their family, being healthy, having a good diet, and more money. But the last outcome might frustrate when there is no proper communication and poor delivery of expectations.

. In simple terms, the unconscious mind is not set out to frustrate or discourage anyone. But it is supposed to help you get that what you have planned and achieving your mission. The downside is when there is no proper communication, a lot of expectation and no plan that is outlined. There will be a constant frustration and eventually more "Lamp Chops" will be served.

At this point, there is a clear general picture of what NLP is. Now, we need to know the technical explanation of NLP and how it is applied. Simply put NLP involves the balance between personal development and communication. It was developed in the '70s in the United States, California by Richard Bandler and John Grinder. There was a link between the three components; the neurological part (Neuro), the language (linguistic) and the behavioral patterns that a person has and developed through experiences (programming). They also believed that there is a chance that the components can be altered and make a person achieve their plans and meet their goals.

Grinder and Bandler believe that the methods used for NLP can sharpen the skills and make people exceptional and that anyone can achieve those skills. And they also state that NLP methods can be used to treat different ailments like depression, tic disorder, phobias, short-sightedness, common cold, allergies, and also learning disorders.

Most companies and hypnotherapists use NLP for marketing; they do that when they organize seminars, workshops, training for single businesses or for agencies of the government. NLP is not a pseudoscience and the claims laid out have no evidence that it has worked. It is believed to be outdated and cannot give actual and accurate information on how the brain works. The theory used in the neurological approach is said to contain errors.

The claims that were made by Grindr and Bandler is said to contain flaws in the methodology used and does not support any claim. It is believed that there more than two studies that have produced better claims as compared to the claims that were considered extraordinary by Bandler and Grinder and even other practitioners. There are some hypnotherapists who have adopted the method an approach. Even companies that deal with marketing and training for government agencies and also businesses

The Police, Fbi And Military Techniques That Are Connect With Npl Or Mind Control

NLP, the mind, and ultimate control

Have you ever wondered how some people are able to handle change constructively and creatively? While some people are knocked off balance by changes in their lives, others seem to fit right in perfectly. Why is it that some people seem to be in the right place at the right time? How comes some people have good relationships while others cannot get it together even for a week? Is there some form of good luck or inborn traits, making some people more successful than others?

One of the professors at the University of California called John Grinder, and his student called Richard Bandler started to work on a behavioral study project in the 1970s. They observed the behaviors of successful people and were more interested in why some people so good at what they do when compared to others. The findings helped them to develop the neurolinguistic programming, which involved observing, codifying, and replicating the behaviors and thought patterns of successful people. The programming explores the relationship between our Neuro (how we think) linguistic (how we communicate) and programs (pour patterns of emotions and behaviors).

The background of Neuro-linguistic programming is that positive behaviors that lead to success can be copied. The professor and the student were interested in the difference between the thought patterns, behaviors, and language use of successful and unsuccessful people. Their findings are the basis of NLP today. Simply put, the researchers claimed that success has very little to do with luck. You do not have to be lucky in order to succeed. Changing your approaches to life can help you to become more successful in relationships, career, social spec, and other situations. Though some people develop natural ways of becoming successful, these ways of thinking, acting, and speaking can be learned by anyone who is willing to give it a shot.

The Neurolinguistic programming was developed years ago, but a lot of redefinition has taken place over the years. Currently, NLP has become a commonly used technique in self-development and therapy. It is used in education, business, military, and above all, for individuals. NLP can be successfully applied in personal life, and a lot of big companies train their staff on how to use NLP with clients.

Basically, NLP is about how we develop mental representations sounds, images, and verbal descriptions of different situations. When we become aware of the internal maps of reality within us, it becomes easier to consciously change our inner landscape and consequently respond differently to people and situations in the outside world.

One of the main benefits of using NLP is that results can be seen very quickly. For instance, people with some kinds of phobias can be treated in a matter of minutes using some of the techniques found in NLP. Further, blockages and fears can be dealt with easily and quickly through the use of NLP. Honestly speaking, NLP has shed a lot of light on how we interact with our physical and social environments and other aspects of life.

NLP, manipulation, and mind control

Can NLP help you avoid negative manipulation and mind control? Yes, NLP can help anyone to fight manipulators. Often, we move along life on autopilot- responding to life in an extensively automatic way. This leaves us vulnerable to manipulation because we hardly analyze situations critically and make strong decisions. When living life on autopilot, we tend to follow what other people are doing (social proof) and also allow other people to influence our choices.

Sometimes go through life drive by those subconscious programs which we have learned and practiced for years – some of them we practice since childhood.

Some self-development advocates and personal change ambassadors can fail to explain to us how we can avoid the specific tools we should apply to improve our lives. On the other hand, NLP lays out the tools you need to implement that change. It informs you that you are responsible for your actions, reactions, and responses to the situations in life. NLP allows you to get behind the steering wheel and take charge of your life instead of having another person drive you around.

NLP is practiced more because of its practicality – The tools are functional, and a wide range of challenges can be addressed through NLP. Some of the issues include;

- Developing better relationships,
- Becoming more healthy
- Overcoming phobias and fears such as fear of public speaking,
- Improving communication
- Being more successful and impactful in your career and family life.

Success in any field of life, be it career, sport, family, et cetera requires excellence. Neuro-linguistic programming is a roadmap for this excellence. Although other factors like luck and innate ability play a role in the success of an individual, the majority of NLP tools must be applied. Success is a predictable result of behaving and thinking in a certain way.

How People Manipulate You?

The type of people that the manipulative people target is low self-esteem people, no boundaries people, and desperate people. Now how do you know if you are being manipulated? If you feel like you are constantly criticized and he makes you feel inadequate, then it means you are being manipulated. If you get into an argument and he's giving you the silent treatment, you are being manipulated. If somebody gives you the silent treatment, which makes you go crazy, you start thinking of every scenario, and you start making assumptions because no dialogue is happening that can reassure or bring clarity to your thoughts, then that is a huge form of manipulation.

Ghosting You

And guys do this a lot, even if it is something as simple as ghosting you. Because it trains you to not get used to hearing from him certain times, and you always have to reach out to see how he is doing and checking out to see if he remembers the date that he set for you. They use their profession or their education to delay you finding out the truth or make you feel like they're always the right one. For instance, if you get into an argument with someone and you are dating a lawyer, they will tell you something like, "I've been a lawyer for five years, and I know what I'm talking about and people that did what you just did need not to be trusted." They sort of use their title to rain over you and make it look like they are the right ones. What happens is that you silently agree to what they are saying because they do know what they are talking about. Because they know when people lie, and they know it through body language.

Demonize your reactions

They tend to demonize your reactions because anytime someone that is manipulating you and they don't want you to be able to express yourself or control the situation, they're going to make you feel like you are the bad guy for reacting the way that you did to the situation. They will flip the script on you because you didn't agree with their actions.

You might tell him, "Hey, babe, I don't know why you just liked this girl's picture on Instagram. I thought that we agreed that you are not going to do this. You show me their stuff. Because it makes me feel embarrassed that my boy is licking the girl's photos and commenting on rubbish on Instagram, and it makes me feel insecure because you are my boyfriend". Then he will say something like, "you are so insecure it's just Instagram, I can't believe that you are seriously talking to me about a comment that I wrote to a girl. First of all, I don't even know her, and she looks nice. Other guys are commenting on her photos, but why do you care because I'm with you". So they demonize you and make you feel like the way you feel is not accounted for. They make you feel like the way you feel is invalidated because he doesn't know that girl and maybe he may even be trying to learn that girl.

Using pity

One of the greatest forms of manipulation is by using pity. Because getting pity out of anybody is going to guilt-trip them, so that they feel bad for you and do what you say and hear you out and like whatever trash you want to slip by because they are feeling bad for you.

For instance, if you say, "I just realized that when we were in the get-together, you were nagging to really hanging out with me. You were just doing your own thing. I don't know everybody there, I felt alone, and I understand that you know everybody, but I didn't feel included. Then he will say something like, "Honey, I'm really sorry that you didn't feel included. However, what do you expect me to do, all the people were people that I grew up with? So I'm sorry that I wasn't holding your hand the entire time. But I did introduce you to some people. You know that I wouldn't do that to you. You know that I am not like that. I was just caught up. Plus I saw one of my girls from high school and we just started talking. Come on, if you really know me, you know that I wouldn't do something like that. I am not like that."

So they tried to play on your emotions so that you will think that they are helping you. To think something like, oh, "I do know him. I'm not sure that anyone will want to invite me somewhere and then drop me off and not even associate with me at all or leave me alone". So you feel bad for yelling at him because it gets overwhelming when you are hanging out with so many people that you haven't seen in a long time.

If you are bothered by the fact that he left you alone, then it means that he left you alone for so long that it became so uncomfortable. It's not a big deal if he's going to leave you for some minutes and go to say hi to someone, but he should introduce you to those people because you guys are in a relationship. So the reason why you are feeling how you are feeling is that something was wrong.

So the best way to combine this is to minimize their actions so that you get to stick around. If he says, "I can't believe you would do something like that. You should say, "What do you mean. You do dumb things all the time". These people that always want to downplay what it is that they are doing so that you will feel stupid and feel like you're overreacting on what the offense was

For instance, let's say that you want to surprise him and leave something cute in his mailbox. So you drive by his house, and you see another car parked in his driveway, and then you notice that another girl is in his house. And then you think that maybe that is one of his guy friend cars so you drive in his car and instead of you to give him a little bit surprised, you get out of the car because you don't know whose car you are seeing. You knock on the door and then he opens the door halfway and starts asking you what things like, "What are you doing here." And then you answer him, "I'm checking in. Are you well? I noticed that there is an extra car in the driveway, and it's not mine. So why are you not letting me in". And he says, "That is one of my home girls from high school we haven't talked in a long time, and she just wanted to drop by and catch up."

So you should say, "why is your friend in your house alone and you didn't even mention it to me. I've never seen this girl in my life, and I never knew that this is one of your home girls. Why am I just finding out about this"? And he says, "Calm down you are just a little extra obnoxious, she's just a friend. She just dropped by to say hi. I didn't even think about mentioning it to you, because it's not about what you think. Because if it was like that, you would just tell me," then he's trying to play ignore and because he wants you to feel guilty. He wants you to feel like how he can cheat on you when in broad daylight when he knows that you can come and visit his house. The best way that this guy's used to hide things is in plain sight eyesight because it's so unbelievable.

Glaring and Unbelievable things

They do glaring and unbelievable things, and then they try to convince you that what you saw wasn't true. And what you saw couldn't be what you possibly think. It is because it doesn't look like you will do anything like that, and he will have to be a real idiot to do something like that to you. He wants to minimize his action and play ignorant like he has no idea what it is, and you are tripping, and both of them are just friends. He also tries to make rude remarks in the name of humor.

It's so important that it's it in your subconscious mind, and whenever you guys are in an argument or in a situation where you feel intimidated, and you're someone that is easily intimidated by other beautiful girls, then what he says becomes your inner voice. So the joke that he makes about how big your nose gets into your mind.

Because you are thinking about the waitress and it's looking like he's flirting with her because she has a nose that he actually likes or he always makes fun of your crooked tooth, and you are very subconscious about that, and the girl over there has straight teeth.

So you must pay attention to things like that in the relationship and in friendships because there is always some sort of truth to those little remarks. There is always some sort of underlying truth if somebody is constantly attacking something about you like your physical appearance or playing on your weaknesses because they know that it is going to get you inevitably. But, remove any responsibility or accountability for what they are saying even though they're trying to make it look like a joke.

Act unapproachable

Another way that you know that you are being manipulated is when something happens, and you are bracing yourself to bring it up, but your spouse tends to act unapproachable. So you on top of making you feel nervous about bringing whatever it is that you want to mention. They tend to make you feel uncomfortable. If he is acting so weird, then you should don't know if it is a good time because he doesn't want you to be upset at you for what he offended you for. He just doesn't know how to approach the situation; that's why he is already acting upset. Because if somebody is already acting unapproachable when they know exactly what it is that took place or that offended you, then the easiest way to get you off their back and to roll over the situation is to ignore you to make it look like you can say anything.

As a lady, think about a situation whereby you have been talking to a guy, and something has offended you, but there is this unspoken energy that he does to make you feel like you can't bring up exactly what it is that you want to say. Because if you do, you will look crazy, you will look annoying, you will look insecure, and he'll stop talking to you. He will give you the silent treatment. Those are manipulative tactics if you don't feel comfortable enough to have a dialogue with him and express yourself and how you feel with him that you are with, and then there is a problem.

Manipulation And Mind Control Through Nlp

L earning the basics of psychology is necessary to get to work as an effective manipulator. These basics make up the skeleton of every technique that allows you to manipulate people, so you can't expect to manipulate people without knowing these basics like the back of your hand.

You can use these inherent human weaknesses to help you as a manipulator, but this doesn't mean you have to use it in a harmful way. Think about it this way: you can see the weaknesses and vulnerabilities in yourself already. It isn't unethical to recognize these same vulnerabilities in other people and use them to manipulate their minds.

Before we start on these topics in psychology, let's look at an example so you can see how psychology is integral to psychological manipulation.

The subject does not seem to be doing well, and you want them to adopt a new belief. (Remember, once again: mind control and persuasion are changing someone's thoughts while manipulation is changing someone's behavior, and mind control is just reading the cryptic brain language expressed through unconscious communication.) In this case, let's say you want them to join your faith. Now, what you are trying to do may be completely different from this, but we don't have the space to examine every possibility, so we will just go with this one.

You see, when the subject is already in a vulnerable state, we can take advantage of it and get them to have beliefs they wouldn't otherwise have. The key is the belief we give them has to give them hope that things can be better since they currently aren't feeling so good.

But this is only the simplest example, because you don't usually deal with subjects who are currently in a negative state. Everyone runs into negative states sometimes, and you can take advantage of them, but it certainly isn't something you can take for granted.

There are also people who seem to be negative all the time and have a problem seeing the light at the end of the tunnel. This makes them particularly easy to mind control — all it takes is convincing them that your system of beliefs and ideas is their light at the end of the tunnel.

We aren't only bringing up human vulnerabilities for the sake of exploiting people when they are at their lowest. Not at all these are only the most basic scenarios, because even as an intermediate-level psychology manipulator, you have to know how to bring these vulnerabilities out of people when they are not already in this negative state.

It may sound like a hard or even an impossible thing to do, but it truly isn't. When you have even just a decent understanding of the basic findings in psychology, you can bring out anyone's weak spots and use them to get people to adopt your ideas — or mind control them.

It doesn't come naturally for everyone. Some people do better in the practice side of things with psychology manipulation, but struggle to adapt their frames in new situations because they don't have a strong enough grasp of the theoretical side. Then others are the opposite: they can explain exactly how these principles of psychology work, but getting use out of them in practice is much more of a struggle.

No matter which position you find yourself in, you still need to learn more about psychology. Even if you think you already understand it, you should know from what you learn that repetition is a crucial part of learning. The more times you repeat these ideas to yourself, the better consolidated the ideas are in your brain, and the better you will be able to apply them on the fly when you are manipulating someone with psychology.

If you feel you already have the confidence to use techniques like door-in-the-face, learning the psychology might seem less important. You think that since you have done similar things before in sales or whatever the setting, you must already have an intuitive idea of psychology.

It may indeed be true that you understand psychology intuitively, but that doesn't mean it is enough to be the best psychology manipulator you can be. Just like the more theoretically-minded person, you need to get these concepts into your brain repeatedly, so they are easier to recall when you need them.

Now that we are on the same page, we will start with the psychological reasons for procrastination. Remember that you will be able to apply this psychology lesson to mind control later on — we are not only telling you this for its own sake, although it can be enjoyed this way as well. The hidden parts of the brain that allow things like procrastination to happen are the kinks in the armor of the mind that you will use to mind control people. What is the kink in the cerebral armor that makes procrastination so prevalent in people?

You should start by thinking of a time you procrastinated yourself. Maybe you aren't the kind of person who puts this off — maybe the very idea stresses you out far too much. If that is you, then imagine that feeling of nervousness that prevents you from procrastinating in the first place. This is all that matters for the purposes of our lesson anyway.

If you have procrastinated before, think about how it feels physically. What kinds of thoughts run through your head when you let this happen?

As usual, we advise you not to overthink it, because what you are feeling at this time should be obvious and easy to point out. You are incredibly nervous when you put things off for too long; you feel your blood pumping through your body more than you usually do. It is as if your house is on fire, because whatever it is that you put off, you can't think about anything besides putting out the fire. Nothing else takes up your attention when you get to this point of procrastination.

This is the subjective vantage point of procrastination. As a psychologist, you want to know the physical and chemical changes that happen in your brain when you procrastinate. The long and short of it is you are feeling two main chemicals flood your veins: cortisol and epinephrine.

Epinephrine is often referred to as adrenaline. It is a chemical that fills our bodies when we need to act quickly. Cortisol is slightly different; it isn't used for life and death situations, but rather it is a general stress-inducing chemical. You might wonder why your body would purposefully put you into a state of stress, but the answer isn't too hard to figure out.

If you were never stressed, you wouldn't be able to survive. You wouldn't be driven to get food to eat or find shelter. Our ancestors needed cortisol for inducing stress a lot more than we need it today. In fact, it is easy to see how people these days are more stressed than they should be.

When people who procrastinate are asked to evaluate the thoughts that go through their heads, one clear pattern emerged in the data. The one thing that kept all of them from doing their work for so long was fear. They were afraid that their work would be bad because they weren't good enough; they didn't even want to think about the work they had to do.

It wasn't because they just wanted to spend their time watching streaming television (although this had to be partially the case). It was because all of them felt a great sense of fear that their work wouldn't be satisfactory.

Hopefully, you can relate to this feeling yourself. Even if you don't procrastinate, you should still be able to relate to the fear that your work isn't good enough. The idea is that people procrastinate because they don't want to face their own perceived lack of skill or competence. If they start doing the work, they will have to confront how imperfect it is.

Now, non-procrastinators still get the increase of cortisol to get them to do their work. But they do it on time because they get the meaning of this chemical signal early on and simply abide by what it is meant to communicate.

Meanwhile, procrastinators have everything working against them from two angles. For one, the longer they put off doing the work, the more the cortisol and eventually epinephrine increase. They already weren't doing the work when the levels were already pretty high, so when they just keep increasing, it doesn't cause them to simply start working. They are unable to use the chemical change as a means to change their behavior, but they still feel the unpleasant feelings it gives them.

The second thing going against procrastinators is that awful feeling of fear stemming from their notion that their work is inadequate. On one side, they have the cortisol and epinephrine trying to force them into doing this work, but on the other, their intense feeling of fear is telling them not to do the work. If they do, they will have to confront how bad (they perceive) it is. As you can see, procrastinators have opposing forces that don't push them either one way or the other. It just keeps them still, and they don't do the work.

That is, until the point of no return comes. For those who haven't procrastinated, this is a hard thing to describe, but in the mind of a procrastinator, something completely changes once the deadline gets too close.

Psychologists say that this is the point where the social consequences become apparent. The procrastinator realizes that if they don't get their act together soon, their boss or their teacher at school will make sure they face the consequences. But the consequences themselves are less of less importance than the social consequences.

Procrastinators still want to have a good reputation with the people they know. They have reached a point where if they don't get their act together, their social groups will not look at them the same way.

Hopefully, this scenario was described in enough detail for someone who has always been responsible and never dealt with this before — because you will have to apply it to psychology and manipulation in a moment. The whole purpose of establishing the scenario was to discuss the kink in the armor of the brain that makes it possible for us to procrastinate.

After all, if you think about it, the fact that we can procrastinate is pretty strange. Why would the brain want to not do things? If you followed along, you have a good shot at answering this for yourself.

The human weakness revealed in procrastination is our tendency to not change our behavior until a powerful chemical reaction changes things. The procrastinator may have been dealing with the fear and the cortisol and epinephrine in the background of their minds, but at some point, these chemicals reach a new height, and they simply cannot ignore their work anymore. Otherwise, these feelings will not go away.

Our last human weakness is actually the number one worst fear that people consistently report. It is speaking in public. We don't have to spend too much time on this one because it has a lot of overlap with the human weakness of feeling inadequate.

It is no more complicated than it sounds. In fact, since the fear is so common, it is likely that you have at least experienced the fear of speaking in front of people, even if you ended up doing it and were fine with it. But public speaking frightens people because they become the center of attention. Their reputation among peers, in their eyes, will completely change if they do something wrong.

Mind Control And Even Undetected Mind Control

People term the word "mind control" as persuasion, seduction, manipulation, politics, sales skills or advertising among others. The truth is that each time we open our mouths to communicate or utter words, we use mind control. The more we try to deny how we will use mind control the more ineffective we are in it.

In our everyday life, the few things we use mind control include motivating children to perform better in their academics, motivating people to buy our product and services, making someone reconsider what he/she believes in and making a group of people feel superior towards other groups.

Whether intentional or not, when you are trying to motivate people to do something, or people do something without asking questions, what is happening is mind control. You need to know how to make use of mind control to your advantage because really mind control is everywhere. Since it involves controlling people's thoughts emotions and actions, several models can be used.

A very common model of mind control is the behavioral conditioning model, which works by giving rewards or punishments based on the behavior of a subject. It deals with a series of step that involves rewarding good behavior and punishing bad behavior.

For instance, if a young boy steals toys from a store, using this behavioral conditioning model, the first step is to reward the boy for being creative, which is for thinking outside the norms of the social behavior. After you make him get used to thinking outside the norm, and you are rewarding him for everything he steals.

NLP model is also used in mind control because this technique treats people as individuals and not a mass of robot, which means each person, is responsible for the change and processes that are unique to them. The major thing why NLP is used as a tool for controlling the mind is to determine ways in which people's processes are elicited. Once you are able to discover these unique processes, there is no limitation to how you can control such an individual's mind.

Like I said earlier mind control is not wrong in itself. For instance, if a group could stay together as one, they would have a better chance to survive anything the world push to them. But if one person's thought does not align with the other people in the group, their survival as a whole could be threatened.

Some parents use the mind control process to take part in every aspect of a child; sometimes, this is done unknowingly. The technique is also employed by most teaching institutions. And, it's no news that in advertising, most industries look for a way to manipulate people to buy whatever they are selling.

There is a need for you to start examining people's efforts to influence you. And importantly, examine how you respond to those influences. It might be on a TV show, conversations, or images. You should learn to ask yourself what those people's intents really are. This way you might find the possible answers to if or not the intention was to control your mind.

Let us take a look at extreme human behaviors. It seems difficult to understand why normal people will behave in a contrary way. For instance, those involved in cultism, ideally no normal human being should want to kill themselves. The question should be, are they crazy? Are they monsters? What could have been led them to do what they did? In cases like this, we try to use our moral acts to understand how other people mind works. But this will block us from being able to understand what is going on. In mind-controlling, you have to put aside your judging and moral analysis.

The study of mind control can benefit anyone. Because sometimes, the more easily we can influence people around us, the easier it is for us to fulfill our basic needs which include money, security, love, even sex.

Sometimes the kind of power you are hungry for can only come to you through mind control.

Learning mind control helps you to be able to evaluate yourself. It also helps you not to be too distracted or annoying about politics or advertisement unnecessarily.

If you need to train yourself on how to control the mind, learning this will require that you read and study it. Studying means you have to make yourself understand the concept at least on an intellectual level; it goes beyond just reading to have a brief surface knowledge about it.

To be good at doing this, you need to study hypnosis, social influence, and brainwashing. These are a few techniques used in mind control.

Hypnosis is described as a cooperative interaction in which someone will provide suggestions, and the other person will respond. Gaining popularity is a form of hypnosis. It is also used for medical and therapeutic importance.

Brainwashing is a type of mind control which involves the process of convincing people to let go of beliefs they had in the past, and enforce them in taking up new values and ideals. Not all brainwashing is wrong, so are right and important to be done. This is quite similar to lying, but it is different. The technique has been used by people about a very time. One of the first things to do is to keep your subject in isolation. This is because if the subject is around other people, there will be receiving influences. After this, you will make them undergo the process of breaking themselves.

After, you then have to create what you want them to believe in. Brainwashing can span into several months or even years.

Social influence is the study on how the interactions between people influence them. An understanding of this will help you to design your environment such that everybody will be under your mind control.

Other forms are mind control involves the use of manipulation, persuasion, and deception. As a matter of fact, anybody can be a victim of being manipulated by mind control. When something is considered as a lack and being insufficient, a normal individual will look for a way around it, sometimes at the cost of other people's happiness and things. The point is that the moment you get in power, or you now have influence over other people, you will see how quick it is to dive into mind-controlling.

Understanding this concept of mind control, of course, there will be a need for you to learn and read about the concept, but the most important thing is that you have to desire to connect deeply with people. You would have to understand how to control people in a way that when you're around them, they like it, and they will always be thankful for the attention you give them.

In learning mind control you have to be curious that means there is no limit to the amount of information you need to know and even study. This curiosity will help you examine everything that you learn about mind control. Another thing is that you have to know how to think in a strategic way and not just the use of tactics.

In mind control, we have three levels of intention, which involve strategies, the stated intention, the hidden intention, and the secret intention. The stated intention includes what you want to tell people from the start, the hidden intention is later revealed as you begin to express yourself and actions, whilst the secret intention is the core reason for your action, this might never be unveiled.

Edgar H. Schein highlighted five steps of mind control. These include identifying a new identity, the use of reward/punishment cycle, manipulating in a mystical way, the use of mind-altering techniques like monotony, hypnosis through excessive chanting, and drawing out the logic confession.

However, the application of this knowledge can be seen in marketing, political action, or even in relationships. The 'dumb blonde mind control" is a definite strategy used by women to control their men. This works in a way that you promise a man sex, and then you combine it with helplessness and vulnerability.

The one who wants to play this dumb blonde mind control game will be able to alternate between being sexy and helpless or being loved and rejected, in such a way that it looks like a swing.

The affection or rejection swing will be as a result of something her subject is doing. The man then begins to change his behavior, thinking he is the one in control of her good moods whereas, he is responding to conditioning. To achieve this real control over your subject as a Lady, you have to make him believe that he had you figured it out; he will be so sure that he has gotten you. This can keep him hooked.

Also, some people use drugs for mind control. An example is a cigarette. You wonder that despite the fact the smoking results in bad health, millions of people are still engaging in it. The same people selling it are the same people advertising that smokers are liable to die young. The producers make you feel they care, yet they produced, but nicotine present in the drug has made them addictive. Another drug for mind Control is alcohol. Alcohol removes inhibitions. However, the effect is for a very short time. It is used to distract the mind from other issues. The class of drugs known as hypnotics, which helps to depress the over functionality of the nervous system and make you be more open to suggestions, are also used for mind control.

Undetected mind control is one of the most useful tools of governments, media, and companies. Think about a time you had low self-esteem. You left your house feeling very good that day—at least until you saw an underwear advertisement with an impossibly slim yet curvaceous woman with a guy whose abs are better than you could ever have the time to develop. The couple in that ad looks so happy and sexy. They are cool, and they are wearing the brand of underwear in the advertisement. You begin to feel ever-so-slightly insecure the rest of the day after comparing yourself to the two beautiful models. Later that night, you see an ad on Facebook or on TV for this same brand. You remember how cool the ad was, and how you yourself want the happy, sexy life presented in the advertisement. You buy a few pairs of underwear online from this brand by the end of the night.

It can be carried out by one manipulative individual on another, or it can be a large-scale project by a big corporation or government. Individuals who engage in undetected mind control to be manipulative and cowardly. They want what they want, but without having to ask or having to cooperate with the person they are trying to control. When undetected mind control occurs in an interpersonal relationship, the manipulator usually chooses a victim who needs something. Someone in need is almost always more open to undetected mind control tactics because having those needs unmet makes them more reward focused. The corollary to this is that being more reward focused makes the victim less aware of consequences; they will be more compliant towards the manipulator because they are focusing on the possibility of being relieved of their unsatisfied needs.

Overcoming Manipulation

Many manipulators will do their best to make sure that the victim doesn't realize what's happening but there are ways to use this to your advantage.

By creating stakes, the manipulator has control over you because they know that either way they win. During those stakes, it's important to recognize that they don't expect you do not play their game.

A manipulator knows how to use dark psychology to make the victim do what they ask. If they are constantly picking on you or making a note of every mistake you've ever made, the manipulator is planning to use this against. Their reactions to the things that disappoint them are important too.

Pay attention to how they respond to you in the beginning because this will change as time passes. The manipulator will take note of how you react to things not going your way. If you are prone to fits of rage yourself when frustrated, the manipulator will know how to use that against you. If you get depressed or are deeply saddened by failure, the manipulator will use that against you. Dark psychology focuses on human reaction to situations and using that to influence a situation.

A manipulator will focus on every reaction, every moment of joy, sadness or anger and twist it to suit their needs. For example, Liam and Cierra are brother and sister. Liam wants Cierra to stay home from summer camp this year because he doesn't want her to ruin his summer. Liam knows that Cierra doesn't like Sarah D. from her grade and would do anything to avoid her. Liam tells Cierra that this year Sarah is going to be at the summer camp and she's going to be bunking in her cabin. Cierra not wanting to spend a whole summer sleeping in the same room as Sarah drops out of the summer camp

Emotional Intelligence 2.0

and now Liam gets to go alone like he wanted. Something as simple as knowing that his sister didn't like another student was all he needed to manipulate her into doing what he wanted.

It's easy to manipulate someone into doing what you ask when you know what grinds their gears. Using dark psychology could make it easier for a manipulator to take advantage, and the victim wouldn't know how they gave them the opportunity to use these weaknesses.

Narcissistically they would believe they are smarter than their victim and pay close attention to how they react to even the manipulator themselves. Manipulators love over sharers, or people who don't care who knows about their lives. These people are easier to manipulate because they lay everything about them on the table.

For example, Tyra is always talking about her bad marriage to John, John's friend that wants to have sex with Tyra knows how bad his marriage to his wife is and knows how John acts, so he portrays the exact opposite of that and manipulates Tyra into sleeping with him by complaining about his own friendship with John.

A manipulator will always make things go their way by using keywords that may trigger a response out of the victim. They may berate them constantly for something small or make them feel guilty for having any reaction to what's happening around them at all. A manipulator's main tool to anything is pulling the wool over the victim's eyes. Dark persuasion is making the victim feel like they have no control over the situation or giving all the "power" to the victim. Prolonging events or constant empty promises may occur.

The manipulator will always show that they are in complete control but it's up to the victim to say they aren't falling for it. They will find ways to make it feel like the victim has the power of choice, but the manipulator has carefully thought out every step from the moment they picked their victim.

Dark persuasion considers age, creed, upbringing, religion and/or sexuality. The manipulator will take all these factors and create a trap for their victim. The victim would be completely unaware of what's happening, but they will feel like the events are correlating with their behavior or with what's happening as the situation transpires.

They won't be able to see how the manipulator has taken control of what's happening and leads them to do what they ask of them without much question. The manipulator is skilled at masking their true intentions of what they are doing, and the victim won't see they are clearly being manipulated.

Manipulators may also get angry over very little things, to make themselves look and feel bigger. They will start fights over someone not listening to them or they will start a fight over the way a person looks at them.

A manipulator will shout especially when they know they are in the wrong and don't want to admit it. As mentioned, if they feel cornered or don't know how to make themselves look like the victim, shouting is the next method. If someone for no reason just explodes the fear they incite can make someone do what they want.

A manipulator would be hyper curious about your life or your friends or family. The victim would voluntarily share this with a boyfriend/girlfriend/partner maybe even a close friend. If the manipulator seems to provide nothing to contribute to the stream of information they get, be careful with what is shared.

Manipulators will make sure that the victim is dependent purely on them, constantly creating a situation where they would be the higher authority and not be able to lose the rank they have over the victim. Taking them out of their comfort zone would be the most important part.

They would never let them go to a place where the victim could be superior.

A manipulator might prevent them from going online or checking their phones or would get mad at them for trying to source check any information they come across during the relationship.

For example, Tom is with Jane. Tom doesn't want Jane to know anything about his past and gets irate with her every time she tries to look up anything. Tom deleted all photos on his social media accounts that had any inkling to him having any former partners as well as his old drug use. Tom doesn't want Jane to see anything before she started seeing him and when she asks about his past, Tom tells Jane he was a good student and didn't get into any trouble.

A manipulator will almost always paint themselves as the hero in their own backstory; the narcissistic part of their personality prevents them from seeing it any other way. A good way to combat this is to not give in to any delusional attempts to lie about something. If you catch them in a lie, question it then and ask for proof. Or just leave the situation and don't further humor them.

Manipulators will always try to make the victim do what they want and sometimes they will use the victim to do it. They may try to lead the victim into believing that they are the one who wants to complete the task they are given. The manipulator will use the right combination of words to make sure that your thinking is lead toward what they want from you.

Manipulators know how to make the victim feel like they have more than they think they have. The victim must see that if something is reoccurring whether it is a conversation or something they've heard from them multiple times, there is most likely a deeper meaning behind this and you should either talk about it with the manipulator.

The manipulator will always play the victim. There is no reason for the manipulator to be the victim, but someone who wants to manipulate another person would never admit to being wrong in any situation. The victim could confront the manipulator and they will direct all attention to either their past or what they believe to be the source of their problems.

The manipulator will be morally incapable of seeing what they are doing wrong. It would be in the cynical responses to possibly saying something hurtful or the lack of regret they contain when something is done to hurt their victim. And when they're cornered, they'll either get aggressive or pretend to be horribly hurt by what occurred during the argument and use that as fuel for their guilt trap.

It's important to focus on the reactions that every single manipulator portrays; it would be in their eyes and in body language. Exposing what they do for what it is can be a good method but this can also be very dangerous. If you suspect someone of being a manipulator it is important that you look at what they do before picking out one single factor.

A manipulator's ability to bend a person's human nature requires using a step by step methodology based on what the victim needs to fall for their traps.

These mind games would keep the victim hooked on and it would keep the imbalance of power from shifting off the manipulator.

How To Manipulate Effectively

Methods of Manipulation

When it comes down to how people manipulate others, there are countless methods that can be used. Some people make use of methods that involve lying. Others try using methods that rely on constant showering and inundation of love or affection. There are many different manners that people can be controlled in and there is no rule that you must use any one method in particular. However, each and every technique that you will see can typically be classified into one of five different categories. Some forms of manipulation are considered positive reinforcement while others are negative, and others still are partial. Some people rely on punishment and others still rely on some form of traumatic event to get someone else to change how they behave.

At the end of the day, being able to understand these five criteria will allow you to better see how the manipulation attempts that you will be learning about will work. You will see that they all vary greatly from type to type, but they are all successful in their own unique ways. We will be going over each and every type of reinforcement within this section—we will be discovering what it means to use each of these types of reinforcement.

Positive reinforcement

Positive reinforcement is a behavioral reinforcement that is meant to make someone continue to perform what they have done. It involves preventing something that is desirable as the consequence of a behavior that was performed. Keep in mind that not all consequences are negative—a consequence is simply the result of the behavior or action that was taken and it can be positive, negative, or neutral.

When making use of positive reinforcement, you are going to be providing the individual that you are manipulating with a positive factor or a positive result when they perform the behavior that you want to see. Usually, you can see positive reinforcement as praise or a reward for doing the right action at the right time. Think of this as providing an allowance for your children if they do all of their chores for the week. You want them to feel incentivized to perform the right behaviors so you will give them the rewards that they need to keep them interested in doing so.

This is often done in manipulation as well—you may use love bombing, for example. This is a method that is commonly done to encourage the other party to behave in a very specific way because they want to continue to be showered with love, gifts, and affection for doing so. If you want to make use of this, you simply need to figure out the positive reinforcement that you plan on using and you provide it every single time that the other person or party does what you want to encourage.

Negative reinforcement

Negative reinforcement is the opposite—it is reinforcing a behavior by the removal of something negative when it is done properly. For example, imagine that you work a job that says that, if you complete all of your weekly work, you can have an extra day off. The catch, however, is that you have to complete that extra work during the week prior to the day. If you finish your work by Thursday evening and have nothing left on your weekly to-do list, you are told that you can have the Friday off. In this instance, having to go in to work for that Friday shift would be the negative reinforce. You would rather not work on Friday, so your production during the week has increased and improved so you can have an extra day off that week.

When it comes to manipulation, the negative reinforce will oftentimes be something that you would least expect. It may be that you are told that you will not have to do as much work if you do what the manipulator wants. It could be that you offer to forgive something if the other person does something else for you in return. It is meant to essentially work by making sure that the other party feels like helping or giving in to what is expected is going to be better than not.

Partial reinforcement

Partial reinforcement is essentially inconsistent reinforcement. It is meant to create a feeling of doubt or insecurity that can be preyed upon. It makes the individual feel like winning or getting that positive result is an option, but they have to sort of take a risk to make it happen. It is meant to instill some doubt or uncertainty into the other person. Surprisingly enough, when the chances of reward is made to be unpredictable, the individual that is going to be trying to get that reward will likely chase it far more often than if someone who was used to regular positive reinforcement would if it simply stopped happening.

This is essentially playing upon those same methods that are used to trap gamblers into continuing to throw money toward their games that they play. They will repeatedly sink money into gambling in hopes of winning because they know that they have to win at some point. After all, statistically speaking, they will at some point in time, so long as they keep playing, and the longer they go without being rewarded, the more they try because they believe that statistically, it will happen at some point soon.

Punishment

Punishment refers to the addition of something negative to the situation. You can add it to either the behavior being performed if you want that behavior to be ended, or you can use it until the behavior is performed until the punishment is ended. When you punish someone else, you are going to be making them uncomfortable or unhappy with the idea of repeatedly not following through with what needs to be done or what you would like for them to do. This can be done in many ways—some of them being more obvious than others. Punishments such as nagging or the silent treatment are two such examples. One continues to bother someone until the behavior is completed while the other refuses to speak to the other person until the behavior is completed.

When you use punishment, you want to make doing the opposite of what you want as unpleasant as possible so the other person decides to follow along with your wishes and gives in to you. When you do that, you ensure that you can get your way—you ensure that you more or less force the other person into wanting to give you what you wanted to make the punishment stop.

Trauma

Finally, the last method of attempting to manipulate someone else is through the use of trauma. Usually, these methods are the most overtly abusive of them all. Some of these will be through the use of verbal abuse. Others will make use of explosive tempers or attempting to intimidate the other person into obedience. Some will attempt to establish some degree of dominance or superiority over the other person and others will attempt to make the person being manipulated so incredibly wary about angering or frustrating the manipulator.

Essentially the manipulator is going to be trying to train the other person to avoid doing anything that would be deemed as contradictory or confrontational. The idea is to make the other person as afraid or intimidated by the idea of annoying or disagreeing with the manipulator as possible so the manipulator can continue to take advantage of the situation. The more that this happens, the more in control the manipulator gets to become, and with some of the most extreme methods of this form of manipulation, they only have to happen once before they become effective.

Detach From Emotions

When tapping into Dark Psychology and its uses, it is important to pay attention to the role that emotions play in your decisions. Many of our decisions will undoubtedly be imbued with emotion. Some of them are relatively easy; others take a great deal of learning and getting through challenges. Often times, we will need to detach from emotions. They can help you to gain motivation, and feeling joy and pride is one of the rewards for living a good life. Emotions are a necessary and ever-present thing. However, you must learn to separate from these experiences and know that they are not necessarily real. It might be hard to tear yourself away from feeling sad. You might not be able to at all. However, you must learn just to let that experience be. You can't let it take over your entire day. You have to let yourself let go of the "importance" of that emotion.

People who are driven only by emotions are carried away in whatever is happening. They are not able to use the logical side of their brain, rather letting their sadness, happiness, joy, or depression take them away.

First of all, let's talk about what we're not talking about. When talking about detaching from emotions, we are not talking about becoming cold and disconnected. This can be a source of coping for some people; they become disconnected and "detached" from emotions and use this to be unhealthy and justify it in their minds. This can be described as being aloof. These people are afraid of intimacy and connection. They are afraid of engaging with the world on an emotional level. Of course, we are emotional creatures, and emotions will always be a part of our experience as human beings. We can't part with this aspect of humanity, thank God. We have to learn to live with our emotions and use them in appropriate ways.

True detachment leads not to disconnection and aloofness, but rather to an ability to be wise. Wisdom is described as the ability to use knowledge. Well, detachment helps along the process of wisdom. We can't use our knowledge if we rely too much on the emotional information that we are experiencing to make a decision. To use the knowledge, we have to make decisions and understand our world; we have to contextualize our emotions. Wisdom comes from this contextualization. True detachment involves acknowledging our emotional states and dealing with them most efficiently. When we are detached from emotion, we are able to still engage in emotion while not letting it take over our decision-making.

We've all heard this one before: "when you assume, you make an Ass out of you and Me." this is an important lesson and understanding ours and other's biases is a big part of not assuming.

The first thing to ask yourself when you are thinking about the reason you assume things are this: Are you a psychic? Do you have a crystal ball that tells the past, future, and present truth? I bet not! For the rest of us, it takes to realize that we are not omniscient and that we can't tell what is going on in other people's minds.

We tend to think of more attractive people as more trustworthy. There are scientific studies that show that people tend to have a bias and assume that physically good-looking people have good personality traits, more than we would assume for people who are less traditionally good-looking. Why is this? On its face, it seems totally shallow and ridiculous. There is an explanation, however, for this tendency, if we look to evolutionary theory. People used to choose partners based on physical traits that they felt would ensure their survival. So, it follows that men who were the strongest and fastest would find mates and women who were determined the most, physically adapted to take care of children, and keep the family functional would be chosen. In men, this led to the propagation of certain traits, and selectiveness for men who are physically tall, powerful, and muscular. For women, this developed into an idealized mate who had a body that appeared fertile and "womanly." However, we are past that now. We no longer need to choose mates that will defend us from the mega fauna of the past. We don't need to choose in this way anymore, but we still have vestiges from the past embedded in our psychology. This has resulted in the expectations of gender that we have inculcated in our population.

Another idea to consider is this: you have no idea what another person is going through. Pain and suffering are subjective. Some people hide their pain from the world. They may present as a happy-go-lucky, content person, but really, they have hip arthritis that makes it hard to walk. People may be hiding emotional pain in just the same ways.

We can't assume that we know that people are going through or how they are feeling internally. Sometimes, we will misinterpret a smile or facial expression. If you have some ideas about a person like if they are mad at you, you may see the smallest physical move, as a move of aggression, or you might find that you interpret their speech too hastily for anger.

How do you stop assuming things? You should analyze your thoughts and see when you are assuming and then try to get to the why of assuming. Why are you doing these things? Sometimes, people start the critical thinking process without having all the facets. They may fill in the information into the process that is untrue; to draw conclusions before they can actually be drawn. We can pay attention to how much our mind is doing this; try to redirect when you are noticing the assumptions. You might find that you have some biases that you had now acknowledged before.

There are three ways of thinking to consider when you are analyzing your thinking. The first is the emotional mind. This mind makes decisions under duress and will only be taking into account the data that is coming from the emotions. The emotional mind will be frenzied, whirling, and unstoppable. It will be passionate and driven by love, art, humor, and romanticism. The logical mind is driven to make decisions without any source of emotional data whatsoever. The logical mind can ignore a crying face. It can deny emotion and prove to the world that it has never felt anything, ever. It was a way to self-denial that can be very satisfying for some people. Most people don't make decisions this way, but some do. The logical mind is not good at fully understanding people; it relies on scientific observations and quantifiable data. The third, more moderate way of thinking is the wise mind. The wise mind takes into account both the emotional mind and the logical mind when it is making decisions. It addresses the problems of emotionality and the problems of logic. It takes input from both of their perspectives; if the emotional mind is saying something, it listens and responds gently. If the logical mind is making its case, it weighs the importance of logic in that situation. The wise mind is a beautiful synthesis of these two forms of human awareness. IT is called the wise mind because it embodies the wisdom that we see in the most intelligent and efficient people. Often, you will find that older people have more wisdom. This is not true for all older adults, but a lot of them. They have acquired more wisdom simply because they have had more practice in making a decision. Over and over again, they have made decisions. Maybe sometimes they had let the emotional mind take over their decisions, and they saw how that played out. They have also witnessed the ravages of the logical mind, a mind that is disconnected and aloof, and seen the effect that that way of thinking has on their decisions. Often, older wise people are known as "not giving a damn." Simply, put, they don' sweat the small stuff. They have a perspective on life that is influenced by having lived through most of it. They know the importance of emotions, but they also know not to get too wrapped up in it.

Free Yourself

Prevention is better than cure and finding a way to spot and stay away from emotionally manipulative people is just as important as finding a way to get out. Through this prevention, you can keep the manipulator from dealing with any damage against you. Here, you will find ways on how to keep yourself from getting stuck in a relationship with a manipulator, as well as what you should do to get out of a relationship with a manipulator if you happen to be in one already.

1.   Things to do to unmask potentially emotionally manipulative relationships

•   Be wary of excessive flattery and flamboyant gestures of love, especially if it's from someone you just met. When you feel that your new suitor is becoming over the top with his flattery and grandiose demonstrations of love, ask yourself "Would someone who is emotionally stable and healthy say and do these things after such a short period of time?"

Once you notice that he is becoming over the top and excessive in his words and gestures, you can try to confront him about it. He may get offended or even angry, but at least he will know that you are not falling for his little traps.

•   Try to get to know him as well as you can before committing to a relationship. People often have different behaviors they put on when faced with different social situations and that is quite normal, but when you find your new friend or suitor is swing from one extreme behavior to the next, i.e. overly polite to one person and extremely rude to another, then you may want to take a step back. Be observant of his actions and reactions in different situations and try to see every side of your potential partner before making any decision.

• Take your time. Although an emotional manipulator may have ways to hide his negative intentions and desires, he can be very impatient. That's why love bombing is common in emotional manipulators; he tries to overwhelm you with such a grand concept of love in such a short time. In this case, time is your friend. Wait it out. If he truly loves you, he will not be impatient or demand answers. When you find your new suitor starting to guilt you or is becoming aggressive, then you may want to steer clear of him.

1. Handling a Manipulative relationship

At this stage, you have a choice - leave the relationship, or change the parameters of the relationship and get the abuser to stop his or her manipulative behavior.

• Be observant of your partner's behavior. See if any of the warning signs apply to your relationship. See if your partner exhibits manipulative behavior regularly and be ready to admit to yourself, and to a professional if need be, that you are being abused and manipulated by someone in your life.

• Know your own feelings. Be sensitive to yourself. Don't allow how you feel to be masked by how another wants you to feel and think. Find validation in your feelings and why you feel that way. Develop more relationships and friendships outside of the manipulative one you find yourself in.

• Stand up for yourself. Manipulative people will often prey on those whom they think are weaker than them. If your partner is constantly putting you down, break his line of thinking, assert yourself and be confident.

• Learn to say NO with finality. When you find yourself being given demands or requests that seem unreasonable to you, then say no and don't take it back be firm but calm in how you say no. Remember that you are your own person and that you have a right to do with your time as you please without feeling guilty or without blaming yourself. How you live your life and what you do with it is your choice. You should never be forced to do anything you do not want to do.

Building Yourself Up

Surviving an emotionally manipulative relationship can leave your identity and self-confidence in shambles. It is important to get up and brush yourself off, build up your confidence once again lest you fall into another abusive relationship. Here are a few tips on how to build up your self-esteem after an abusive and manipulative relationship.

1. Complement yourself

Being subjected to a constant and exhausting barrage of insults or belittling of your emotions can have a big effect on your confidence and your belief in yourself. Try to take the time each day to focus on positive things about you and complement yourself. Notice how pretty or handsome you are, how nice your hair is, or how well you can do certain things. Continually reminding yourself of the positive aspects of yourself can help build your confidence back up.

2. Find the good things in life

Find something to be grateful for in your life, whether it is good friends, a steady job you love, or your own independence. Be positive in seeing your life and try to see how much of a whole you already are without others. Develop friendships based on generosity, kindness and respect. This will make you a happier and better-rounded human being.

3. Develop new interests and skills

Excelling or even just learning to do something new can give a big boost to your ego, not to mention keep your mind off any negative thoughts. It is a fundamental human need to improve oneself, and finding new interest that you can learn or even just improving a skill can make you feel fulfilled and independent.

It is important to build yourself back up before venturing into a new relationship. Whatever insecurities you may have already had can only be worsened after being in a relationship with an abusive and manipulative partner. Give yourself time to grow and know yourself as a person before letting someone else into your life again. You can only be a better partner if you learn to love yourself.

Become The Master Before Attempting To Master Others

Know your outcomes

The first key that we need to take a look at when it comes to mastering ourselves is to know what you want, no matter what the situation is about. If you have no idea what you are aiming for, it is impossible to know which strategy is going to be the best, and which one you should pursue. Always go into a situation with a good and clear objective in mind. Realize that any kind of objective, even if it is not perfect, is going to be better than having no objective in place at all. You do have the option to adjust your goals and refine them as you go, but at least start out with some kind of goal in mind.

It is important that you make the intended outcome, also known as your target, as specific and clear as possible. You will be able to do this as you go along and learn what works for you. But you never want to make the goals too vague, even in the beginning, because then it is impossible to measure these goals, and how can you assess how far you have come. Make sure that when you are picking your goals, you go with something that is definitive, which you can measure the progress for, and which has an ending that is clear.

Know your values

At this point, you have now gone through and established your intended outcome, and then linked it back to one of the main things that will motivate your lie. This is very powerful, but to make sure that you can really increase your self-mastery to a new level, you will need to establish your values and then link them back to the intended outcome as well.

There is no point in us taking the time to suggest which values you would like to consider because this is a very personal topic. Just think about the things in life that are going to matter the most to you. And then write down the values that are going to be unable to help you keep those things. Once you have been able to establish all of the major values, take some time to rank them from the most powerful to the lead powerful, just like we did with the drives earlier. Once you have your top three values figured out, you can write them down on their own pieces of paper.

Just like what we did with the drivers earlier, you will want to go through and link your values into not only your outcome but also to your drives. You want to ensure that all of these factors are going to be in alignment, to ensure that you are focused on a deep and a subconscious level to achieve your own outcome. This may take a bit more time to accomplish, but it really does some wonders when it comes to ensuring that all of your motivations are going to reinforce each other, and keeps you away from isolating each one.

Your motivation can be temporary, but your habits are not

To make sure that you are able to achieve your intended outcome, you must make sure that you fully understand your values and drives. To motivate yourself about the outcome that you want, you must think about all of the ways that you are going to feel once you have been able to achieve that goal. For example, if your goal is to get that big promotion at work; imagine how you are going to feel, and what will change in your life, once you actually get for that promotion.

Once you have a clear idea of what your goal is and what achieving that goal is going to mean for you, you will find that it is much easier to stay motivated and to control yourself in order to reach that goal. However, motivation is easier to attain that it is to keep around for a long time. That's way, once you have your motivation, you should use it to help you build up the proper habits that are needed to support the outcome. If you don't make that effort now, you will end u falling into patterns that don't support your values and your influence in life.

Let's look at an example of this. To form a budget, you will need to form the habits of recording you're spending for a period of time, adding up all that you have to spend, and then split it up between the different categories. You need to get into the habit of looking for ways to cut back on spending, such as always going with special offers or generic options at the store. You can even form the habit of balancing your budget against your income to make sure you are reaching your goals.

It isn't enough for you to just establish some habits, and have motivations in place, but they are done in isolation. It is so important that you are able to link them together. You can do this by ensuring you link the motivation to the habits that you want to carry out on a regular basis. You may find that the anchoring technique from NLP can work for this. For this one, you would trigger your state of motivation by envisioning the good feelings that are triggered when you achieve the goal. You would then use a repeated physical gesture, such as touching your wrist when you carry out the routine habit.

Using this gesture is going to link the feeling of motivation to your physical gesture. You can then trigger this motivation just by doing the physical trigger. It is that easy. Once you have had the time to create these habits, you are going to keep going through and following through with them, even when you have lost out on some of the motivation. There are going to be days that are tough and days when your motivation is going to be very low. But if you develop the habits early on, you will continue to work towards your goals, and you will achieve them, even when things aren't as easy as they once were.

One of the hardest things to work on when it is time to start working with NLP is to learn how to master yourself. Once you have mastered how to handle all of the goals and dreams of your own, then you will have more control over dealing with control over others.

Subconscious Techniques For Persuasion

Persuasiveness is an effective aptitude everybody ought to learn. It is helpful in incalculable circumstances. For both your business and your personal life, are inspiring and influential to others will be the foundation for accomplishing objectives and being successful.

Learning about the traps of persuasion will give you knew awareness for when they appear in sales messaging you read? The greatest advantage your cash stays in your pocket. It literally pays for you to understand exactly how sales representatives and marketers offer you items that you don't really require. The following are some persuasive techniques that work on a subconscious level.

Outlining Impacts Thought

Let's say you're thirsty, and someone hands you a glass of water not-quite full. "The glass is half full." An optimist would "outline" the reality of your glass of water in that way. Outlining is used as an approach to modify how we classify, connect, and attach meaning to every aspect of our lives.

The headline "FBI Operators Surround Cult Leader's Compound" creates a mental picture strikingly different from another version of the headline for the same story: "FBI Specialists Raid Small Christian Gathering of Women and Children." Both headlines may convey what happened, however, the selected words affect the readers' mental and emotional responses, and therefore direct the impact the target events have on the article's readers.

Outlining is employed by apt government representatives. For example, representatives on both sides of the abortion debate refer to

477

their positions as "pro-choice" or "pro-life." This is intentional, as "pro" has a more positive association to build arguments on. Outlining an event, product, or service this way unobtrusively utilizes emotional words strategically to persuade individuals to see or accept your perspective.

Creating a convincing message is as easy as selecting words that summon strategic pictures in the minds of your audience. Indeed, even with neutral words surrounding it, a solitary stimulating word can be powerful.

Reflecting as Persuasive Strategy

Reflecting, often called "the chameleon effect," is the act of replicating the movements and non-verbal communication of the individual you want to persuade. By mirroring the actions of the individual listening, you create an appearance of empathy.

Hand and arm motions, inclining forward or reclining away, or different head and shoulder movements are types of non-verbal communication you can reflect. We, as a whole, do this without much thought, and now that you're becoming aware of that, you'll notice not only yourself but others do it, as well.

It is important to be graceful, thoughtful about it and allow just a couple seconds to pass between their movements and you reflecting them.

Highlight Scarcity of a Product or Service

The concept of scarcity is often employed by marketers to make products, services, or associated events and deals appear to be all the more engaging on the grounds that there will be restricted accessibility. The belief is that there is a huge amount of interest for it if availability is scarce. For example, an ad for a new product might say: Get one now! They're selling out quickly!

Again, it literally pays to know that this is a persuasion strategy that you will see everywhere. Consider this concept the next time you settle on your buying choice. This principle triggers a feeling of urgency in most individuals, so it is best used when applied in your marketing and sales copy.

Reciprocity Helps Make a Future Commitment

When somebody helps us out, we feel responsible for providing a proportional payback. All in all, the next time you need someone to accomplish something beneficial for you, consider doing something unexpectedly pleasant for them first.

At work, you could pass a colleague a lead. At home, you could offer to loan some landscaping tools to a neighbor.

The details, where or when you do it, won't make a difference; the key is to supplement the relationship without being sought out first. Lead with value and give it freely, without overtly expecting anything in return, and their response will come.

Timing Can Bolster Your Good Fortune

Individuals will be more pleasant and accommodating when they're mentally exhausted. Before you approach somebody for something they may not otherwise participate in, consider holding back until they've recently accomplished something mentally challenging. Consider making your offer toward the end of the work day, for example, when you can get a colleague or collaborator on the way out of the office. Whatever you may ask, a reasonable reaction could be, "I'll deal with it tomorrow."

Enhance Compliance to Acquire a Needed Result

To avoid cognitive dissonance, we all try to be true to how we've acted in the past. A reliable technique business people use is to shake your hand as they are consulting with you. We have been taught that a handshake equals a "sealed deal," and by doing this before the arrangement is really sealed, the business person has taken a step to persuade you into believing the deal is already done.

One approach to employing this yourself is influencing individuals to act before their minds are made up. Let's say that you are roaming downtown with a companion, and you decide you want to go see a movie at the local theater; yet, your companion is undecided. Compliance can come into play if you begin strolling toward the theater while they are still thinking about it. Your companion will probably consent to go once they realize you are strolling in the theater's direction.

Attempt Fluid Discourse

In the natural flow of our speech, interjections and reluctant expressions act as fillers when we need a moment to think or select the "right" word, for example, "um" or "I mean," and obviously the newly pervasive "like." These fillers have the unintended impact of making us appear to be unsure and doubtful and, in this way, less convincing. When you're certain about your message, others will be more effectively persuaded.

If you have trouble finding the right words at the right time, practice some free-flow association every day in front of the mirror for 60 seconds. You can add it to your morning ritual, or you can do it while having a shower, like I usually do. Basically, your goal in these 60 seconds is to jump from one topic to another very quickly, by associating words; do your best to avoid "um," "like," or other fillers.

Example: The water on my back right now is so hot; it reminds me of the hot weather in California. I love Cali; I like the food there. Mexican food is so spicy and hot, like Mexican women. I remember Marcella, that one Mexican girl I met last time I was there; she was probably the only blonde girl from Mexico. She was blonde like a Swedish model. I've never been to Sweden, but I've heard it's cold out there...

And so on, until you get to 60 seconds without pauses or interjections. Once you reach that point after some practice, you can aim for 120 seconds. Once you've done that, the next step is to practice this game with other people. You don't need to go on for a full two minutes straight, but while you're talking to someone, you can go on a tangent for 20 seconds and practice the free-flow association skill. You'll practice and improve tremendously, while they'll be wondering "This guy is interesting. I really want to know what he's going to say next..."

Group Affinity Can Affect Decisions

We have a much higher tendency to imitate or be persuaded by somebody we like or by somebody we see as an influential leader.

A compelling approach to make this work for you, bolstering your good fortune, is to be viewed as a leader by your target audience—regardless of whether you officially have the title. It helps to be enchanting and sure, so individuals will have more confidence in your message. Keep improving yourself, and you'll soon become more magnetic than everyone else.

If you're interacting with an individual who doesn't consider you to be a powerful person (for example, a rival at work or your irritating in-laws), you can, in any case, exploit group affinity. For example, if you praise a leader that individual respects, that praise then activates the positive associations in that individual's brain about that admired leader, which creates a mental space where they can relate those qualities with you.

Create a Photo Opportunity with Man's Best Friend

Give your target audience the idea that you're trustworthy, and motivate them to be loyal to you, by taking a photo of yourself with a pooch (it doesn't need to be your own puppy). This can make you appear kind and cooperative, but keep these kinds of photo-ops to a minimum; setting up an excessive number of pictures looks amateurish. On a side note, it pays to know your audience; if you know they share a lot of cat pictures, maybe try a picture or two with a feline friend, too.

Offer a Drink

This might seem too easy, but giving the individual you want to persuade a warm drink to hold while you're conversing with them can be persuasive in itself. The warm vibe you've offered their hands (and their body) can intuitively make them see you as candidly warm, affable, and inviting. Offering a chilly drink can do the opposite! As a rule, individuals tend to feel "frosty" and seek out warm beverages when they're feeling stressed or overwhelmed, so take care of that need keeping in mind the end goal to make them more open.

Start with a Simple "Yes" Question

Start the discussion with an inquiry that creates a "Yes" reaction. "Nice weather we're having isn't it?" or "You're searching for a great price on a car, right?"

When you get somebody saying yes, it's anything but difficult to motivate them to proceed, up to and including "Yes, I'll get it." You can counter this in your daily life by giving cautious answers to even the simplest questions.

Gently Break the Contact Boundary

You could be sealing a deal or asking somebody out for coffee, and touching them (in a modest and suitable way) can enhance your odds of hearing "Yes," because you have intuitively triggered the human yearning to connect.

In a professional setting, it is normally best to "touch" verbally by giving consolation or acclaim, as a physical touch could be seen as lewd behavior.

In sentimental circumstances, any delicate touch from a lady will more often than not be taken well. Men will need to proceed here with extreme caution—keeping in mind the end goal is to abstain from making a lady feel uncomfortable.

Control Through Confusion And Compulsion

I n any sensibly sound relationship between couples, there is about in every case some cognizant or oblivious manipulation and intimidation. Be that as it may, relationships, for the most part, develop towards some parity if they are to stay steady and reliable.

In a profoundly manipulative relationship, the level of influence is solidly in the manipulator's camp. The manipulator opposes all endeavors to adjust the relationship-since they need unlimited authority, now and again by making their victim think they have some control.

The most noticeably awful relationships happen when an exceedingly manipulative individual enters a relationship with somebody exceptionally prone to manipulation.

The consciousness of how manipulation works, and of what makes a victim prone to manipulation, will help people break free from the move of duplicity they get captured in.

The trap is opened.

The starting sentimental, manipulative relationship is vague from some other. The manipulator gives visit positive strokes, particularly when their victim demonstrations in the way they wish to develop.

It is difficult to perceive any difference at this phase to a typical sentimental relationship. The two partners usually are mindful to one another, giving regular affirmation and positive strokes. Also, they rush to get things done for the other.

If not, things are headed toward a terrible start, as of now.

Sooner or later, the victim has been adapted to positive reinforcement (recollect, people who are progressively powerless to manipulation frequently have low confidence and are regularly people pleasers). Hello and we as a whole like positive reinforcement and assertion that we are extraordinary to somebody.

Presently, the manipulator ordinarily starts to lessen the positive strokes.

Around this time, the manipulator will likewise start tossing in specific actions to befuddle their partner. They will start to grin less and may look exhausted with the victim. A typical strategy is to stroll around the house with a glare, making their 'partner' feel restless about what they may have done. Asking the manipulator will typically get the victim a 'nothing is the matter...Why?'

The general purpose is to muddle the victim and make them restless.

The victim is currently entering the unsure stage; regularly, things appear to go well; however, from time to time, they seem to have started on a crazy ride of vulnerability. The stress levels have begun to construct.

The goad is put in the trap.

Around this stage, the manipulator regularly lures the trap. An immediate or hidden idea of a significant reward is made. At work, it could be the potential for advancement or a continuous activity. It may be the idea of sex in individual relationships, or maybe the likelihood of marriage.

Numerous men will be comfortable with the-come here, leave, come here, leave, come here, and leave ladies that keep them moving. Additionally, innumerable ladies have moved to the potential draw of a marriage for a considerable length of time. The switch of these jobs moreover happens.

What's more, everybody is powerless to the carrot of more significant compensation and advancements at work.

The guarantee of the big reward ordinarily brings recharged exertion and excitement, what's more, restored confidence in the relationship or profession in the brain of the victim.

The manipulator can utilize the big carrot and the big stick now. An implied threat of withdrawal of the 'prize' is periodically used to expedite expanded weight the victim, to keep them dubious and consistent.

Presently, the victim's stress levels have expanded further. They are questions about their relationship and future. The harder they work in their activity or relationship, the less and fewer rewards they appear to get.

Creating compulsive behavior

At this point, the manipulator is well while in transit to have the victim well and tangled in their strings. The monotonous routine of manipulation and the stress and vulnerability in the victim keep them from seeing and stepping back the big picture of what is occurring to them.

Outside onlookers will frequently (however not generally) see checked differences in the character of the victim when they are within sight of the manipulator, to when they are in an increasingly typical relationship.

In any case, this is certainly not a clear pointer. Generally, the manipulator will modify their behavior when others are near, with the goal that the relationship seems increasingly adjusted. The victim may not understand why they are frequently more joyful when they are in other organization.

Manipulators, as a rule, have a fine sense for their victim's passionate state. If it starts to ascend for a long time, they will hose it down — continually yo-yoing their victim's feelings.

At this point, the victim might be adapted by intermittent and random threats and rewards. These are given with no apparent link to the victim's behavior. This kind of treatment can make a condition of compulsive behavior in the victim.

Researchers have found that people (and creatures) can create compulsive behaviors when they get rare and random rewards or threats.

While there is a clear link between an action and a reward, an individual more often than not stops that action rapidly, when the bonus stops. However, when constant and predictable rewards for a response is changed gradually to inconsistent and random rewards, people regularly prop the work up long after they got their last award.

Another variety for creating compulsive behavior in victims is to utilize intermittent and regularly random negative strokes. Shouting, annoying, and misuse is usual. When the victim is delicate and is dubious what prompts this behavior from their 'partner,' they tread lightly.

Gradually, through intermittent and random utilization of little positive and negative strokes, and progressively rare utilization of the big stick and carrot, the manipulator annihilates increasingly more of their partner's feeling of self. What's more, the victim turns out to be increasingly stressed. Without acknowledging, they are frequently gotten in compulsive behaviors that they would think odd if they saw it being finished by others.

Synopsis

We are for the most part prone to manipulation somewhat, however some substantially more so than others.

If you are prone to manipulation, the initial step to breaking free is to perceive the indications of manipulation in others.

The subsequent step is to start to comprehend what makes you powerless to manipulation.

The third step is to start to comprehend what is being done to you. For example, utilizing the intermittent random carrot and stick treatment to befuddle, bewilder, and stress you.

The fourth step will be to learn obstruction methodologies.

Approaches To Understand Human Behavior

There are five major approaches to understand human behavior.

The Psychodynamic Approach

The psychodynamic approach was propounded by Sigmund Freud in which he believed that there are three personalities that develop the approach of the person. One is the development of the illness factor. This factor was discovered in the year 1993, when Freud was able to discuss the advantages of the illness emanating of the child. This theory was further comprehended with the passage of time and the people believed that it was able to make the functionalities of the personality look better. Another theory was about the conscious and the subconscious manner. This theory believed that people are able to delve into the personalities of the person in an effective manner. The conscious mind is the mind that is aware of all the pros and cons of living. Whereas, the subconscious mind is the mind, which heralds some of the important aspirations of daily life According to Freud, the subconscious mind clearly stores a lot of information in the minds of the public and with the passage of time; the person is able to have a strong version of interest in it. The idea of the construction is quite similar to the game because the psychodynamic approach will give you strong comprehension about the functioning of the mind. The system will thereby make you believe in it and with the passage of time, you will be able to have a stronghold on the construction effectively. Therefore, the psychodynamic approach helps you to psychologically listen to the minds of the people and understand them effectively.

Behavioral Approach

This is a kind of approach which makes the behaviors of other people understandable through experiences and external stimulus. By many psychologists it is also referred to as the classical conditioning method and the conditioning is done by altering the external stimulus of the public. The public gets to know the major ingredients of the development of behaviorism and with the passage of time; the people get to know the true nature of all the components of real life. The idea is simple and straight here that to make sure that how the people are able to have more strategic interest in their coming, the behavioral approach is possibly maintained and implemented. Therefore, the behavioral approach is an approach, which needs to be strengthened by all means and it tends to give strong reservations in the coming time. So, the reason for making the humans look more understandable and adjustable, the people must not make the hectic decision of life and try its best in making the reasons go way bound.

Predicting Human Behavior

The human behavior of humans can be predicted in the following ways.

The use of Homecourt

This is the manipulation technique in which the individual uses his or her home as an advantage for his own benefits. The psychological demeanor was used to define the crux of the people, who were under the liability of the people. For the substantiation of this case, it is important to understand that the people, who are in a psychological condition to manipulate others, are very smart. The first rule is that the public must come into consideration of the psychological master and then the master will navigate his thoughts. First and foremost, the master uses the court to manipulate the personalities and then the public first advocates the use of manipulation to be just and obscure.

Establishing the stance first and then looking for weaknesses

In the manipulation of psychology, it is important to understand that the establishment of the stance is first. The stance needs to be manifested first and then it is established so that the people, who are listening to the track, come under the way of the manipulator. Once the stance of the manipulator is established then the maneuvering is very easy. The people have to understand the use of the stance easily and then they have to use the words of the manipulator as a source of manipulation. The people can easily be thrown into the abyss when the manipulator asks a lot of questions. The idea is that the public first navigates the stance and then the manipulator can use the stance to find its justification. If the manipulator wants to find the essence of the stance and if he finds some distortion of the stance then he can avoid the crux of the stance very badly.

Manipulation of Facts

If you want to assert the significance of the psychology of manipulation, then the facts stated can be used to deceive. The facts can be of any statement and that can be used to defy the logic of the people. For instance, if the manipulator is using the fact sound of one thing then that thing can be used to defy as well. People that can assess the logic of the personalities can manipulate by navigating them through their own lies. This is the act of manipulation if people are using the effects of deviance in an effective manner.

Overwhelming with facts and statistics

First and foremost, the fact and statistics can be used to defy the personalities of the public. The facts are to be constructed in an effective manner so that the manipulator can be used to defy the odds of manipulation. So, for a strong manipulation, you have to overwhelm the facts and statistics with the people. The people can be used to come under the clout of statistics if the public is not able to use a strong mode of psychological messages. Therefore, it is important that psychology can be used to interpret the essence of the public in a logical manner.

Overwhelming with procedures and Red tape

In order to maintain the crux of other personalities, the manipulator uses procedures and red tapes to give more defying reasons to the public. The manipulator will use the procedural versions, in which the public has to be manipulated in a stringent manner. The manipulator can be harnessed in a strong way so that the public can give concrete methods to it. For this reason, to be constructed, the manipulator uses some procedures and advantages through which the normal public comes into oppression. This oppression is used to defy the lands of the public and the public comes under the manipulation of the manipulator. So, in order to manipulate the people, the psychologists can use the crux of procedures and some secretive tapes that can be used in a strong manner.

Raising the voice and Displaying Negative Emotions

The manipulator in order to make the voice of the public effective has to raise the voice of him. The manipulator uses some strong means and modes through which he is able to forecast a shadow of darkness. This darkness is used to construct the methods of manipulation among the stakeholders and the people can come under effective modes of destruction. Also, the negative emotions, give the value of harsh realities among the public and they get severely neglected by the personalities. Therefore, it is important to understand that the public is not able to get manipulated if they see the raised level of voice and hence there is a display of festering emotions among the people.

Negative Surprises

The negative surprises are another mode of manipulation by the manipulator. The manipulator can be using harsh negative surprises through which the people are not able to understand their nature.

These negative surprises also affect the effects of the mentality of the public and with the passage of time; the people do not get easily comfortable in this essence. The negative surprises show a strong moment of disinterest among the public and there is a culture of disassociation among the public through the negative surprises. The negative surprises give a sense of bad omens for the public through which the people are not able to give standard modes of deviation for the public.

Giving you a little or no time to decide

The time that has been given to you is either less time or there is no time. The manipulator wants to get his thing done because only then he is effective in his mode. The manipulator would cast his means to come in front of the public. The time that has been slotted for the manipulator has a strong version of connectedness with the people and thus, there needs to be a strong sense of affection for the people. Therefore, the time of decision that has been given to you are a tool of the manipulator so that the public is able to give more directions for the public. So, the time has to be a motive interest for the public to understand in an effective manner.

Use of Negative Humor

The negative humor is a manipulating tool to disassociate you from your being. The manipulator would cast negative humor on you and will do his best to make you feel bad about the situation. This manipulation is further designed by the manipulator to disempower you and with its continuous bolstering; the use of negative humor could be very harsh and brutal for you. Therefore, the use of negative humor could be used to induce isolationism and fanaticism in public and could be very pernicious for you as well. If the use of negative humor could be bad for you then manipulation could be a stringent maneuver to showcase in-effectiveness among you.

Consistent Judgment

The consistent judgment could be a harsh tactic to induce fright among you. The manipulator could use the essence of judgment to make you feel discomfort able. How it can be done? This is as follows: Suppose, you are sitting in a room and the manipulator is sitting in front of you and you are able to hear the statements of the manipulator and with the passage of time, the public is not able to define the essence of the judgments properly. The public is quite effective in harboring the essence of the manipulator and if the manipulator is successful is dissing you with his judgments then finally you are under his claw. The consistent judgment will make you feel very demotivated and with the passage of time, you will be feeling delusional.

Silent Treatments

When the manipulator wants to harbor his mechanism then he uses the edifice of silence. This silence is very haunting. It is very managerial and with the passage of time, it induces a bad version of manipulation among you. You get affected by the silence of the manipulator and in time, this becomes very pestering among you. The silent treatment is also very haunting at an individualistic level because at times, the public is not able to see the results of it in a discomforting manner. Therefore, silent treatments can be used to haunt the premises of the individual in a bad manner.

Thus, these are some of the mechanisms that make the prediction of human behavior look way too easy. Therefore, human development needs to be adopted with the passage of time properly.

The Fear And Relief Technique

The fear and relief technique is a commonly-employed dark psychology technique used to control people. It uses emotional influence and mind control to help you achieve your motives.

Understanding the Fear and Relief Technique

This dark psychology technique feeds on the emotions of the person you wish to influence. To manipulate someone, you use his/her fears against him/her to, first, stir up intense emotions, and then to appease them by providing some relief.

A great example of this is an instance where you don't want your partner to accompany you on a work trip, but you know that he or she will insist on accompanying you.

In such an instance, you can upset him/her or cause some discomfort. Then, you can play the role of calming him or her down by apologizing for your behavior while at the same time using compelling language to get him or her not to accompany you.

Once the other person feels bad, he/she retreats into a deep shell of low self-esteem. At this point, because you know the person now wants your comfort, you put some emollient on his/her wounds in the form of kind words, affection, and care.

This warmth and comfort displayed through peace offerings such as apologies, kind words of appreciation, accepting your mistake, and even gifts will leave the person feeling better. As soon as the person feels better about you, he\she forgets the hurt you inflicted. At this point, you covertly insert your demand and trick him/her into agreeing to what you want.

Since this strategy capitalizes on the emotions of the other person as a means for control, once you have him/her under your influence, you can control and influence his/her mind into taking the desired action.

The correct implementation of this technique helps you control and influence others:

How to Implement the Fear and Relief Technique

While the technique can sometimes feel unfair, it can also come in handy when you want to stimulate others to do their work or listen to you.

For instance, when you want your kids to listen to you or your team members to pay heed to your instructions, you can use the fear and relief technique to your advantage.

Here's how to implement it:

1. Be clear on the goal you want to achieve; clarity will help you plan your moves accordingly.

2. Have enough knowledge on the insecurities and weaknesses of your target; you will need this knowledge to implement the strategy successfully. If you know your team members are afraid of job loss, use that to manipulate them into working harder. If you are aware that your sibling is dependent on you for financial sustenance, use that fear to encourage him to quit smoking.

3. When talking to your target, use the right words. Never approach your target directly. Always start the conversation with an interesting topic, something the person considers exciting. After capturing the person's interest, drive the conversation towards your motive.

4. When you change the direction of the conversation, first talk about and build on your subject's fear. Once you cement a sense of unease, suggest your desired goal as a means to relieve the fear and unease. For instance, if you want a particular team member to push his/her limits and produce quality work, talk about how substandard work can lead to job loss, as has been the case in the past. Once you sense a growing sense of fear, talk about how the person has the talent to prove his/her situation if he/she is willing to go the extra mile.

5. Make your manipulation subtle, and strike when the iron is at its hottest, which is when your subject shows signs of immense fear.

6. When providing relief to your target, do so in the guise of taking care of him/her interest, accepting your mistakes, apologizing to your target, offering extra help and care, and saying kind words.

That said you may not want to be the victim of similar manipulation, which is why you need to learn how to block the strategy.

Here is how you can block manipulation from this technique.

How to Block the Fear and Relief Technique

Blocking the fear and relief technique is not too difficult. You just need to act tactfully and make the right moves at the right time.

Here is what you should do.

1. First, gain clarity of what you consider good and bad for you. You need to know what does and does not work for you, and set boundaries for yourself and others accordingly. If you know you don't believe in breaking workplace rules, you should not agree to it even if your coworker, who happens to be a good friend, approaches you with a related scheme.

2. After crystallizing your beliefs, make an effort to read people's energy. If you keenly observe someone for a few days, you will get

some idea about how the person talks and behaves when he or she wants something. For instance, by being observant, you can tell when someone who approached you with a request you denied resorts to using fear-based manipulation to trick you into agreeing to his/her terms. Stay on your guard at this time as your controller is likely to make a move.

3. If the person approaches you for a favor, analyze it under the light of your beliefs. If the request contradicts your beliefs and the relational boundaries you have set, say no firmly and resolutely. Politely, but firmly, tell the person her how what he/she wants does not comply with your beliefs and how much you'd appreciate it if he/she stopped bothering you with similar demands in the future. As you say this firmly, remain friendly by pasting a smile on your face.

4. At first, the person may act 'sweet,' but when your stance fails to budge, he/she is likely to retaliate by using the 'fear' element as a way to push your buttons. Stay strong and maintain your ground.

5. At this point, the wisest move is to extricate you from the situation. If that person lives with you, go out for a walk. If that manipulator is a coworker, head out to see your boss or take a break from the discussion. If a heated discussion with your controlling parent happens in the lounge, go into your bedroom.

6. If someone approaches you again and tries to resume that conversation, firmly say you don't want another discussion.

7. If the person persists, switch on your deaf ear mode and do not pay heed to whatever else the person says. The person may resort to calling you names, gas lighting, blaming you for weird things, and imply that you don't care about him/her. Do not believe a word the person says and continue ignoring him/her.

8. When the person calms down, politely, but firmly tell him/her how you tolerated that behavior because you do not like to create chaos.

With the same level of firmness, tell the person that if he/she puts up a similar show again, you will have no choice but to take drastic action. For instance, if the person is a colleague, you can state that you will file a report, and if the person is an abusive loved one or friend, you can intimate that you will leave.

9. Do not fall into the 'fear' trap the person tries to set up. Take action by gradually limiting your interactions with the person. Creating some distance will save you a great deal of mental energy that you can direct to other worthwhile undertakings.

Use this strategy every time someone tries to trick you using the fear and relief technique. Your goal should be to keep the person from scaring you, which will stop him/her from making the next move.

Conclusion

It appears that you are serious to learn about dark psychology and its effects on those who are the targets as well as why a person would employ this psychology's techniques.

We are all subject to dark psychology. Advertising is the master at using it to get people to pay attention to their product and buy it. We may know someone who has one of the personalities outlined in the Dark Triad; perhaps a narcissist who demands that it's all about them and for them all the time.

Before you read this book, you may have thought that dark psychology was only practiced by psychopaths or sociopaths and not "normal" people. That is far from the truth. That charming, charismatic person you like and think the world of maybe just the type to practice dark psychology to get their way and no one really notices that about them.

The next step is to make sure that you use these techniques to protect yourself against manipulation, persuasion, and NLP in your daily life. There are always people trying to persuade you and manipulate you— and while some of these are going to do so in a beneficial way that can help not only them but also you, most individuals who use manipulation are only interested in getting what they want and aren't concerned about how it affects you at all.

This guidebook has spent some time taking a look at manipulation and persuasion, as well as how the victim can often get stuck in this kind of cycle, thus providing benefits to the manipulator even though it may not be suitable for them, without even realizing what is going on. We then looked at some of the ways to recognize what is going on and to know the signs and break free so that the victim can live the life that they want, free from the manipulator.

When you are ready to learn more about the world of dark psychology, manipulation, persuasion, and NLP tactics, make sure to read this guidebook to help you get started. Sometimes, the act of manipulation can occur right in front of us, and we don't even know it. Why? It's because we miss the signs, signals, and body language cues that indicate that there might be more to that person than meets the eye. We have all, in one way or another, been guilty of manipulation—or we've been the victim of a manipulator's underhanded tactics. There are many aspects that build manipulation: persuasive words, body language, and tone of voice are all channels to convey or communicate manipulative messages. However, is manipulation harmful—or is it a case of a little harmless persuasion that won't hurt anyone? Why is manipulation wrong and what if it is done for the good of the one manipulated? The book will play a key role in helping you understand the dark psychology of the human mind, as well as how to identify the subtle body language signals all around you!

EMPATH

PART FIVE

Empath

The definition of empathy is the ability to understand and share the feelings of another. When you are an empathic person you have the capability of acknowledging what someone else is going through and offer genuine concern and compassion, perhaps even going through it emotionally yourself. When someone else is expressing a feeling or an emotion as they talk about their life circumstances or a current issue they may be having, your ability to feel their pain is an act of empathy.

Empathy is an amazing skill and gift that we should all try to nurture. We are all people living our lives looking for hope and happiness. When you share your feelings with others you are sharing a part of yourself and your story. What we all want is to feel that others will hear us and make us feel welcome, secure, and part of a community. Being an empathic person allows you to have that energy of affirmation that none of us is alone and we are all sharing a life story together.

Being an empath is different. When you are able to sense and feel another person, place, or thing as if it were your own experience, emotion, or pain, it is altogether another story. An Empath is a person who can viscerally feel, either through the emotions, the physical body, or the intuitive sense, how someone else is feeling. This can be a very challenging thing to experience, especially if you are not fully aware of your gift and how it can affect you.

The Empath will struggle with determining which feelings and emotions belong to them, and which belong to other people and the world around them. It happens to be a very direct influence and even if you think that you are just an emotional person, the Empath is actually someone who absorbs the energy of emotions into their own senses and lives with that energy inside of them. If you cannot determine the difference between someone else's sorrow and your own, you can have a very troubled and difficult life as an Empath.

Empaths are highly sensitive to more than just feelings and emotions. They can also be heavily influenced by aromas and odors, loud noises and crowded places, bright lights, and a variety of stimulants, like alcohol, drugs, caffeine, and sugar. Whether it comes from an innate disposition from childhood and early life programming or is gained as a skill over time as an adult, being and becoming an Empath has its challenges as well as its gifts. Empathy and being an Empath are different and it is what you need to understand about being an Empath that will help you realize how empathy works. We are all highly sensitive people and many people choose or are not capable of, being aware of that. As a human being, you have a very sophisticated internal technology that is very adept at sensing and feeling the world around you. How do you think we survived extinction? Part of our survival mechanisms is to look and listen to everything that could harbor danger or offer us safe shelter, food, and an ability to make it to the next day.

Fortunately, we're no longer living in the age where death by a wild animal is as likely, but our instincts have remained intact in our brain stems, allowing us all to sense and perceive what will likely cause some kind of effect in our immediate environment.

In the case of empathy, as you are sitting next to someone or something, you are sensing and perceiving their energy to determine whether they are trustworthy, kind, good, etc. Much of this actually occurs on a subconscious level and we are not always aware of the fact that we are naturally "reading" the energy output of another person. It can be very strong when you are sitting next to a grieving mother who has lost her son, or next to a person who is angry and frustrated by everything you are saying. You feel all of the energy with your own sensory receptors and not all people are as skilled or as predisposed to having such a strong perception of this kind.

Empaths are incredibly sensitive to the energy of another person. Without an awareness of this gift, an Empaths will have a lot of emotional turmoil and will often feel like something is wrong with them and that their emotional state is just an unfortunate part of who they are, not realizing that their state of depression, anxiety, or frustration is the result of perceiving someone else's unraveling energy and absorbing it.

Empathy is not as complicated. When you are sitting next to a coworker and are an empathic listener, you might act as an available friend who will offer support while they talk about their recent divorce. You will have a very strong ability to connect with them and sense their pain, but you won't necessarily absorb those feelings and make them your own, as an Empath would.

There are a lot of people in the world who are Empath who have studied their gifts and still struggle with maintaining a healthy balance and emotional groundedness. It can be very challenging to always identify their feelings from those of another. As an Empath myself, I have had times when I have walked into a room and sensed the angry argument that happened between a married couple just before I arrived for dinner. I worried the entire time I was eating with them that they were unhappy with my presence there until I realized later that I was just sensing their feelings about each other and the fight they were having before their dinner guest arrived.

If you are an Empath, you will feel everything a lot more than other people do and it is not a bad thing. It can be a very good thing to help you understand who you are and what the world has to offer from a sensory perspective. The key is to know yourself well and to trust your instinct and intuition so that you are not carried away with fear and doubt that doesn't actually belong to your true feelings and is coming from something else outside of you.

Empathy is a powerful resource for all people and learning to develop your general empathic skills will help you to connect to others in a more impactful, personal, and meaningful way. The truth of being empathic is that you are a supportive listener and that you are able to allow another person to have their own emotional experience without making it about yourself. You offer kindness and intentional offerings of understanding while another person is given space to share their emotions with a person who might know what it feels like to be going through something like what they are feeling.

An Empath will offer the same support but will actually sense and feel it before words are even spoken about it. True Empath always perceives through the senses and will pick up on the slightest intensity of feeling from the person standing just behind them at the grocery checkout. A true Empath will notice when someone is putting on a façade to pretend that they are fine but, under the surface, holding back tears of anguish and sorrow.

There are a variety of ways Empaths experience empathy and the next segment will elaborate on how empathy works for the different types of Empaths that are known to exist.

Jealousy In Relationships

How come a person feels jealous? Maybe the relationship was too weak to start with? When the relationship is strong and both are committed, should one feel jealous at all? Or is there something in an individual's genes? How can somebody be jealous if every little thing seems to be exercising just fine? Does it associate with one's past? Or why must she feel envious? But envy is still a fact of life. It can be there, whether we like it or not. Let's analyze better what jealousy is and where it originates from.

Let's take a look at a basic example. Say, your son or daughter likes your neighbors and her or he is every bit mindful of them. Can you feel envious of this or happy with this? Can you try to remove your child from the next-door neighbors or forbid them to go? Can you face the next-door neighbors? You may do nothing at all. What if your little one is substituted with your partner? Your response may be completely different. What's the difference in both circumstances? It's the suspicion, the dream and the creativity that something might be going on.

The primary distinction is belief. You have a total belief that the child may run around and have fun with a ton of people round the day. But he/she'll go back to you during the night, or maybe starving, or perhaps harm? Am I right? It's not required to share the precise same belief together with your lover/spouse. And that's the main reason for envy. Somewhere in your ideas, you're always curious about how you look your intelligence, your relationship skills and all sorts of extra factors that could break your relationship, making your partner more susceptible to enter another relationship.

Can any relationship that depends on such slippery ideas be thought about a happy relationship? Will it survive the test of time effortlessly? No. The most convenient way out would be to go over without doubt every little thing in your thoughts together with your spouse/lover and expose all of your worries. Be completely open. Try to discover everything that is included in the mind of the partner in the same way. Discuss every little thing and choose whatever the best alternative is since your relationship is not going anywhere quickly. Hand that dedication and take that commitment in exchange. And enjoy life forever without troubling about enviousness. If in the end of the day, the 2 of you arrived at the conclusion that it isn't working any longer, the commitment isn't strong enough for one another, and after that perhaps you should produce a tidy break. Jealousy is readily available in our minds as we do not know the love and commitment. Take correct care of that to live a pleased life.

Understanding the true reason, you're battling with a jealousy relationship ordeal is strongly liberating. In the end, when you're taken in with enviousness, it's not tough to think that your life is spinning unmanageably. Once you have taken the logical steps to fix this sort of feeling, you will notice that your scenarios are not as frustrating as they seem.

The essential thing to defeating your feelings of enviousness is conversation. In the end, among the best reasons for envious emotions is an unvoiced grudge. You may silently detest someone for winning a competition or scoring greater on the test than you. You may sit, tense and dissatisfied, as somebody compliments your romantic partner. Nevertheless, in voicing the beginning of the misery, you have the ability to steer clear of the trouble of envy relationships just before beginning. You will not just be venting your concerns and disappointments, but individuals around you can assist it ends up being clear that this sort of sensation is unreasonable.

Keeping a journal is a completely different way to conquer your enviousness relationships. Writing, in the end, is recognized as probably the most therapeutic means of dumping your stress and anxieties. It's not only a great way to clear the mind, but you will find the benefit of having the capability to really appreciate every day the event once you have calmed down just a little. This allows you to certainly see the issue from new perspectives.

In case your jealousy is starting to hinder your individual life or at work, you may want to think about treatment as the 2nd alternative. A therapist can give you a calm, neutral listening ear to vent your problems to. In contrast to your friends or members of the family, there's no predisposition or hesitation to let you know precisely what you ought to know. She or he can also get a notified, qualified background for dealing with your own personal problem. Your therapist will have the capability to suggest approaches to beat your envy in your relationships, but she or he might also be in a position to uncover the primary underlying reasons of this problem. Once you have learned this, you will notice that it's substantially simpler to see your emotions of anger and enviousness for what they truly are: insecurities.

Romantic Jealousy

With views to romantic enviousness, it's not hard to lapse into negative thinking. You might, for example, feel angry at the person you are romantically thinking about for picking another person. You may even feel mad at the person she or he chose. You might want to check out this relationship and face them to eventually choose her or him, or you. This sort of sensation is totally natural, and you should not be embarrassed about it. Nevertheless, you should not allow these emotions to rule your life either. What you do with it, is what matters most.

Even though the frustration may be squashing, it will not last forever and ever. Understanding that is among the best steps in dealing with romantic envy. You might feel at that time you won't ever find other individuals. Nevertheless, after a while, the rough immediacy of those emotions will fade, and you will notice that this event is practically no need to resign you to a life filled with distress. You will find somebody else, probably, and there is a lot of convenience in that.

How will you overcome romantic enviousness? While the death of time is usually important for the process of recovery, there are a lot of other approaches for you to ease your discomfort.

Romantic emotions come and go. Just comprehend that it has a lot to do with hormonal agents, public opinion, oxytocin, dopamine, and other situations. It can be associated with the emotions of loss and grieving; the same emotions people have when a loved one dies, and a modification of strategies. We, as humans, normally like to know what will happen in the future, but we just don't. I remember I dated a guy and when it was over between us, I was quite upset. Not devastated, I think, but it still harms, and a long relationship had ended in a bad way. Little did I know I would meet my terrific husband to be a few months later.

How To Stop Insicurety And Grow Confidence

Build Your Self-Esteem

Your self-esteem is evident in your gestures and how you speak about yourself. Remember, the manipulative person is looking for those signs of weakness and submissiveness in the way you communicate verbally and through your body language. If you have low self-esteem your actions and conversation will display this.

High Self-esteem is having a good sense of self-worth. This is having a respectful and healthy view of yourself, when you have good self-esteem; you will be comfortable with yourself and are confident in most situations. You have a positive self-image, and you will surround yourself with people that treat you with respect. You will have a good opinion about yourself and will not be overly concerned with the opinions of others. You will believe that you deserve to be happy and that you deserve to be loved. You will value your happiness and you believe that you should have a good life and that you do not need to change yourself for other people. You believe that you deserve respect and fair treatment from others.

When you have good self-esteem, you are confident that even if things go wrong or you have difficult relationships, you can work things out. You have a firm belief that you can manage what comes your way in life, knowing that if you are faced with challenges or struggles, you believe that you can take care of it. You are self-assertive, think for yourself and have faith in your capability to direct your own life. You believe that you can create a good life for yourself and handle things that need to be handled.

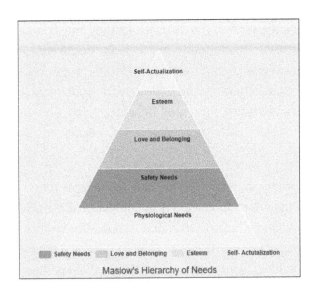

Maslow's Hierarchy of Needs

It has been discovered that if we are deficient in any of these needs, we are prompted to fulfill them. When fulfilling the needs for love and belonging we seek approval. Many times, looking outside of ourselves to others for that approval, if one is lacking self-esteem or feeling bad about them, they may become overly dependent on the approval of other people.

It is important not to worry about what others think about you and just value your qualities and attributes. You cannot control everyone's opinion of you or worry about it. Wanting to improve the opinion of everyone else has of you is an exhausting and unrealistic goal to set. It is not logical to try and persuade everyone to like you. It is not workable to have your entire self-esteem based on the opinion' others have of you. You must have firm boundaries about what you allow in your life. You do not have to let the opinions of other people control what you want to do in your life. Stop caring about compliments as well. By doing this you will observe from a very neutral perspective and be less likely to get offended or be hurt by the opinions of others. Keep in mind other people's views are based upon their own thoughts and are not reality, just opinions.

Another thing to consider is that we cannot satisfy our self-esteem without addressing our morality. It has been discovered that personal morality is another aspect of having good self-esteem. Be sure that you are aligning your behaviors and actions with your morals and do not permit anyone to push you into behaviors that you believe to be immoral. Do not exchange your own beliefs in exchange for acceptance.

You can improve your self-esteem in a few simple ways. One way to begin increasing your self-esteem is valuing yourself, appreciating what you have done and what you like about yourself. Another is becoming part of a group or organization. Being productive is also another method of building your self-esteem. Learning something new brings up our self-confidence, so furthering your education or taking up a new hobby is a perfect way to do this. Another good way to raise your self-esteem is to set goals and achieve them; this will build up your self-worth.

Your self-esteem is very malleable, and you can improve it easily. Our self-esteem is based upon our thoughts of ourselves. You must be aware of the words you use to describe yourself and your abilities to others. You should take the personal time to journal your thoughts and recognize the way you are feeling and the way you speak to and about yourself. There a few techniques that you can follow that will build self-esteem when practiced routinely and incorporated into your inner dialogue.

One technique is to find out what your purpose is. Think to yourself what you would do if you had all the time and money in the world. The answer to this self-inquiry will tell you about yourself and your inner drive. See if you can work your way towards that goal, even if it's only on a smaller scale.

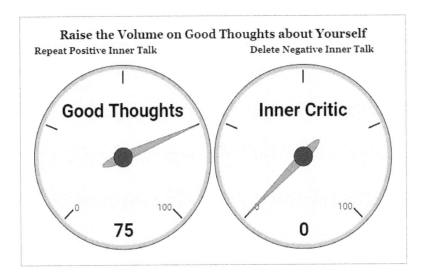

Raise the Volume on Good Thoughts about Yourself

Repeat Positive Inner Talk   Delete Negative Inner Talk

Good Thoughts   Inner Critic

0   100   0   100

75   0

There is a suggested visualization technique that has helped some people to change their inner dialogue that may help you. Meditate on those qualities for a bit. Whenever you have a negative thought picture pressing a delete button and do this for any negative thought you have whenever they come up.

Another practice that will help build self-esteem is mediation. Meditation provides you with the ability to recognize your thoughts. Once recognized you could dismiss these negative thoughts and re-frame them with positive thoughts. The more a thought is repeated you will eventually believe it, so the more you re-frame your thoughts and counter these negative thoughts with more positive views of yourself the sooner you will begin to believe it. Think things like "I have value", "I am a good person" and "I'm worthy of good things."

Having a daily awareness practice combined with meditation will help you to realize when you are entertaining self-defeating thoughts and enable you to counter them quickly by saying to yourself "that's not true." The more you practice the better you will become and eventually, you will no longer have this negative self-talk sabotaging your self-esteem.

Finally, make it a daily practice to start repeating to yourself statements that are up-building to your self-esteem. What will happen is you will begin to believe these statements about yourself once you repeat them to yourself and this will build self-confidence and raise your self-esteem?

Be Assertive

Being assertive is an important part of avoiding manipulation, being assertive means that you value yourself and have a strong sense of self-awareness. When you are assertive you have self-confidence, know who you are, your strengths and your boundaries. When you are assertive you are sure of who you are and what you will and will not do. There is nothing about you that a manipulative individual would recognize as weak or insecure, in other words, you would be lacking the traits that they look for.

You can relate to others but not from a needy and catering perspective, but rather from a healthy self-reliant perspective. You can support and encourage others because you know the value of yourself. You will contribute your time and effort once you have given yourself time to consider a request and are sure you have the desire and ability to do so. In other words, you value yourself and your time and though you care for others, you will not be pushed into overextending yourself.

Being Assertive means that you can accept that people are imperfect and when confronted by an individual who is manipulative you understand that this is just their behavior. You do not take their slander personally. You would not absorb their actions, nor would you let them drag you into a dramatic argument just to get what they want. When you are assertive you will consider yourself and make the decision that is best for you, before caving to the demands of others.

To build your self-assertiveness work on communicating your thoughts and decisions clearly, making sure you are being firm about your boundaries. If someone asks you for a favor take the time to consider if this is something you can do, if not then be direct and tell this person you are just unable to help them. If someone tries to lure you into an argument, accuses you of being selfish or not caring about them, just let them know that you understand their feelings, but that does not mean your decision will change. If you find that you are getting a little uncomfortable or stressed by their behavior just politely excuse yourself.

To be truly self-assertive you must remain in your integrity, knowing that you are not dependent on the opinions of others for validation. You are sure of yourself and you are not swayed by the pressure others put on you because you value your time, yourself and respect your needs.

Feed Yourself: Practicing Self-Love

Now that we have explored self-confidence and being assertive it is a good idea to begin to feed you with positive thoughts and inner dialogue. Self-love is a good way to begin to change the inner dialogue that you have from a negative one to a more optimistic and positive one. How do you this?

Practice gratitude as much as you can and be happy with where you are. Gratitude will encourage optimism and positivity. Do not attach to your thoughts, especially negative thoughts. Let your thoughts just flow through your mind objectively. Monitor your thoughts and accept them and redirect those thoughts. If you are worried or stressed about something, tell yourself "I am capable. I can handle this, and everything will work out fine." End your self-criticism and allow yourself to be who you are and how you are. Accept yourself as you are and know that you are good enough. You should accept the things about yourself that you cannot change and know that it does not make you less deserving of love, happiness, and good things. Take care of yourself; this self-nurturing is key to you feeding your self-worth and building your confidence. Get out in nature it will clear your head and it will help you remain emotionally balanced.

Speak to yourself in a loving and caring manner; your thoughts will dictate what type of day you have, so make sure you are feeding yourself with only positive and uplifting thoughts. Make sure you say positive affirmations to yourself every day. Get out of habits and situations that are in your comfort zone but are not good for you. Make it a point to reach out to new people, go to new places and explore new experiences. Do not focus on other people and their lives. Do not compare yourself with others as their life has its own share of trials. You need to focus on your life and be accepting and joyful in the life that you are living in. You are a unique person and you have many attributes and qualities that are worth enjoying and being proud of.

Take care of yourself and do things that make you happy. If you have a hobby takes the time to invest more yourself in that. If you have a good circle of friends, make plans with them and reflect on the support you get from the If you have the time to take a vacation then do so. Take yourself out on the town or go explore a new club or activity. Try new things that you may have been interested in but fearful of trying due to your insecurities. Take time for yourself and be sure to do things you enjoy at least once a week if possible. When you practice self-love and feeding your emotional well-being you will find that your good days will increase, and your bad days are a thing of the past.

How To Improve Your Positivity

Positive reasoning has been comprehended and utilized in different ways, sometimes to the extent of an entirely inappropriate meaning. Individuals misuse the influence of this incredible practice and recommend that it will draw in cash or wealth: "Be positive, and you will have anything you need!"

No, you will not! And it is not the reason for practicing your mind to think along these lines. This is actually one of the principal reactions to the book, "The Secret." Just by doing great, you can have anything you desire. That is a lie, period!

The advantages of reasoning and feeling positive are, in reality, beneficial. They will trigger other positive marvels throughout your life. You will put both your soul and body in an exceptional state with the capacity of achieving great things. Joy and euphoria will emanate from you wherever you go. Life will appear to be greatly improved. Your frame of mind will improve, as well as the world's disposition toward you.

The reward for thinking positively is a delightful life full of energy and motivation. Likewise, it will unquestionably help you in your financial undertakings. These are some of the incredible practices that will put you destined for success in your everyday life:

Help others in need.

You know, it is not about you. Help other individuals and really care. Try not to do it only for the sake of doing it, however. Demonstrate some sympathy and empathy. Have a go at placing yourself in their shoe and view the world through their perspective. At that point, do your best to support them. You have no clue what this can accomplish for you.

Get used to walking outdoors.

The impact of this single walking outdoors can be incredible. Indeed, even research demonstrates that this activity can support your state of mind, all things considered. Get it done and see the outcomes.

Laughter is the best medicine.

Our body is the instrument of our mind, yet it is additionally obvious that our contemplations and demeanor are particularly identified with our body due to the manner in which we work. We will, in general, think according to what we see, hear, taste, smell, and feel. So, if you smile, you can quickly feel it, and your mind will react to this. You will begin feeling better and with positivity. It will not just lift up your state of mind; it will influence every other person who interacts with you to feel the same way. You can choose to smile only for the sake of it, or you can think about a circumstance, an occasion, an individual, or anything that puts you in a state of joy. Both of them will work great. You can simply head toward your mirror, take a gander at yourself and will yourself to smile. This works incredibly well. Very soon, it will end up infectious. Have in mind that giggling and grinning can also fix maladies and wretchedness! That is, as of now, deductively demonstrated. Smile regularly and your energy will continue to expand more every time you do it.

Volunteer and contribute more to your community.

Think about the different ways in which you can improve your community. Maybe you can help with cleaning the parks in your neighborhood? Shouldn't something be said about helping people in the neighborhood library? This one will be peculiar yet surely intriguing. What about visiting detainees and helping in reaching out? Keep in mind that the more you give in your everyday life, the more you receive something in return. Life will consistently remunerate you ten times for each good thing that you do. Choose how you can give back to the community, and after that, do what needs to be done. Inspiration will turn into your characteristic mindset that appears to make your organization consistent.

Participate in yoga and meditation.

These two exercises will never neglect to support your inspiration. They will assist you in gaining control over your considerations, and your mindfulness will be increased. You will end up being mindful at the present minute and what is happening in your mind. Positive considerations will end up normal as you practice these abilities.

Exercise more.

Truly, this is a significant undertaking for your health and mind. Pick any physical activity that you like and practice it routinely. You can run, climb mountains, or take swimming lessons, or you can take classes in hand-to-hand fighting. You will be enthusiastic about life, energetic, and motivated. Your state of mind will change as well. It is highly unlikely that physical activity will not make you feel positive. Do what need to be done for your mind and body.

Offer thanks every day.

Write an appreciation diary, or essentially compose on a sheet of paper five things that you are thankful for. Read this list multiple times every day, starting at the beginning of the day and then around early afternoon and before sleeping. The more things you can incorporate into the rundown, the better. These things should make you feel better and positive about yourself and life when all is said and done. Appreciation is the key to a tranquil, cheerful, and positive way of life.

Sing a little more.

When life hits you hard, or you make a mistake, sing your problems away. Pick a tune that truly makes you feel happy and begin playing it in your mind until stress leaves you. The melody can be one that makes you feel glad. It very well may be one that incites giggling and delight in your heart. Is there any tune that you can consider your happy song? This may be something that instantly puts a smile all over face each and every time you hear it. Great music has consistently been an incredible instrument for changing one's temperament. It will never fail to make you feel positive, so consider singing whenever you can, especially at trying times.

Remember that everything that happens to you is on you.

You can't blame others for the outcomes you get in your life. Every one of our outcomes comes as an immediate consequence of our activities and behavior in our everyday life. Our activities and behavior are the immediate consequences of our considerations, decisions, and sentiments. Only you have the ability to control your frame of mind involved your considerations and emotions. You pick the things that you give your regard to, so instead of whimpering and whining, quit accusing the conditions, the government, the economy, and God. It is your fault that you have given these things a chance to happen. Assume full liability to your actions, and your life will turn out to be considerably more positive!

Make a compliment to other people regularly.

If putting the blame on others makes a person feel awful, the opposite of it, which is giving compliments, can make you feel better. The person receiving your compliment will feel better, but you will also feel good. When was the last time you gave a true compliment to somebody and this compliment came straight from the heart? In the event that you can't recollect it, the time has come to consider doing this whenever you see someone you know. Keep in mind that in case you're searching for the great sides in others, this is an impression of the great sides in you. What's more, be sincere and real when you compliment individuals!

Breathe in and out regularly.

Have you realized that our awareness is exceptionally associated with our method of relaxing? In particular, yogis and priests have found, in the past that our considerations are legitimately associated with the manner in which we relax. When we begin breathing gradually and somewhere down in our tummy, by using 100% of our lung's limit, our contemplations appear to back off, and we become progressively loose. Life essentially backs off; all types of pressure leave both the mind and body and the person who inhales this way picks up lucidity and mindfulness. This training will not just quiet you down; it will influence your well-being and regulate your blood flow better. It will support the movement of your cerebrum, and it will never neglect to improve your state of mind. Breathing is the embodiment of life; begin mindful breathing as a daily exercise. Essentially, begin practicing this until it turns into a consistent propensity. Inhale somewhere down in your stomach and fill it like an inflatable. Rather than breathing in shallow breaths in the chest, extend your midsection as much as you can. The more you practice this system, the more profound and progressively viable your breaths will become. Your cognizance will be clearer, and lucidity and internal harmony will take place. This will never neglect to support your general inspiration.

Be in a positive environment.

What are your companions like? Does your manager at work have a positive temperament? Is it accurate to say that they are fun and diverting or not so much? Great organizations consistently make a difference! If you happen to associate with negative and burdensome individuals, you can stand to change your way of life in the same way.

It is important that your environment is positive since it will be the source of your vitality. It will influence you each and every time.

More often than not, we are affected by a huge amount of cynicism in our lives. We are always besieged with weight and upsetting circumstances, yet it is our decision on how we will react to them. We can assume liability and choose to be in full control over our frame of mind, or we can live step-by-step, letting the influx of life take us wherever it goes.

Carry on with your life in the manner that you want to live it! Quit being a casualty of outside conditions and choose to pick a positive point of view. Also, make a recollection. It is the little things that have a significant effect on our lives. So, take a full breath at the present time, and state how thankful you are for everything in your life.

How To Analyze Yourself

Through self-awareness, you gain an understanding of yourself and your personality. You can also get to know about your behaviors and tendencies. Part of this process is coming to accept the unsightly corners of your own mind that you would rather keep locked away. It is through embracing our whole being (even the darkness) that we are able to achieve true contentment. There are some strategies listed below that will allow you to take a closer look at the person that you have become.

Be Aware of Your Feelings

Notice your thoughts

Your thoughts are essential in defining who you are. They will assist in guiding how you feel and your attitude and perceptions of situations. You should keep in touch with your mind. You need to be able to tell whether they are harmful if you are pinning yourself down, or within which areas you are hard on yourself? This reflection to encompass all of your perceptions, even the ones that need to change

Keep a Journal

Keeping a journal can be a wonderful way to stay in tune with your patterns. Emotions and reactions will be documented.

Be Conscious of Your Perceptions

Your perceptions can lead you astray, thus making you have the wrong conclusions about what occurred or what you saw. For instance, you can blame yourself that your friend was mad at you during lunch break; thus, you will think that you did something wrong. When you are conscious of your interpretation of her mood, this can assist you in knowing why you came to the conclusion that she is mad at you.

With such situations, you are supposed to take your time to study your moves and beliefs about what happened. Write down what you saw, heard, or had feelings about that made you understand the situation the way you did. You must be able to get answers about what made your friend moody, and if there are any outside reasons, you should be aware of it.

Identify Your Feelings

The feelings you have will readily tell you the person you are from the way you react to situations you have at hand and the people around you. You are supposed to try and analyze your feelings and how you respond to different topics, interactions, tonal variations, facial appearances, and body language.

You should be able to tell why you have certain feelings and why you experienced such emotional responses. You should be able to understand what you are responding to, and what directed you to make such choices. You are allowed to use physical cues to assist you in understanding how you feel.

Scrutinizing Your Values

Know Your Values

When you are aware of what you value, this can give you an overview of who you are at your core. Many of your beliefs are based on your individual experiences. They will change, the more you get to know about yourself. You may find it very difficult to identify your values at times. The concept can be intangible and unclear.

Identify Your Values

Values are the beliefs that you remain loyal to. They are usually based on morality. There are some things that you believe that others may not agree with. One of your core values may be to never steal. This is an idea you have thrown meaning behind, and you hold to this sentiment even when theft would benefit you in a significant way.

Your values describe the type of person you are. The caliber of friend or partner you are (to someone else) may be based upon these ideals; the things that you consider important. Defining unmoving moral mission statements can take some work! Imagine knowing off-hand, every aspect of yourself that you consider to be worthwhile. Most people aren't able to do this.

Start identifying your values by inscribing answers to questions like:

Think two people you admire, what qualities do they have that make you admire them? What particular thing do they believe to make you admire them?

Think of the person you hope to be in the future and write down all the positive aspects of their character.

What are you passionate about?

What good thing have you done, even when it would have been easier to walk away or take advantage?

Plan Your Core Values

When you have answered the above questions, you should have an idea of the qualities that you consider important. Writing these values down will allow you to create a map. Pick one or two of these at a time and form a plan for being the sort of person who better embodies these beliefs. You have always been completely in control of the person you are. It can be so easy to forget that we are steering this vessel. Our daily grind can fog up the lens of our abilities. YOU decide all of the things that you wish to embody.

Do you look up to people who are brave? Right this moment, plan an activity that places you outside of your comfort zone. Do you want to be charitable? Call that homeless shelter, right this instant, and offer your services. You are being the steering wheel. You can be as cool, well-red, honest, or kind as you want to be.

Discover Yourself

Write Your Story

Writing down your story can be both fun and rewarding. This is your chance to document the events that changed you and the beliefs that you hold dear. Not only is this a brilliant way to pass the time, but it can also allow you to look back on your life, like a spectator. Can you imagine the feeling of accomplishment that will come from completing a project of this nature?

Evaluate Your Story

After writing down your story, you should be able to evaluate yourself by asking yourself questions like:

What are some of the themes that recur in your narrative? Are you always saving people, or you are the one who is always saved? Is your story based on a topic? Is it a love story, drama, comedy, or some other genre?

What is the title of your story?

Have you labeled yourself and others in the story?

What kind of words are you using to talk about yourself and the others? Are you using positive language?

Resolve What Your Analysis Means

You have to decide what your story means after writing it down. What is interesting about authoring your own account, for review, will be referred to as narrative therapy. It will highlight your moments in life when you felt essential or worthy. It will also show you the way you see yourself and the path of your life up to where you are.

For instance, you can tell your story as if it were a drama, due to a feeling that your life is dramatic and very intense. If it was written as a comedy, then you will think that your experience has been full of fun up to where you are. Or maybe it feels like a cosmic joke? A love story could indicate that you are a romantic.

Put it in Your Mind That It Takes Time

You can follow all the steps, but still, you have to remember that it will need to take time. You should be aware that it's vital to analyze yourself and put your ideas into action. The person you are will change in the days to come.

Track Your Sleeping

When you lack sleep, exhaustion will have some negative impacts on your body. This can encourage stress. You should be able to look at the hours you spend sleeping every night. Amount of sleep needed for an individual varies. This can result in your anxiety levels getting higher than they should be. When you don't sleep:

You will think and learn slowly.

There will be an increase in accidents.

A lot of health challenges will be experienced.

Increase in depression and forgetfulness.

Lower libido.

You will age faster.

Weight will fluctuate.

You will have impaired judgment.

You should have a list of things to help you to enhance your overall life experience. This will aid you in a thoughtful self-analysis. Brainstorm ways to promote growth. You should always see yourself evolving and changing based on your ambitions and life experiences.

It's extraordinarily vital to take your time and engage in self-analysis. This will assist you in changing into the person that you are meant to be. You can live by your own values. You can make the rules and steer yourself toward realizing your goals.

Emotional Intelligent

Intelligence is of different types, and it is important to understand each of them and how to use them in our daily lives. Intelligence is measured in quotients, and the most common type is the intelligence quotient or IQ. This refers to the ability to reason things out logically and memorize stuff. Another common type of intelligence is the curiosity quotient or CQ, which measures the ability to learn a new concept or subject.

Emotional intelligence was introduced by two researchers – Peter Salovey of Yale University and John Mayer of New Hampshire University. It refers to the ability to perceive, analyze, and influence a person's emotions and the emotions of others.

Emotional intelligence shows you how to use your intelligence in the right way. It helps you recognize, assess, and use your emotions correctly. In summary, it evaluates a person's emotional state.

Research shows that individuals who possess high EQ are always creative, result-oriented and succeed more in business than those with high IQ and low EQ. this is because emotional skills have been found to affect business performance more than technical skills.

Emotional Intelligence Model

In the 1990s, Peter Salovey and John Mayer devised an emotional intelligence model that can be used to define a person's ability to control emotions. These two researchers broke the model into four parts, namely:

• Self-awareness which is the ability to understand and acknowledge individual emotions

- Self-motivation which refers to the ability to stay focused on achieving set goals despite the level of impulsiveness and doubt

- Need management. This is the capability to handle emotions maturely based on the current situation

- Relationship management is the ability to handle disagreements and mediate between conflicting parties

This model indicates that if you are in total control of your emotions, you can easily control your reactions and actions. Through this, you can develop strong communication and social skills, and also be compassionate about others. Many researchers suggest that emotional intelligence is essential for leading a fulfilled life.

In summary, emotional intelligence comprises of two aspects

- Recognizing, analyzing and managing personal emotions

- Recognizing, analyzing and influencing other peoples' emotions

Emotional intelligence is mostly seen when a person is under pressure. It is measured using standardized psychometric tests. The result of these tests is referred to as the Emotional Quotient or EQ. Although the concept has been received with a lot of criticism, EQ has gained a lot of interest from the general public, especially in organizations. Most employers incorporate EQ in their search and selection processes, as well as in leadership training.

Importance of Emotional Intelligence

Although emotional intelligence is not as popular as IQ, research shows that emotional intelligence is one of the most important aspects when it comes to learning new ideas and skills. It has been found that the level of success in learning boils down to how a person can control their emotions and confidence. It is also affected by how well the learner is able to communicate, cooperate with the teacher, and manage their elatedness.

Several scientists have related emotional intelligence to organizational aspects such as individual and group performance, leadership, and change management. High emotional intelligence comes with several benefits. Here are some of them.

Improved Physical Health

Taking good care of our bodies impacts overall wellness and helps reduce stress levels. The ability to do this is largely influenced by our emotional intelligence. If you are aware of your emotional state, you will react to circumstances cautiously, and this can result in less worry and stress.

Mental Health

Emotional intelligence affects individual attitudes and motivation. Being self-aware helps to reduce anxiety since the person is able to overcome mood swings easily. High intelligence often translates to a positive mood and attitude. This means that the individual will generally live a happy life.

Better Relationships

Since high EQ helps you to manage your emotions, you will communicate your feelings more accurately without hurting others. It also helps you to connect with other people's emotions. Therefore, you will easily understand how to talk, treat, and relate with them on a personal level. EQ also helps you to determine how to respond to people's needs and questions in a way that does not affect them negatively.

Resolves Conflicts

When you are able to understand the emotions of others, it is easier to settle disagreements as soon as they start. High EQ means high negotiation capability since the person is able to understand the needs of others.

Leads to Success

High EQ acts as internal motivation. It increases your level of confidence, reduces procrastination, and keeps you focused on the objectives of your assignments. It helps you to develop better support networks that can be useful where resilience is required to complete a task. EQ improves your ability to relay timely gratification, which directly impacts your success.

EQ Benefits for the Workplace

EQ enables you to control your emotions when in the workplace. In the old working setups, employees were not allowed to express their emotions at work. However, these days, most employers allow this at work since they have understood the benefit of allowing employees to express how they feel. This is where EQ comes in.

In most organizations, people are required to work in teams. EQ seeks to ensure that each team has a healthy environment to work in since it makes individuals aware of their emotions and the emotions of others. In most cases, people with high emotional intelligence tend to be more flexible and adaptable when it comes to working in teams.

Leaders who possess high EQ tend to raise happier subordinates. This automatically translates to higher productivity. Nowadays, companies' higher candidates whose EQ is high enough to enable them to fit in the existing teams. As a result, most organizations incorporate EQ testing in the hiring process. Let us have a detailed look at the importance of emotional intelligence in the workplace.

Improved Team Performance

A team comprising of highly intelligent members is likely to produce the best results on an assignment. It is easy for such members to get along without disagreements, and since each is curious to learn, research becomes easy. The members will know how to communicate with each other. They will have confidence in each other, value each other's opinions, and respond to questions and suggestions positively. They also share ideas with ease and are less likely to dominate a situation without consulting others first. They are thoughtful and have the interest of the group at heart.

High Adaptability to Change

When introducing something new to an organization, most employees tend to resist it. Emotional intelligence equips employees with the ability to handle and deal with any form of change. It helps employees develop a positive attitude towards change items. Such employees can easily inspire other members of a team to embrace the new concept, idea, or process positively too.

The reason why high EQ individuals adapt to change easily because they are well prepared to handle anxiety, stress, and concerns without a struggle. They are, therefore, able to adjust more easily to new environments that suit the business.

Good Negotiation Skills

High emotional quotient allows you to engage in touch conversations within the organization. For example, you may encounter an angry customer or difficult employee that needs to be calmed down. In such circumstances, difficult conversations may arise, and with the right EQ, you can easily connect with the emotions of such people in an attempt to offer a solution to their issues. By using EQ in the workplace, it is very easy to control individual emotions and reach an agreement for each disagreement. Doing this creates a positive work environment that increases the motivation of employees and customers at large.

Networking

Emotional intelligence makes it possible for you to build trust around people. High EQ facilitates good communication since you are able to empathize with those around you. This is a key phenomenon for leaders who must build networks within and outside the organization. A great leader seeks to understand people in terms of how they work and what they need to stay motivated. This is essential for steering teams in the right direction.

Common Vision

As individuals spend the day at work, both positive and negative emotions may arise. In such circumstances, each person can apply emotional intelligence to demonstrate consistent behavior and communicate any challenges or strengths to the rest of the team. By doing this, the team can come up with a common vision for all the members since each of them is able to control their emotions and remain focused on the goal.

In most cases, individuals who are emotionally intelligent remain optimistic however difficult a work assignment gets. They have a mindset for growth and are able to endure all obstacles to ensure completion of a project. The motivation for such employees is not external – it comes from within. They derive their joy from completing work projects successfully. This means that emotionally intelligent employees will work extra hard and not give up easily. They measure their merit on how effective an assignment has been done, and it is important that organizations keep such employees motivated and happy.

Improved Communication

It is always difficult for people with low emotional intelligence to express themselves. Highly intelligent people connect with others with ease. They are able to earn respect from others and create lasting relationships within a short time span. They remain calm in case of challenges and easily accept input from others. Because of this, they can easily communicate and influence the behavior of others. This creates an environment for them to succeed within a short time.

Great Office Environment

Emotional intelligence boosts the morale of staff, creating a better office environment. Each organization desires that its many staff respect and get along with each other. Some organizations list this as one of the cultures, but sometimes it becomes difficult for employees to work together, especially if they have unresolved differences. A good office environment motivates employees to enjoy their work and also the people they are working with. As co-workers get along with each other, they will be able to discuss ideas and projects that can be of benefit to the organization. This creates a sense of belonging for each of them as they will be sure of each other's' support. Office managers are often given the responsibility of ensuring this happens by creating room, activities, and events that bring employees together.

Increased Self-Awareness

One great advantage of emotional intelligence is that it guides employees in understanding their strengths and weaknesses. Employees who have identified their development areas can easily accept feedback as well as positive criticism. Such can easily be convinced to improve in some of the areas they are weak in. Mostly, managers become defensive when offering feedback to employees. This can reduce the effectiveness through which the feedback is received, resulting in reduced productivity levels. It is also difficult to work with employees who do not understand their weaknesses. Managers can use EQ as a tool to make employees understand themselves better. Once the employees understand themselves, they will be able to view constructive criticism positively and beware of what they should do to improve on their performance.

Control Your Emotions

Dealing with your feelings is especially an issue of decision. Would you like to, or not? So much has been expounded on feelings and how to manage them adequately, yet numerous individuals can't control this everyday issue. Why? Overseeing feelings viably is really similar to building up an ability or a propensity. It is a method for improving, and as people, we battle with change the most.

Changing the manner in which you generally accomplish something isn't simple and it is much increasingly troublesome with regards to feelings. At the point when we are feeling 'passionate,' the exact opposite thing we need to do is quiet down and attempts to manage the circumstance star effectively; we frequently need to yell about what is upsetting us.

On and when we comprehend somewhat more about how our feelings work, we are in a vastly improved situation to utilize this data to further our potential benefit. Figuring out how to control your feelings can be perhaps the best aptitude you will ever create in your life. Your feelings lead to the moves you make and, in this way, make the existence you are encountering now, all aspects of it.

Our enthusiastic piece of the mind, the limbic framework, is perhaps the most established part when looked at, for instance, to our prefrontal cortex, which is our 'thinking' part. Since our enthusiastic part is so old, and in this way an incredibly solid piece of the mind, it is justifiable that it feels like our feelings run us and seize our intuition on occasion. The normal individual's enthusiastic piece of the cerebrum is more than six billion times more dynamic than the prefrontal cortex.

The fact is, your feelings will normally capture your reasoning—this is guaranteed—yet there are still approaches to manage this.

To keep things basic, how about we take a gander at what you can do to flip this circumstance around. Disregarding feelings, stifling them or not managing them will return to haunt you! Stress and uneasiness originate from smothered feelings, so on and when you believe that managing your feelings by disregarding them is getting down to business, you are woefully offbase.

As indicated by numerous neuro phonetic programming methods, there are three components to any expertise or conduct. These 3 components are interconnected and when you change one, you consequently change the others.

To start with, there is the outside conduct which is the thing that the individual really does or says. Furthermore, the individual's inside procedures or musings and thirdly the individual's inward states or feelings. Following are 2 simple and basic approaches to deal with your feelings successfully. Utilize this basic technique to oversee disappointment, outrage, bitterness, dread or some other negative feeling. These are fundamental Neuro semantic programming systems.

1. Change your physiology.

Changing your physiology is presumably the least complex Neuro etymological programming system to change your feelings in a split second. You can prepare yourself to change your physiology so as to feel certain, excellent, rich, glad, settled or grateful. To do that, become mindful of your physical body when you're miserable, baffled or terrified of something. Is it accurate to say that you are drooped or slouched over? Any tight muscles in your shoulders, back or legs? Are your eyebrows wrinkled, your eyes squinted or perhaps your jaw gripped? At that point, change your physiology immediately, move, lift your hands over your head or bounce around as high as possible. As you do this, see how your feelings and thinking have changed.

2. Change your reasoning.

It's less of what you think yet how you think it. I took in a basic Neuro phonetic programming procedure year prior called the cloud method. You can likewise consider it the entryway strategy. Envision 2 entryways or 2 mists before you, one to your left side and one to your right side. At the point when you experience a negative feeling, which is spoken to by a cloud, step away from it (the feeling and the cloud). Ask yourself the 2 after inquiries: does this feeling serve me in that circumstance? Ideally your answer is no. At that point asks yourself: what other helpful feeling I would require in that circumstance. At the point when you think that it's, make as though it was the subsequent cloud or the subsequent entryway and start strolling to the entryway or bouncing in the cloud in your creative mind. You just ventured away from a negative feeling and submerged yourself into an increasingly clever state.

With training, you can ace your feelings. It can take you 10 minutes to do it the first run through, yet it will just take you seconds with training.

You can't generally control what befalls you, yet you can control your reaction. It isn't tied in with disregarding how you feel, rather you have to comprehend your feelings and utilize this comprehension to pick your reaction to a troublesome circumstance. Doing this work will lessen the impact of weight on your wellbeing, improve your basic leadership and backing everyone around you in accomplishing ideal outcomes.

Here are ten stages to take to deal with your feelings in those profoundly charged minutes.

1. Distinguish and name your feelings. Check in with yourself a few times each day to see how you are feeling. On and when you wind up utilizing general words like fine, OK, or great to portray your feelings, drive yourself to be increasingly explicit and perceive the nuances of your feelings. On and when you can't locate the correct words, possibly you have to grow your passionate jargon. A web search on

"arrangements of feelings" will yield arrangements of feelings that you can use as a source of perspective.

2. Recognize feelings and contemplations. Contemplations and feelings are inseparably connected. Much the same as the incredible chicken and egg banter that researchers have had for a considerable length of time it is hard to figure out what starts things out? Yet, our contemplations do make a passionate encounter. Your contemplations can make physical sensations as your body responds to what you state as though it were genuine. Construct consciousness of your "self-talk" and the physical sensations related with various feelings this procedure of becoming more acquainted with yourself at an alternate level will fabricate your mindfulness and capacity to deal with your feelings.

3. Skill to quiet yourself down and postpone your response. It might be as straightforward as taking long moderate breaths. The old procedure of tallying to ten really works as a method for quieting enthusiastic responses and giving time for viewpoint. In any event, concentrating on taking notes, or a doodling an image for you, can be a gainful imaginative discharge. Keep in mind; you have control of your responses. You can't stop the breeze however you can give it a chance to spill off your sails! Before you respond to a circumstance, give yourself an opportunity to think and pull it together to abstain from saying something that you are probably going to lament.

4. Acknowledge your feelings. Overseeing feelings isn't tied in with passing judgment on a feeling as either fortunate or unfortunate and afterward covering the awful ones. Emotions don't leave since you overlook them. The dreamer technique of disregarding your emotions may give impermanent help yet it's conceivable that the sentiments will return considerably more grounded then previously. A little dissatisfaction can prompt outrage or slight worry to freeze. Acknowledge your feelings as data about yourself.

5. Turn the spotlight internal to reflect and get yourself. Consider the circumstances or individuals that annoyed you. Do you see any

examples in your responses? Burrow further to comprehend your responses and hot catches. What are your programmed examples of thought? What suppositions would you say you are making as you make inferences from your perceptions? Are you over-summing up, mind perusing, accusing or foreseeing what's to come? Gain from your reactions and the responses they trigger in others, deciding how you may react in an unexpected way.

6. Build up a propensity for positive self-talk. The running critique in your mind is with you day in and day out and can affect your recognitions and frame of mind. In the event that your self-talk is negative, it will make your own negative reality. Consider the objectives that you need to accomplish and afterward recognize progressively beneficial musings that help these objectives. Whenever you get yourself in negative self-talk, stop and check whether you can re-outline your reasoning utilizing these progressively profitable considerations.

7. Exercise. An extraordinary method to consume off disappointment and stress is work out. Any physical action is a solid outlet for enthusiastic vitality, and it will enable your body to be increasingly impervious to push. Start gradually, however has an ordinary program of physical action with the goal that when the weight is on, you are stronger and ready to keep your cool.

8. Express your emotions.... appropriately. Feelings are the magic that binds connections. In the work environment the passionate vitality of the pioneer can help characterize the way of life. Be that as it may, there is a major contrast between conveying everything that needs to be conveyed deferentially and "giving them a chance to have it". Talk and recognize how you feel, however consistently know about the effect on others. Feelings can demolish a culture, or they can help make a working environment that is loaded with vitality, bounty, good faith, advancement, and trust - prompting achievement.

9. Now and again you simply need to vent. Discharging our feelings can go about as a security valve - easing pressures, much the same as steam out of a pot. On and when you truly need to vent, discover somebody you trust outside the circumstance that will simply hear you out. Perceive that in spite of the fact that blustering may feel great at the time, it is a way to nowhere, except if you set aside the effort to reflect and comprehend your feelings. Additionally, fuming may simply fan the fire and exacerbate the situation.

10. Practice, practice, practice. The more you practice the means over the more you will flex, manufacture and deal with your enthusiastic muscle.

METHODS TO CONTROL YOURSELF

If you feel like your life happens without you, it doesn't have to stay this way.

In order to be in control of your life, you need to feel in control. There can be a sense of safety to feeling like other people make the decisions for you. For one, the pressure is off of you, and you are not responsible for when things go wrong. However, it comes at a price. You will have to watch others decide your fate. You will never achieve success if you do not stand in your own power.

There are things in life that you cannot control. Things that happen outside of you and the choices other people are going to make fall into this category. You will never have control over your life if you do not learn to recognize the difference between what you can and cannot have any impact on. The first thing you need to remember here is that the only thing you truly can control is your actions and your reactions to stimuli.

This is not to say you cannot be provoked or tempted to lose your temper. When someone says or does something rude to you, it will only be natural to feel anger. You will have fleeting thoughts of acting out in anger. However, if your thoughts become a reality and you actually follow through with your impulses, you must hold yourself accountable for it. Everything we do is a choice we make. No one can make anyone else react in a certain way. It will be an empowering moment when you realize you have the power not to react when someone provoked you.

People who have hacked their minds place themselves in a position of having control over their lives. People who do not control their lives put themselves in the passenger's seat. They allow others to decide what is going to happen in their life. Everything a person does, they are gaining something from it. When someone relinquishes control over their life, they are able to place the blame on others when something goes wrong. That is one of the most prominent benefits of playing the role of a victim. If they are let go from their job, it is because their boss had it out for them from the start. If they never accomplished a goal they wanted to, someone held them back (the person they are in a relationship with tends to be the one this particular bit of blame is placed on). They can still be in a foul mood by the evening about a minor rude gesture from this morning, such as being cut off on the way to work. The problem with having this type of mindset is that you will always be unhappy and feel unfulfilled. Even if you shift the blame onto others, you will still feel a sense of shame within yourself.

If you want something, you have to hold onto it with both hands. If you want a music career, you have to create music and put it up somewhere that people will hear it. If you want to write a book, you need to start putting words down onto a page. If you want to start a business, you will need to bring in customers and develop a sellable product. All of these endeavors will require a lot of time and effort. Anyone who is famous for achievements such as these put in such work and had to pick themselves back up after a lot of rejections.

You must learn how to deal with rejection in a healthy way instead of internalizing it if you ever hope to be successful. When you are developing your career, especially in the beginning, you will deal with a lot of rejection. Many young people today find themselves dejected because they are sending out job applications every day and either not getting any replies or being met with letters that tell them their application was declined. If these rejections are taken personally, the person is at risk for developing what is known as post-graduation depression. This means they are worried that they will never find employment or start their future. This anxiety causes them to want to avoid it. This means they will stop sending out applications or any other behaviors to seek employment. This is what happens when you interpret rejection as a personal failure instead of what it really is.

When you are rejected by a business or a person, you were just not a good fit for that particular situation. For example, if you ask someone out on a date and they turn you down, they are not trying to say you are undesirable. They are just not romantically interested in you. Your job application being declined does not mean you aren't hirable. There are only a certain number of people they can hire. They had to look through a lot of resumes and they saw someone whose credentials matched what type of person they were looking for. This time it was someone else. You will suffer indefinitely if you internalize rejection because it continues to happen to everyone throughout life.

This is something else not to lose sight of. Misfortunes happen to everyone. No one gets what they want all the time. It is an extremely unhealthy thought pattern to fall into, to start buying into the idea that everyone else is given everything while you are denied. This will cause a number of ill effects. For one, you will likely fall into a state of depression. You will also come to be resentful of others. You will spend a lot of time angry, which is not good for any aspect of your health.

While you need to chase the things you want, there is one caveat to this. There are things you will not obtain no matter how hard you want it, most often this comes in the form of unrequited love or trying to fit into a certain social group. It could also be when you are trying to convince a friend not to make a decision you know is a bad one, and you can foresee the consequences it will mean for them. None of these situations are ones you can change. This is because the power lies with the other person. In order to have a relationship, both people need to want it. If the other person does not love you back, it will never be real. If you don't have someone's approval, no amount of effort will gain it. It is actually an act of taking back your power to stop trying relentlessly to obtain the impossible.

All have us have looked at a friend or colleague and thought how easily success comes to them. They seem to ooze confidence and make the right decision, every time. Even if something does not go their way, they seem to take it in stride. Maybe they even say something like "Well, I can chalk that up to experience." They make a mental note of the event and how things went awry to be dissected later. What you do not see those doing is hurling negative thoughts onto themselves because this is a derailer that has nothing to do with attaining their goals.

It is important to visualize your goal to the point that you can really see yourself accomplishing it. You can consciously change your thought patterns to suit your path to success. "Don't sweat the small stuff" is a commonly known aphorism, but it can be hard to put into practice. To some, it does not come naturally where there is an inclination to overanalyze what one does and how one appears in his/her interactions.

Removing negative thoughts from your mind before they have a chance to take root can free up a great deal of space in your mind before they have a chance to impede you on your journey to prosperity. The concept is sort of like Disk Cleanup on your computer. You can focus on the positive and tidy up the space in your mind.

Along with your own negative thoughts, we all have situations that cause stress for us. Some of those are unavoidable like the line being especially long at the grocery store or the traffic being particularly congested when it rains. However, we should also explore ways we can remove frustrations from our lives that are a matter of choice.

Let's delve into some situations and, as we do, perhaps you can think of personal examples. First, there is a restaurant very near your house. Sometimes when you go, the experience is great; you have a good time and enjoy yourself. However, there is one particular waitress who is negative to the extent that her expression is constantly unhappy and even her voice shows little liveliness and vigor. When you eat your meal in this type of environment, it is bad for digestion and the mood lingers into your afternoon. You have a couple of options such as trying to ignore her, but instead, you can go to another restaurant down the street if you peer in the window and see her there. Another example could be that you are playing your favorite video game, and someone is typing vile things on the screen and it is impacting your mood. Most games have a block player function so you can return to having the pleasurable distraction that your game was designed to be. Lastly, training your mind away from self-destructive behaviors such as looking at your ex-partner's social media is vital to your path to success. This is an exercise in futility and will create bad feelings that will contaminate your path to success.

You can literally train your brain to stop obsessing over things that will cause feelings that will you stress inhibiting you from favorable outcomes. When stopping one behavior, it's important to replace it with something else that is better for you. Writing down goals you want to achieve is an important step to making them a reality. The fact that you have begun to remove negative thoughts from your mind, staying away from situations that cause anxiety which will rip thoughts of your goals from your mind and moved on to positive thoughts will leave you energized. Your mind is clear, and your thoughts are calm. Meditate on your goals and visualize yourself doing the steps that will take you to them. Is your goal to learn another language? Visualize yourself purchasing a book and signing up for a class. See yourself making flashcards for yourself so you can quiz yourself on your vocabulary words. Envision that you decide to do all the questions because you want to get more practice and learn more. As you think deeply about this goal, you can make decisions such as assigning yourself moments where you will find someone to practice with and/or begin to think in your new language, perhaps for an entire afternoon.

With your freed up "disk space," your brain is working faster, thinking ahead about your goals. You are giving yourself positive affirmations, so you are no long defeating yourself before you even set out to accomplish your goals. You are making plans that will take you closer to your goals.

Importance Of Emotional Intelligence

Being academically bright and lacking the ability to interact with others socially will result in poor performance in places of work, affect relationships with others and it could also have an impact on your health as an individual.

Below are the benefits of having emotional intelligence.

11-   Emotional intelligence helps in building better social relations

By nature, human beings are created to be social beings. For us to coexist well with each other, we need to know how to communicate with each other effectively. An individual with emotional intelligence is likely to have good social relations with people around him or her.

He or she can easily read emotions and know how to act when to act and understand situations that require no action at all.

This can also go a long way in impacting positive performance in the workplace or in any set up that deals with working with other people toward a common goal.

12-   It changes the way we view other people

How we perceive others affects how we relate with them. Individuals that are considered to have high emotional intelligence often portray the right image of themselves to other people.

They tend usually have self-regulation, and they are empathetic towards others. This is an aspect that earns them respect and makes them trustworthy.

One is likely to feel comfortable around such people and quickly form strong relationships with them.

13-   Emotional intelligence boosts one's confidence

It becomes self-liberating when you are aware of your emotions and know how to regulate and manage them. It gives you a grip over your self-control, which makes you feel secure in your actions and in who you are.

Your confidence levels increase as you learn to master your emotions courageously.

14-   It results in better intimate relationships

Mastering emotional intelligence will help one create strong bonds with friends and intimate partners. EI allows you to know the other person and to understand how they behave and also aid in identifying their emotions.

You get to understand why they act in a certain way and get to a point where you do not judge their decisions since you know them from a personal aspect. This kind of understanding leads to the establishment of unbreakable bonds that last forever.

In a situation whereby both partners have high emotional intelligence, then the relationship is likely to last long.

15-   Emotional intelligence can result in great academic achievement

Emotional intelligence has been attributed to, resulting in excellent academic performance. An individual with EI learns to control their emotions effectively. This factor can aid in stress management.

You find that this individual is highly unlikely to suffer from depression. As a result, emotional inhibiting factors become a non-issue, which leads to high performance. This person can learn without struggles about the emotion that results in boosting their earning for optimum results.

16-   It aids in psychological well-being

Having the capacity to master one's own emotions and understand the feelings of others can help in getting a great and satisfying life. Your confidence levels are boosted, which results in high self-esteem. It lowers an individual's level of insecurity and allows you to feel secure. By doing so, you find that things get more comfortable since you can feel good about yourself.

17-   It allows one to have self-compassion

Individuals with high emotional intelligence tend to love themselves and feel secure about which they are. You find that they identify their emotions and learn how to manage them.

They can make the right decisions when faced with a challenge. Also, they appear as being rational and tend to give excellent and informed advice. Self-love is very crucial for an individual's well-being.

A person with self-compassion tends to have an overall high performance in different life sectors.

18-   Emotional intelligence promotes functional leadership abilities

A good leader requires attaining high emotional intelligence. He or she should be able to read other people's emotions and know how to act and how not to work, depending on the situation at hand.

It is also crucial to identify what inspires the people you are leading so that you can know how to motivate them into giving excellent results. As a leader, you need to individually interact with the people for you to easily relate with them and come up with strong bonds that can last a lifetime.

Acquiring people's trust is also essential as it makes you a competent leader that people believe in. Having high emotional intelligence will impact your leadership abilities and make you a good leader that people can trust and follow. Aspiring leaders need to acquire emotional intelligence to be at a better state of high performance.

Constructive Emotions And Destructive Emotions

Negative thoughts strengthen in intensity every time you react to them. If you feel angry with your kid and react to the anger by yelling at him or her, or if you throw a huge fit in reaction to something demeaning your sibling said to you, you will only feel more upset, remorseful, and frustrated later.

Reacting to something means you pay heed to the very first irrational thought you experience. To illustrate, if you feel a strong urge to quit your job when your boss does not give you the raise he promised, you may actually quit your job without thinking about the implications of this decision.

Similarly, if you feel upset, you are likely to react to that sadness by holding on to it and overthinking that very emotion. You fixate on it for hours, days, and weeks only to understand its implications when it turns into a chronic emotional problem.

To let go of the negativity, stop reacting to the emotion and **make a conscious effort to respond to it**. Responding to an emotion, a negative thought, or any situation means that you do not engage in the very first reactive thought that pops up in your head, and instead, you take your time to think things through, analyse the situation, and address it from different aspects to make an informed decision. If you carefully respond to your emotions and thoughts that trigger negative behaviours, beliefs, and actions, you will get rid of the negativity in your life and replace it with hope, positivity, and happiness. Here is how you can do that:

- Every time you experience an emotion that stirs up a series of negative thoughts in your head, stop doing the task and recognize the emotion.
- Very carefully and calmly, observe your emotion and let it calm down on its own without reacting to it.
- You need to fight the urges you experience at that time to react to the emotion. Therefore, if you are depressed and keep thinking of how terrible you are, and you feel the urge to lock yourself in your room, control it by just staying where you are.
- Give your emotion some time, and it will calm down.
- Try to understand the message it is trying to convey to you. If you are angry with yourself for not qualifying to the next round of an entrepreneurial summit and have lost the chance of winning the grand prize of $1 million, observe your anger and assess it. Ask yourself questions such as: Why do I feel angry? What does the loss mean to me? Asking yourself such questions helps you calm down the strong emotion and let go of the negative thoughts you experience during that time. Naturally, when you stop focusing on the intense emotion and the negative thoughts it triggers, and you divert your attention towards questions to find a way out of the problem, you gently soothe your negative thought process.
- Assess the entire situation in depth and find out ways to better resolve the problem at hand. When you focus on the solution and not the problem, you easily overcome negative thoughts and create room for possibilities.

It will be difficult to not react to a strong emotion, but if you stay conscious of how you feel and behave, and make consistent efforts, you will slowly nurture the habit to respond to your emotions, which will only help you become more positive.

List of Different emotions

Emotions can usually be categorized into two different types. However, these types come in different forms. Some experts categorize emotions into two types: emotions to be expressed and emotions to be controlled. Others categorize emotions as: primary emotions and secondary emotions. One thing common with both classifications of emotions However, is all kinds of emotions are usually either positive or negative? Whether an emotion is primary/secondary or expressed/controlled, it will either be negative or positive. Often, people believe that positive psychology is centered mainly on positive emotions but this isn't quite true. In truth, positive psychology leans more towards negative emotions because it is more about managing and overturning negative emotions to achieve positive results.

Firstly, positive emotions may be defined as emotions that provide pleasurable experience; they delight you and do not impact your body unhealthily. Positive emotions, as expected, promote positive self-development. Basically, we are saying that positive emotions are the results of pleasant responses to stimuli in the environment or within ourselves. On the other hand, negative emotions refer to those emotions we do not find particularly pleasant, pleasurable, or delightful to experience. Negative emotions are usually the result of unpleasant responses to stimuli and they cause us to express a negative effect towards a person or a situation.

Naturally, we have different examples of emotions groups under positive and negative. But most times, you can't authoritatively state if emotion is positive or negative. In fact, there are certain emotions that could be both positive and negative. The best way to discern between a positive and negative emotion is to use your intuition. For instance, anger could be both, positive and negative. So, the best way to know when it is negative or when it is positive is to intuitively discern the cause and the context of the anger. This book is, of course, going to focus more on negative emotions and how you can embrace them to create positive results for yourself.

Anger and fear are the two prominent negative emotions which most of us erroneously assume we have to do away with. To be realistic, we cannot allow these emotions to rule our lives yet; we must also understand that they are a necessary part of our experiences as humans. It is impossible to say that you never want to get angry anymore; what is possible is to say that you want to control your anger and get angry less. Mastering negative emotions such as anger is about recognizing and embracing the reality of them, determining their source, and becoming aware of their signs so that we can always know when to expect them and how to control them. For example, if you master an emotion like anger, you naturally start to discern which situation may get you angry and how you could avoid this situation.

A list of negative emotions includes;

- Anger
- Fear
- Anxiety
- Depression
- Sadness
- Grief
- Regret
- Worry
- Guilt
- Pride
- Envy
- Frustration
- Shame
- Denial...and more.

Many people regard negative emotions to be signs of low emotional intelligence or weakness but this aren't right. Negative emotions have a lot of benefits as long as we do not allow them to overrun us. You aren't completely healthy if you do not let out some negative emotions every now and then. One thing you should know is that negative emotions help you consider positive emotions from a counterpoint. If you do not experience negative emotions at all, how then would positive emotions make you feel good? Another thing is that negative emotions are the key to our evolution and survival as humans. They direct us to act in ways that are beneficial to our growth, development, and survival as humans. Anger, mostly considered a negative emotion, helps us ascertain and find solutions to problems. Fear teaches us to seek protection from danger; sadness teaches us to find and embrace love and company. It goes on and on like this with every negative emotion there is.

When we talk about negative emotions, we don't actually mean negative as in "bad." The negativity we talk about in relation to certain emotions isn't to portray them as being bad but rather to understand that they lean more towards a negative reality as opposed to positive emotions. Negative emotions, without doubt, can affect our mental and physical state adversely; some primary negative emotions like sadness could result in depression or worry. We must understand that they are designed just for the purpose of making uncomfortable. They could lead to chronic stress when not checked, making us want to escape these emotions. What you should however know is that we cannot completely escape negative emotions; we can only master them so they don't affect us adversely. Often, some of these emotions are geared towards sending us important messages. For example, anxiety may be a telling sign that there is something that needs to be changed and fear may be a sign that a person or situation may endanger our safety.

Overall, what you should know is that these negative emotions you experience aren't something to be gotten rid of. Rather, they are meant to be mastered so we can employ them in achieving the high-functioning, full-of-purpose life that we desire and deserve. Just like positive emotions, negative emotions are meant to protect us and serve as motivation for us to live a better, more qualitative life and build/maintain quality relationships with people around us.

Note: Negative emotions in themselves do not directly have any impact on our mental and physical health and well-being. How we process and react when we experience negative emotions is what actually matters to our health.

Meditation And Mindfulness

The reason that we might experience such a high level of stress is that we aren't allowing ourselves to be present at the moment. Rather than focusing on the things that are going on around us, we might get hung up on things that have already happened or situations that might still come about.

It can be easy to go over what we have already lived through. You might play through past scenarios and think about, "What if," or "I could've, I should've, I would've," situations. You might wish that you could go back in time and do something completely different than how it played out originally.

Fearing the future and what is to come can be just as terrifying. You can play the "what if" game with things that might happen down the line as well. You might worry about what could go wrong in small ways, or often find yourself zoning out and thinking about the worst-case-scenario.

Don't allow yourself to keep these kinds of feelings around. Instead, keep your mind centered on reality. When you keep yourself in the moment and stay present in what is unfolding around you, it becomes that much easier to de-stress and remove you from any situation causing mental anguish.

If you've tried mindfulness before and found that it didn't give you the total results you wanted, remember that this is something that needs to be practiced often. The first time that you practice mindfulness, your anxiety isn't going to be cured. Unfortunately, it is not a pill for instant release that will be able to carry you throughout the rest of the day the first time you try it. The more that you practice this, the easier it will be for you to find relaxation through these methods.

The first benefit of mindfulness you will see is that you are enjoying the present moment more. You can have more fun in situations that are already exciting, and you can even find ways to make it through the most challenging and painful conditions.

It will be a chance for your brain to clean itself up and come back even better than before. You will remove yourself from the past or future scenarios in which your mind is stuck and be able to bring yourself right to this present moment.

The benefit of meditation is that you will eventually enable yourself to meditate anywhere you want at any moment to stay grounded in the present. If you are having a panic attack at work, you can go to your car and have a moment of meditation or mindfulness. If you are stressed at a family event, you can head into the bathroom and try to de-stress.

This is helpful for chronic stress because it is a way to breakdown the tension that we have built. Even when you aren't stressed, you should practice being mindful, and meditation is necessary every day even when you might be in a very good mood and a peaceful environment.

Mindfulness Exercises

Mindfulness merely involves looking around at the things which already surround you and becoming more aware of the reality of the things occurring in this present moment. You are making your mind focus on the things that matter, and this moment that you are currently present in rather than focusing too specifically on minor things that you have no control over.

Mindfulness can be as simple as playing a computer or phone game. When you play Sudoku or do a crossword puzzle, this can be helpful as well. When we are stressed, it can be as if we are free-falling down a pit of hopelessness that could eventually lead us to be depressed. If you are mindful, it is like you are grabbing onto something so that you at least stop falling in this moment, giving you the mental clarity needed to get back out of this hole.

Look at the objects in the room around you. A simple exercise you can do to pull you back into the moment is to pick out all the things with the same color. Maybe you see everything that is green. This could be a houseplant, a pen, a throw pillow, a picture frame. That's it! Doing this quick activity can is enough to stop panic or rumination and bring you right back to where you are.

Group mindfulness activities are great as well. If you have a group of friends who are all anxious frequently, or if everyone is always turning and looking at their phones whenever they get the chance, these could help. When one person is anxious around others that also experience stress, then this can be something that allows everyone to calm down at once. Look for more games that involve multiple players that you can participate in so that everyone is having a better time. You might try playing charades, a board game, or something else that keeps the attention of everyone in the room. Games, where you can work together to figure out a solution, will be the best option.

Keep an extra table out with a puzzle set up that anyone can go up to and try to figure out as they please. Rubik's cubes and other hand-held puzzles are great as well. Keep picture books as coffee table ornaments so guests will always have something to keep their attention. Always look for new ways to be mindful.

Positive Body Scan

A body scan is a great way to keep you mindful and ensure that you are present. It will involve looking at your body and starting from the top, working your way down so that you can better focus on keeping yourself grounded.

For this, what you will want to do, which differs from traditional methods of mindfulness, is to decide on one thing that you like about yourself as you go through each body part and focus on that. A traditional body scan might make you aware of these body parts and tell you to flex these muscles or something else to acknowledge this part of your body. This exercise is different. Instead, say one thing that you like about this body part. Even if you are having deep issues with your body or there is a specific part that you wish were different, look for the one thing that you do like.

Start with your head. What is it that you like about your head? Maybe you have mesmerizing eyes, a cheerful smile, or your hair is well-kept. Look inside your head as well. Do you have great ideas? Are you a compassionate listener? What quality do you like about your mind rather than just the physical aspect?

What about your shoulders and arms? Maybe there's just a small freckle on your shoulder you like, or you have good posture. If you can't think of physical features, again, what can these arms do? Maybe they hold onto your loved ones, or you use them to create inspiring art.

Your chest Perhaps you like your toned chest, or maybe you are proud of the breasts or pectoral muscles that you have. Inside the chest, what about your heart? Do you love others fiercely? Do you have empathy, unlike anyone else?

Your stomach Maybe you are a great chef and always know what food to cook. Perhaps you have a gut feeling and sharp intuition that has helped you through some challenging scenarios.

Your legs, hips, and thighs again, even if you don't like these physically, where have these legs taken you? How have they allowed you to bend and sit?

Don't forget to even go all the way to the tips of your toes. Where have your feet taken you? As you work your way through your body, you will become more present in the moment while also allowing yourself to become aware of the reality that you live in.

Who, What, Where, When, Why, and How

This will be an exercise you can do, no matter where you are, at any time. Pick out one object that you see.

Answer the "who" of this object. Who bought it? Who made it? Who uses it?

Now ask yourself the "what." What is it? What's its purpose? What are all the parts of it? The inner workings

Where did this object come from? Where is it now? Where was it before that?

When was this item purchased? Consider all questions of time as you go through this. When will it last until?

Why is this object here? Why was it made? Why did someone buy it?

How does this object affect what's around it? How are you able to get use to it?

You don't have to go into a detailed explanation for this. You can start small and get more complicated if you need to come back to this moment even more. This is just a simple and fun activity that will keep you thinking about the "now" rather than anything else that might be causing you stress.

Methods of Meditation for Stress Relief

Meditation is something that you are going to have to practice. Meditating, for the first time, can be hard and might even make you feel uncomfortable. If you struggle to start this, then trying out a guided meditation can be great in order to keep you present and in the moment

It will all start with you identifying the purpose of why you will begin to meditate. Are you trying to connect deeper with yourself? Are you doing this so that you can eliminate the stress in your life? Perhaps you are meditating so that you will be able to get peace over past trauma. It will all start with intention, and then you can move onto the actual practice.

Find a spot to meditate. This can be anywhere that you want, as long as it is a spot that you will use specifically for meditation and nothing else.

Make sure that all distractions have left your brain. Sit comfortably and as any thought comes into your brain, simply push it away. Each time a thought passes into your brain, good or bad, push it out. The focus here is going to be on thinking about nothing at all. The only thing that you need to do in this situation is to relax.

Focus on different breathing exercises and stick with one that makes you feel comfortable. Keep up with the same breathing pattern to keep you more and more centered on becoming relaxed.

Keep your eyes closed. Avoid the temptation to open them as this might give you a visual stimulus that breaks your meditation.

As thoughts come into your mind, push them back out as best as you can. You might only be able to go ten seconds before another thought passes into your mind, but that's fine. Watch as it passes out just as easily.

Again, you might start only being able to do it for five minutes or less. Eventually, you will be able to meditate for over thirty minutes at a time. This process will help relax your mind, body, and soul.

How To Protect Yourself From Mind Control

N ow we get how the whole thing works, we're not that fond of it, but we understand the basics. The main question now, though, is how do you guard against it? That's really what we've been trying to figure out this whole time, isn't it? How do you prevent someone from pulling all that NLP mumbo jumbo on you when you're not looking?

Well, you're in luck because we have a few pointers for you.

Beware of Matchers

The first thing you're going to want to do is to take in and apply everything you've just learned. Remember all that stuff about matching and mirroring? Well, now you need to be on the lookout for it. When you are speaking to someone who you think is trying to control you, make a point to note how they are reacting to your body language. Are they sitting in the same pattern you are? Are they copying your movements as well?

If you're unsure, try testing it out by changing your posture and then wait to see if they mimic it. With pro NLP practitioners, the mimicking may be a bit more subtle and a bit more delayed, but the unskilled ones are a total giveaway. They'll copy the posture right away, and automatically, you know what you're up against.

Now that you know, you can either call them out on their behavior or, if you want to have a little fun, start applying NLP on them to confuse them! Not only will you catch them off guard, but if you can pull it off, you can get them to tell you what their whole ploy was all about and who put them up to it. Total win!

Consciously Infuse Randomness in Your Eye Movement

When it comes to confusing your opponent and playing them at their own game, there is little that is going to give you the same amount of satisfaction as random play. Random eye movements are like going to the gym with your iPod on shuffle. It's basically like trolling your manipulators in real-time and it can be quite fun.

Any NLP user worth their salt is going to go in hard with the whole eye movement thing. This is because your eye movements tell them how you assess and store information, which is precisely why some people can tell if you are lying or cheating just by looking at your eyes. When they say your eyes speak volumes, this is what they mean!

So how do you avoid being read by an NLP practitioner? Simple, use random eye movements, as you are speaking, make a point to look left or right or up or down. You can even make a game of it. Left for every complex sentence, down for every question, and simple sentences can go right or up, depending on whether they start with a vowel.

Sounds fun?

We guarantee it is going to drive your manipulator bat-shit crazy. But hey, #SorryNotSorry, right?

Protect Your Personal Space

What else do you need to do?

Well, this one may seem a little obvious, but we'll tell you anyway—be protective of your personal space. Do you remember how in P.E. class they taught you all about your personal space bubble (as far as your arms stretch to your sides, and in front and behind you)? Well, you need to go back to your basics.

Remember what we covered in anchoring?

Sure, it's all candy and fluff when someone good is doing the anchoring, but when your NLP practitioner is just a master manipulator out to make you feel like a ten-day-old sack of manure, you need to steer clear.

How does this happen again?

Allow us to refresh your memory. Let's say that, for whatever reason, you are in a pretty unstable state of mind. Suddenly your resident NLP master comes up to you and moves to hug you or to even give you a light tap on your shoulder. Do you know how you just associated that touch with a sense of calmness? Yeah, you just got anchored, meaning your whole state of mind now depends on whether or not this person decides to give you another hug or tap on the shoulder and makes you lose control, all over again.

How about, no?

Pick Up on Ambiguity

One of the tricks that NLP kind of sneaks in from hypnotherapy is the full use of vague, unclear language, a great example of the use of this technique is Donald Trump's Make America Great Again Campaign.

Even though the now-president went around campaigning about making a better version of America, he never really broke down what that meant. It was such a vague term that it could mean anything to anyone, and that was precisely what he wanted.

Whenever anyone starts using stuff like that on you, such as "release your inner troubles and feel the world move slowly around you in conjunction with your prospective earthly successes," what you're doing is allowing hypnotherapy to program your internal state in a specific form. Anytime you feel that someone is trying to do something like that to you, force yourself to snap out of it and ask specific questions, "What exactly do you mean by 'great'?" or "What potential are you talking about?"

Remember, all you have to do is point it out. Once you've done that, you're home free!

Be Hypersensitive to People Permitting You to Do Stuff

When a person says something like "you can do XYZ" or "Feel free to make yourself at home" or even something tempting like, "If you want you can borrow the new Avengers movie from me," what they are doing is preparing you to enter into a trance state. You see, experienced NLP users never outright tell their subjects to do anything. They suggest, recommend, or allow. In this way, the subject feels like they are in control, whereas in reality, control was wiped out a long time ago!

Read Between the Lines

We're onto reading between the lines. You have to keep in mind that people who use or people who are using NLP to control you or to manipulate you tend to use specific controlled langue, and nine out of ten times you are not going to know what hit you.

How do they do it?

Double meanings

And you'll find them in the most unlikely places, so skilled NLP users who are good at what they do know how to use double meaning infused sentences to get you to think the way they want you to. Imagine that you are the evil witch's neighbor from the Hansel and Gretel story; now you don't eat kids, but you do have a thing for snacks. Your NLP user, A.K.A the evil witch, comes up to you and says, "Children make nutritious snacks, just in case you were wondering." Sure the witch claims she was talking about their production capacity, but what you heard and processed was something a little different, and already you're a bit more inclined to take a little nibble.

Be Attentive

Another thing you need to be very careful about is how much attention you are paying to your surroundings and to what's going on in them. This may sound a little extreme because obviously who stays alert all the time, you're hardly a cop on the stakeout, and even if you were how you are supposed to be attentive all the time!

Okay, so look, we get you can't always be super alert, but you need to know that when you aren't alert; you are vulnerable. So, an important tactic that employers use when negotiating salary packages is waiting until the employee in question seems a little off and then jumping in and saying that they haven't negotiated a pay difference for Tom, Dick, and Harry, and don't foresee a lot of change in the other employees as well. Not much change at all, they repeat.

Automatically, now that you are asked how much change in salary you expect, you say not much change – Congratulations! You've just been programmed!

Watch Your Mouth

Watch what you say. Master manipulators tend to create a false sense of urgency where they will make you feel that you have to do this particular thing by this specific time or else something drastic will happen.

You don't have a choice. You have to do this now! What do you do?

Well, nothing.

Yes, seriously nothing. Never make any important decisions at the drop of a hat. Chances are you're not the president of the United States, meaning no nuclear codes lie with you, which of course means that you don't need to make any immediate decisions without consulting people. Really, you don't have to make any immediate decisions at all.

Trust your gut

And your final rule, which also happens to be your most important, is to trust your gut. Your instincts know a lot more than you do, mostly because your subconscious mind is processing signs and symbols at a rate your conscious brain can't even begin to fathom. So if it is out there telling you that something is up and that something needs to be done about it, then you need to make sure that you are on your guard ready to get things done because like a used car salesman, you are more likely than not in the hands of a master practitioner.

REWIRE
YOUR BRAIN

PART SIX

Introduction

I f you came to buy " EMOTIONAL INTELLIGENCE MASTERY " it is not by chance, but you understood that something must change in your thought habits and this book will take you by the hand as Virgil did with Dante in that universal work that is Dante's hell. We will go through the flames and, armed with awareness, we will face those monsters that one after the other will try to take us down and finally we will reach heaven, the light, going through different stages to transform those thought schemes, making them help you, not stop you.

In the animal kingdom, metamorphosis gives a new shape to a living being, and, just like those species, we will have to undergo a metamorphosis from caterpillar to butterfly. It will not be an external change, but we will work from the inside, from the roots, to produce better fruits, understanding how thoughts are formed and correcting harmful though habits, gaining more and more awareness about certain mechanisms.

It all starts from the inside; we will explore the darkest corners of our mind and look in the third person at those stages and understand why we behave in a certain way.

Nothing happens by chance, but everything follows a

process.

We will dissolve from the inside of your mind those unconscious blocks and dark sides you try to hide, which are part of you, and you cannot avoid them: it would be like running away from yourself and escape is not the solution. If you've always avoided them, now is the time to finally understand them and evolve.

It's time to evolve into a new man, who takes his life into his own hands and, step by step changes his destiny. First, we will understand how our operating system works and why we do what we do; then, chapter by chapter, we will go deeper and deeper to understand what makes us stumble once and for all. Let's start this journey within yourself to clean up your mind and get rid of that little voice that has always haunted you and you never figured out how to deal with it.

You're smarter, don't get fucked!

How Unconscious Works

T he unconscious mind was discovered in our modern age by Freud, who was the first to show society that there was this part inside us that sustains our whole life. The metaphor used by Freud is that of the iceberg that lies on the surface of the sea and shows of itself only a small part but, the hidden part corresponding to the unconscious is submerged, much larger than the one emerged.

The unconscious as we know it is divided into 3 distinct parts. Lower, middle, and higher unconscious.

The mistake that 99% of people make when they speak of the unconscious is that they use the word subconscious as if it were synonymous with the word unconscious, which indicates the middle unconscious.

The funny thing is that many trainers use the word subconscious to define the unconscious but is not really like that. The word subconscious indicates only the middle unconscious.

It's a bit like saying that a 100-meter tree is equivalent to a small tree or that the Gospels are the same as the Bible. The Gospels are 4 books, the Bible consists of 73 books. So, the Bible (unconscious) is wider than The Gospels (subconscious). Four is not synonymous with 73.

Now be careful because I will explain how the unconscious is divided and structured in all its parts.

Lower Unconscious

There are no clear divisions inside the psyche, on the contrary, everything is in constant connection.

The lower unconscious is the oldest and most primitive part of the human being. It is the place of consciousness where we store all those experiences that we removed because they are judged not to be integrated with the idea we have of our personality. It is the headquarter of all impulses, obsessions, and of all that doesn't fit the image we have of ourselves. We can say that it is that part where we locked up our shadow, all those aspects of us that we don't need, we don't desire, and that for some reason we removed.

The thing you need to know is that in this area of the unconscious we buried everything we don't like about ourselves and, for the principle of psychological projection, we project it onto others.

So, everything you hate, that bothers you, everything you don't appreciate about others actually you feed it too but you don't accept it and so you bury them in the deepest part of the unconscious.

This part of the unconscious represents your past and more

or less all those experiences you had within the first six years of your life, and if you let this part take control of yourself, you will continue to live in the past. You will be limited by what confined them in the past and especially you won't enjoy the present moment because your recurring thoughts are oriented towards something that no longer exists.

Conscious Mind

The conscious mind is that part of your psyche which is reading at this very moment, it's that part you use to make a reasoning.

The most common mistake is to consider this part as if it was the totality of a human being, but it is a small drop in an ample ocean.

It is only a small part that is greatly limited.

The Ego

Along with this conscious part, there is the central self, which is the one who hears, who feels, who sees, who experiences the various situations, the various emotions, perceives and, understands that part that is not unitary, but it consists of many different voices. You will never have a central self since the ego is a conquest of years and years of work on you.

In 99% of people, the ego is fragmented, there are many different selves with opposite desires. For example, one of your egos wants to join the gym, another of yours doesn't. One of them promises eternal love to your partner, another one betrays him. With one ego you decide to stick to a diet, with another one you decide not to respect it and not to eat as healthy as you were imposed.

The problem of the modern man is to possess a central self, but this ego is a conquest, not a prize given to you at birth. That is why you have to take a path of personal growth otherwise you have no will because a self-desires one thing, another one wants its opposite.

A centred self is created through the effort to remember oneself, through the effort of being present here and now.

Medium Unconscious Or Subconscious

It is the place of consciousness easily accessible through the 5 senses as everything that crosses the 5 senses ends up in this area of the unconscious.

Also, the content of this area of the unconscious is easily accessible through memories.

It is the only area of the unconscious which is in direct contact with the conscious part because all other parts of the unconscious are far away from the conscious side.

The conscious part cannot access these areas directly but needs several intermediaries.

Higher Unconscious

It is the place of all the higher faculties of a human being. It is also the most important area as it is the seat of all the higher faculties. All talents, superior abilities of a person are enclosed in this area.

The higher unconscious can only be "contacted" by working on themselves and taking a path of personal growth.

The most extraordinary intuitions come from there. Since this area is not in direct contact with the conscious part, how do you find out what qualities are inside of it?

You just need to analyse which people you admire, because, for the mirror mechanism, you admire people with the same qualities you have.

If you analyse the situation carefully, those qualities you yearn for, you already have them too, but in a minor way.

Those people manage to express them more than you do.

Those qualities to be able to be admired are also in you.

If the lower unconscious represented the past, the higher unconscious represents the future.

What's beyond the higher unconscious?

Higher Self

It's what we are. It is our truest essence, and it is free from all conditioning.

He feels no fear, he has no doubts, he doesn't feel negative emotions, but he feeds on higher emotions and it represents the splendid promise of what we must become.

Collective Unconscious

It is a term coined by Carl Gustav Jung and you as a person, you have not only a personal unconscious, but you are also immersed in the unconscious of humanity.

There is a collective unconscious that is influenced by the behaviours and way of thinking of all the people of the world. This collective unconscious has recorded every information, every emotion, every conviction of humanity and allows every new-born to find the psychological mechanisms of the majority of people in the place where he was born.

You have to keep in mind that in all those situations where an event involves many people, the collective unconscious, teems with those emotions, and although we are physically separated from each other, at the level of the collective unconscious we are all one, we are all connected.

So, you can't feel anger, hate, or annoyance without it influencing the people around you. If these emotions are experienced by thousands of people automatically the flu will shift and, it will cross the lives of millions of people.

For example, if there is a limiting way of thinking regarding money in Italy, all the people who will be born there will have this way of thinking and, even if this person was born in Austria, he will tend to have that specific limiting way of relating to money.

That is why it is important to work on oneself to break away from these limits located in the collective unconscious.

How Does the Unconscious Communicate?

The unconscious communicates mainly by symbols and on him have a strong impact on the rituals.

By rituals, I mean whatever is done in a certain order and which follows a certain procedure.

Why does the unconscious use symbols to communicate?

Of all you live the most important part is the symbolic part that lies behind the event you are experiencing.

Let me explain better, for the unconscious, it's different if you have a sore throat rather than a stomach ache.

The unconscious constantly tells the conscious part of what to improve and tells him exactly what he needs. Most people, for lack of knowledge of these mechanisms, and not realizing that everything is symbolic, will never improve on certain aspects.

When a person doesn't understand there are internal causes that create external behaviours, he usually tries to fix the external causes that caused those behaviours instead of fixing the internal ones.

Another thing you need to know about the way the unconscious communicates is the fact that it first sends a message to the conscious part, to indicate to them what it needs and what it needs to integrate. If the conscious party rejects this message, the unconscious mind sends another message of greater intensity. He communicates with him more forcefully.

If this message is ignored again, the unconscious part sends another one even stronger.

So, the message which originates from the unconscious progressively increases in strength if the conscious party rejects it.

Let's assume that a person has not accepted an event that happened to him in his life and therefore the unconscious sends the message to the stomach, so you will feel pain in the stomach as if you didn't "digest" something in the past.

If a person ignores this type of message, then the unconscious will make you find yourself in situations that will make you understand even more that you need to change certain behaviours and it will always increase in intensity until the appearance of a disease.

So, beware of the "subliminal" messages that our unconscious sends us because they hide something bigger and more dangerous which originates from our repressed emotions that appear under the guise of a symbolic language.

The interesting thing to understand is the fact that since the unconscious works with symbols, the second you realise something on a symbolic level, it feels like you achieved it.

If you have to manage the fear about something and act on a symbolic level, this action of yours leads to an impact on the unconscious.

Let me give you an example: imagine sitting on a chair and having in front of you another chair. Sat on that chair there is the negative emotion you struggle to manage, perhaps a particular fear of yours. Imagine having a dialogue with it. What happens is that fear is giving you messages and intuitions, helping you handle it. An intuition you've never had despite you've been trying for a long time. Doing so you can act on a symbolic level to understand or satisfy a certain desire which the unconscious needs to be accomplished. Another consideration about how the unconscious communicates is that whatever is repressed tends to manifest in various ways. For example, singers, artists, and poets represent these repressed emotions in their works like songs, poems, and, through this symbolic channel, they tend to represent their emotions. It could be anger against the government or anger for the end of a love story; they both express the theme of anger.

It is something that has been incorrectly processed. But this is not art, but it is something artistic.

Some artists have as their strong point the ability to express their emotions in a creative form, and it is their way of managing certain states that, by writing them on paper, take shape giving it meaning. Some painters paint fear, many poets write about anxiety and it is much better to reveal their inner self in this way rather than keeping it inside. Emotions can be vented either through art, but if you don't have certain skills, it could be difficult, or through sport, another form of outbursting emotion. Physical activity helps to remove certain energies and discharges the stress tension accumulated during the day.

Reality Doesn't Exist

One thing you don't know is that there is a secret that can change your vision of what your results are, and it is the secret of life: it's the ability to see things from above. When you can see things from above, to elevate your mind and look from above like a drone you detach yourself emotionally from everything is happening *and you start doing the actions that need to be done!*

Let's do a simple exercise.

Let's imagine for a moment that we see ourselves as a robot, everything that comes to us from the outside is a programming *input*. For example, I'm giving you content right now, your robot absorbs this content and processes it. This content stimulates different results based on how you process data. These results generate feedback that produces a new programming input. So basically, you trigger a continuous mechanism of input, output, and feedback.

The problem is that the majority of people have no idea what's going on in our minds and they believe everything they see is always real.

Now, let's imagine looking at a mountain, every different person looking at it has a different *"perception"* of it: the mountain gives to each of them a completely different input.

So, we absorb information, and what you believe determines your way of perceiving reality. Always and anyway. Read this passage again because it is crucial.

That's why if you believe that wealth, freedom, and money are something intended for the few, you will never get close to the goals you want to achieve.

Many people don't even try to achieve their goals because they already know they won't succeed in them.

And do you know why? Because maybe in the past they tried and failed.

That's how it works.

I have beliefs, those beliefs lead to actions, and those actions lead to results, those results give me perceptions, and those perceptions will increasingly feed what our beliefs are.

Each of us has a different perception of reality. Reality does not exist. It's not the same for everyone. Each of us has something different and so the perception you have of yourself right now is not real, but it's just your perception.

Let me give you an example: there's a thoughtful girl because her boyfriend is two hours late.

What does she start to think, knowing her boyfriend is an adorable and good person?

She's going to call him and ask him if everything is okay.

But what happens if the boyfriend has already got in trouble in the past and suddenly, he is two hours late? What does she start to think, knowing she discovered and suffered a betrayal?

She's going to think he is cheating on her, maybe with a prostitute...

Is it true or not?

It's the same situation, with completely different perceptions.

I repeat this because it is important to emphasise it: what you live every day is not reality but only your perception.

The greatest thing that will get in your way will be the *perception you have of yourself.*

If you look in the mirror what do you see?

Every day lots of people fight against themselves, and that's why they can't achieve their goals. They are too committed to fighting and they have no time to go through their problems.

Now if you try to achieve your goal or your dream, *staying always the same person,* I'm sorry to tell you, it will never happen.

The sooner you understand it, the better.

What you have to do is become the person who can achieve any kind of result, and only then this kind of gap will be bridged.

And that's the secret.

Instead of swimming upstream to achieve your dream, you must become the person who can achieve that dream.

I have a suggestion that allowed me to keep my mind always focused and never fall back. I always carry it with me and it's my diary.

But if you prefer, try to keep an agenda where you write your goals daily.

It also helps me write positive affirmations and rewrite my goals every single day because it pushes me to move towards them.

Positive affirmations help you create an even better image of yourself. For example, in the morning and the evening after brushing my teeth I repeat to myself in the mirror: "I AM A CONFIDENT PERSON, I AM PROGRAMMED TO WIN, I FEEL

INVINCIBLE!" Every morning.

It is a very powerful technique to build a new mental image of you.

Even a house is built with the laying of the first brick. The first step is to start.

Changing the Mindset

"A problem cannot be solved if you do not change the way of thinking of who created that problem", Einstein said that, and I don't think there's anyone who can contradict him.

What is the problem caused by?

By our personal reality model that doesn't have immediate information to solve that particular situation.

How can I be successful if I have only collected failures so far?

What do I need then to get out of my vicious circle? A new way of thinking.

Thought precedes change.

If you think you can't do it, what do you will be the result? The answer is obvious. You're not going to make it. Would it be enough to think of achieving it?

In this case, there is a different strategy of thinking but there would still be no action.

We are still in the field of thoughts, things must be done, we cannot only imagine them. But without a vision, there is no starting point.

I need a vision. I need to create a model of what I want.

Reality changes if the dream changes.

So, if you change the point of view, it also changes reality.

If you've always been paid an hourly salary, you'll struggle to start your own business, especially if your parents have always been employees because the environment you grew up in only got that kind of information. If you want to start your own business, you have to radically change the way you think and change your point of view.

If I currently earn $1,500 per month and I want to get paid

$10,000 per month, I have to change the model. Maybe I'll start by wanting 2,500 dollars, moving step-by-step to the goal of $10.000. So that the model gradually evolves.

The model I own now ($ 1,500 model) is my way of observing the world around me. Let's take it as a springboard and not as an endpoint.

If you want to change, it's not you who needs to change but the model, if you're still thinking you won't make it, of course, you won't make it. You'll have to tell yourself to change the model, change, the new software is now YOU CAN DO IT.

If you start trying to do that and focus on the new way of thinking, do you know what really changes?

Your reality changes.

If you change the way you perceive, you also change your experience.

What do you really need to change? Only the model, its operating system, or the information you have. The ones you've had so far haven't led you to achieve your goals.

When we changed the information, we received advantages, didn't we?

Okay, that's what's called evolution.

Success exists in any profession, I didn't say that, but to achieve that success, or a better situation, what do you need?

The information. Organise the information to do the thing you set your mind to together with the vision, the thought that leads you to portray that goal in your mind and act. Act. Without acting no leaf moves.

Change Your Thinking from Negative to Positive

We all know that theories are important but what makes the difference is practice.

And there's an area of positive thinking where all of this applies perfectly. Because we all know very well that we can influence our thoughts and if we had more positive thoughts our lives would be better, lighter, things would roll off our backs and we would be able to manage more easily stress and difficulties and we would achieve our goals. Yet almost all of us are stalled.

Almost all of us fail to implement any kind of change that really changes the dynamics of our thoughts. The most typical reaction is saying: "Yeah I know but it is difficult".

The point is that most of the important things in life are difficult, and very few are really easy. Most of the paths that life proposes to us have a high difficulty level, but this is not a good reason to give up choosing that road.

And people may think that thinking in a positive way is a trivial, banal and a little superficial choice, to such an extent that in modern culture we tend to say that if one is too positive it's a little silly, a little foolish and he isn't that smart.

And if I'm smart, if I'm cultured, I must have understood the bitterness and negativity of life. That's how our society works.

In fact, many years ago many psychologists gave birth to the current of positive psychology, they wrote many books about it and today there are a lot of data and knowledge which tell us positive thinking is not at all a superficial thing and can make a huge difference in achieving a higher degree of happiness. Today on the neuroscientific level, happiness is no longer considered as an emotional state but rather as a habit.

Happiness is built through daily habits that, by being exercised every day, become the reality of your thought.

It is said that the neurons that light up together end up bonding together.

So, as you exercise a certain kind of thinking, it will become easier and easier to exercise that kind of thinking, even negative thinking.

As you give more and more space to negative thinking, it will become more and more automatic and rooted in you.

There are profound reasons why this is happening, it is not simply a matter of choice.

We have a strong tendency to recognise negativity and hold it back and an equally strong tendency not to fully savour positive things, and this applies whether we talk about real events or talk about thoughts.

And why it is like that?

Because evolutionarily having a particular ability to recognise negative things coincides with a great ability to perceive the danger and therefore to save your life.

So it is clear that on the evolutionary level nature has made us more careful to the negative side of things rather than to the positive one; but in the modern world, especially in a situation where evolution has given us such an evolved cerebral cortex and a reflexive capacity on our life, this very ancestral mechanism ends up hurting us.

We can agree that the ability to recognise danger is sacrosanct, but a constant and repeated over the years tendency to see everything negative leads to a huge decrease in the quality of life.

And so, you have to learn well a basic concept: *awareness*.

The first step in modulating our thoughts is to raise the level of awareness.

If I can figure out what's happening to me in my brain, I've taken a huge step toward adjusting my thoughts and it will help me evolve toward a new self, fitted with new information and new keys to reading my problems.

The Key

I personally repeat myself quite often a concept that helps me to raise the level of awareness: "Here it is coming back".

Every time I recognise it and I realise that I'm thinking

negatively, or I'm criticizing myself, I recognise this kind of thought that comes to mind and I say the magic formula "Here it comes back" or "Here it is".

Just try to say: "Here's the negative thinking coming back" and recognise him for what he is. It can be real, or it can be invented and is held in your mind.

The moment you become aware of this, the negative thinking mechanism begins to slow down and opens up a chance in your emotional sphere to better see positive things.

Automaticity is the real trap for all of us, if we want to really live our lives to the full and to use our full potential.

When things are automatic and we don't recognise them, it's a huge rip-off, because for evolutionary reasons it's easier to stabilise a negative habit than a positive habit.

And the moment you don't recognise it and let it act undisturbed, it ends up prevailing, because you're training that negative possibility much more than the positive one.

What needs to be done is a simple brake mechanism, a slowdown in the automaticity that could start from recognition. Think of the sentence "Here it" every time you perceive a negative thought that comes to your mind and it will act as a *brake* opening the possibility to positivity, through this pause in automaticity.

Awareness is the key to turning off negative automaticity and to discover your own positive dimension.

Limiting Convictions: How to Delete Them.

The important thing to understand is that our deepest beliefs determine how much of our potential, which determines what kind of actions we're going to take, we use and we must remember that we can achieve our results thanks to our actions.

So, the key is that if you want to change your results, you have to change your beliefs. Is it possible? Of course, it is.

To do this, you need to follow these five steps:

1. Link Pain With Old Convictions

Pain and pleasure determine everything we do.

Every change happens because we associate pain with the old way of thinking.

Or pleasure with the new.

Start thinking about how much it costs you to keep old beliefs in your life. What things could it limit in the future?

How many other unsatisfactory situations could it cause in the future? How many other opportunities could you miss? And in general, how much will it make you suffer?

So, ask yourself, how much will it cost me emotionally not to abandon this belief?

The thing to understand is that people don't know about their limiting convictions.

Therefore, you can hardly associate pain with your limiting conviction if you do not realise you have it.

You just need to see what kind of actions you do and what are the results you have.

If your health results are poor, it's because you don't do enough "effective" health actions.

For example, you do not play sports, or you do it once a week, you do not eat healthily... in this case there is a limiting belief.

Analyse the variables of your life, consider your dull results and if you pay attention, you will find a limiting belief.

2. Create Doubt

A limiting belief is a sense of certainty about something, so if you question everything based on this belief, that belief will be purged.

There are very powerful questions you can ask yourself to see if that's the case.

For example:

What are my references that confirm it? Who I got it from?

Are there people with better results who have an opposite belief to mine?

Is that person worthy of being taken as a model?

It is useful to ask questions that may create doubts about the usefulness of your belief.

3. Choose a New, Empowering Belief

Identify which new idea you want to turn into a new belief.
Then locate a new empowering belief.

4. Look for References for the New Belief

Let's pretend to time travel and imagine yourself while applying this new belief and managing to achieve different results.

Then ask yourself, are there any other people who have achieved good results by applying this belief?

5. Combine Pleasure with the New Conviction

How will your life change by following this new belief?
Find all the reasons why this belief will improve your life.
Write them down. In a way that affects your brain and visualise how your life will change thanks to this new belief.

Wiring Up Your Brain

Every belief we have, every thought we formulate has both a cognitive aspect and an emotional-affective aspect. Every idea is not just an image, it is not only a thought, but it is a representation, therefore also physiology.

Changing an idea means changing physiology, changing internal chemistry. Plato had already understood these things. In his famous book "The Republic" he said as early as 400 BC that men are asleep.

They live in a cave and they stare at the walls, they see images, shadows, and they believe in those, which are not reality but only projections of reality. If one of them manages to come out of the cave, he will see reality as it presents itself and recognise the truth.

At first, his eyes will hurt for a while, because of the bright light, but then he will be contemplating the infinite beauty of the outside world.

So, what he's going to do? He will go back and wake up the others. Will they thank him? Of course not. They will kill him.

So, the attachment to toxic ideas becomes something vital for our survival. Have respect for other people's ideas, whatever they are. Because at that moment their lives are based on those ideas, their identities speak to you.

If you're skilled, you can explain to someone that their ideas are toxic and, if there is a good relationship between the two of you, they may change their minds.

Remember that the primary concepts of the human mind are two: belonging and identity.

We internalise ideas by belonging. Belonging means affection, life confidence; non-membership means exclusion, death. Changing your unconscious mind means dying.

If we believe we are only made of our conditionings and our personality, we just have to suffer them. If we discover we are something infinitely greater, precious and sacred than just those few things, then we realise even for a moment that we usually tend to look for self-confidence where there isn't.

It's not easy to do it yourself, because it means getting out of the cave.

Model = Your Perception of Reality

The brain lives imprisoned in a box and it needs the sense organs and therefore a pattern to find out what's out there. Without a model the brain does not have access to the outside world, any correlation with the outside world must be modulated and filtered by the model and the instructions determined by the model have their limit but also their advantage.

The model is a limit itself since it can never represent the whole reality: it can only show us a portion of it.

Often when you talk you refer to a fraction of the whole, but then you end up swapping that fraction for the whole, and so you swap your model for reality. However, if I recognise that my model is relative to a portion of reality, and so I accept its condition of relativity, this allows me to be able to change. If the model, my operating system, stiffens and raises its defences, changing perspective becomes more difficult. If the programs of my model give me the impression of being open and malleable, I can have problems but also solutions but, if my operating system is rigid, closed, it means that my reality is limited to my model.

If I'm sick, where's the problem? In the model. If I am okay, where it is? In the model. Both disadvantages and advantages are expected in the model. If I want to change my disadvantages to advantages, I have to change the model or include other perspectives. It seems natural to do so, but this is not the case because there are internal resistances. The model depends on the direct or indirect information we have. Our limit is that every expression we express is always an expression of the pattern. How is it possible to break the impasse? I have to use other areas of the brain.

Why do ethologists study animal behaviour? Because they

study the laws that govern reinforcement, which is the stimulus-response to understand how humans work.

We use such prehistoric areas of our mind so often that we just need to study a chimpanzee to understand what people will do when they won't use cognitive thinking.

Stimulus-response-motivation are relevant to the emotional brain. If I'm in a state of fear, I'm still using that area of my brain meant for survival and I'm not evolving. The more I protect myself, the less I grow, because I don't use higher cognitive activities. Stress also blocks cognitive activity, all the part of the neocortex (the part of the brain with the more recent development that accounts for 90% of the brain mass) needs to be wired. Change must be built.

If we analyse the brain divided into three parts, we'll see that the reticular conformation has control over everything.

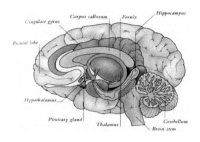

"The headquarter" is represented by the limbic system, which knows everything that passes through the body and accepts it. On the "second floor" there is the neocortical brain and it is divided into 2 hemispheres, left and right. The inputs are scanned by each party according to their point of view and it is difficult to put both the interpretations together. This is the stage that may confuse you a bit. The part of the brain that interests us is the neocortex, we can modify it —let's say educate it—because the cortex is already wired.

We build the model on our own and we need a mechanism to act on the model and so to change reality. All parts of the brain are separated and each of them has a specific function. The frontal lobe is the most evolved area, while the neocortex deals with the most sophisticated data analysis. When nerve impulses arrive in this area, however, they have already been filtered and only a small part of them will come to you: that's why the model can never be the reality. What really comes to you is conditioned by the filters and the model of belonging. Our 5 senses are influenced by past models. All you see will be what you have already seen, experienced; what you will experience will be what you have experienced before.

When you process information, it has already undergone several processes, including acceptance by your past. When you think, your thoughts have already been compared to your past ones. When a thought is born, if it is consistent, the filters will get it to the upper cortex. Otherwise, they won't.

From this point of view personal experience is a major

energy disadvantage, in fact, initially, it has a positive function but then it takes on a neurotic value.

If you were to ask me to lend you a pen, to do so, I would first have to know what a pen is, and then I have to draw on memory, from the past. But perhaps if I saw a pen stuck in someone's neck in my past, today, when I look at any pen, I'll always recall that scene.

This is the advantage and the limit of the past. To overcome these limits, we need to learn to dissociate negative and limiting information. This is one of the obstacles to our way of personal change.

The Model and The Environment

Every person we meet, man, woman, or child represents a set of information. When I say "information", taking inspiration from the philosophical language, I mean "giving a shape", modelling according to a sketch, like a potter who creates the vase, as in following certain directives. Information shapes a sequence of data, whatever object is in front of you, perhaps this book, a car is the "fit" of certain information. For us humans, we take some information from our DNA, and some from the model: the data form our genetic code aren't enough to create a perception of reality. Every newborn acquires his genetic legacy from his parents and thus he possesses the information to "put shape", to model the atoms that will form the cells, the various organs, the tissues, the bones, and the nerves that will make up the body.

Meanwhile, the child grows and, what does he do? It's not a closed system, it's open. And as soon as he's ready to get instructions, he starts storing information.

You create the template.

The variety of information received means that the child will be "put in shape" in a certain way.

If the mother is stressed and the child perceives stress information, his body will shape itself in a certain way.

If the mother is calm and loving, the child will acquire another model.

In any case, it will be conditioned by the information it receives. From this, I deduce another truth. The environment is conditioning.

If the brain was a simple recorder, it would reproduce the voice as it receives it.

This means that there is no processing in a recorder. The brain doesn't act like that. It does something more, it doesn't just receive signals, but once it is stored, *it processes it, and while doing so, it changes it. By changing the information, it modifies the tatement itself.*

The information processed by the brain is put "in shape" in a different way. This processed information is called a "model".

Let's take an example, if you and I participated in a certain event, we would mentally record the same information derived from that event.

The question is, would we both elaborate it the same way? And would the others who were present do the same? If we were recorders, we would record the information identically and we would reproduce everything exactly in the same way. Unfortunately, our brain processes the information received and we would remember the episode differently.

This happens not because of the event itself, but because of our way of processing it. We process information in a very personal way, based on the experiences we accumulated over the years and each of us will respond differently depending on the "model" installed in its brain.

First rule: *the model is not the reality.*

If it were, it would be the same for everyone. The model is the sum of the environment, the DNA information, and the processing of each. Not all of us are in the same environment.

If I was born in Iraq or Afghanistan with the war always going on, I would live in a very different environment to the one in which, fortunately, you and I grew up. If I have a certain DNA sequence and I was born in Rome with parents who over the years move to Mumbai, would I always be the same? Of course not.

Yet the DNA is the same. It just changes the environment and the DNA inserted in another context gives me a different result. DNA + ENVIRONMENT = ME.

My way of developing data is the sum of DNA + ENVIRONMENT + MODEL.

They are not the result of the environment, they are rather the product of the model, in other words of my perceptions of reality. Since the environment is unique, the experience is individual.

What happens to me has no relevance, it is important what I think of what happened to me, what meaning I attributed to it.

The subjective interpretation of reality is its elaboration. Processing modifies the event itself, and so, how I interpret it. You will wonder why everyone processes reality differently.

Filters select which kind of data can enter the system and which cannot. You could suppose that since it's just information to change, you instead don't do so. Certainly not. My self-awareness makes me say that I am the same of yesterday, of today and of tomorrow, but nor physically or on the conscious and behavioural level, I am the same person of 10 years ago, 5 years ago, 6 months ago, a week ago; tomorrow I will be even different. What changes is the information. That means that any experiment carried out on me is not replicable because I'm not yesterday's, and I, you, and everyone, change every day. This is because the brain does not process information now and then but constantly, continuously. We can define the brain as an information processor and in the act of processing it, it changes the information itself every single moment.

Self-sabotage

You can consider self-sabotaging anything that limits you, anything that blocks you in achieving your goal or expressing your potential. It doesn't come from the inner world but yourself, from the deepest part of you.

Why does a person self-limit?

This happens for several reasons: perhaps someone may not feel inward that they deserve to achieve a certain goal and so they do everything not to achieve it. You could think of self-sabotage as a person who should run a marathon and shoot himself in the foot. Despite having all the skills to run this marathon, they will never be able to run it because he "hurt" themselves.

This example gives you an idea of what I intend as "self-sabotage".

I identified how these mechanisms manifest themselves, however, before I speak about this, I want to explain to you why these mechanisms are there and why your unconscious considers dangerous achieving a certain goal.

If you obtain certain results, your unconscious thinks it's dangerous for you. Why?

Because you might not be able to emotionally handle the

fact that you achieved that goal. What does that mean? Let me give you an example.

If you become a millionaire, then you have to manage those millions without harming you. The unconscious through self-sabotage prevents you from reaching something that could be dangerous for you. But why some goals could be dangerous for you? Imagine being in charge of Microsoft, so you become the CEO of the company, we're talking about one of the most important companies in the world. It wouldn't be a success for you but instead, it would be a huge problem because you have to learn how to handle the incomes, the criticism of the press, the televisions, the people around you and a whole range of things.

The unconscious to prevent you from living these experiences blocks you before you can even reach them since you unconsciously don't believe to have the proper skills to manage that goal.

In conclusion, self-sabotage exists for your good.

Although they are indeed very annoying

and you have to learn to delete them, they are fundamental for your survival, especially when they protect you from achieving certain goals that for your unconscious are dangerous.

Another common self-sabotage is trying to stop smoking. The thing is, if you've been smoking for 20 years, you won't be able to quit smoking in just one day. It's a longer and more complex process.

Another situation may be that you are a runner, you have a marathon tomorrow, but you get sick the day before.

Another example may be having all the information to start what you want to do, such as that online business you've been studying for months, and never act. You keep procrastinating and waiting for the right moment.

Common ways of self-sabotaging

The most common form of self-sabotage is to find justifications and blame something else instead of you.

From now on you must pay attention when you make excuses because it's nothing else than self-sabotage. Another very common form is perfectionism. People instead of acting immediately, they waste time by trying to do something perfectly. The so-called paralysis-analysis. This is wrong because to achieve the goals you need to act. You need to act now! Yes now. Get off your ass and move, do something in the direction of what you want to achieve.

Perfectionism is related to judgment, to the fact that you judge yourself and others too heavily and this worsens the quality of your life. *You don't have to be perfect; you have to act.*

As Jim Rohn said, "You don't have to be great to get started, but you have to get started to be great." Another very common self-sabotage is trying to achieve goals bigger than us. It's not bad to think big but it's better to do it gradually. If you haven't exercised in 20 years and you're aiming for the Olympics within 1 month, this is a way to self-sabotage.

Another method by which people self-limit is procrastinating. They never do what needs to be done and so they postpone it to better times. They postpone until tomorrow what they could do today and so on.

Procrastinating makes sense when you postpone doing bad things for you. For example, don't light your cigarette if you're trying to quit smoking or, if you're on a diet, don't eat the dish isn't on your diet plan, or, postpone that uncomfortable phone call that needs to be made. And so on for every other situation in your business or activities.

Another method that people use to self-sabotage is giving up. People usually start doing something, encounter the first difficulties, and give up, and they start doing something else.

Now that we've seen an overview of self-sabotage, let's see what strategies you need to use to permanently eliminate them.

Strategies to stop self-sabotaging

The first strategy that allows you to find a solution to self-sabotage is:

- Find the worst thing that can happen to you and find a solution

Let's take an example: if you're trying to learn Italian and you want to talk to someone because you're training to speak a foreign language, you meet an Italian and let's say you want to talk to them.

If you let your brain control you in these situations, there will be thoughts of fear and you won't talk to that person. All you need to do is imaging the worst-case scenario that can happen to you, perhaps this person slaps you as soon as you try to talk to them. What do you do?

You think that person is not normal, they may have some brain disease and that's not your problem.

At best, you'll have a conversation and maybe you'll get the information you need. Most of the time we freak out for stupid things, and these brain defence mechanisms damage us the most.

When you find a solution to what is the worst-case scenario, you *accustom your brain* to find a solution to the worst-case scenario and, if you managed to do it in this case, what limits you to find solutions in normal and daily scenarios?

It's clear they are manageable situations, it is not a monster to fear, you can overcome it.

- Hang out with people who got the results you want

If you can't meet them in person listen to their podcasts, read their books, or otherwise spend time with people who have already both physically and virtually achieved that goal.

- Convince yourself you can do it

For example, if you have to run a 30 km marathon, you have to say to yourself that that's just a number and that you can do it. You can record an mp3 track with your motivational messages or positive thoughts and you can listen to it when you are on the bus, while you are driving or when you are working out.

Over time, the repetition that this goal of yours is feasible for you, it will go from *the conscious mind to the unconscious mind* and so you would do more concrete actions. Eventually, you will fall, but you will rise because you know down deep that you can achieve it. The secret is to transfer every situation from the conscious mind to the unconscious mind and it can only happen by repeating hundreds and hundreds of times that message. You have to stick it on your head.

"Repetita iuvant" said the ancients. And it means "repetition helps". The purpose of this sentence is to tell you that if you repeat it many times, you end up learning it. Like driving. At first, you have to think of engaging the different gears. After a while, everything comes to you automatically without thinking about it. This also applies to the goals you want to achieve.

The fact is that people get tired pretty quickly and end up giving up before they see results.

Thanks to this guide you'll understand the innate

mechanisms that limit you.

Be constant and repeat, repeat, repeat, repeat, and repeat.

If it can get into your head even 1 concept of this book, let it be this.

- Stop telling yourself limiting things

You should ever say "I can't" or "I'll never achieve it". You need to understand the concept that it's only a matter of time, that you just have to find the right way to do it: don't think negative, you need to tell your unconscious you are absolutely capable of reaching your goal.

It is also true that it will take some time, but it's vital that in the meantime you convince yourself you can do it. As we said before, you need to repeat positive messages to achieve your goals.

You have to stop criticizing yourself, stop listening to negative people or TV shows, don't let the outside environment limit you in any way.

Letting your brain know that you can accomplish something is the first step to make it happen because if you are the first to not believe it, that thing will never come true.

Avoid as much as you can people who criticize you such as family, friends because it is important to stay focused and limit as much negative exposure as possible, even TV shows about crises or misfortunes can have a bad influence. Isolation allows you to focus on your goals.

When I was building my online business, the morning from 5.30 am to 7.30 am was the most productive time of my day because I was alone in my studio planning all the actions needed to be taken with no one around. During the day, my children, work emails, colleagues, and meetings kept me away from what I had to do for my start-up business. Only isolation from external negative sources made me succeed in promoting and selling products online.

- Split your target into smaller parts

Another strategy I recommend is taking small but steady steps in the direction you are moving to reach the goal you want. Don't do it all right away. Segment your actions to make them smaller, they will also seem less demanding and more manageable. This will make it much easier for you to create an important change for you. The mistake that many people make is that they want to accomplish something that is too far beyond their capabilities when they need time to develop the skills necessary to achieve that goal. If you won't hurry and, above all, you will work hard by doing certain actions every single day, I assure you that consistency will take you where you want to go.

- Keep your goals in mind

Another technique that Bob Proctor uses is to write down on a piece of paper your goal. Just a post-it notes. I keep my five principal goals in my wallet and every time I open it I have them in front of me. I use my computer desktop as a blackboard with a list of things and, every time I look at it, it reminds my conscious what I want to achieve.

Whether it's a post-it, a piece of paper, or whatever, the important thing is that is something you can look at many times during the day.

Be Careful

By reading successful people's biographies, your brain will begin to believe that, if they have accomplished such great things, you can do it too.

Beware the environment that surrounds you and pay attention to the messages that pass to your conscious sphere because then they will also get to the unconscious sphere. Be especially careful with the people around you because you need them to be as empowering as possible.

Get rid of anything that limits you in any shape and any way. Watch out for the books you read, the films you watch, and especially the people you hang out with because it might frustrate the efforts you've made so far.

Many years ago, when I was 18 years old, my first form of entrepreneurship business was in the field of network marketing. I had told pretty much everyone, my family, my closest friends, my uncles, and I was really excited about my first business. My dream has always been to be independent, not to have a boss, who decided how much my work was worth per hour and to whom I had to ask permission to go to the toilet. In short, I told them that it was a fantastic business, that would change their lives and that they would even benefit enormous economic and health benefits from these products.

Unfortunately, they didn't understand my intentions and, their reaction was really negative, they told me I was no one, I had to stay humble and I would never succeed. Especially my mother, who had always been programmed since she was young to have a secure job with a fixed salary at the end of the month, didn't understand my idea of finding my way.

In fact, they tried everything to make me give up, they tried to convince me I was wasting time and money. Instead, I thought it was a great investment in myself and in a business that would soon make me change my life. At that time, I was working in a warehouse preparing orders that were then shipped to customers in the evenings.

My friends made fun of me, they told me to be careful, that network marketing is a scam, that people were brainwashing me in those meetings, that I couldn't see the truth of things...

The fact is that no one supported my cause, indeed, no one understood me, I was the weird one, the one that in a few years changed his life in online sales.

The teasing bothered me at the time, very annoying, but those laughs fuelled my will to win, my desire to assert myself, to change the course of my life.

The derision was the fuel to my desire to win.

I was as hungry as the lion that remains in the savannah flattened in the grass, waiting for the right moment to jump on its prey. Unfortunately, I abandoned that network marketing business. Taunted and mocked by my friends, not understood by my parents, I quit after one year and a half. With few results and a warehouse full of products to sell.

This experience, however, which in many ways was a complete failure, laid the foundations of my mindset. All I did was read personal growth books, everywhere. During the evenings I just studied, I spent my little free time in training myself. I listened to motivational videos while driving, I was just thinking about training more and more in the field of personal growth and how to help others achieve their goals. Even though I was far away from mine. I thank my girlfriend, today my wife, who has always supported me in those years of experiments to find my way. It's hard to be close to someone as obsessed with personal freedom as I was.

All these efforts and failures of these years helped to build my "forma mentis" and after 5 years of experience, I made more than $100,000 per month with my online sales.

I give you a valuable piece of advice, which I understood afterward; protect your dream, don't talk to anyone if you know you wouldn't be understood because they might damage it. They could be envious, or they could try to stop you from achieving your goal.

When I was designing my new online business, no one knew what I had in mind, I looked back to my experience and I decided not to make the same mistake. They knew afterward, thanks to my results in my dashboards.

Don't talk, show the results, they make much more noise.

Remember, it's all in your mind, if you can think of it, you can accomplish it.

The 40% Rule

You've never had that situation when you say ENOUGH! I CAN'T TAKE IT ANYMORE!

It is a very common phrase when you do a very demanding workout, an endless study session, or a really hard work.

Marathon runners call this feeling the 30th-kilometer wall.

When they have done about 30 km they start to collapse, practically they can't go on anymore and the brain starts screaming to stop!

Yet out of 10 people who start a marathon, 8 of them complete it. The limits our brains impose on us aren't that real.

You have to imagine our mind as a circuit breaker: as soon as it senses a slight danger it triggers right away; this mechanism has been fundamental to our survival and evolution over the last 200,000 years.

But when we talk about modern daily challenges, our brains

confuse warning signs which aren't that dangerous. This actually limits our real potential.

So?

What should I do when my brain tells me to stop?

In this situation, I like to come up with a very useful rule.

The 40% rule.

I first read about it in a book by Jesse Itzler an American businessman who had for 31 days as a personal trainer a former Navy Seals, the U.S. Navy Special Forces.

On the first day of training, the man asked the American entrepreneur to do as many pull-ups as possible.

Jesse managed to do 10 with great effort.

After 30 seconds, the man asked him to do 10 more. And Jesse could only do eight.

Another 30 seconds passed, and the Navy Seal asked him to do 10 more.

Jesse was destroyed and could barely do any more than six.

Another 30 seconds passed, and he asked him to make another 100 pull-ups, he wouldn't let him go until he completed the exercise.

Jesse took a whole day to do all of them, he did 2, then 5 more, then 8 more, and eventually he got to complete the 100 pull-ups.

At the end of that field day, the soldier reveals to him what is the 40% rule.

When you've reached the limit and think you can't get ahead, you're only at 40% of your potential. I don't know if this percentage can be applied to every area or challenge of life, but it made me think a lot.

We set ourselves too many unnecessary limits, we build golden bars from which we can no longer get out. But above all, we waste our lives not expressing our full potential.

Remember, when you want to give up, when you think you're throwing in the towel, then think you're only at 40%.

Antagonist's Law

In this chapter, we will talk about the absolutely fundamental principle you need to know to achieve your goals which is called "antagonist's law".

Most people ignore this law and find it very difficult to achieve their goals. If you learn to use this principle in your favor, you can achieve an innumerable amount of goals.

When a person sets a goal, three distinct and separate steps will take them from where they are to where they want to go.

The Phase of The Impossible

In the beginning, when you decide a goal, the first step of your journey is the impossible phase.

Once you start doing the first actions and moving towards it, the first difficulties appear.

It's the time when you put your mind to something, you have your dream but it won't come true, because you don't have the resources, you lack the skills, you don't have the knowledge, you don't know the right people, you miss pretty much everything you need to achieve your goal but you're determined to pursue it. At this stage there are two fundamental things you need to focus on: first of all, you need to *believe in yourself in order to see.*

If you convince yourself you can make it, if you make enough effort, if you are disciplined and you put all your commitment and your money, there's no doubt you will achieve your goal.

What you need to say is not "if I see it, I believe it" but "if I believe it enough, I will see it realised".

This is the first thing that people struggle to understand, because you have to see it in your mind first and then fulfil it practically with your actions. The majority of people want to be reasonable and need to see it before it's realised. That's why they're never going to achieve anything.

What was reasonable when the two Wright brothers in 1905 designed a plane?

What was reasonable when Henry Ford created the first car while everyone used to ride a horse?

The second very important concept is, as I already said: the fewer the people you talk about it the better. And I don't want to dwell on it, I hope the concept is clear.

The Phase Of The Possible

Once you have set yourself the goal, take concrete actions to achieve it: learn skills, knowledge, techniques, strategies, allies that will help you to really make your dream come true. The point is that right at this stage, just when things are starting to go well, you'll struggle. This is the law of the antagonist. The bigger your goal is, the bigger the difficulties you will encounter. But what is the most important thing to understand?

First, difficulties are never greater than your real skills. You can also remember the story of David and Goliath where David beats the giant Goliath.

The giant symbolically recalls the difficulties you'll encounter along your path, that appears to you as an invincible monster, but you can actually overcome them easily.

The point is that people experience difficulties only in this stage and not in the others: difficulties tell you can accomplish that goal and most importantly they show you which inner aspects you need to work on. If you are afraid, the difficulty shows you fear in such a way that you can get rid of it to reach your goal. If you have any doubts, that difficulty shows them to you: any hesitation, fear, limiting conviction you have is there to show your limit and help you get over the obstacle.

The law of the antagonist is a mechanism that always tries to do your good, in the sense that it does everything to show you the path you need to follow, it is like a finger pointing inside you that shows you what limiting beliefs, what fears and what doubts you have and you need to get rid of.

What you need to understand is that the moment you start to struggle, it means you can accomplish that goal and you need to start to work hard because you're getting closer to your goal. You have to be happy because life is testing you to see if you're worthy of the prize. Only who is climbing a slope encounters this difficulty, only who have set an ambitious goal, because, if you think about it, going down the slope is much easier.

When you try to elevate yourself, you attract difficulties and they are there to show you what aspects you need to go to work, and that's where you have to put all your energy into it and believe it more. Now, given these two phases, that of the impossible and that of the possible, we get to the third phase.

The Phase of The Inevitable

This phase indicates that this goal is achievable for you and it's only a matter of time or maybe you've already realised it and so you're setting yourself another goal.

At this stage, the main problem you will encounter is the envy of other people, or at least their attempts to diminish the results you obtained. As if they said, "I told you you'd make it".

Actually, the moment you accomplish a goal or, when you're striving to build your business and you're achieving excellence in a given industry, people, instead of looking at yourself with admiration to try to learn from you, because you're elevating and they are trying to elevate too, as a consequence they'll try to lower you to their level.

It's a bit like the technique of the crabs in a bucket. If you put crabs in a bucket and one of them realise, he's trapped in a different environment and would like to escape, his attempt to climb vertically involves a blocking attitude from the other crabs. So, the ones below will make it fall down. The ambitious crab will try again and those below will do the same thing. Doing so, the ambitious crab will get tired and lose hope of escaping from the bucket.

Our society works in the same way, the people around you will always try to knock you down. They will do anything to throw up roadblocks because your excellence is a finger pointed at their mediocrity.

If you think about it every great man has had to overcome enormous difficulties, Socrates, Jesus, Buddha, Nicola Tesla, Edison have all had enormous difficulties in their lives.

If you maintain this vision, that a goal must go through these 3 stages, I assure you that the moment you experience difficulties and remember the law of the antagonist, you will continue to do the actions that will lead you to achieve your goal.

In the inevitable phase, comes the time to put your mind to an even greater goal, to look at the horizon and try to reach new and even more ambitious goals. Some people think they will be supported the moment they set a goal, but you're alone. Then when you'll get the first results, the people who will believe in you will pop up, but first, you have to deal with yourself.

Focus Creates Reality

So, can you change? Sure! You can only change.

The question to ask is another. Can we drive change? In any case, it's possible to influence the change by changing the degree of energy we give them.

How so?

With the focus.

Let's pretend you have a 25-watt light bulb that fires energy in all directions.

It will have some influence on the surrounding environment.

The laser has 25 watts, but all centred at a single point.

What result can an energy beam have on a single point rather than on the whole room?

It will hit that point in particular, while on other points in the room will arrive a few bounce photons. When you meditate or focus on something, your attention focuses on that thing, on a single point, with the result that we can change that thing more effectively, intentionally and consciously. That's the difference.

When I come out of meditation, a part of my operating system has changed forever. So, I can change the entire operating system or model?

The answer is yes, even radically, but we need energy. Don't think you can change something with flying thinking, a one-off.

Energy flows where attention goes, it can be directed, intentionally, and consciously.

The programs work at the subconscious level and, even if I did not have a conscious intention at this time, I would have a program that supports the information in any case.

It's the DNA + MODEL.

Your DNA tells you that you are incompetent: What do you have to do to change the program?

You can't change it by thinking the other way around. That is, you can do anything you can think of. You have to act on the operating system that controls that program.

You have to change the way you think. You have to change your behaviour; you have to behave like those who are convinced they'll make it; it is a positive exercise on how to keep the focus on this positive attitude.

Repetition is keeping the focus on this new way of being, where there is the focus you create reality.

The brain is a computer: as it changes the new information, my next actions will be different from the previous ones since there's been a change in the processing. However, if I think of the laser example and focus on that part of the program, that increased energy projected on the target will change the information. If the information changes, so does my reality. I repeat the concept so that it is clear.

If I work automatically using my DNA combined with the model, I only reproduce my past, but if I want to create a new future, I have to use intention + awareness. I need to add new information. Focus energy combined with new information changes the result.

So, you have to add new information to the ones the model already possesses.

Reading this book, you are adding information and editing the model, this way you will also change your reality. That's the change.

Dominate Your Internal Dialogue

Internal dialogue must be managed, must be dominated and self-control derives from the command over our thoughts.

There is a consideration that needs to be done: conscious thoughts have their strength, but unconscious thoughts are much more powerful; this does not mean that conscious thoughts should not be managed.

Managing one's thoughts is one of the pillars in a path of personal growth and it is a good lifestyle. It's not something you can do just now and then, but you have to do it every single day for a lifetime.

You must know that the mind is like a pendulum, it is constantly moving with thoughts that look to the past and thoughts that look to the future. So every single day your mind behaves like a crazy monkey: it makes you focus on all the reasons why you can't achieve your goals, or it makes you focus on problems with colleagues in your workplace, or the argument you had with your girlfriend and so on.

Perhaps it makes you focus on your future; you are stressed and anxious because of the exam you are about to take because of the task your boss gave you which is too burdensome for you.

We continually move our minds between the past and the

future, constantly generating anxieties and worries.

So, you have to make a conscious effort to manage and give direction to your thoughts because having constant pounding, limiting or obsessive thoughts is not good for you.

Given this premise, let's see what are some exercises that you can apply right away.

- Exercise No.1

Repeat a sentence for 3 minutes. It is a basic exercise, very easy, even a first-grade child can do it.

You have to focus your mind for 3 minutes on a short sentence.

Repeat it as a mantra, and only after you've become good at it you can move on to the second exercise.

To know if you've done properly, you have to check that you respect the 3 minutes "without wandering". It sounds easy but it's not because we always tend to lose our attention. This first task, through practice, will also improve your concentration when you try to stay focused on the things you're doing.

- Exercise No.2

Repeat a short sentence for 5 minutes while watching a film.

You have to understand the plot as you repeat the words but also stay focused on that short sentence.

So, you are splitting your focus, part of your attention goes to the plot of the film and the other part is aimed at repeating your thoughts.

When you become good at this exercise, move on to the next exercise.

- Exercise No.3

Don't complain for a week.

Not complaining involves managing your thoughts; usually, the mind tends to focus on everything that doesn't work, everything that's wrong, everything that's not how it should be. How do you do that?

Simply keep your desire to complain inside you. For example, it's hot: try not to say anything about the hot weather. It doesn't mean you don't take precautions, but you do it without complaining. Because you can solve that problem without having to talk about it, so either you find a solution, or you shut up.

Do this exercise for a week. Dominate your behaviour when you're working with colleagues, in front of a TV personality, and so on.

- Exercise No. 4

Repeat every day for a week these four words "I believe in me".

You have to take into account that in our lives there are 3 very important relationships.

The relationship with our mother, our father, and ourselves.

Focusing on the sentence "I believe in me" is a useful thing.

We live in a society that has low self-esteem and so, even if it does not make a big difference, you have to use the first tools to dominate your internal dialogue: repeat this phrase mentally all day every time you remember it. When you're in your office, stuck in the traffic, at the supermarket, with your mother-in-law or at the post office. Every moment you think of it, do it because it's important.

In fact, who meditates find it is "easier" to control one's thoughts because they are locked in a room in the dark. Managing ourselves when we're experiencing our daily routine is not easy at all. We need to learn to manage ourselves in all different situations and manage our internal dialogue regardless of what happens to us.

- Exercise 5

Analyse which word you use more frequently and try not to use it for a week.

I used the word "it seems to me" and for a week I tried not to use it because I knew that pronouncing it gave me a sense of approximation, not precision, and apathy; I used it almost unconsciously. I couldn't even notice it.

I had not to use this form in my speeches and when I happened to use it, I immediately recognised it and analysed the situation.

Finally, after ten days of effort, I realised that I had replaced it with more precise words.

You should focus for a day on which words you use most often and which you can also delete from your vocabulary (NEVER, I CAN'T, and so on) and on Monday you pledge not to use it.

It's not something you can change in a day, but with practice and consistency, you get good results.

It is not important what results you get, but the effort you put into dominating and managing yourself.

- Exercise No. 6

Take a quick tour of your house, go through every room, and pay attention to the details and how things are arranged. Then you sit down, close your eyes, and try to rebuild your entire home in every little detail. So, try to rebuild in your mind your whole house by mentally reproducing every single room.

The moment there's something you don't remember, you can get up and go check which elements you haven't put into your imagination. Then you go and sit down again, close your eyes, and imagine the room adding those elements.

- Exercise No.7

What I propose now requires maximum concentration.

It is one of the key principles so read the following pages and then apply it as soon as you have some free time.

First of all, isolate yourself, find a quiet and peaceful place where you are not disturbed, better if dark.

Close your eyes.

Take slow, deep breaths. Count up to 10 breaths.

Bring your focus on the lower lip until it creates a sensation right on the lower lip. This concentration of thought leads to a feeling.

Then move the vantage point, from the lower lip to the corner of the mouth, first to the left and then to the right. And the feeling shifts depending on where you move your attention.

Focus your concentration on the area until you feel the sensation on the spot of your lip. Focus on one point at a time, feel the feeling on where you focus your attention, and you'll see that by shifting the focus to the corners of your mouth the feeling will shift too.

You can move the focus later to the tip of your tongue, or between your eyes.

To do this operation it takes such a concentration that you do not get any other thought. Impossible. If more thoughts come to your head, kindly bring your thoughts back to the part of your face that you were thinking of.

Do this for 5 minutes and you got the wonder. Inner silence.

These pieces of advice are practice interventions, they work, but it takes your commitment to apply them consistently.

The latter is not only used to free your mind but then it is necessary to go to the "control room" where, with the appropriate moves, you can start at your leisure the dynamo of positive emotions.

So, we can say we are sovereign of ourselves, only if we know how to go into the "control room", where we can press the button and the dynamo of positive emotions turns on.

In whatever situation we feel at this precise moment, we can disable negative thinking and activate the dynamo of positive emotions.

We're our owners here. Sovereign of ourselves.

The one who can produce positive emotions for himself is the master.

Without depending on the interaction with others. I'm happy regardless of the behaviour of the other people around me.

It's the same thing as money. If a state cannot print money but has to borrow it, it's not sovereign.

We decide our inner politics without being hostage to our emotions.

Mental Images

Mental images are the key to our realisation, everything we want to create in our lives goes through mental images, these are, in fact, imprinted in the subconscious mind and become the matrix or the template of the subconscious mind itself.

Even a house before taking shape needs a thought. This thought thinks the object of desire and realises the project. The project with all its details is carried out and, brick by brick, the house takes shape. It all starts with an idea.

We have to be very careful about which mental images we keep in our minds in a predominant way: we must avoid at all costs to imprint mental images that we do not want.

Many take for granted the ability to imagine because it' so cheap and affordable we almost give no value to it when instead it is one of the most powerful faculties of the human mind.

Imagination is one of the most important faculties for 2 essential reasons.

1. *It is a border faculty.*

It activates with the conscious mind, (because we intentionally think of our "goal") but draws on the resources of our subconscious and spiritual mind to bring us what we want.

2. *It does not distinguish imaginary experience from real experience.*

The subconscious mind can't determine whether the image is real or imaginary and, in both cases, the nervous system elaborates the data that is communicated to it by the brain.

It accepts everything we send to it if we send to it our best desires it will work towards them, but if we cannot control our imagination and we always think of the worst, for example, an affair went wrong, the never-ending expenses, our old catastrophic relationship, what do you think comes to our subconscious?

Lack, scarcity, disappointment, anxiety.

And what results do you think you will achieve by always imagining things in the worst scenario?

I'll let you answer that.

How do you plan to attract abundance if your mental images and thoughts are always directed at what you don't possess?

Creative imagination is not only relegated to poets and writers but is part of all our acts, our action or non-action are consequences of imagination and not of will as is commonly believed.

A human being acts and operates according to what he thinks and imagines to be true about himself and his environment, everything we create with our mind consists of a model, a matrix for the subconscious which will automatically tend to transform the mental reality into objective reality.

Picturing doesn't just mean reproducing; it means constantly creating.

This is the immense power of mental visualization, if you do not reproduce it first in your mind, it cannot take shape; we are the creators of our destiny, the captains of our soul.

Thanks to the fact that the experience of imagination activates the same processes as the experience of reality, with the conscious visualization we continually recreate our reality.

You can constantly change your reality, this means that every mistake of the past can be recreated and transmuted into our minds in a positive way and therefore we always hold the keys to open the doors that were once locked and open them to create everything you want. If you have failed in the past, you must remember that you are not your past and you can change the path you chose in the past by choosing a new one. It all starts with your thinking. Who are you? Have you ever asked yourself?

What image do you have of yourself?

The winner? Or the loser?

When do you think of doing a certain job, do you think about winning?

Or do you think you're not able to do it and so give up?

It all comes from the mental images you make, from the fantasies you have in your mind.

If you're in the wrong business, what forbids you from getting into the right one?

If you have a job you don't like because in the past you thought you'd only do that, nothing forbids you from finding a new one.

And if you're in a toxic relationship, what stops you from finding one that makes you feel good?

Limits are only in our minds. Ghosts, which cloud the vision and do not allow you to see in the distance, just like when you're driving and it's foggy. You're driving and you can change your ways. Turn off autopilot and start taking control of your life.

Everything you think is not real, but the result of years and years of mental programming caused by your environment.

You can change your programming by changing your mental images.

Creating and maintaining in one's mind a specific mental image that represents one's ideal or aim is the first step to bring yourself to the next level.

However, these images too often take the shape of daydreams that we create like pipe dreams or fantasies to which we do not give weight.

That's why we all have to learn to be precise when we ask our subconscious, we have to be scientific in asking why they are not daydreams but the scheme or plan to create our future.

Always take well care of your plan, re-create it daily in your mind and remember that no one can set your limits, only you can. Self-sabotaging. I dedicated a chapter to self-sabotage, to recognize, and to overcome them. Understanding that you are self- sabotaging is the beginning, many people do not even acquire an awareness of that.

Ideas must first take a mental form, as we said before about the project of a house, then you can jot down your project keeping the image imprinted in your mind and it will gradually approach you. Eventually, you will become what you want to be.

Here are 3 steps to create effective mental images.

1. Idealisation

It's a fundamental step because idealizing helps planning your project which you'll follow to build your goals. As mentioned before, you, as an architect, you have to think of every detail and establish exactly "your home" completed in your mind even before you lay the first brick.

As a child, my sister cut out images of houses she liked and put them in her diary, at the age of 20 her first home took shape. It was an early example of visualising and realising her intentions, a mental plan that made her dream possible. She managed to achieve it all alone with all his might thanks to her strong will.

2. Visualising

In this second step, your mental imagine gets more and more complete and limpid in your mind and your "blueprint" takes shape.

3. Holding

It's about holding back mental images as much as possible and visiting them every day not only to create new ones but to reinforce our creations to feel them alive. You cannot think about them today and for the next two days, you completely forget them. It lacks the flame, the spark that keeps you going. This is why they need continuous nutrition to get used to and to repeat to your unconscious what you want.

Whether it's a new machine, the house, or your new business, let the images guide you to your goal and, thanks to the burning desire, your unconscious will automatically push you towards reaching it.

Kill the Monster
While It's Still Small

In this chapter I will talk about the 4 mistakes that impede you from facing your fears.

Fear is something physiological, a necessary thing for growth and it is very well manifested by children who, as they face their fears, grow, strengthen, and then become adults.

Courage should not be seen as the lack of perception of fear but simply as an overcoming of fear itself, so a brave person is not necessarily a person who doesn't fear anything but rather a person who makes sure to manage his fears and learn to overcome them.

One of the things that are considered absolutely dangerous in an individual is the absence of fear because it would lead a person to underestimate the risks and to make mistakes more easily than a person who perceives fear but somehow learns to manage it, to face it and to overcome it.

Between these two extremes, between the person who does not perceive any fear – who could have dangerous behaviours – and a person who perceives fear – who understands the risk and is able to manage it – there is also the third hypothesis of a person who perceives fear and freezes.

646

You need to understand if fear hinders your behaviour and functionality. In that case, it would be a problem.

If fear is something that makes your life more difficult than it might be, if it something that affects your choices, which leads you to avoid certain developments then it becomes a serious problem that somehow needs to be managed.

In the next pages, we will talk about 4 common mistakes and then we will find 2 possible solutions or 2 possible strategies to better address the problem.

These 4 mistakes are:

1. Trying to overcome your fear.

Trying to control a fear is a lost battle. Fear is manifested through circuits that are much more primordial, basic, than those of conscious control. It is as if conscious control was not able to affect this type of behaviour. On the contrary, the centres that perceive fear, and that give life to it, read your attempts of consciously controlling your preoccupation as another danger or another fear and it just increases your level of tension.

So, trying to control fear is quite ineffective.

2. Talking about your fear.

This behavior does not lead to a solution: talking to your

friends, your partner, or your parents, could give you the impression of letting off steam but in reality, it does nothing but leaves untouched the core from which the fear develops and talking about it never really faces it. You talk about the dynamics, explain the evolutions but you never get to face it head-on.

3. Avoiding your fear.

Avoiding putting yourself in all those conditions that could arouse a certain degree of fear. The most common example may be not calling that person I need to contact because I'm too afraid of a negative response. In this case, you are not expressing fear but what is likely to be created with this mechanism is the fear of fear. Because you're actually putting yourself in a mechanism that can't lead to growth but an absence of exposure.

4. Constantly asking for help.

Overcoming fear through the support and help of others is something that necessarily leads to the fact that you are not able to overcome that fear on your own.

For example, every time you ask your colleague for help as soon as you doubt what is going on in your workplace, it implies that you are not overcoming your fear, but you are transferring it to another person.

Strategies to Overcome the Monster

We've seen the fundamental types of fear but let's see if there are at least a couple of strategies that can be useful to overcome these difficulties.

- Step 1:

Tackling fear in small doses is a very effective way of training in overcoming it. A small calculated exposure causes your immediate strengthening.

If I managed to do a little step, why I shouldn't do the next one? And so the third step and so on.

My first step years ago was to open a company in the business I was entering, and I had to do open an LTD company in order to be in good standing with the revenue office.

At that time I was an employee, and taking this step was for me a quantum leap and it cost me a lot of effort and a lot of thoughts, but this first push gave me the energy to face even the second step that was buying the products, creating the sales page and so on.

Small steps, which you overcome, give you the strength to take the next step, and then another one and again and again. To the end. Until I reach my goal. Up to cash the money of the first sales, up to climb the business with a second, third, fourth, and fifth product.

Are you afraid to speak in public? Start with to speak it in front of 3 people, then 5 and then 10.

And continue until you increase your audience. As you do this, eventually you'll talk to hundreds of people and it'll grow stronger in you the belief that wasn't a big deal, after all.

You can do the same thing with any form of fear.

If on one hand, you keep running away, you'll see the fear behind me and you'll see it getting bigger and bigger,

but thanks to this strategy I'm looking at the fear face to face and I'm dealing with it.

So, I'll decide how frequently I'll expose myself to this fear (one step at a time), and if the exposure dosage is defined correctly, I will not react negatively, and what will I develop? Courage.

ven though I have overcome a fraction of this fear, it is always a form of courage.

I was able to deal with it and I overcame it.

- Step 2:

The Latin people called it "premeditatium malorum": practice the worst fantasy in small doses.

They trained to predict the worst and by doing so, which is actually a very concrete way of training the mind to face fear, it helped to reduce the feeling of fear.

Because it was as if you already emotionally felt the fear. While most people try not to do what scares them, so they try to avoid fear to avoid getting hurt.

In this chapter, I provided you with 4 mistakes to avoid and 2 strategies to overcome them.

When you will eventually face your fears, and you will, read these pages again and you will see that fear will deflate like a balloon.

And then you'll say: Is that it?

Our Malaise

Malaise.

It may sound like a strong word but having to deal to work with many people every day, I realised that discomfort is widespread and, I do not even know how to identify it precisely.

It's not a disease but it's more a feeling that makes most people not fully enjoy life.

That's why I really like the concept of living to the full, basically, that's what should be our deepest goal and that's also what's missing in the lives of many people.

Scientists tried to identify what may be the causes of our malaise and why it is so widespread in our society; they identified 2 phenomena that are somehow very closely related to each other. And it's hypervigilance and hypo-satisfaction.

Hyper-vigilance, already the term explains itself quite well, means a state of excessive vigilance. Our central nervous system works like a radar, so it is able to constantly measure and evaluate the reality we live in and it sorts the environment by dangerous values. Our nervous system is very capable, but in a society where natural reality is now non-existent and where reality is perceived in different ways for each of us, it is inaccurate. It feels the danger where there is no danger and when it perceives danger, it triggers a whole series of responses that are nothing else than combat and escape impulses, which would trigger if there was a mammoth or a hungry tiger in front of you.

Maybe there isn't a tiger chasing you but there's a hassle that lasts several days because of your employer or a colleague who doesn't like you. That's why long-term stress response becomes highly harmful and exhausting.

Hypervigilance is a situation in which we find ourselves almost forced by the environmental situation in which we live and which we unknowingly amplify because of our perceptions, elaborations, our thoughts that instead of blunting the corners very often exacerbate the conflicts.

The second point is the hypo-satisfaction, which is this vague, widespread, latent feeling among people that you never have enough, that you never get enough, that you always want something more, that you do not settle, that you do not observe the things that life actually gives you because you are always busy thinking about something else. Hypo-satisfaction is something that leads to very profound behavioural alterations, perhaps people try to find satisfaction in other things, such as food, alcohol, or drugs. These attempts of looking for satisfaction from the outside are caused by a lack of pleasure that comes from the inside. Unfortunately, this is something that is spreading a lot among young people, who very often have an inability, since adolescence, to enjoy the beautiful things of life. Logically, a strategy to address these 2 issues, hypervigilance and hypo-satisfaction should ideally lead to reverse them; we should try to enter a state of hypo-vigilance and hyper-satisfaction, but one might think that it would be unnatural. And instead, our basic, ancient condition was probably like this.

200,000 years ago, humans lived in a depopulated world and became hyper-vigilant when there was a physical danger, but their lives were interspersed with very long periods of stillness and – we could say –of complete boredom. Now I want to mention 5 important points that can help you restore a balance between vigilance and satisfaction.

1st point: learn relaxation techniques.

We can never avoid being stressed in the modern world, none of us can avoid traffic, tensions, colleagues, your boss (if you are an employee) but we can learn to counterbalance them and to do so we need techniques.

These relaxation techniques are scientifically proven, they are effective in reducing stress levels and is nothing more than a workout. It's just like training your muscles, your heart, your relaxation techniques; it could be meditation, autogenic training, Thai Chi, or yoga, but the important thing to understand is that it is a technique and it must be repeated over and over to have an effect.

2nd point: pruning the dry branches.

It's a crude word, but that's how it should be.

Each of us during our lifetime fills up with commitments and sometimes we do not realise which of them we can get rid of because they do not give us anything. And it's not a matter of selfishness, it's a matter of self-protection. You will not be able to cut everything but there are some dry branches that you need to cut off to free yourself. To give oxygen to the rest of the plant. Because otherwise, you'll struggle to ensure a balance that isn't at the expense of your well-being.

In the end, the time will come when you've collected all of this, but you haven't enjoyed anything.

3rd point: dwell on the details.

Pruning the dry branches, getting out of some unnecessary commitments makes it more likely that you will be able to dwell on the details, to enjoy the experiences.

When you're under too much pressure nothing can be pleasant. If you're able to get rid of unnecessary commitments, one of the important consequences is that you'll be able to enjoy the details.

The idleness. Sitting for a few minutes on a lawn, watching nature or looking at the view, staying there for a while, and doing nothing.

What happens when you allow yourself to do this? You notice the details. For example, colours, scents, and a whole range of things that disappear when you're under pressure.

4th point: Give yourself daily goals to give you satisfaction.
If you can plan something that every day leads you to feel deep satisfaction and a deep sense of contentment, you'll definitely have a satisfaction effect over time of your overall levels of contentment in your life.

Think, if every day you could help someone, even a very small gesture, it would help to give you a sense of satisfaction. In fact, we know that helping others is one of those things that gives more satisfaction to human beings. But if you don't have any free time, everything slips away, but you have to find something in your day that allows you to give something to others, and then in return, you'll receive a sense of satisfaction. It might just be helping your children every day and seeing how happy they are.

5th point: Have fun.

Having fun is the most valuable antidote to hypervigilance and hypo-satisfaction. Having fun causes an immediate reversal of these 2 phenomena. If you laugh nicely and use your body in fun, it means you're safe. If you set yourself the goal of making your child laugh for 2-3 minutes, it's extra fun for you and in exchange, you'll get a sense of contentment.

Hypervigilance and hypo-satisfaction are two important problems in our society that lead to alterations in our behaviour and these are effective strategies to reverse these two phenomena. Good luck with your work.

Conclusion

We have come to the end of this journey within the mind.

I've shared all my knowledge I acquired over the years to give you the best and to help you figure out how to redirect your mind through mental re-programming and understand the mechanisms behind the actions we do to be the best version of ourselves.

This new man makes conscious and courageous choices, he dares, goes beyond his limits and gets rid of fears, embraces fear, faces fear with courage and awareness to get everything that is aligned with himself, with his values.

If you have to ask yourself a question, ask yourself, who are you?

It's the most important question and it's crucial to ask yourself where you are now and where you're going. Ask yourself, what makes you feel good?

Why are you happy when you do the things you love? Because that's all in the end.

Do what's aligned with yourself.

If you're doing a job you don't love, it's because it's not aligned with your values.

Do you know why you're sick at your workplace? Because deep in your soul, in the most secret part of you, you know, you're worth a lot more than what you're getting paid today.

Free the champion in you, not the loser. We all have a champion waiting to be freed. He's there, waiting for you to order him to go wild.

You're not your thoughts, you think you're those, but it's just ghosts, mental lies you believe in. Throw away all those thoughts that form in your mind automatically, learn to recognize them, and direct yourself in life towards those thoughts that do you good, that energise you. Throw away the trash.

Observe the thoughts that pass in front of you, like the traffic when you're at the side of the road. Get out of your mind and in the third person observe your thoughts, watch them pass in front of you, and ask yourself, how are they?

Do they empower you or are they rubbish? Trash is the thing that separates you from the one thing that matters, this moment. And when you'll be in the present moment, you'll be amazed at what you can do.

So, what are you going to do now? What thoughts do you choose to keep in your mind?

You have the power to choose. You have the power to dominate your mind. This is the real power that no other being in the world is able to have. You have the free will to think about what you want at any time. It's all in your hands.

If you liked this book, leave an opinion on Amazon. I would be deeply grateful.

CPSIA information can be obtained
at www.ICGtesting.com
Printed in the USA
BVHW041249100222
628586BV00011B/684